Disaster Management

There is a perennial gap between theory and practice, between academia and active professionals in the field of disaster management. This gap means that valuable lessons are not learned and people die or suffer as a result. This book opens a dialogue between theory and practice. It offers vital lessons to practitioners from scholarship on natural hazards, disaster risk management and reduction and developments studies, opening up new insights in accessible language with practical applications. It also offers to academics the insights of the enormous experience practitioners have accumulated, highlighting gaps in research and challenging assumptions and theories against the reality of experience.

Disaster Management covers issues in all phases of the disaster cycle: preparedness, prevention, response and recovery. It also addresses cross-cutting issues including political, economic and social factors that influence differential vulnerability, and key areas of practice such as vulnerability mapping, early warning, infrastructure protection, emergency management, reconstruction, health care and education, and gender issues. The international team of authors combine their years of experience in research and the field to offer vital lessons for practitioners, academics and students alike.

Alejandro López-Carresi is founder and director of CEDEM Centre for Disaster and Emergency Management in Madrid, Spain.

Maureen Fordham is Principal Lecturer and Enterprise Fellow at the Department of Geography, Northumbria University, UK.

Ben Wisner, who has worked in development and hazards for 47 years, is a research affiliate at University College London, UK.

Ilan Kelman is a Senior Research Fellow at the Center for International Climate and Environmental Research – Oslo (CICERO) in Norway.

JC Gaillard is an Associate Professor in the School of Environment at the University of Auckland, New Zealand.

D1292275

Disaster Management

International lessons in risk
reduction, response and recovery

**Edited by Alejandro López-Carresi,
Maureen Fordham, Ben Wisner,
Ilan Kelman and JC Gaillard**

Routledge
Taylor & Francis Group

LONDON AND NEW YORK

First published 2014
by Routledge
2 Park Square, Milton Park, Abingdon, Oxon OX14 4RN

Simultaneously published in the USA and Canada
by Routledge
711 Third Avenue, New York, NY 10017

Routledge is an imprint of the Taylor & Francis Group, an informa business

British Library Cataloguing-in-Publication Data
A catalogue record for this book is available from the British Library

Library of Congress Cataloging in Publication Data
Disaster management: international lessons in risk reduction, response and
    recovery/[edited by] Alejandro López-Carresi, Maureen Fordham, Ben
    Wisner, Ilan Kelman and JC Gaillard.
    pages cm
    Includes bibliographical references.
    1. Emergency management. 2. Crisis management. 3. Risk management
    —Planning. 4. Rescue work. 5. Disaster relief. I. López-Carresi,
    Alejandro.
    HV551.2.D556 2014
    363.34—dc23   2013014593

ISBN13: 978-1-84971-347-4 (hbk)
ISBN13: 978-0-415-71744-1 (pbk)
ISBN13: 978-0-203-08253-9 (ebk)

Typeset in Times New Roman by
Florence Production Ltd, Stoodleigh, Devon, UK

Contents

Figures

Tables

Boxes

Contributors

David Alexander is Professor of Risk and Disaster Reduction at University College London. His books include *Natural Disasters*, *Confronting Catastrophe* and *Principles of Emergency Planning and Management*. He is Editor-in-Chief of the *International Journal of Disaster Risk Reduction*, Co-editor of *Disasters* journal, and a Founding Fellow of the Institute of Civil Protection and Emergency Management.

Mihir Bhatt has led the All India Disaster Mitigation Institute (AIDMI) work since 1995 on reducing disaster risks through action research.

Camillo Boano is an architect, urbanist and educator. He is Senior Lecturer at The Bartlett Development Planning Unit, University College London (UCL), Director of the MSc in Building and Urban Design in Development and Co-director of the UCL Urban Lab. He has over 18 years of experience in research, consultancies and development work in South America, Middle East, Eastern Europe and South East Asia in urban development, disaster management and recovery and informal urbanism.

Jake Rom D. Cadag is currently undertaking his PhD at the University Paul Valéry in Montpellier, France. He is pursuing his professional specialties in disaster risk reduction and management. He is an aspiring community worker who has a great interest in the development of participatory tools involving communities and integrating all potential stakeholders in disaster risk reduction.

Ana Maria Cruz is an international expert in risk management and emergency planning for conjoint natural and technological (Natech) disasters in Japan, Europe and the United States. She has a unique background having work experience as a chemical engineer in industry, and holding a PhD in Environmental Engineering from Tulane University in New Orleans, USA. Her research interests include risk analysis of flooding, storm, earthquake, tsunami and climate change-induced impacts on infrastructure systems; Natech accidents and consequence analysis; and disaster risk management. She has published over 40 peer-reviewed articles.

Maureen Fordham is based at Northumbria University, Newcastle upon Tyne, UK, where she teaches on the MSc Disaster Management and Sustainable

Development. She has been researching disasters since 1988. She has a particular interest in marginalised groups in disasters including women and children. She is a founding member of the Gender and Disaster Network in 1997 and Radix: Radical Interpretations of Disaster.

JC Gaillard is Associate Professor at the University of Auckland in New Zealand. He trained as a geographer with particular interest in disaster risk reduction (DRR) in Asia and the Pacific. His present work focuses on developing participatory tools for DRR and in involving marginalised groups in disaster-related activities with an emphasis on ethnicity, gender, and on prisoners and homeless people. JC also collaborates in participatory mapping and community-based DRR training with NGOs, local governments and community-based organisations. More details from: http://web.env.auckland.ac.nz/people_profiles/gaillard_j/.

Marianne Karlsson is a researcher at CICERO in Norway. Her research interests are coastal livelihoods and social aspects of resource management in small island states. Her research is currently focused on small-scale fisheries in Belize.

Ilan Kelman is a researcher at CICERO in Norway, where his main research focuses on island sustainability and disaster diplomacy – how and why disaster-related activities do and do not reduce conflict and create peace. He also co-directs the non-governmental organisation Risk RED (Risk Reduction Education for Disasters). See http://www.ilankelman.org.

Joachim Kreysler, a German of refugee origin, a physician with public health interests in emergencies, spent his professional life in Sub-Saharan Africa with the Max Planck Institute, WHO and the Red Cross. Also an ophthalmologist, he has recently returned from Tamil Nadu, working with ARAVIND eye surgeons on equity issues in preventable blindness. He is 77 years old and still married.

Allan Lavell has a PhD in Geography from the London School of Economics. For the past 25 years he has been an associate researcher at the Latin American Faculty of Social Sciences (FLACSO) in Costa Rica. He is a founding member of LA RED (http://www.desenredando.org/) and has published over 70 specialized items on disaster risk.

Alejandro López-Carresi is the founder and director of the Center for Disaster and Emergency Management (CEDEM). Alejandro has over 20 years of experience working in emergencies, disasters and international development in countries such as Bolivia, Ecuador, Panama, Sudan, Kosovo, Pakistan and Indonesia. Alejandro combines field missions with research and training.

Tania López-Marrero is an Assistant Professor at the Department of Geography and the Department of Latino and Hispanic Caribbean Studies, Rutgers University. Her research interests include vulnerability and resilience to natural hazards, and ecosystem services and drivers of change in the insular Caribbean.

Emmanuel M. Luna is a Professor of Community Development at the College of Social Work and Community Development, University of the Philippines. He was one of the conveners of the DRR Net Philippines, a network of civil society organizations in the Philippines. He co-edits the international journal *Disaster Prevention and Management*, published by Emerald.

Jessica Mercer is an independent consultant, focusing on disaster risk reduction and climate change adaptation. Previously Jessica has worked for academia, NGOs and UN agencies in similar fields.

Lourdes Meyreles is a sociologist with an MA in Gender and Development Studies. Lourdes is an Associate Researcher and the Coordinator of the Social Studies of Disaster Project at the Latin American Faculty of Social Sciences (FLACSO), in the Dominican Republic. She is an Associate Professor at the Instituto Tecnológico de Santo Domingo, and co-author of the GDN's *Gender and Disaster Sourcebook*.

Mehul Pandya is a senior advisor at AIDMI.

Tommy Reynolds was a senior specialist at AIDMI.

Rajib Shaw is an Associate Professor in the Graduate School of Global Environmental Studies at Kyoto University, Japan. His research interests are: community-based disaster risk management, climate change adaptation, urban risk management, and disaster and environmental education.

Koichi Shiwaku is the program officer in OYO International, a consulting firm, based in Tokyo. His specialisation is disaster risk reduction education.

Yukiko Takeuchi is an Associate Professor in Kyoto University with a specialization in disaster risk communication.

Dewald van Niekerk is a Professor in disaster risk reduction, the founder and the current director of the African Centre for Disaster Studies at North-West University in South Africa. He holds a PhD and is the Editor-in-Chief of the international peer-reviewed journal, *Jàmbá: Journal of Disaster Risk Studies.*

Krishna S. Vatsa is at present working as the Regional Disaster Reduction Advisor with the UNDP in New Delhi. With a DSc in disaster risk management from the George Washington University, Washington, DC, Krishna has been an active practitioner in the area of disaster risk management and recovery since 1995.

Juan Carlos Villagrán de León is a Guatemalan citizen and has been engaged in disaster risk management, early warning and emergency response efforts since 1995. In 2004 he joined UNU-EHS in Bonn and in 2009 he joined the UN-SPIDER programme. He has authored, co-authored and edited more than 70 scientific and technical publications.

Ben Wisner works with the Aon Benfield UCL Hazard Research Centre, University College London (http://www.abuhc.org/) and GNDR (http://www.globalnetwork-dr.org/). He studies complexity, local knowledge and interactions among livelihoods, governance, natural environment and risk. He has taught in Africa, the USA, the UK and Switzerland over three decades while researching in Africa, Asia, and Latin America. Now he consults, advises and writes. Ben is the lead author of *At Risk: Natural Hazards: People's Vulnerability and Disasters* (2004) and lead editor of *The Routledge Handbook of Hazards and Disaster Risk Reduction*, (Routledge, 2012).

Acknowledgments

If it takes a village to raise a child (and it does!), then how many people does it take to produce a book? The answer is nearly the number of PhDs it takes to change a light bulb: many, many!

First, we have to thank the large number of *friends, colleagues and loved ones* who have not only patiently supported but also provided substantive comments along the way to each of the five editors. In particular, we thank Marta Cabarcos Traseira, Sonia Kruks and John Fordham.

We also need to thank the tireless *editorial staff at Earthscan* for their patience and for the support and encouragement they have given.

Finally, we are extremely grateful to a *panel of practitioner-advisors* who reviewed chapters and also made general suggestions that helped us keep the primary focus of the book on the needs of those who make decisions, fund, guide and practice disaster risk reduction in the real world and not merely in ivory-coloured towers (not real ivory any more since we all want our grandchildren to enjoy live elephants). These include Loy Rego, Mayfourth Luneta, Suranjana Gupta, Aniello Amendola, Garry de la Pomerai, Tim Radford, Terry Gibson, Anne Castleton, Zenaida Delica Willison, Jo Kreysler, Rajib Shaw, Lena Dominelli and Annelies Heijmans.

Abbreviations and acronyms

ACDM	Committee on Disaster Management
ACLU	American Civil Liberties Union
ADB	Asian Development Bank
ADPC	Asian Disaster Preparedness Center
ADRC	Asian Disaster Reduction Center
AECID	Agency for Development Cooperation
AfDB	African Development Bank
AHTF	ASEAN Humanitarian Task Force
AIDMI	All India Disaster Mitigation Institute
ALNAP	Active Learning Network for Accountability and Performance in Humanitarian Action
AP	Asia-Pacific
ARPDM	ASEAN Regional Programme on Disaster Management
ASCE	American Society of Civil Engineers
ASEAN	Association of Southeast Asian Nations
AU	African Union
AUC	African Union Commission
AUDMP	Asian Urban Disaster Mitigation Program
CA	Change Agents
CAPRADE	Andean Committee for Disaster Prevention
CARICOM	Caribbean Community
CBDM	community-based disaster management
CBDO-DR	citizenry-based and development-oriented disaster response
CBDP	community-based disaster preparedness
CBDRM	community-based disaster risk management
CBDRR	community-based DRR
CBO	community-based organisation
CCAD	Central American Commission for Environment and Development
CCIB	Chamber of Commerce and Industry for Small Businesses
CDEMA	Caribbean Disaster Emergency Management Agency
CDERA	Caribbean Disaster Emergency Response Agency
CDKN	Climate & Development Knowledge Network

CDM	comprehensive disaster management
CDMP	comprehensive disaster management programme
CEDAW	Convention on the Elimination of All Forms of Discrimination Against Women
CEPREDENAC	Central American Coordination Center for Natural Disaster Prevention
CICERO	Center for International Climate and Environmental Research – Oslo
CIPDSS	Critical Infrastructure Protection Decision Support System
CMR	crude mortality rates
CPP	Cyclone Preparedness Programme
CRED	Centre for the Epidemiology of Disasters
CRRH	Central American Commission for Hydraulic Resources
CSIRO	Commonwealth Scientific and Industrial Research Organisation
DCC	Disaster Coordinating Council
DEC	Disasters Emergency Committee
DHS	Department of Homeland Security
DM	disaster management
DMC	Disaster Management Centre
DRR	disaster risk reduction
ECB	Emergency Capacity Building
EDRR	Education for Disaster Risk Reduction
EGS	Employment Generation Schemes
EM-DAT	Emergency Events Database
EPS	Emergency Planning Society
ESCAP	United Nations Economic and Social Commission for Asia and the Pacific
ESD	Education for Sustainable Development
FEMICA	Central American Federation of Municipalities
FSWW	Foundation for the Support of Women's Work
GA	General Assembly
GBV	gender-based violence
GDN	Gender and Disaster Network
GDP	gross domestic product
GEHI	Global Emergency Health Initiatives
GEIS	Global Emerging Infections Surveillance and Response System
GFDRR	Global Fund for Disaster Risk Reduction
GHSI	Global Health Security Initiative
GIEH	Global Initiatives for Emergency Health
GII	Gender Inequality Index
GNDR	Global Network of Civil Society Organisations for Disaster Risk Reduction
GOARN	Global Outbreak Alert and Response Network

GOI	Government of India
GPS	Global Positioning System
GPSA	Global Pathogen Surveillance Act
HAC	Health Action in Crises
HEICS	Hospital Emergency Incident Command System
HFA	Hyogo Framework for Action
IAEM	International Association of Emergency Managers
IASC	Inter-Agency Standing Committee
IATA	International Air Transport Association
IAWG	Inter-Agency Working Group on Reproductive Health in Crises
ICS	Incident Command System
IDNDR	International Decade for Natural Disaster Reduction
IDP	internally displaced persons
IFAD	International Fund for Agricultural Development
IFRC	International Federation of Red Cross and Red Crescent Societies
IHR	International Health Regulations
IIASA	International Institute for Applied Systems Analysis
ILO	International Labour Organisation
IMF	International Monetary Fund
INGO	international non-governmental organisation
IPCC	Intergovernmental Panel on Climate Change
LAC	Latin America and the Caribbean
LDC	Least Developed Country
LESLP	London Emergency Services Liaison Panel
LPG	liquefied petroleum gas
LRRD	Linking Relief, Rehabilitation and Development debate
MFI	micro-finance institution
MISP	Minimum Initial Services package
MPA	Marine Protected Areas
MSV	Many Strong Voices
MTUS	Multinational Time Use Study
NAIS	National Agricultural Insurance Scheme
NAPA	National Adaptation Programme for Action
NCDM	National Council for Disaster Management
NDMD	National Disaster Management Directorate
NDMG	National Directorate of Meteorology and Geophysics
NEO	near-Earth objects
NGO	non-governmental organisation
NIPP	National Infrastructure Protection Plan
NREGS	National Rural Employment Guarantee Scheme
NSET	National Society for Earthquake Technology
NTD	Neglected Tropical Diseases

NTHMP	National Tsunami Hazard Mitigation Program
ODI	Overseas Development Institute
OECS	Organization of Eastern Caribbean States
OED	Operations Evaluation Department
OFDA	Office of Foreign Disaster Assistance
OSDMA	Orissa State Disaster Mitigation Authority
P3DM	Participatory 3-Dimensional Mapping
PAHO	Pan American Health Organization
PCCSP	Pacific Climate Change Science Program
PCDPP	Pan Caribbean Disaster Preparedness Project
PCVA	participatory capacity and vulnerability analysis
PLA	Participatory Learning and Action
PNG	Papua New Guinea
PONJA	Post-Nargis Joint Assessment
PPEW	Platform for the Promotion of Early Warning
PPP	public–private partnerships
PPPiE	Private–Public Partnerships in Emergencies
PREDECAN	European Union-Financed Disaster Prevention Project for the Andean Countries
PREVDA	Central American Environmental Vulnerability Reduction Project
PROMISE	Program for Hydro-Meteorological Disaster Mitigation in Secondary Cities in Asia
PRRM	Philippine Rural Reconstruction Program
PRSP	Poverty Reduction Strategy Paper
R2D	Relief to Development
RHRC	Reproductive Health Response in Crises Consortium
Risk RED	Risk Reduction Education for Disasters
RNA	Rapid Needs Assessment
SAARC	South Asian Association for Regional Cooperation
SDMC	SAARC Disaster Management Centre
SESP	School Earthquake Safety Program
SEWA	Self Employed Women's Association
SIDS	Small Island Developing States
SMEC	Sapang Maisac Evacuation Center
SNET	National Service for Territorial Studies
SRGDI	Sustainable Rural Growth and Development Initiative
STI	sexually transmitted infections
TCG	Tripartite Core Group
TEC	Tsunami Evaluation Coalition
U5MR	Under-Five Mortality Rates
UN	United Nations
UNDESA	United Nations Department of Economic and Social Affairs
UNDP	United Nations Development Programme

UNDP BCPR	United Nations Development Programme-Bureau for Crisis Prevention and Recovery
UNDP–RBA	United Nations Development Programme–Regional Bureau for Africa
UNECA	United Nations Economic Commission for Africa
UNEP	United Nations Environmental Programme
UNESCO	United Nations Educational, Scientific and Cultural Organization
UNFCCC	United Nations Framework Convention on Climate Change
UN-INSTRAW	United Nations International Research and Training Institute for the Advancement of Women
UNISDR	United Nations International Strategy for Disaster Reduction
UN/SCN	United Nations Standing Committee on Nutrition
UNU-EHS	United Nations University – Institute for Environment and Human Security
UP	University of the Philippines
USACE	United States Army Corps of Engineers
USAID	United States Agency for International Development
USGS	United States Geological Survey
VCA	vulnerability and capacity analysis
VGF	vulnerable group feeding
VSA	Village Social Analysis
WASH	water, sanitation and hygiene
WB	World Bank
WHO	World Health Organization
WWF	World Wide Fund for Nature

1 Introduction

Who, what and why

Alejandro López-Carresi, Maureen Fordham, Ben Wisner, Ilan Kelman and JC Gaillard

Who needs this book?

We have produced this book for practitioners. Too much valuable research and reflection on disaster, hazards, vulnerability, risk and risk reduction has been written in technical language and published in either expensive or obscure places, or both. The editors have worked closely with practitioners at various scales for many years, probably well over 100 years if you total up our careers. We remain closely involved with networks that include many practitioners: the Gender and Disaster Network, Many Strong Voices, the Global Network of Civil Society Organisations for Disaster Reduction, the Emergency Capacity Building (ECB) Project, Periperi U, Duryog Nivaran, the Community Based Adaptation project and the RADIX network. At a further distance, we are also engaged with the Overseas Development Institute's (ODI) Humanitarian Practice Network, the Sphere Project and ALNAP, among others.

Recognising this gap, we tried to fill it with a book that digests research and reflection on good practice, edited specifically for practitioners. Our work was made easier by the fact that our chosen authors are to varying, but close, degrees engaged themselves with the world of practitioners – or are practitioners themselves – and come from many corners of Planet Earth.

What is a 'practitioner'?

If we parse the term 'practitioner', we find many kinds of people: the policymakers, project managers, extension workers, regulators, teachers, members of scientific research councils, **community** leaders – all of them found at different scales of government service; the staff of civil society organisations and their volunteers and pro bono advisors that number in the tens of thousands around the world; the professionals working with international non-governmental organisations (INGOs) and the larger national non-governmental organisations (NGOs); the employees of the UN and international agencies that have 'mud on their boots' (or if they are now in administration, once had that mud). Bilateral and multi-lateral donor team members are also practitioners, and again, those working in the field or closely involved on a day-to-day basis with partners are most likely to enjoy and benefit from this book. So, too, perhaps, may some of the policymakers and advisors in donor headquarters, but likely not the political appointees who rule development assistance organisations (with minor exceptions).

This large cross section of people work in vastly different organisational cultures, pursue quite different careers, are younger and older, and are professionals and volunteers. Their lives differ greatly in terms of income, health care, housing, education for their children, safety of their own neighbourhoods and provision for their old age. They believe many different things about 'life, the universe and everything'. All these characteristics affect the way such **knowledge** workers take up, interpret and apply new knowledge. They also affect the manner in which they search for knowledge, together with the time and resource constraints that go with

---

Box 1.1 Some resources for practitioners

- ALNAP (Humanitarian learning network): http://www.alnap.org
- Climate & Development Knowledge Network (CDKN): http://www.cdkn.org
- Community Based Adaptation project: http://www.iied.org/cba7-seventh-international-conference-community-based-adaptation/
- Duryog Nivaran (South Asian practice network): http://www.duryognivaran.org/
- Emergency Capacity Building (ECB) Project: http://www.ecbproject.org/resources/resources-and-learning/
- Gender and Disaster Network: http://www.gdnonline.org/
- Global Network of Civil Society Organisations for Disaster Reduction: http://www.globalnetwork-dr.org/
- La Red (Latin American practice network): http://www.desenredando.org/
- Many Strong Voices: http://www.manystrongvoices.org/
- ODI's Humanitarian Practice Network: http://www.odihpn.org/
- Periperi U (African practice network): http://riskreductionafrica.org/en/home
- RADIX network: http://www.radixonline.org/
- Sphere Project: http://www.sphereproject.org/

their job descriptions. We have tried to take these existential realities into account in our choice of topics and authors.

The Drum Beat Network (2012) has carried out large surveys of development practitioners in order to find out what sources of knowledge they use. The results show that that they tap a wide variety of sources and that the gap between 'theory' and 'practice' or between 'academia' and 'the real world' is not as great as some might think. Some 1183 people completed the 2012 survey, from over 200 different agencies. Respondents included people with 121 nationalities, based in 115 different countries and covered a full range of primary job functions – with five roles having over 100 respondents: executive or decision-making; information or knowledge management; programme communication; programme management; and research or technical work. There was a good spread of primary areas of work – with the five top roles being health, education, governance, social and economic policy and gender.

In answer to the question: 'How do you keep up to date with the latest develop-ments in your field?', more than 50 per cent replied: publications, colleagues within and outside my organisation and professional conferences. The survey further asked: 'Outside your organisation what kinds of professionals are you most in contact with?' Top of the list were: academics and technical experts (72 per cent), communication professionals (53 per cent), programme managers (53 per cent), and community or civil society leaders (51 per cent).

Other audiences for this book

We also think researchers and students will find this book useful: in particular, academics who are part of a rising wave of interest in interdisciplinary approaches to human development, security, environmental management, hazards, risk and disaster. Communication across and among disciplines has been made easier with the increased funding of teams that work hard to understand one another's language and approach to problems such as the ones just listed. This book can, among other things, help to encourage and validate such team approaches. However, our aim is more ambitious: it is also to encourage a young cohort of 'engaged' academics.

While our primary audience is those knowledge workers described above, we recognise as well that in the twenty-first century the 'engaged' scholar, researcher and academic is becoming an increasingly common figure. 'Engaged' has a meaning that overlaps somewhat with the more common term, 'applied'. In many disciplines inheriting their power structures and cultures from earlier centuries, 'applied' work is still considered second class, something that ranks 'below' highly theorised contributions and 'pure' science that are published in the 'top ranking' journals and earn for their authors recognition and job security. While this archaic bias persists, increasingly some have simply ignored that polarity and defined themselves as 'engaged'. This term describes researchers and scholars (outside as well as inside the academy) who have a long-term relationship of mutual respect and trust with people in communities and institutions with whom the engaged researcher co-produces knowledge. Taking such a stance, attempting to 'walk in the shoes' (or rubber sandals) of her/his interlocutor, the engaged knowledge worker must adopt methods and frameworks that break down disciplinary and professional silos. As Marcus Oxley, coordinator of the GNDR (Global Network of Civil Society Organisations for Disaster Reduction) has put it: in villages and urban neighbourhoods, people conceive problems, threats and opportunities holistically.

Why is this book necessary?

Confronting the new normal without comforting rhetoric

In the shabby tradition of political rhetoric that has promised 'no child shall go hungry' (Henry Kissinger in 1975) and 'health for all by the year 2000' (World Health Organization), the **Hyogo Framework for Action**'s (HFA) expected outcome was 'The substantial reduction of disaster losses, in lives and in the social, economic and environmental assets of communities and countries' by 2015 (UNISDR, 2005:3). The midterm assessment of the HFA and subsequent reports show that the world cannot expect such a reduction (UNISDR 2011). On the contrary, the mounting evidence suggests that, notwithstanding many solid initiatives from community teams to national legislation, vulnerabilities continue to increase.

Sorting through the statistics is not an easy task, because for comparisons to be made across years, the changing baselines must be taken into account. That is, populations, communities and infrastructure are not the same from year to year. So the Emergency Events Database EM-DAT (http://www.emdat.be) reports that from 2005–2011, the number of deaths from disasters involving environmental events decreased from 2005–2007, jumped significantly in 2008, was extremely low in 2009, spiked in 2010, and dropped again in 2011. Specific disasters made a big difference, such as the 2008 earthquake in China just nine days after Cyclone Nargis struck Burma – with each event causing tens of thousands of deaths.

The events which cause the spikes are not the anomalies. Instead, they are symptomatic of the systemic vulnerability existing around the world, indicating major disasters just waiting to happen. This 'new normal' – or, in reality, not so new – is one of precarious existence for a large part of humanity produced by the negative, worsening influence of multiple crises: violence of all kinds, climate change, unplanned urbanisation, polarisation between rich and poor, **corruption** and bad government practice and the instability of a globalised economy. This means that disaster management and disaster risk reduction (DRR) cannot be seen as 'technical' matters. They are deeply political. Figure 1.1 suggests a wide range of interconnected processes at work that combine to produce and reproduce, generation after generation, conditions in which marginal people are allocated to marginal places; the weakest in society are placed in harm's way, usually not through their own choices.

The challenges apply to rich locations as well. The USA lacks neither wealth nor power, yet chooses and perpetuates allocations of that wealth and power that create and continue vulnerability. What can a disaster manager practitioner do

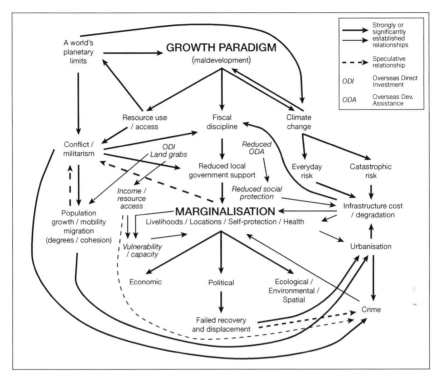

Figure 1.1 Spaghetti of doom: some complex interactions that link the dominant
development approach to marginalisation and the creation of disaster risk

against the long-standing system in Figure 1.1 that encourages the destruction
of wetlands along Louisiana's shoreline and forces poor people to live behind
inadequately managed flood control works, thereby permitting Hurricane Katrina's
storm surge to inundate New Orleans in 2005, killing over 1500 people? New York
City is not going anywhere, meaning that emergency management practitioners
must deal with the millions of people (rich and poor) and hundreds of billions of
dollars of infrastructure in the flood zone, as demonstrated by Hurricane Sandy in
2012. These are the realities of vulnerability.

Frameworks that are supposed to guide the **policy**, programming and projects
aimed at reducing disaster risk, such as the HFA, either completely ignore what
one sees in Figure 1.1 or talk about these processes in vague ways that do not help
practitioners. The framework we offer in Chapter 2 and the rest of this volume
will hopefully begin to fill that gap.

The buzzword is not mightier than the sword

One only has to look at what the HFA lists as '**underlying risk factors**' to see
that huge gaps exist. Corruption is not mentioned (Transparency International 2005,
2011; Lewis and Kelman 2012). There is no reference to land grabbing (LDPI

2012) in the name of 'modernising agriculture' or addressing 'the climate imperative' with production by foreign companies of biofuel for export on what was once land used by small farmers or herders (Wisner *et al.* 2012).

Again, the HFA makes much use of the phrase 'community participation', but large surveys at the grassroots conducted by the Global Network of Civil Society Organisations for Disaster Reduction in 2009 and 2011 showed that very little of what is done with money for DRR in national capitals 'trickles down' to localities (GNDR 2009, 2011). While **local governments** are the lynchpins for linking up community and civil society efforts with national resources, local government itself is starved of adequate resources (O'Brien *et al.* 2012).

Similarly, many other phrases, buzzwords, and concepts compete for attention and cause confusion. Just some of the examples are vulnerability, sustainability, resilience, resiliency, complexity, holistic, adaptation, adjustment, capacity, capability, surprise, transformation, and security. They all have their place and they all have the potential to confuse (Box 1.2).

But ultimately, dealing with disasters is about people and communities, not about words and phrases. Any practitioner (and academic) must keep in mind that words do make a difference, so it is important to clarify definitions and vocabulary

---

Box 1.2 Terminology

A new word is like a fresh seed sown on the ground of the discussion.
– Ludwig Wittgenstein

People use words such as 'disaster' and 'vulnerability' in many ways. There are 'common-sense' meanings, and these also vary from language to language. In addition, there are many 'technical' uses in different disciplines such as economics, politics, sociology, engineering, and climate science, among others. None of these uses are 'natural' or foundational. They all have histories and contexts, and to that extent are 'constructed'. Political, social, economic and gender power are evident in the choice of words and the meaning(s) they are given. Land-use changes that are 'resilient' over time in the face of climate change from the point of view of overseas agribusiness investors in an African country may not at all be 'resilient' from the point of view of small farmers or herders who are displaced from the land.

At a minimum, the core terminology used in this book has been standardised so that seeds of confusion are not sown together with the seeds of productive discussion. On the whole, we follow the usage recommended by the UNISDR (http://www.unisdr.org/we/inform/terminology). Where we differ, these key terms are discussed fully in Chapter 2. There is a Glossary of key terms used in this discipline on p. 310, and the Glossary word is emboldened on its first occurrence in the chapter.

to ensure that concepts are accepted and agreed upon. Then one must rapidly move on to the real work in terms of understanding the processes leading to disasters and how to solve those. Why do people live in certain places in certain ways? What options and **resources** do they have and not have? How do they interact and not interact with other sectors of the community and those further afield? How could that situation be changed without undermining or marginalising others? These questions are tackled on the ground and by the authors in this book.

What will you find in this book?

Part I Prevention and disaster risk reduction (DRR)

Part I deals with prevention of disaster and DRR. There are seven chapters. The section begins with a framework that has guided our organisation of the book and has also been found to be useful in operational contexts. The framework uses some basic concepts – **hazard**, **vulnerability**, **capacity**, **risk** and **participation**, and it is found in Chapter 2. Then, Chapters 3 and 4 firmly ground this book in the place where most practitioners are most at home: the community, and it explores a theme that is central to work by practitioners on DRR as well as **livelihoods**, health and empowerment, namely gender.

The community focus continues with Chapter 4 on the origin and development of **community-based DRR** (CBDRR), while Chapter 5 reviews the experience of people-centred early warning systems. Schools may act as centres of DRR in the community and are structures and functions in the community that must have priority protection. This is the argument of Chapter 6, which is taken up and amplified by a discussion of public awareness and adult education for climate change adaptation in Chapter 7.

The final chapter of Part I provides a thorough overview of the kinds of damage to structures and infrastructure that are vital to the entire built environment: from megacities and towns to neighbourhoods and villages to those in isolated locations – the built environment that is humanity's 'second nature' – as well as critical to economic activity and livelihoods. Without demanding expertise in engineering, this chapter also suggests ways of preventing or limiting such damage.

Part II Response and recovery

Five chapters delve into the issues surrounding response to and recovery from disaster. Chapters 9 and 10 are mirrors of each other. The former lays out the state of knowledge and practice as regards professional management of emergencies, while Chapter 10 enters the murky realm of mythology that attends such events. It covers persistent myths concerning disease, cadavers, social disorder and looting. The 'irrationality' of the common human response to disaster stands in contrast to the precarious rationality of the Emergency Operations Centre.

Health, micro-insurance and recovery are the subjects of Chapters 11, 12 and 13, respectively. They take us back to the community focus of this whole book since a robust primary health care system is shown to be a precondition for DRR in Chapter 11. Meanwhile, formal micro-insurance is a fairly recent outgrowth of the decades-old breakthrough known as microcredit. Chapter 12 discusses the need for micro-insurance and how it has functioned so far in a pilot in India. Recovery, in Chapter 13, is then shown on the basis of much experience to be successful only where communities are deeply involved in the design and implementation of rehousing and other sectors.

Part III   Regional perspectives

Chapters 14, 15 and 16 trace the outlines of policy and practice in the face of regionally specific sets of hazards over the past few decades. These regional perspectives provide the context for understanding why implementation of the HFA has been difficult and why so few of the processes pictured in Figure 1.1 have been addressed. Yet they do narrate some progress, especially as regards engagement with communities, a shift from an exclusively technical focus on hazards to a consideration of comprehensive vulnerability and the establishment of mutual aid and co-learning arrangements among countries in these regions. Chapter 14 discusses Africa; Chapter 15 takes us to Latin America and the Caribbean; while the focus of Chapter 16 is Asia and the Pacific.

Part IV   Tools

Part IV includes two chapters that both talk about tools that have been found useful as aids for CBDRR (Chapters 17 and 18). In the recent past, there has been an explosion in the availability and use of many different tools and methods with which communities may assess their own vulnerabilities and capacities, map hazards and plan systematically for increased safety.

The book ends with a special sort of Conclusion. We have asked a number of practitioners with long experience to review the chapters and to help us draw out lessons and recommendations for policy and practice. The conclusion is based on this correspondence. This is timely in the context of 2015 when the entire current architecture for reducing disaster risk, helping people adapt to climate change and implementing the Millennium Development Goals is up for grabs. Much improvement is needed in all these efforts, and they have to be tackled together, not from isolated 'silos' acting as distant, top-down command centres.

Under an improved regime for DRR, including climate change adaptation and nested within a New Development Agenda, practitioners will hopefully have more freedom to develop plans together with communities, to help implement them and to evaluate the effects. Our hope is that this little book can provide help for practitioners in doing precisely that.

References

Drum Beat Network (2012) *2011 and 2012 Survey Results.* Available at: http://www.comminit.com/en/children/content/survey-results-information-needs-and-practices-international-development-professionals-a (accessed 27 November 2012).

GNDR (2009) *Clouds but Little Rain: Views from the Frontline: A Local Perspective of Progress Towards Implementation of the Hyogo Framework for Action*, Teddington: Global Network of Civil Society Organisations for Disaster Reduction. Available at: http://www.preventionweb.net/english/professional/publications/v.php?id=9822 (accessed 17 November 2012).

—— (2011) *If We Do Not Join Hands: Views from the Frontline 2011.* Teddington: Global Network of Civil Society Organisations for Disaster Reduction. Available at: http://www.globalnetwork-dr.org/views-from-the-frontline/voices-from-the-frontline-2011/ (accessed 17 November 2012).

LDPI (2012) 'Land Grabbing II', International Conference, Cornell University, Ithaca, NY. Available at: http://www.cornell-landproject.org (accessed 27 November 2012).

Lewis, J. and Kelman, I. (2012) 'The Good, the Bad and the Ugly: Disaster Risk Reduction (DRR) Versus Disaster Risk Creation (DRC)', *PLoS Currents Disasters*, 21, June 2012. Available at: http://currents.plos.org/disasters/article/the-good-the-bad-and-the-ugly-disaster-risk-reduction-drr-versus-disaster-risk-creation-drc (accessed 27 November 2012).

O'Brien, G., Bhatt, M., Waunders, W., Gaillard, JC and Wisner, B. (2012) 'Local government and disaster', in B. Wisner, JC Gaillard, and I. Kelman (eds) *The Routledge Handbook of Hazards and Disaster Risk Reduction*, London: Routledge, pp. 629–40.

Transparency International (2005) *Global Corruption Report: Corruption in Construction and Post-Conflict Reconstruction*, Berlin: Transparency International.

—— (2011) *Global Corruption Report: Climate Change*, Berlin: Transparency International.

UNISDR (2005) *Hyogo Framework for Action 2005–2015: Building the Resilience of Nations and Communities to Disasters*, Geneva: UNISDR.

—— (2011) *Hyogo Framework for Action 2005–2015: Building the Resilience of Nations and Communities to Disasters. Mid-Term Review 2010–2011*, Geneva: UNISDR.

Wisner, B., Mascarenhas, A., Bwenge, C., Smucker, T., Wargui, E., Weiner, D. and Munishi, P. (2012) 'Let them eat (maize) cake: climate change discourse, misinformation and land grabbing in Tanzania', paper presented at Land Grabbing II, International Conference, Cornell University, Ithaca, NY. Available at: http://www.cornell-landproject.org/papers (accessed 23 November 2012).

Part I

Prevention and risk reduction

2 Hazard, vulnerability, capacity, risk and participation

Ben Wisner, Ilan Kelman and JC Gaillard

A framework for practitioners

Existentialist Søren Kierkegaard said of the huge system of ideas built by the philosopher Hegel that '[he was] like a man who builds an enormous castle and himself lives alongside it in a shed' (Kierkegaard 1840). In this chapter, we offer practitioners a way of framing the quest for reduced **vulnerability** to disasters, not by giving answers, but by suggesting useful questions. In Chapter 1, we critiqued the international frameworks generated both by individual disciplines and international agencies such as UNISDR (United Nations International Strategy for Disaster Reduction). They rarely help with the complexity that confronts local practice, the details and **root causes** of people's vulnerability, and their creativity and **capacity**. Let's see if we can do better with a grounded framework that has been built up from our observations in communities over many years.

Many causes but one clear truth: disasters are not 'natural'

Hazards

Human settlements and **livelihoods** depend on the Earth's variations and variability, past and present, in the form of geology, topography, bathymetry, geomorphology, climate, and the distribution of biota and fresh water. At the same time, these variations and variability pose potential threats, sometimes termed natural **hazards**. Extreme movements in the Earth's crust release energy experienced as earthquakes. Volcanic eruptions and tsunamis are other geological extremes. Climate extremes such as hurricanes release gigantic amounts of energy. Heat waves, blizzards, and ice storms are other climate extremes. Floods and mass movements such as landslides, rock falls, and avalanches are generally more localised but can be destructive and deadly, as are tornadoes and lightning strikes. Drought is a slow-onset hazard, but is nevertheless associated with large mortality, great economic cost, and significant displacement of people.

Hazards, however, are not in themselves a problem for humanity. As with the tree falling in the forest with no one around to hear it fall, every day thunderstorms flash and rumble around the world in uninhabited areas and over the large surface of the planet covered by oceans. Ice, rock, and debris slides are a normal part of the erosion and deposition cycle, and many take place in uninhabited regions. To mention an extreme case, a near-Earth object entered the atmosphere and exploded over Tunguska, Siberia, in 1908, flattening 80 million trees over an area of 2000 square kilometres. But there were no human settlements nearby (Rincon 2008). Had the event occurred over Nairobi or Mumbai, the outcome for humanity would have been quite different – as demonstrated in February 2013 when a near-Earth object disintegrated over a medium-sized town in Russia causing over 1,000 injuries, mainly from the shockwave shattering glass.

At the other extreme, data on frequent but small hazard events show that they erode people's livelihoods and make them more vulnerable to the occasional large events (UNISDR 2009). These events include the hundreds of small-scale landslides which every year slip down the hills and mountains of Nepal and bury farms and roads (Sudmeier-Rieux *et al.* 2012), the tide-associated recurring floods in the Philippines which destroy crops and prevent kids from attending schools (Gaillard *et al.* 2008), and the slight variations in temperature and rainfall leading to unnoticed frost episodes and droughts of damaging consequence for local households (Reyes and Lavell 2012).

Vulnerability

Chambers (1983) highlighted the term 'vulnerability' in his analysis of rural poverty, aptly titled *Rural Development: Putting the Last First.* It came as one of five elements interlocking with each other, producing what he termed the 'ratchet effect' or 'deprivation trap' (ibid.: 112): a condition of 'integrated rural poverty' from which it is difficult to extract oneself. The other elements were political powerlessness, physical weakness (ill health), isolation, and income poverty.

Chambers had in mind *social vulnerability* when he used the single noun of 'vulnerability'. This has to do with the degree to which one's social status (culturally and socially constructed in terms of roles, responsibilities, rights, and expectations concerning behaviour) influences differential impact by extreme and everyday natural events and the chances of recovery. Thus, depending on the society and situation, social characteristics such as gender (e.g. Enarson and Morrow 1998) and sexual preference, marital status, age, occupation and caste, immigration status and national origin, race, ethnicity, and religion may have a bearing on potential loss, injury, and life chances in the face of hazards and the nature of one's recovery trajectory.

In addition to such socially differentiated vulnerability, there is what has elsewhere been called 'generalised vulnerability' (Wisner 2003). *Generalised vulnerability* is a characteristic of the poorest of the poor in every society, especially those who suffer income poverty and are marginal. This means people who have no voice in government (politically marginal), who live in urban squatter settlements or in remote rural locations (spatially marginal), whose livelihoods are based on **access** to meagre natural resources or who live in degraded environments (ecologically marginal), and who have poor access to markets and other economic resources (economically marginal) (Wisner 1993).

The poorest and most marginalised groups in a society live with chronic indebtedness, malnutrition, ill health, degraded physical surroundings, and often violence. For them, any additional stress can have catastrophic results, such as losing land or meagre assets to moneylenders, losing children to famine, or losing their place in a **community** as they are forced by circumstances to migrate. In this sense, whatever is on the local geographic menu could impact them – flood somewhere, landslide elsewhere, and coastal storm or earthquake in yet other places.

If it is possible to identify the poor and the marginal, then their numbers and locations are a starting point, crude as those figures might be. Without falling into the trap of assuming that **poverty** equals vulnerability, one can zero in on these groups, determining, for example, their initial well-being, their capacities, and the existence and extent of **resources** accessible to them. Bankoff *et al.* (2004), Chambers (1983; 1995), Wisner (1993), and Wisner *et al.* (2012) among many others further explore the relationships among vulnerability, capacity, and poverty.

The Hemispheric Congress on Disaster Reduction and Sustainable Development, made up of researchers and practitioners in the Americas, emphasised highly vulnerable populations (Maskrey *et al.* 1998: 18). They highlight the same points we make: 'lack of resources in daily life' that increases vulnerability, a 'vicious cycle that further marginalises those already at greatest risk', inflexibility in **policy** and practice in dealing with a wide range of domestic arrangements and modes of self-assistance, and 'policies reinforcing marginalisation on the basis of ethnicity, culture, national origin, age, gender or social class'. They specifically mention migrant labourers, refugees, women, children, and the extremely poor as examples.

The characteristics of vulnerability have causes. These causes relate to access to a wide variety of resources, and these causes are rooted in the workings of political, social, and economic structures in each particular society. These relations are summarised in Figure 2.1. The idea of access to resources is explained in the next section.

Capacity

Most people, even the poorest and most marginalised, have **capacities** (resources, networks, **knowledge**, and skills) that they can put to work in order to prevent, resist, cope with, and recover from stresses and shocks such as hazardous natural events (Figure 2.2).

Access to Resources

The capacity to protect oneself, one's family and assets from hazardous events as well as to recover from any damage or loss inflicted by such events depends on

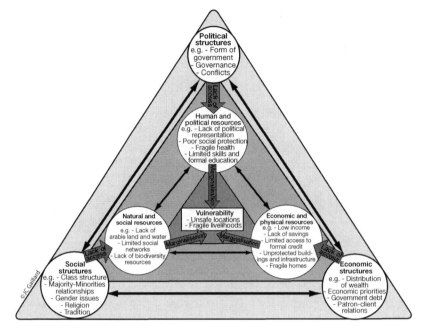

Figure 2.1 The triangle of vulnerability
Source: Wisner *et al.* (2012: 27).

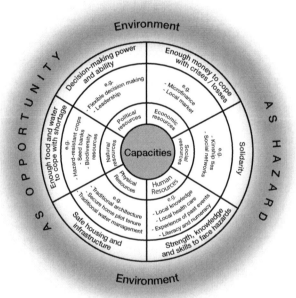

Figure 2.2 The circle of capacities
Source: Wisner *et al.* (2012: 28).

access to resources (Wisner *et al.* 2004: 12). 'Resources' are defined broadly to include all bundles of assets that can produce a livelihood, as well as the institutional, political, and social preconditions for using those assets. Thus, for example, land and water are assets that farmers can use to grow food, but there have to be conventional rules for governing the farmers' access to the land, or, as in many countries, formal legal title to the land. Markets for buying and selling assets, goods, and services are also usually necessary for a **household** (rural or urban) to realise values that provide a livelihood. Income is often taken as a short cut to identifying 'poor' and 'less poor' households; yet income is only part of many livelihood systems. Production for one's own consumption remains important in many parts of the world. Also, many income sources are not usually counted, such as remittances from family members working abroad or in another part of the country, along with bartering and other parts of the so-called informal economy.

Networks and social resources

Groups of people – neighbours, extended family members, members of faith communities and other civil society organisations – can be active in their own interests when facing the possibility or reality of an extreme natural event. Little of this knowledge, skill, sharing of knowledge and material goods, mutual aid, or emotional support is visible to many government planners and researchers. It is much less valued in economic terms. Yet the complex interactions among different kinds of resources (social, human, institutional, and natural) may have positive outcomes for preventing disasters triggered by hazardous natural events. They are critical for preparing for such events, for warning, for immediate relief, and for subsequent recovery. It is well known that the vast majority of people rescued during sudden-onset hazardous events (e.g. earthquakes, landslides, and flash floods) are saved by non-professionals, namely loved ones, neighbours, and passers-by. As Sun (2011: 1135) writes, 'Disaster survivors engage in over-whelmingly prosocial behaviour and victims-turned-resourceful-first-responders rationally assess danger and work assiduously to save their neighbours and communities'.

Under most circumstances, investments in strengthening and preserving social and human resources (e.g. education and health care) produce a 'two-for-one' or win–win situation. These investments are likely to increase productivity and welfare in normal situations and also strengthen communities against hazardous natural events.

Knowledge and skills

Seven important features of local knowledge can be used as examples to illustrate the importance of local knowledge for DRR (Box 2.1) – without denigrating the need for non-local as well, to be combined with local knowledge.

Box 2.1 Seven important features of local knowledge that are important for DRR

1 Local knowledge, like all knowledge, is social. There can be no knowledge that is completely separate from what others know and have known in the past.

2 Local knowledge is not entirely 'traditional' (passed on by earlier generations). So-called 'indigenous' or 'traditional' knowledge is only part of the picture. Local knowledge may incorporate versions of outside specialist knowledge. For instance, weather or climate forecasts on the radio may be interpreted and modified according to local weather signs and past experience.

3 The tendency to mix or hybridise knowledge is increasing. Mobility is important to livelihoods (for instance, because family members send home money). They may also send or bring knowledge home.

4 Within a community, local knowledge is not uniformly distributed. Not everyone has access to secret knowledge or knowledge associated with local skills such as building, finding water, or midwifery. Occupations and special skills come with subsets of local knowledge that may not be widely distributed in a **locality**.

5 Local knowledge is gendered and age graded. It also varies according to the standpoints of people in different life situations; for example, local knowledge of people living with disabilities, knowledge of people with chronic health problems, or knowledge of people who constitute an ethnic or caste minority in a community.

6 Local knowledge may be a source of power and status. For example, in Sierra Leone, rice farmers have been known to compete with each other in breeding new varieties of rice, some simply for the beauty of the plant (Richards 1985). This is a source of praise and prestige.

7 Local knowledge may not be explicitly spoken about by those who have it. It is sometimes tacit or implicit in their practices – for instance, where on a slope with different soil characteristics to plant different crops. Western-trained or Western-oriented experts find the idea that knowledge is tacit hard to accept, yet it can be made explicit through patient discussion. People may 'know' something without knowing that they know it.

At the local scale, people experience and understand threats in a more comprehensive way than specialists who design practices focused on one hazard or several. Poverty, violence, inequity and many different natural and other hazards including climate change confront people at the scale at which they live, work, raise children, celebrate, and suffer. Local efforts to deal with one of these challenges generally involve dealing with the others, yet there is sometimes a lack of trust between communities and governments or non-local institutions. This influences how local people's knowledge and practice match or clash with advice they receive from the outside. Ideally, outside specialist and local knowledge should complement each other. But to get the best of both, mutual respect and trust are required. Trust and partnership must be built; they cannot be assumed. Without trust and mutual respect, the exchange of knowledge and production of a useful hybrid of outside and local knowledge are not possible.

People are constantly coping with threats. They share knowledge with neighbours, may draw knowledge in from far away, and work out ways to apply it locally. Local communities are workshops of knowledge production, not just museums of tradition. Thus, for the outside specialist, the locals are as much sources of new ideas to be tested, refined, and shared as the outside specialists' skills are a source for local people. Possibilities exist for a broad and deep partnership in knowledge production for DRR that are seldom achieved.

Policy implications of our framework

Decentralising, building partnerships and co-producing knowledge

National governments could do more to develop local capacity by training locals and then devolving responsibilities and control to subnational and local authorities. This is not just a problem for low-income countries. Response to disasters in Japan, the USA, and Taiwan have suffered from over-centralisation in the cases of the earthquake that hit Kobe in 1995, Hurricane Katrina along the US Gulf Coast in 2005, and again following Typhoon Morakot and its deadly landslides in southern Taiwan in 2009. This does not preclude the need for national support of subnational jurisdictions during times of such troubles, but a balance must be sought between (1) centralisation inhibiting disaster risk reduction (DRR) and response and (2) local authorities having the capability to accept responsibility.

Two points must be emphasised. First, simply devolving responsibility without budgetary resources, training and technical means could cause more DRR problems than it solves. Certainly, lack of funding can be used by institutions as a scapegoat for not fulfilling their responsibilities, but that does not deny the need for adequate resources to do the required work. Budgetary resources, including for training, are necessary, but not sufficient for decentralised responsibility for DRR.

Second, even with such resources and responsibilities decentralised, without a working relationship with people and communities based on trust and mutual respect, little can happen. The key is not absolving central governments of responsibility, but ensuring an adequate balance and partnership among governments, civil society, communities, and institutions at all scales. For example, as Chapter 3 shows, often women's and girls' potential contribution to DRR is overlooked by a male-focused, macho culture derived from years of so-called civil defence and the culture of first responders (police, fire and ambulance services). This must change – but without alienating the frontline workers who have the needed skills and experience.

Once local partnerships are established, consultations with locals should reveal their knowledge of hazards and local capacities for preventing, coping with, and recovering from extreme events. This local knowledge should provide a foundation for discussing outside specialist knowledge, and thus suggest actions for moving forward with local hazards, vulnerabilities and capacities (Gaillard and Mercer 2013).

But close collaboration for DRR between government units and communities does not always happen, as three recent global studies agree. The UNISDR's *Global Risk Assessment 2009* (UNISDR 2009) and the GNDR's 2009 and 2011 *Views from the Frontline* (GNDR 2009; 2011) came up with the same quantitative and qualitative result: the international and national scale knowledge and the practices based on that knowledge are not 'trickling down' and penetrating local communities fast enough to achieve the **Hyogo Framework for Action** (HFA) goals (see Chapter 1). Other than absence of mutual respect and trust, one of the main reasons why partnerships between **local government** and communities are often lacking is that national governments are not decentralising sufficient finance and technical assistance to local governments, according to these studies. Even where local governments are involved, there can still be a tendency to ignore or devalue community-based practice and knowledge, such as that of women and girls (see Chapter 3).

Building assets and livelihoods

In many cases, the capacities available locally will not be sufficient. Poverty remains one of the principal obstacles to local partnerships and action plans even when there is ample political will. So DRR often depends on broader programs of asset and livelihood building.

The notions of sustainable livelihoods, social networks, and access to resources are common to current ways of thinking about human development linking with DRR. A striking example is the way microcredit schemes have proliferated following the success of the pioneering example of the Grameen Bank in Bangladesh (Yunus 1999) – see Chapter 12 in this book as well. The importance of remittances from abroad to rural and poor urban households is acknowledged to have become an increasing part of livelihood systems. Some international initiatives have attempted to streamline the electronic transfer of funds while introducing lower-cost alternatives to established oligopolies that charge large transfer fees.

In the area of DRR, the transfer of funds from individuals abroad to assist recovery has been a notable feature of disasters such as the 2001 earthquake in El Salvador (Hernández *et al.* 2002). In addition, policy and practice in DRR have come to acknowledge many of the same asset-building processes, including, for instance:

- diversification of income sources;
- development of microcredit small banking systems and micro-insurance;
- diversification of agricultural production;
- development of local networks and knowledge base;
- strengthening local capacities;
- development of storage of crops and seeds.

While asset and livelihood building hold much potential for reducing disaster risk, such initiatives contradict the dominant tendency in the world toward reduction of the scale and functions of government and encouragement of privatisation caring about only short-term profit. In view of the trend toward state withdrawal and irresponsible privatisation, new forms of private sector accountability and hybrid public–private forms of banking, insurance, and service provision will have to emerge if the livelihoods approach is to be anything more than a comforting theory. In particular, supporting small, responsible businesses matches both privatisation and local livelihoods. In many places that must come in tandem with reform of access to land, water, and other resources or else the livelihood and asset-building approach will stall and prematurely falter.

Conclusion

Hazard, vulnerability, capacity and **risk** are inextricably bound up together. Their connections are not a matter of definition or semantics. If one takes a people-centred point of view, then livelihoods and the risks and opportunities of daily life anchor one's analysis and guide practice. Issues of DRR have to be seen in this context, where little distinction is made among risks such as violence, loss of one's house or land to speculators and landlords, or the impacts of environmental hazards such as hurricanes, floods, and disease. Partnerships between ordinary people and local authorities are a way of reducing risk while also strengthening livelihoods. So far, top-down investment in new laws, national government institutions, science, and technology are not 'trickling down' to this primary level. A new effort is required to decentralise, build partnerships, and to develop action plans together with locals.

References

Bankoff, G., Frerks, G. and Hilhorst, D. (2004) *Mapping Vulnerability: Disasters, Development and People*, London: Earthscan.
Chambers, R. (1983) *Rural Development: Putting the Last First*, London: Longman.
—— (1995) 'Poverty and livelihoods: whose reality counts?' *Environment and Urbaniza-tion*, 7(1): 173–204.
Enarson, E. and Morrow, B. (1998) *Gendered Terrain of Disaster: Through Women's Eyes*, New York: Praeger.
Gaillard, JC and Mercer, J. (2013) 'From knowledge to action: bridging gaps in disaster risk reduction', *Progress in Human Geography*, 37(1): 93–114.
Gaillard, JC, Pangilinan, M.R.M., Cadag, J.R. and Le Masson, V. (2008) 'Living with increasing floods: insights from a rural Philippine community', *Disaster Prevention and Management*, 17(3): 383–95.

GNDR (2009) *Clouds but Little Rain: Views from the Frontline: A Local Perspective of Progress Towards Implementation of the Hyogo Framework for Action*, Teddington: Global Network of Civil Society Organisations for Disaster Reduction. Available at: http://www.preventionweb.net/english/professional/publications/v.php?id=9822 (accessed 17 November 2012).

—— (2011) *If We Do Not Join Hands: Views from the Frontline 2011*, Teddington: Global Network of Civil Society Organisations for Disaster Reduction. Available at: http:// www.globalnetwork-dr.org/views-from-the-frontline/voices-from-the-frontline-2011/ (accessed 17 November 2012).

Hernández, R., Menjiva, R., Alvarado, J. and Paniagua, A. (2002) *Thanks to Family Remittances*, San Salvador: Social Watch El Salvador Initiative; Association of Women for Dignity and Life (LAS DIGNAS); Maquilishuati Association (FUMA); Intersectorial Association for Economic Development and Social Progress (CIDEP). Available at: http://www.socialwatch.org/node/10776 (accessed 8 December 2012).

Kierkegaard, S. (1840) *Journals and Papers*, Book III. Available at: http://www. naturalthinker.net/trl/texts/Kierkegaard,Soren/JournPapers/III_A.html (accessed 18 December 2012).

Maskrey, A., Bender, S.O. and Peacock, W.G. (1998) *Inter-American Dialogue on Disaster Reduction*, Lima: Red de Estudios Sociales en Prevención de Desastres en América Latina and Intermediate Technology Development Group, ITDG-Peru.

Reyes, L.R. and Lavell, A. (2012) 'Extensive and everyday risk in the Bolivian Chaco: sources of crisis and disaster', *Journal of Alpine Research*, 100(1). Available at: http://rga.revues.org/1719 (accessed 13 December 2012).

Richards, P. (1985) *Indigenous Agricultural Revolution*, Boulder, CO: Westview Press.

Rincon, P. (2008) 'Fire in the sky: Tunguska at 100', *BBC Online*, 30 June. Available at: http://news.bbc.co.uk/2/hi/science/nature/7470283.stm (accessed 19 February 2013).

Sudmeier-Rieux, K., Jaqueta, S., Derron, M.H., Jaboyedoff, M. and Devkot, S. (2012) 'A case study of coping strategies and landslides in two villages of Central-Eastern Nepal', *Applied Geography*, 32(2): 680–90.

Sun, L. (2011) 'Disaster mythology and the law', *Cornell Law Review*, 96: 1131–208. Available at: http://www.lawschool.cornell.edu/research/cornell-law-review/upload/Sun-final.pdf (accessed 1 September 2012).

UNISDR (2009) *Global Assessment Report on Disaster Risk Reduction 2009*. Available at: http://www.preventionweb.net/english/hyogo/gar/report/index.php?id=9413 (accessed 14 June 2012).

Wisner, B. (1993) 'Disaster vulnerability: scale, power, and daily life', *GeoJournal*, 30(2): 127–40.

—— (2003) 'Turning knowledge into timely and appropriate action', in O.D. Cardona, *Information and Indicators Program for Disaster Risk Management*. Manizales, Colombia: National University-IDEA/ IADB/ ECLAC. Available at: http://idea.unalmzl.edu.co/ documentos/Ben%20Wisner%20EM%20Barcelona%20Nov%202003.pdf (accessed 23 September 2012).

Wisner, B., Blaikie, P., Cannon, T. and Davis, I. (2004) *At Risk: Natural Hazards, People's Vulnerability and Disasters*, 2nd edn, London: Routledge.

Wisner, B., Gaillard, JC and Kelman, I. (eds) (2012) *Routledge Handbook of Hazards and Disaster Risk Reduction*, London: Routledge.

Yunus, M. (1999) *Banker to the Poor: Micro-lending and the Battle against World Poverty*, New York: Public Affairs/Perseus Books.

3 Gender aspects of disaster management

Maureen Fordham and
Lourdes Meyreles

Lessons for practitioners

- Disaster situations are not 'freak' events but reflect the unequal structures of the societies in which we live.
- In disasters and conflict situations, gender gaps in everyday life chances not only persist but can widen with lower socioeconomic status.
- Disaster management continues to be resistant to, or dismissive of, gender concerns and fails to both recognize and facilitate **participation** by all social groups.
- The inclusion of women (and other marginalized groups) in disaster and development decision-making processes still has to be demanded: it is not automatically provided, despite widespread rhetorical commitment to equitable **policy** and practice.
- Organized constituencies of women delivering pro-poor, disaster risk reduction (DRR) actions, have already accomplished much, represent consid-erable potential for the future and deserve greater national and international recognition.

Introduction: why focus on gender in disaster management?

Despite the amount of literature that has been produced on gender in all its aspects, the everyday living conditions, and the differing impacts of disasters on men and women, boys and girls, make it essential to continue to ask the questions: Why focus on gender in disaster risk reduction? Why especially women and girls? This topic has been studied from different perspectives: including sociology (Enarson 2012); anthropology (Hoffman 1999); development studies (Bradshaw 2004; Cannon 2002), and geography (Cupples 2007) among others; and through varied approaches of practitioners in the field (Ariyabandu 2006; Ariyabandu and Wickramasinghe 2004; IASC 2006). From the earliest analyses of the situation of women, there has been not only a recognition of their practical needs and strategic interests (Moser 1989), but also a broadening of the analysis to include other related issues such as those of human rights and development (Enarson and Fordham 2001), and of gender in the wider sense, incorporating the experiences of men

(Fordham 2011), and people of other sexual orientations (Balgos *et al.* 2012; Gaillard 2011; Pincha 2008a, 2008b; Wisner 2001). Whatever the perspective or the approach, there is one best answer to this question, and that is: a focus on gender is necessary because of the continuing prevalence of inequalities within societies between men and women, boys and girls (Sen 2001).

If we take a close and objective look at the ordinary living conditions of most people in most societies, we will identify gender gaps, which impact upon the basic elements necessary for survival, before, during and after disasters: human rights, **resources**, services, and the satisfaction of basic needs. While the capture of the complexity of such interlinked and cross-cutting issues is always problematic, indications of such disparities are reflected in data from the Global Gender Gap Report 2011. Figure 3.1 provides a global (135 countries, representing over 90 per cent of the world's population) snapshot of the gender gap in just four aspects. It shows some considerable advances in reducing the gender gaps in health and education outcomes on a global scale but gender gaps in economic and political empowerment outcomes remain wide (Hausmann *et al.* 2011: 7–17).

Data on a global scale are helpful to a degree but they conceal wide variation among (and within) countries and indeed within single categories such as 'women'. So while the high scores for educational attainment are welcome, UNDP's Gender Inequality Index[1] (UNDP 2010a) reveals that in eight countries (Afghanistan, Benin, Central African Republic, Haiti, Liberia, Mozambique, Niger and Togo) women have less than half the years of schooling compared to men (ibid.: 38). Furthermore, *quantity* of education does not equate to *quality* of education although data on quality is even more difficult to find (ibid.: 40). Gender inequalities reflect unequal distributions in human development more generally: those countries with an unequal distribution of human development also experience high gender inequality. Among the countries doing particularly badly in both human development and gender inequality are Central African Republic, Haiti and Mozambique (ibid.: 7).

Disaster management in many of the most disaster-prone countries of the world must also be set against a continuing trend in globalization, characterized by an increase in neo-liberal economic policies, deregulation, combined with oppressive, externally imposed, structural adjustment programmes. Furthermore, in many parts of the world, disaster and development pressures exist alongside conflict which create the kind of complexity that practitioners find hardest to manage:

> However, contexts in which conflicts and disasters overlap are daily realities for people who are affected, as well as for many humanitarian and development practitioners. Effective programmes to manage crisis interventions need to reflect conflict-disaster complexities and respond to them in a holistic and integrative manner. Experience has also shown that development interventions that do not recognize the link between disasters and conflict in at-risk countries can worsen tensions and increase risk . . . The overlap of disaster and conflict worsens gender-related vulnerabilities and violence.
>
> (UNDP-BCPR 2011: 7–8)

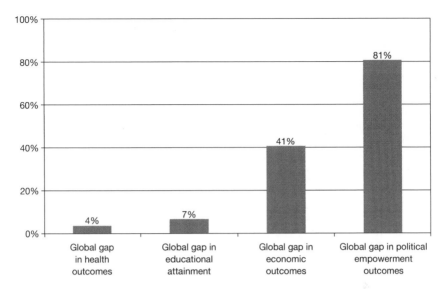

Figure 3.1 The gender gap in outcomes for four subindexes: health, educational attainment, economic participation and political empowerment

Note: Global averages; scores are weighted by population.

Source: Adapted from Hausmann *et al.* 2011.

In such a context, the impacts on the economy, the environment and on women can be 'catastrophic' (Guerrero *et al.* 2000: 273; Plümper and Neumayer 2006).

In emergencies and disasters, and in conflict situations these gender gaps not only persist but may widen with lower socioeconomic status (Neumayer and Plümper 2007), and also may determine the outcome of efforts and resources invested in dealing with these situations (Hammami *et al.* 2009; UNISDR 2009).

Disaster situations, far from being different or 'freak' events, reflect the structure of the societies in which we live and the way systems in society function (systems such as the economy, the government bureaucracy, the legal system, the education system, etc.). Approaches to disaster situations have been changing within the last few decades, due in part to the imperative of increasing disaster events and losses, but also due to a growing understanding of the complex dynamics behind disasters (Wisner *et al.* 2004). The concept of disaster risk and the understanding that this **risk** is both constructed and manageable have begun to contribute to new outlooks and to understanding the roles that social relations, in all their complexities, have in creating or minimizing disaster risk (Enarson *et al.* 2007). However, it has to be stated that the management of disasters is still determined and governed by patriarchal[2] structures and processes which, despite the advances of recent years, continue to be resistant to, or dismissive of, issues of gender and fail to recognize the necessary involvement of all social groups in disaster risk reduction. A gender focus is too often seen – even now – as an unwanted luxury in an emergency; what has been called 'the tyranny of the urgent' (BRIDGE 1996).

Gender relations and the differences they generate are a basic element of social structure and will therefore play an important role in the ways we manage risk in disasters, mitigate and respond to emergencies, and recover from them. Efficient disaster management, therefore, must entail an understanding of these gender gaps; and our **capacity** and disposition to consider them will be part of a positive transition toward more secure and egalitarian societies. Because these factors represent the **root causes** of gender inequality in disasters, we next spend some time laying out the evidence.

Gender: from nature to culture

What is gender?

Differences between men and women originate in both nature and **culture**. With the help of feminist anthropology and sociology, we have been able to understand that biological differences between men and women – signified by the term 'sex' – must be distinguished from the social and cultural differences between them, for which 'gender' is the appropriate term. This is important, given that because the word 'sex' has other connotations, 'gender' has been adopted as the more decorous means of referring to both biological and social differences. Such a lack of differentiation is only one of many examples of how blurring the distinction between biological and social factors has been the means by which women have become the subordinated sex. Sherry Ortner (1972) argues that, since that subordination is not biologically determined, but nevertheless is common to every culture, then it is some particular shared component of cultures which explains the universally inferior position of women. This she concludes is to be located first of all in the way societies value 'nature' less than they value 'culture'. Second, women are seen as 'closer to nature' due to a perceived association of women's bodies and functions with the 'naturally' creative life; the menstrual cycle, childbirth and child rearing. Whereas men, because of a physiological difference, which prevents them from giving birth, have instead to be culturally creative – using tools and symbols. This leads to the inevitable identification of 'woman' with the domains of nature, the domestic and the private, as opposed to the social, public and technical domains occupied by men: a distinction which is manifest in other sets of socially constructed negative or positive associations: e.g. weakness/strength; dependence/independence; instinct/intellect; passivity/activity.

So, what does this have to do with disaster management? After disasters, those tasks that are seen as 'naturally' the realm of women (childcare, household management and other caring roles) can become much more difficult to carry out. However, as they are seen as women's natural role (not real work but just 'what women do'), they do not attract extra support or even substantive recognition as do those matters more clearly in the public realm such as business and the economy. Furthermore, if women are identified with the private space of the home, then they will find it harder to claim a place in pre- and post-disaster planning which are generally located in the public realm and dominated by the men of any **community**.

An example of an organized response to the post-disaster exclusion of women-identified needs and concerns was in the aftermath of Hurricane Andrew in 1992. As in many other disasters around the world, the (mostly) male members of the business community of Miami formed a foundation for its reconstruction. This group, named 'We Will Rebuild', raised and distributed many millions of dollars, which were mostly devoted to the reconstruction of the business district. However, such a strategy failed to meet the specific needs of many crisis-hit, and especially poor, women and their families, whose priorities were more basic: health care, protection from gender-based violence, education and other essential needs. In reaction to the gender blindness of the business group, a coalition of women's groups (more than 50 at its height) formed 'Women Will Rebuild' in an attempt to redress this imbalance and make visible these marginalized dimensions (Enarson and Morrow 1998).

Sex and gender: the danger of false assumptions

Underlying these socially embedded sets of oppositions is the false assumption that there is a direct relationship between biological sex and cultural/social differences and **capacities**; but the urgent consequence, for which there is increasing evidence, is that continuing to rely on such assumptions and not recognizing the particular needs and interests of subordinated groups, such as women and girls, results in their greater disadvantage in disaster situations and their proportionately dying in greater numbers. It is the contention of the present writers that, in order to alter a prevailing social order in which women and girls continue to be subordinated, we need to re-establish the clarity of distinction between sex and gender. It has to be acknowledged, for instance, that sexual differences do not vary with race, caste, class, ethnicity and religion but that gender differences do. Furthermore, they can vary in respect of such factors 'over time', and are thus fundamentally alterable (Murthy and Kappen 2006). This is to emphasize that 'gender' and not 'sex' refers to 'socially ascribed roles, responsibilities and opportunities associated with women and men, as well as the hidden power structures that govern relationships between them' (Riquer 1993, in Aguilar 2009: 13). The power structure in which 'gender is a first order structural variable which affects all social processes and organizes the social system' is that which is fundamental to 'patriarchal societies' (UN-INSTRAW 2010: 20). It is to a continually dominant patriarchy, then, that challenges need to be made in the interests of the effective reduction and management of disaster risk. This makes disaster management a social and political endeavour rather than simply a technical one.

Beyond women: other vulnerable groups

In order to ensure that false assumptions and socially constructed prejudices do not extend to other vulnerable groups, the needs of women and girls in disasters need to be located within the wider framework of social relationships in which they exist.

Masculinities

The analysis of gendered power relations, then, must be made within the context of established yet contestable notions of identity governing conventional behavior and which, paradoxically, can sometimes put men and boys at greater risk. For example, in Hurricane Mitch (1998), despite the significant vulnerabilities of women, more males died. This was interpreted to be a result of men's and boys' socialization to take greater risk and consequently of the dangerous roles they play in search and rescue operations (Delaney and Shrader 2000: 5; Bradshaw 2004). Another example is the higher numbers of deaths of elderly men, especially African-American males, in the 1995 Chicago heat wave (Klinenberg 2002). Here the reason is again sociological more than biological; the men who died had lost their social connections and networks that might have looked out for them and seen to their needs.

Sexual orientation

The complexities of masculinity in turn demand that due recognition is given to other less visible, yet no less vulnerable, gendered groups. Consistent with the results of anthropological and social studies of women, there have recently been challenges to the simple binary division between male and female; a continuum or a spectrum better represents the range of difference because not everyone identifies with a masculine or feminine gender or even a male or female sex. For instance:

> Transgender people identify as or express a gender that is different from their sex at birth. This includes transgender women who were assigned male at birth but live and identify as women, or transgender men who were assigned female at birth but live and identify as men, and also people who are gender nonconforming and may not identify as male or female.
>
> (National Center for Transgender Equality 2011)

The needs and interests of gays and transgender people in disasters have begun to be recognized. For example, Chaman Pincha (2008a; 2008b) has raised awareness of the situation of Aravanis (also known as Hijras or Jogappa) in India who do not fit into a two-gender system. They may be apparently male or inter-sex by birth but do not normally identify as either women or men. In refusing to accept either a male or a female label, they are in turn rejected by mainstream social institutions, which can include their own families who cannot accept the consequent stigma. Aravanis face serious gender discrimination and were invisible as a group during the 2004 tsunami. Since applying for a ration card or other social welfare services is deeply humiliating to them (because they must choose between a male or female category), they do not enjoy the benefits such as appropriate post-disaster shelter or compensation available to most other Indians.

Other examples include those from the Philippines (Gaillard 2011), Indonesia (Balgos *et al.* 2012), Nepal (Knight and Sollom 2012), Haiti (Laguerre and Nixon 2011), Japan (Ozawa 2012), Australia (Gorman-Murray and Dominey-Howes forthcoming) and the USA (Wisner 2001; D'Ooge 2008). The magnitude of the problems of recognition for such groups is evident in the fact that sexual orientation is still currently subject to the imposition of legal sanction in many parts of the world, and disagreement and controversy among the disaster studies community. The Gender and Disaster Network (GDN www.gdnonline.org) listserv recently discussed this topic[3] in which a range of such views were represented.

Gender, class and age

Keeping in mind that societies have a complex structure, we must consider that gender is only one of the elements to take into account when analyzing stratification systems, or the ways in which people are placed differently in societies. Social class – which incorporates the subcategories of occupation, income, lifestyle, education, race and religion – is of primary importance in the way that it impacts on subordinated gender groups. Women, like men and others defined by gender, are not a single homogeneous group. The inequalities that pertain to all of these categories exist along a continuum which places men and women, boys and girls in a variety of social positions: depending on which position is occupied, an individual's risk in a disaster situation will be likely to lessen or increase. Hurricane Katrina in 2005, for instance, hit the USA badly but not uniformly. Katrina's victims were more likely to be African-American women and their children; these impacts were not solely attributable to race or ethnicity but rather to their being poor, lacking health care and earning low wages (UNDP 2010a; see also Gault *et al.* 2005; Williams *et al.* 2006). Also noticeable here are cases in which children and elderly men are particularly vulnerable. Statistical data from disaster events are not always available but an analysis of available sex-disaggregated data between 1981 and 2002 has shown that 'natural' disasters kill more women than men or kill them at an earlier age thus reducing their life expectancy (Neumayer and Plümper 2007). Although, currently, it is a regrettable fact of disaster statistics that factors of sex, age and other social characteristics are not always recorded, those examples where we do have the data invariably reveal significant insights into gender relations. Here, for instance, it is noticeable that:

> Sex/gender and age matter in terms of how people experience natural disasters and armed conflict. Scholarly and academic publications and UN, INGO, NGO and CSO reports clearly and overwhelmingly reflect that there are often

significant differences in experiences of natural disasters and armed conflicts in terms of access to essential, life-saving services based on a person's sex/gender and age.

(Mazurana *et al.* 2011: 3)

Recognition and human rights: why women and girls?

Despite the welcome inclusion of a broader conception of gender, it is women and girls who comprise the largest gender category to be disadvantaged in disasters and for whom we have the most evidence. Although examples of excessive male deaths in some instances must be of major concern, they perhaps provide the exceptions to prove the rule. During the 1991 cyclone in Bangladesh, 90 per cent of the 140,000 fatalities were women and children (Ikeda 1995). The fact that women continue to be vulnerable in disasters is why the remainder of this chapter will argue for a strategically necessary, primary focus on women and girls.

Gender and discrimination

Such figures as those above are all the more surprising given that, since the 1970s, there has been ostensibly widespread international recognition of the ways in which women and girls have traditionally suffered under the domination of patriarchal societies. The United Nations Convention on the Elimination of All Forms of Discrimination Against Women – CEDAW – was adopted in 1979: its aims were to enhance equality between men and women and set out a number of areas on which governments are obliged to take action. As of November 2012, 187 governments have agreed to do the following:

- eliminate gender prejudices;
- eliminate any behaviour (modify social and cultural patterns of conduct) that is based on the presumed inferiority of women and superiority of men;
- eliminate practices that are based on stereotyped roles for men and women;
- ensure that the common responsibility of both men and women in bringing up children is recognized.

(CEDAW, 1979, Article 5)

In the specific context of disasters and risk reduction, gender priorities were integrated into the report of the World Conference on Disaster Reduction which was held in January 2005 in Kobe, Hyogo Prefecture, Japan. Here was adopted the 'Framework for Action 2005–2015: Building the Resilience of Nations and Communities to Disasters': now abbreviated to HFA (**Hyogo Framework for Action**). Among its recommendations for policy and action is the specific priority (d) that '[a] gender perspective should be integrated into all disaster risk management policies, plans and decision-making processes, including those related to risk assessment, early warning, information management, and education and training' (UNISDR 2007a: 4).

Subsequent UN platforms and conferences have continued to state that the vital role of women in disaster risk reduction is still not being recognized. For example, the 61st General Assembly observed that gender mainstreaming and the encouragement of women's participation in DRR decision-making processes needed to be 'speed[ed] up', while the Global Platform for DRR (GDN 2007) noted the lack of recognition of women's contributions to disaster prevention, and consequently their 'potential [being] untapped'. Similar kinds of observation were made at the Manila Declaration for Global Action on Gender, Climate Change and Disaster Risk Reduction (Manila Declaration 2008), which noted the general lack of 'a gender perspective in the global agreements on climate change'; and further calls upon governments for 'commitment to gender mainstreaming' were made by the Beijing Agenda for Global Action on Gender-Sensitive Disaster Risk Reduction (2009) (Aguilar 2009: 10–11). The UNISDR 2011 *Global Assessment Report* reports that gender is still not being adequately addressed in disaster risk reduction; and the UNISDR took as its focus for the 2012 International Day for Disaster Reduction 'Women and Girls – the [in]Visible Force of Resilience'.[4]

Given this volume of attention and the number of times women's (and to a lesser extent girls') **vulnerability** is mentioned, one would have expected the battle to have been won. Nevertheless, it is still necessary to press the case for a gender focus or risk their particular interests being lost in universal claims of need and rights. This is the case whatever the scale of analysis or practice. While the Global Network of Civil Society Organisations for Disaster Reduction provides its own evidence base from the community level, to balance that of the UN's country level reporting for the biennial progress reviews on the HFA (GNDR 2011), those advocating for the needs of grassroots women's groups still find the need to produce their own report (Huairou Commission 2009) to ensure that the voices of grassroots women are heard. Their report identifies the following key findings, which are now becoming all too familiar:

1   Women report they are excluded from emergency preparedness and response programmes.
2   There are information gaps between national programmes and grassroots women's organizations.
3   DRR stakeholders lack a shared definition of effective risk reduction in poor, vulnerable communities.
4   Organized constituencies of women delivering pro-poor DRR practices represent untapped potential.

The question to be asked now is, despite the various declarations of intent and commitment, why has there been so little progress?

Material inequalities

The answer to that question is located not so much in disaster management itself, but in the very structure and fabric of the world's societies. The general condition that the CEDAW undertaking responded to in 1979 remains essentially unchanged. When we analyze data regarding different aspects of social life and how men and women are situated within it, the statistics reveal that women still occupy less privileged positions and social spaces, have less **access** to resources, and participate much less than men in decision-making processes (UN Women 2011). This is characteristic of an everyday reality: in the event of a disaster, such differences and inequalities are merely more evident; their effects, however, are greatly exacerbated. The following list adapted from Aguilar (2009) and UNDESA (2010) provides, on a global scale, a summary of the basic inequalities with which women are daily confronted:

- Approximately 70 per cent of those who live on less than a dollar a day are women.
- Women work two-thirds of the world's working hours, yet receive only 10 per cent of the world income.
- Women own only 1 per cent of the world's property.
- Women comprise the majority of the world's food producers (50–80 per cent), but own less than 10 per cent of the land.
- Women represent just 7 out of 150 elected Heads of State; only 11 out of 192 Heads of Government.
- Women occupy an average of just 17 per cent of seats in national parliaments.

The overwhelming evidence, then, is that women face, sometimes severe, discrimination around the world. At its most extreme, this is revealed through population figures that show that there are 57 million more men than women in the world (UNDESA 2010: 2), concentrated in (but not restricted to) the world's most populated countries – China and India. This underpins a social order in which females are not only awarded lower status, but may not survive pregnancy and birth. Female infanticide, prenatal sex selection and systematic neglect of girls are part of a global, systemic abuse of women and girls (Sen 2001; UN 2009; Watts and Zimmerman 2002). The United Nations conclusion is that: 'Gender inequality remains a major barrier to human development. Girls and women have made major strides since 1990, but they have not yet gained gender equity' (UNDP 2010a: 90). In disasters it may mean that women's and girls' lesser cultural value results in a distraught father, struggling to rescue both his children in a storm, lets go of his girl child in order to save his son who will carry on the family name (Haider *et al.* 1991, in Fothergill 1996).

Roles and conventions

The primary visibility of men and its repressive potential are continually being reinforced. The position or status we occupy in society inevitably governs the performance of our social roles; the parameters of which are defined by conduct and behavior according to established norms and regulating conventions. 'Gender roles' refer to the differing responsibilities that men and women have within any given culture or society. Traditionally these roles are historically defined and will go through changes, but on an everyday basis they are part of what constitutes the totality and relative stability of social relations. Because they are socially embedded, internalized, and customary, the performance of them will inevitably determine the degree to which men and women are able to gain access to society's power and resources. It has to be stated that these traditional roles are changing. Around the world, women are occupying more decision-making positions; they may dedicate more time than before to productive activities, especially in more 'modern' societies; and men are beginning to participate more in household tasks. Yet, despite such emancipatory gains, the public world in which life-affecting decisions are made and carried out is still under the control of men; women predominantly occupy the private, domestic space; and their responsibilities remain primarily reproductive. Even in more highly socioeconomically developed countries with major gains in gender equality, recent evidence (Kan *et al.* 2011) indicates a persistent gender gap. While women's domestic labor has declined somewhat as men's has increased, women still carry out the majority of routine domestic tasks. Men's contributions to domestic work tend to support more those non-routine tasks identified as more masculine (Kan *et al.* 2011: 238).[5]

Vulnerabilities and capacities

These differences in roles are a key part of what maintains social inequalities: the unequal capacities between men and women, and hence their resultant vulnerabilities. The danger for women in particular is that these differences create and perpetuate situations of discrimination, in which the less powerful member of the group can be subjected to ill treatment and violence and deprived of her rights; the disadvantage for humanity in general is that such disparities greatly hinder the development of the potential inherent in both males and females. In patriarchal societies, this is characteristic of both everyday and extreme events. Nevertheless, as Table 3.1 reveals, while established or traditional gender characteristics are liable to increase risks, it is the changing experiences of women that can greatly increase capacities for dealing with disasters.

The corollary of the above is that, despite the, sometimes insurmountable, disadvantages that women face, there is, because of their experience of disasters and the skills and capacities that they have accumulated, equal if not greater potential among women for disaster risk reduction. More particularly, as the second row, middle column suggests, these capacities are in areas of human experience that are essentially outside the official domain of disaster management represented by the technical, professional, and often military apparatus of a masculine 'command and control' model of disaster response.

Table 3.1 Gender and disaster risk

	Women	Men
Characteristics that increase *risks* in disasters	• Higher levels of poverty • Extensive responsibilities of caring for others • Victims of domestic violence • Low status women's occupations	• Internalized norms of masculinity • 'Breadwinner' and protector roles in the family and in the home • Search and rescue responsibilities
Gender experiences that increase *capacities* for managing disaster situations	• Social networking • Caring abilities • Extensive knowledge of communities • Management of natural and environmental resources • High levels of risk awareness	• Professional and leisure networks • Technical abilities • Limited childcare responsibilities

Source: Adapted from Aguilar (2009).

New developments and strategies

These different forms of 'expertise' are being adopted and incorporated into strategies for addressing the new global risks that threaten women: primary among these in disasters are those that follow in the wake of climate change. According to a recent UNDP report (UNDP 2010b: ii), it is particularly in the developing world where such risks 'threaten to reinforce gender inequalities and even erode progress that has been made towards gender equality'. The most vulnerable again are '[p]oor women [whose] limited access to resources, restricted rights, limited mobility and voice in community and **household** decision-making can make them much more vulnerable than men to the effects of climate change' (ibid.: ii). There are opportunities now for women to have equal participation in programmes for adapting to climate change: particularly those which are locally instigated and community based, but experience has shown that the inclusion of women in decision-making processes still has to be demanded: it is not automatically provided, despite widespread commitment to equitable policy and practice. In response to their continuing exclusion, women are producing their own gender-sensitive strategies and programmes for disaster risk reduction.

Women-led initiatives: recent achievements

Significant advances have been made by a number of women's groups working on disaster issues or simply caught up in disasters in their locations. The Huairou Commission and GROOTS International (one of its main member networks) have been pioneers in encouraging and facilitating action by women in disaster and development; their programmes for action are indicators of meaningful women's participation. Given the consistent reports of slowness to put into practice the UN's policies and recommendations on gender, the HFA (UNISDR 2007a, 2007b) was used as a framing device for monitoring the progress of women's inclusion and participation. Structured on the HFA's five Priorities for Action, GROOTS proposed a series of strategies for implementing the HFA's recommendations, which they call 'en-gendering'. It is a report of what grassroots women's groups have actually achieved and an analysis of what is required to foster the engagement of others (GROOTS and Huairou Commission 2009) (see Box 3.1).

Among the many initiatives they have supported, encouraged and facilitated are the Swayam Shikshan Prayog group's work in Tamil Nadu; the Comité de Emergencia Garifuna de Honduras; and the Ntankah organization in Cameroon (Fordham and Gupta 2011). Characteristic of the kinds of progress that have been made is the Foundation for the Support of Women's Work (FSWW) of Turkey – a non-profit organization founded in 1986 – which has had a significant impact in Turkey for women in general and in disaster conditions in particular. Following the Marmara earthquake in 1999, grassroots level women's organizations mobilized and organized themselves in disaster recovery; an experience that enabled them to have the confidence to gain access to resources, to negotiate with officials concerning their needs and priorities, and to develop a capacity to assume leadership roles. This resulted in a higher public profile for these women and established for them a vital role both in the process of long-term sustainable development and disaster risk reduction. The experience in Turkey and those of other countries have demonstrated that:

> Post-disaster situations open up opportunities because decision makers are more open to participation and partnerships. Post-disaster conditions created socially acceptable reasons for women to participate in the public arena. When future disasters strike, these women will be better placed to resist, respond and recover as a result of the strategies and processes that they have put in place.
>
> (Fordham and Gupta 2011: 57)

Such initiatives[6] continue to be made in the wake of disasters. Women felt compelled to make their own 'shadow' analysis after the Haiti earthquake in 2010. The use of a gender perspective in analyzing the post-disaster impact on displaced women made it possible to recognize gender-specific situations and the psychological consequences for women and girls. Among a range of adverse impacts on women were those concerning both their productive and reproductive work: the loss of **livelihoods** and homes caused a severe reduction in women's usual activity; there were significant changes in care-giving responsibilities, where, for instance, women took on the care of children belonging to deceased neighbours and relatives. As with many disasters, there was sexual violence against women and girls both during the emergency and in the post-disaster phase in the camps, without any accountability mechanisms being implemented or concern for the disease-related effects (MADRE 2012). The Haiti Equality Collective produced its own

Box 3.1 Enabling the active engagement of women in DRR and the five HFA Priorities for Action

Priority 1: Ensure that disaster risk reduction is a national and a local priority with a strong institutional basis for implementation.

- Ensure that gender is recognized as a cross-cutting concern requiring action throughout all phases of disaster reduction planning.
- Ensure grassroots women are formal negotiating partners with decision-makers at all levels.
- Ensure funding mechanisms allow participation of locally focused women's groups and civil society representatives.

Priority 2: Identify, assess and monitor disaster risks and enhance early warning.

- Identify the ways the daily routines and social conditions of women and men, girls and boys place them differently at risk, and engage them in multiple networks of communication.
- Identify mechanisms for the inclusion of women- and girl-focused risk **mapping** as a tool to mobilize, raise awareness and negotiate enhanced community security.
- Identify gender-balanced local stakeholder platforms to implement community actions after risk mapping is completed.
- Incorporate grassroots women's priorities into local disaster risk reduction plans and budgets.

Priority 3: Use knowledge, innovation and education to build a culture of safety and resilience at all levels.

- Ensure the collection of gender-disaggregated data and information is the rule and not the exception.
- Resource grassroots women's groups to function as information generators and communicators (organizing peer learning exchanges; promoting grassroots trainers).

Priority 4: Reduce the underlying risk factors.

- Reduce the **underlying risk factors** which result in differential levels and occasions of vulnerability and endangerment, and which shape the capacities and resources of women and men to minimize harm.
- Implement, strengthen and/or enforce gender equity and anti-discrimination laws, in particular against sexual violence, sexual harassment and human trafficking.

- Ensure women are facilitated to negotiate with governments to guarantee secure housing, basic services and livelihoods for their communities.
- Strengthen IDP camp security, shelters and services by targeting gender-based violence, malnutrition and disease.

Priority 5: Strengthen disaster preparedness for effective response at all levels.

- Promote the inclusion of women in disaster-related professions where they are under-represented.
- Scale up existing effective solutions of grassroots women's groups to enhance community resilience.
- Formally recognize grassroots women's organizations as key actors in emergency response, including training and organizing disaster response teams.

Source: Adapted from: GROOTS and Huairou Commission (2009); Gupta and Leung (2010); GDN (2007); Collectif Haïti Égalité (2010).

preliminary Haiti Gender Shadow Report (Collectif Haïti Égalité 2010), echoing actions needed in line with the UN Guiding Principles on Internal Displacement: participation; non-discrimination; capacity development; accountability; and transparency (ibid.: 41). Specifically, it made a number of recommendations for policymakers, donors, civil society groups and all Post-Disaster Needs Assessment stakeholders. These and others formulated by GROOTS International and the Gender and Disaster Network are combined in Box 3.1. The content represents a model for all gender-sensitive programmes for disaster risk reduction. Notable in such recommendations is that it was the event of the disaster that uncovered and highlighted the already-existing vulnerability of women in ordinary social exist-ence. Gender disadvantages and risks in disaster situations are attributable to the fundamental inequalities of the general social condition; it is only by addressing the deficiencies and injustices of the social system itself – the root causes (Wisner *et al.* 2004) of disaster vulnerability – that significant reduction of disaster risk can be achieved.

Conclusion

From the above outline of the historical role of women in disasters and of the potential they can have in disaster management, we must conclude that con-sideration of the vital factor of 'gender' is essential in ensuring that the use of all the world's human resources is maximized in the progress towards significant disaster risk reduction: particularly when we face the increasing challenges of climate change. Women and girls, as well as other minority groups, have for too long been overlooked in disasters or relegated to positions of vulnerability and passivity. However, because they continue to die in greater numbers in emergency situations, it is a matter of extreme urgency that issues of gender are addressed now and in the shorter term; for the long-term future, the groundbreaking and innovative actions of women themselves have demonstrated that it is to them that we must look for strategies that will produce a genuinely sustainable reduction in disaster risk, and climate change adaptation.

Notes

1   The Gender Inequality Index (GII) is a measure that captures the loss in achievements due to gender disparities in the dimensions of reproductive health, empowerment and labour force participation. Values range from 0 (perfect equality) to 1 (total inequality) (UNDP 2010a, p. 26).
2   Patriarchy: A system of unequal social, sexual and economic relations between the sexes which produces and maintains men's authority and power over women (Buck 1992).
3   GDN archives can be found at: http://groups.preventionweb.net/scripts/wa-PREVENTIONWEB.exe?INDEX but to access them, registration with GDN is required at: https://www.gdnonline.org/profile/register.php.
4   Those with long memories will recall that we have been here before; the IDNDR's 1995 World Disaster Reduction campaign was on the theme of 'Women and Children: Key to Prevention' (IDNDR 1996).
5   Data come from the Multinational Time Use Study (MTUS), a harmonized database of large nationally representative time use diary surveys collected from the 1960s to the 2000s. Data were selected from 14 countries: Australia, Austria, Canada, Denmark, Finland, France, Germany, the Netherlands, Norway, Slovenia, Spain, Sweden, the UK and the USA.
6   For more examples, see also the 'Women and Girls on the Map initiative', available at: https://womenandgirlsonthemap.crowdmap.com, which was part of the 2012 International Day for Disaster Reduction 'Women and Girls – the [in]Visible Force of Resilience'.

References

Aguilar, L. (2009) *Training Manual on Gender and Climate Change*, GGCA, IUCN and UNDP.
Ariyabandu, M.M. (2006) 'Gender issues in recovery from the December 2004 Indian Ocean tsunami: the case of Sri Lanka', *Earthquake Spectra*, 22(S3): 759–75.
Ariyabandu, M.M. and Wickramasinghe, M. (2004) *Gender Dimensions in Disaster Management*, Colombo: ITDG.
Balgos, B., Gaillard, JC and Sanz, K. (2012) 'The warias of Indonesia in disaster risk reduction: the case of the 2010 Mt Merapi eruption in Indonesia', *Gender and Development*, 20(2): 337–48.
Beijing Agenda for Global Action on Gender-Sensitive Disaster Risk Reduction (2009). Available at: http://www.preventionweb.net/english/professional/publications/v.php ?id=9538 (accessed 11 March 2012).
Bradshaw, S. (2004) *Socio-economic Impacts of Natural Disasters: A Gender Analysis*, Santiago de Chile: United Nations.
BRIDGE (1996) 'Integrating gender into emergency responses', *Development and Gender in Brief*, 4: 1–3.

Buck, C. (ed.) (1992) *Guide to Women's Literature*, London: Bloomsbury.

Cannon, T. (2002) 'Gender and climate hazards in Bangladesh', *Gender and Development*, 10(2): 45–50.

CEDAW (1979) *Official Full Text of the Convention*. Available at: http://www.un.org/womenwatch/daw/cedaw/text/econvention.htm (accessed 8 June 2012).

Collectif Haïti Égalité (Haiti Equality Collective) (2010) *The Haiti Gender Shadow Report: Ensuring Haitian Women's Participation and Leadership in All Stages of National Relief and Reconstruction*, Haiti: A Coalition Gender Shadow Report of the 2010 Haiti PDNA. Available at: http://www.genderaction.org/regions/lac/Haiti/gsr.html (accessed 21 July 2012).

Cupples, J. (2007) 'Gender and Hurricane Mitch: reconstructing subjectivities after disaster', *Disasters*, 31(2): 155–77.

Delaney, P.L. and Shrader, E. (2000) *Gender and Post-Disaster Reconstruction: The Case of Hurricane Mitch in Honduras and Nicaragua*, World Bank Draft Report. Available at: http://www.gdnonline.org/search.php?cx=007943428441901963700%3Asutepfneabq&cof=FORID%3A11&q=Delaney (accessed 27 June 2012).

D'Ooge, C. (2008) 'Queer Katrina: gender and sexual orientation matters in the aftermath of the disaster in Katrina and the women of New Orleans', in B. Willinger (ed.) *Katrina and the Women of New Orleans*, New Orleans: Newcomb College Center for Research on Women, Tulane University.

Enarson, E. (2012) *Women Confronting Natural Disaster: From Vulnerability to Resilience*, Boulder, CO: Lynne Rienner Publishers.

Enarson, E. and Fordham, M. (2001) 'From women's needs to women's rights in disasters', *Environmental Hazards*, 3(3): 133–6.

Enarson, E., Fothergill, A. and Peek, L. (2007) 'Gender and disaster: foundations and directions', in H. Rodriguez, E. Quarantelli and R. Dynes (eds) *Handbook of Disaster Research*, New York: Springer, pp. 130–46.

Enarson, E. and Morrow, B.H. (1998) 'Women will rebuild Miami: a case study of feminist response to disaster', in E. Enarson and B. Morrow (eds) *The Gendered Terrain of Disaster*, Westport, CT: Praeger, pp. 185–200.

Fordham, M. (2011) 'Gender, sexuality and disaster', in B. Wisner, JC Gaillard and I. Kelman (eds) *The Routledge Handbook of Hazards and Disaster Risk Reduction*, London: Routledge, pp. 395–406.

Fordham, M. and Gupta, S. (eds) (2011) *Leading resilient development: grassroots women's priorities, practices and innovations*, New York: UNDP and GROOTS International. Available at: http://huairou.org/sites/default/files/Leading%20Resilient%20Development%20GROOTS.pdf (accessed 21 July 2012).

Fothergill, A. (1996) 'Gender, risk and disaster', *International Journal of Mass Emergencies and Disasters*, 14(1): 33–56.

Gaillard, JC (2011) *People's Response to Disasters: Vulnerability, Capacities and Resilience in Philippine Context*, Angeles City: Center for Kapampangan Studies.

Gault, B., Hartmann, H., Jones-De-Weeve, A., Wershkul, M. and Williams, E. (2005) *Women of New Orleans and the Gulf Coast: Multiple Assets and Key Assets for Recovery Part I: Poverty, Race, Gender and Class*, Washington, DC: Institute for Women's Policy Research. Available at: http://www.iwpr.org/publications/pubs/the-women-of-new-orleans-and-the-gulf-coast-multiple-disadvantages-and-key-assets-for-recovery-part-i.-poverty-race-gender-and-class (accessed 17 March 2013).

GDN (2007) 'Oral statement of the Gender and Disasters Network to the Global Platform for Disaster Risk Reduction', First Session, 5–7 June 2007. Available at: http://www.

gdnonline.org/resources/GDN_OralStatement_GPlatform_DRR07.pdf (accessed 17 March 2013).

GNDR (2011) If We Do Not Join Hands: *Views from the Frontline*, Teddington GNDR. Available at: http://globalnetwork-dr.org/views-from-the-frontline/voices-from-the-frontline-2011.pdf (accessed 17 March 2013).

Gorman-Murray, A. and Dominey-Howes, D. (forthcoming) 'Queering disasters: on the need to account for LGBTI experiences in natural disaster contexts', *Gender, Place and Culture*.

GROOTS and Huairou Commission (2009) *En-Gendering HFA: grassroots women's strategies for implementing the HFA (Hyogo Framework for Action)*, New York: Huairou Commission and GROOTS International. Available at: http://www.disasterwatch.net/resources/En-Gendering-HFA.pdf (accessed 17 March 2013).

Guerrero, S.H., Asis, M.M.B., Españo, A.J., Taberdo, T.I., Dayo, H., Rovillos, R. and Kintanar, T.B. (2000) 'Impact of globalization on women', *Review of Women's Studies*, 10(1–2): 268–74.

Gupta, S. and Leung, I. (2010) *Turning Good Practice into Institutional Mechanisms: Investing in Grassroots Women's Leadership to Scale Up Local Implementation of the Hyogo Framework for Action*, New York: Huairou Commission and GROOTS International. Available at: http://www.preventionweb.net/files/18197_201guptaandleung.theroleofwomenasaf.pdf (accessed 25 March 2013).

Hammami, R., Dewi, S., Syam, A., Zayyan, H., Wishah, H., Suyapno, E. and Iriarte, Y. (2009) *Towards Gender Equality in Humanitarian Response: Addressing the Needs of Women and Men in Gaza*, New York: UNIFEM.

Hausmann, R., Tyson, L. and Zahidi, S. (2011) *The Global Gender Gap Report 2011*, Geneva: World Economic Forum.

Hoffman, S. (1999) 'The regenesis of traditional gender patterns in the wake of a disaster', in A. Oliver-Smith and S. Hoffman (eds) *The Angry Earth: Disaster in Anthropological Perspective*, New York: Routledge, pp. 173–91.

Huairou Commission (2009) *Women's Views from the Frontline*, New York: Huairou Commission. Available at: http://www.preventionweb.net/files/10154_10154Womens ViewsFromtheFrontline.pdf (accessed 17 March 2013).

IASC (2006) *Women, Girls, Boys and Men, Different Needs, Equal Opportunities* (Gender Handbook for Humanitarian Action), IASC. Available at: http://www.humanitarianinfo.org/iasc/pageloader.aspx (accessed 17 March 2013).

IDNDR (1996) *IDNDR Day 1995. Women and Children: Key to Prevention*, Geneva: UN Department of Humanitarian Affairs.

Ikeda, K. (1995) 'Gender differences in human loss and vulnerability in natural disasters: a case study from Bangladesh', *Indian Journal of Gender Studies*, 2 (2): 171–93.

Kan, M., Sullivan, O. and Gershuny, J. (2011) 'Gender convergence in domestic work: discerning the effects of interactional and institutional barriers from large-scale data', *Sociology*, 45 (2): 234–51.

Klinenberg, E. (2002) *Heat Wave: A Social Autopsy of Disaster*, Chicago: University of Chicago Press.

Knight, K. and Sollom, R. (2012) 'Making disaster risk reduction and relief programmes LGBTI inclusive: examples from Nepal', *Humanitarian Exchange Magazine*, 55. Available at: http://www.odihpn.org/humanitarian-exchange-magazine/issue-55/making-disaster-risk-reduction-and-relief-programmes-lgbtiinclusive-examples-from-nepal (accessed 17 March 2013).

Laguerre, S. and Nixon, A.V. (2011) 'LGBT activism in Haiti through SEROvie: Steve Laguerre in interview with Angelique V. Nixon', in *Theorizing Homophobias in the*

Caribbean: Complexities of Place, Desire and Belonging. Available at: http://www. caribbeanhomophobias.org/steevelaguerre (accessed 17 March 2013).

MADRE (2012) *Struggling to survive: sexual exploitation of displaced women and girls in Port au Prince, Haiti,* MADRE. Available at: http://www.madre.org/images/ uploads/misc/1326210740_Haiti%20SE%20Report%20FINAL%20pub%20011012.pdf (accessed 17 March 2013).

Manila Declaration (2008) 'Manila Declaration for Global Action on Gender in Climate Change and Disaster Risk Reduction', in Third Global Congress of Women in Politics and Governance, on Gender in Climate Change Adaptation and Disaster Risk Reduction (2008). Available at: http://www.unisdr.org/files/8731_maniladeclarationforglobalaction ongenderinclimatechangeanddisasterriskreduction1.pdf (accessed 17 March 2013).

Mazurana, D., Benelli, P., Gupta, H. and Walker, P. (2011) *Sex and Age Matter: Improving Humanitarian Response in Emergencies,* Medford MA: Feinstein International Center, Tufts University. Available at: https://www.care.org/careswork/whatwedo/relief/ docs/sex-and-age-disag-data.pdf (accessed 17 March 2013).

Moser, C. (1989) 'Gender planning in the Third World: meeting practical and strategic gender needs', *World Development,* 17(11): 1799–825.

Murthy, R.K. and Kappen, M. (2006) *Gender, Poverty and Rights: A Trainer's Manual,* Bangalore: Visthar.

National Center for Transgender Equality (2011) *Making Shelters Safe for Transgender Evacuees,* Washington, DC: National Center for Transgender Equality. Available at: http://www.gdnonline.org/resources/MakingSheltersSafe_Aug2011_FINAL.pdf (accessed 17 March 2013).

Neumayer, E. and Plümper, T. (2007) 'The gendered nature of natural disasters: the impact of catastrophic events on the gender gap in life expectancy, 1981–2002', *Annals of the Association of American Geographers,* 97(3): 551–66.

Ortner, S.B. (1972) 'Is female to male as nature is to culture?', *Feminist Studies,* 1(2): 5–31.

Ozawa, K. (2012) 'Relief activities for LGBTI people in the affected areas', *Voices from Japan,* 26: 21–2.

Pincha, C. (2008a) *Gender Sensitive Disaster Management: A Toolkit for Practitioners,* Mumbai: Earthworm Books for Oxfam America and NANBAN Trust. Available at: http:// gdnonline.org/resources/Pincha_GenderSensitiveDisasterManagement_Toolkit.pdf (accessed 17 March 2013).

Pincha, C. (2008b) *Indian Ocean tsunami through the gender lens: insights from Tamil Nadu, India,* Mumbai: Earthworm Books for Oxfam America and NANBAN Trust, India. Available at: http://www.gdnonline.org/resources/Pincha_IndianOceanTsunamiThrough theGender%20Lens.pdf (accessed 17 March 2013).

Plümper, T. and Neumayer, E. (2006) 'The unequal burden of war: the effects of armed conflict on the gender gap in life expectancy', *International Organization,* 60(3): 723–54.

Sen, A.K. (2001) 'The many faces of gender inequality', *The New Republic,* September 17, pp. 35–40.

UN (2009) 'UN Secretary-General's campaign to end violence against women', UNiTE, UN Department of Public Information, DPI/2546A, November 2009. Available at: http://www.un.org/en/events/endviolenceday/pdf/UNiTE_TheSituation_EN.pdf (accessed 17 March 2013)

UNDESA (2010) *The World's Women 2010: Trends and Statistics,* New York: United Nations. Available at: http://unstats.un.org/unsd/demographic/products/Worldswomen/ WW_full%20report_color.pdf (accessed 17 March 2013).

UNDP (2010a) *Human Development Report 2010: The Real Wealth of Nations: Pathways to Human Development*, 20th Anniversary Edition, New York: United Nations.
—— (2010b) *Gender, Climate Change and Community-Based Adaptation: A Guidebook for Designing and Implementing Gender-Sensitive Community-Based Adaptation Programmes and Projects*, New York: United Nations. Available at: http://www.seachange cop.org/seachange/files/documents/2010_10_UNDP_Gender_Climate_Change_and_CBA. pdf (accessed 17 March 2013).
UNDP-BCPR (2011) *Disaster-Conflict Interface: Comparative Experiences 2011*, New York: United Nations Development Programme Bureau for Crisis Prevention and Recovery.
UN-INSTRAW (2010) 'Crossing borders II: migration and development from a gender perspective', Dominican Republic: UN-INSTRAW.
UNISDR (2007a) *Hyogo Framework for Action 2005–2015: Building the Resilience of Nations and Communities to Disasters*, Geneva: UNISDR.
—— (2007b) *Words into Action: A Guide for Implementing the Hyogo Framework*, Geneva: UNISDR.
—— (2009) *Making Disaster Risk Reduction Gender-Sensitive: Policy and Practical Guidelines*, Geneva: UNISDR, UNDP and IUCN. Available at: http://www.prevention web.net/files/9922_MakingDisasterRiskReductionGenderSe.pdf (accessed 17 March 2013).
—— (2011) *Global Assessment Report on Disaster Risk Reduction: Revealing Risk, Redefining Development*, Geneva: UNISDR. Available: www.preventionweb.net/gar (accessed 17 March 2013).
UN Women (2011) *Progress of the world's women, 2011–2012: Justice*, UN Women. Available at: http://progress.unwomen.org/pdfs/EN-Report-Progress.pdf (accessed 20 March 2013).
Watts, C. and Zimmerman, C. (2002) 'Violence against women: global scope and magnitude', *The Lancet*, 359(9313): 1232–37.
Williams, E., Sorokina, O., Jones-De Weeve, A. and Hartmann, H. (2006) *The Women of New Orleans and the Gulf Coast: Multiple Disadvantages and Key Assets for Recovery. Part II: Gender, Race and Class in the Labor Market*, Washington, DC: Institute for Women's Policy Research. Available at: http://www.iwpr.org/publications/pubs/the-women-of-new-orleans-and-the-gulf-coast-multiple-disadvantages-and-key-assets-for-recovery-part-ii.-gender-race-and-class-in-the-labor-market (accessed 20 March 2013).
Wisner, B. (2001) 'Notes on social vulnerability: categories, situations, capabilities, and circumstances', paper presented at the annual meeting of the Association of American Geographers. Available at: www.radixonline.org/resources/vulnerability-aag2001.rtf (accessed 20 March 2013).
Wisner, B., Blaikie, P., Cannon, T. and Davis, I. (2004) *At Risk: Natural Hazards, People's Vulnerability and Disasters*, 2nd edn, London: Routledge.

4 Community-based disaster risk reduction and disaster management

Emmanuel M. Luna

Lessons for practitioners

- Local communities are the first line of defense in facing disasters.
- The members of local communities display different forms of skills, **resources** and **knowledge** which all prove useful in facing natural **hazards** and disasters.
- Community-based disaster risk reduction (CBDRR) and community-based disaster management (CBDM) foster the **participation** of local communities in assessing the risk of disaster, reducing that risk, managing actual disasters and recovering after such events.
- CBDRR and CBDM are bottom-up processes which should integrate support from the top-down.
- CBDRR and CBDM should be integrated into the larger framework of development planning at both local and national levels.
- Practitioners of CBDRR and CBDM must have a good prior understanding of the local context to avoid **community** fragmentation.

Introduction: the community focus

Community-based disaster risk reduction (CBDRR) and **community-based disaster management (CBDM)** can be traced to the rise of the concepts of community development in the 1950s and participatory development in the 1960s and the 1970s. These were the decades when the less affluent countries found themselves struggling with underdevelopment and the expanding gaps between the rich and the poor. Participatory development was born, challenging the economic and political relations among nations at the macro level, and placing the people at the center of development at the micro level. The aim of CBDRR and CBDM is to reduce disaster impacts and risks through community participation (Uy 2004). It is sometimes referred to by other names or concepts such as community-based disaster risk management (CBDRM) and community-based disaster preparedness (CBDP). This chapter explores the history and growing use of community-based approaches with examples drawn from the Philippines, where the author is based, and from India, Bangladesh, and the Solomon Islands.

Community development was introduced in many countries in order to improve the living conditions of ordinary people by strengthening the democratic processes at the local level, the use of local leadership and community workers as facilitators and stimulators, and the use of coordinated teams of experts from various agencies. It was a self-help approach to community improvement (Polson 1964). This approach constituted a shift from an institution-based delivery system that was non-participative, top-down, externally dependent and non-empowering (Luna 1999, 2006b, 2009).

Community development work in the Philippines began in the 1950s (Luna 1999). The 1970s and 1980s were years of dictatorship in the Philippines. The Cold War and high- and low-intensity conflict due to ideological differences and the proliferation of authoritative regimes further pushed the call for a new world order and change on the national scene (Kuitenbrouwer 1976; Szymanski 1981; Bello 1994). A community-based, participatory approach was adopted, particularly by the civil society organizations desiring change in governance (Bello 1994; Villarin 1996), and thus the participatory development and community-based approaches in the Philippines then had a very strong political undertone. A more conflict-oriented community development, as contrasted to the functional community development in the 1950s, resulted from the growing inequity and human rights violations during the Marcos dictatorship from 1972–1986. The concern was not just limited to material delivery of the services but included components such as education and the raising of consciousness about the oppressive regime, community organizing and mobilization, advocacy for people's causes, and even outright confrontation with the dictatorship.

After the overthrow of the Marcos dictatorship, participation was utilized in many ways including in a health program (Osteria *et al.* 1988), resource management (Osteria and Okamura 1986; Borlagdan 1987; Flor *et al.* 1993; Ferrer *et al.* 2001), **livelihood** promotion (Braid 1993; Luz and Montelibano 1993), agrarian reform (Hayami *et al.* 1990; PhilDRRA 1997), irrigation (Korten and Siy 1989), governance (Garcia *et al.* 1993; Villarin 1996) as well as disaster risk reduction (DRR) and disaster management (DM).

In 1987, the Citizen Disaster Response Center and its partners that comprise the Citizen Disaster Response Network adopted the Citizenry-Based and Development-Oriented Disaster Response (CBDO-DR). The CBDO-DR approach looked at disasters as a question of **vulnerability**, recognized and strengthened people's existing **capacities**. It contributed to addressing the roots of vulnerabilities and to transforming or removing the structures generating inequity and under-development. It considered people's **participation** as essential to DRR and DM, and put a premium on the organizational capacity of vulnerable sectors through the formation of grassroots disaster response organizations. It also advocated the mobilization of less vulnerable sectors of society for partnership with the vulnerable sectors in DRR, DM and development work (Heijmans and Victoria 2001).

In 2003, a more holistic DRR and DM framework was introduced that included CBDRR and CBDM. While maintaining the four basic components in the disaster continuum such as emergency response, post emergency, prevention and **mitigation**, and preparedness, four other concerns were integrated namely the reduction of **risks**, the protection of development gains, sustainable human development and mainstreaming DRR into development (Delica 2003b).

Community-based disaster risk reduction and community-based disaster management

Concepts, goals and elements

CBDRR and CBDM refer to both concepts and processes. CBDRR and CBDM are meant to transform passivity and powerlessness into action and resilience. It is an alternative to the reactive and dole out approach during emergencies meant to alleviate the pains and difficulties during disasters. From this temporal response, CBDRR and CBDM go beyond emergencies and encompass risk reduction before, during and after disaster events. The greatest enemy that can be created by relief and development work is dependency: when the local people resign in apathy, look at outside help as the only answer to their misery, and refuse to take action to fix their own situation. With this kind of attitude, the people become more vulnerable and unmindful of the dangers that may come. CBDRR and CBDM are strategies to address this. Their specific goals include: (1) the reduction of people's vulnerabilities; (2) public safety and reduction of impacts on lives, property, resources and environment due to hazards; (3) empowerment of individuals and community institutions; and (4) the transformation of structures and relationships that generate inequity and underdevelopment (Luna 2004a, 2004b). There are social conditions that perpetuate vulnerability such as **poverty**, poor governance, inequitable **access** to resources, and unjust economic relations. In CBDRR and CBDM, these concerns are at the core of the agenda since they are the ones that induce the vulnerability of people and communities. Empowering communities also means instituting changes in these conditions to reduce risks.

One of the early institutions that promoted CBDRR and CBDM through its training programs is the Asian Disaster Preparedness Center. It defines both CBDRR and CBDM as:

> A process ... in which at risk communities are actively engaged in the identification, analysis, treatment, monitoring and evaluation of disaster risks in order to reduce their vulnerabilities and enhance their capacities. This means that the people are at the heart of decision making and implementation of ... activities. The involvement of the most vulnerable is paramount and the support of the least vulnerable is necessary ... Local and national government are involved and supportive.
>
> (Abarquez and Murshed 2004: 9)

Working with the communities means that the external organizations such as government agencies, non-governmental organizations (NGOs) and other key players need to appreciate and adopt CBDRR and CBDM in their own risk reduction programs. This will minimize the imposition of programs from above and will encourage the local people to actively participate in risk reduction activities. An example of how this can be done is illustrated by drawing up a strategic plan in integrating CBDRR and CBDM in socio-economic development processes. In the Philippines, where participation is mainstreamed in the development processes, stakeholders are involved in formulating government policies for DRR and DM. One of the initiatives was the identification of elements of good CBDRR and CBDM practice (Box 4.1) by both the government and NGO practitioners that were adopted in the strategic plan (Office of Civil Defense 2007).

CBDRR and CBDM Strategies

Participatory analysis for hazards, vulnerabilities and capacities

The scientific community provides comprehensive, objective, rational and relevant information and assessment of the hazards and the vulnerabilities of communities. They are equipped with the advance competence in providing the people with the data for risk identification and analysis. However, most of the experts come from outside, such as government agencies, NGOs and academics. The local people have a lot to contribute in understanding and assessing their hazards and vulnerabilities (OXFAM 2002; Wisner 2004). They have local and indigenous knowledge that serves as an effective resource in reducing disaster risks and responding to disasters. What they need is access to studies and dialogues and for them to be listened to in appreciating their situations. The process encourages the people to express their own assessment of their conditions. Previous disasters could leave behind hurts and questions that were not answered, causing the people to feel inhibited, lose confidence, and become subservient. By allowing the people to reflect and share their experiences of disasters, the process becomes educational and liberating as they understand the conditions and the causes of their vulnerability. Digging into their assets and capacities will show that they can contribute in the process of reducing disaster risks, responding to disasters and rebuilding their communities.

Participatory community counter-disaster planning

While the national planning bodies formulate macro and meso plans for DRR and DM, communities have to come up with their own plans (Luna 2000; Heijmans and Victoria 2001; Jayakaran 2001; Wisner *et al.* 2004). The first plan is a comprehensive one that could be short- to long-term, annual to a three- or ten-year plan. It lays down the long-term needs of the communities and the socio-economic, political and physical investments to respond to development needs and reduce disaster risks. Land use is an important component of this plan. The other one is a counter-disaster plan that stipulates operational action points before, during and after the disaster event. From the results of the participatory capacity and vulnerability analysis (PCVA), the people attend workshops where they set goals

Box 4.1 Elements of good practice in CBDRR and CBDM

1 *Community ownership*: The community manages the implementation of the DRR and DM measures though the CBDRR and CBDM process may have been facilitated by outsiders, be it NGO or government agencies, and takes control of future plans and actions in risk reduction and disaster management.

2 *Use of local knowledge about the hazards*: Recognition of existing coping mechanisms, capacities, local know-how and resources of people and communities.

3 *Communities as ultimate beneficiaries*: Community as key resource and front line in CBDRR and CBDM implementation; priority given to the most vulnerable groups, families and communities.

4 *Multi-stakeholder participation*: Local people are the main actors and prime movers in reducing disaster risks, with wider participation of other key players.

5 *Education and capacity building*: Increasing the community's capacity and the people's skills, resources and readiness to undertake DRR and DM.

6 *Gender sensitivity*: Recognition of the different needs, activities, perceptions and priorities of men and women.

7 *Cultural appropriateness*: Recognition and respect for the community's **culture**, traditions and customs.

8 *Sensitivity to local structures*: Recognition of the community and people's organizations, their resources and coping strategies.

9 *Harmony with local, indigenous and scientific knowledge*: Incorporation of people's perception of vulnerability and capacity with experts' knowledge of hazards assessment.

10 *Complementarity of top-down approach*: Involvement and all-out support of local and national government and civil society.

11 *Demonstration of potential for building economic resilience*: Building upon and strengthening the community's coping strategies and capacities to reduce conditions, factors, and processes of vulnerabilities, including poverty, social inequity, and promoting a safer environment.

12 *Transparency and accountability in procedures and processes*: Accountability to the people first and demonstration of individual and collective actions for DRR and DM.

13 *Communication design*: Observing early warning information dissemination and sustained public awareness.

14 *Exit strategy with sustainability mechanisms*: Sustaining CBDRR and CBDM beyond project funding and termination by setting up mechanisms for sustainability.

(Office of Civil Defense 2007)

and objectives to reduce risks at the various stages of disaster. Strategies are laid down, with corresponding mechanisms such as committees composed of community leaders and volunteers.

Community-based early warning

Early warning is a very effective tool in preventing losses in times of disaster. Identification of potential hazards allows the community to warn each other, evacuate, and avoid losses when the hazard comes (Luneta and Molina 2008; OXFAM 2009; and Villagrán de León, Chapter 5 in this volume). This is true for hazards that have a slow onset, meaning there is sufficient time between the identification of the hazard and the time it impacts the community, such as typhoons, volcanic eruptions, tsunami, flood, and droughts. An early warning committee is tasked to observe the hazards, facilitate in the development of an early warning system that is understandable by the people, and communicate this to the whole community. In communities near the river, the most common signal is the marking that shows the elevation of the river. If the water reaches a specific level, that indicates corresponding action. For example, a height of 15 feet means that the families must be prepared; at 18 feet they must evacuate; and at 20 feet everyone should leave their home. When there is a potential threat, the warning signals are activated. These include the blowing of horns, ringing of the church bells, sirens, and volunteers running from house to house to inform the families of the incoming threats.

Building of people's organizations and disaster action teams

Community participation is effective if the people are organized. The people's organization serves as the instrument for assessment, planning, mobilization, and evaluation activities (Heijmans and Victoria 2001; Luna 2004a). Committees are formed to handle specific aspects of DRR and DM efforts. There can be a committee for mitigation, for early warning, for search, rescue and retrieval, for relief distribution, for evacuation management and for relocation and recovery. Committees can be formed also for training and education, health, security, children's welfare, resource generation and volunteer management.

Inter- and intra-collaboration and coordination

There are many stakeholders in DRR: the communities, the people's organizations, NGOs, government agencies, international humanitarian organizations, the private sector, faith communities and academia. In CBDRR and CBDM, the community takes the center stage but the other organizations play a supporting role through the provision of assistance in search, rescue and relief, capacity building, mainstreaming DRR measures in development plans, and disaster recovery. Non-coordination among the support groups can lead to overlapping of tasks, unhealthy competition, poor accountability, diffused responsibility, inefficient resource management, and program failure (Heijmans and Victoria 2001). The provision of external support is not done, however, in a top-down and domineering fashion but through consultation and coordination with the affected communities.

Use of local and indigenous knowledge

A very powerful strategy in CBDRR and CBDM is utilizing the local and indigenous knowledge. This knowledge includes information and skills acquired through education or experiences and have become part of the community and a normal part of everyday life (Luna 2006a; Mercer 2012). People have developed through their past experience ways of preparing, warning, and responding to disasters. Examples are warning signals provided through the observation of the sky or animal behaviours. People structure their houses to make them resilient and practice farming methods that can adapt to the natural environment. Local knowledge incorporates understanding and skills which may have come originally from the outside but have been assimilated by the community people in their practice.

The CBDRR and CBDM process

Prior to the emergence of CBDRR and CBDM, the community-based approach was used in many development programs. When disasters affected the communities, community development strategies such as organizing, mobilization, participatory planning and the like were adapted in DRR and DM process. NGOs that were doing development work with communities pursued relief operations when the communities they were serving were affected by disasters. They adopted participatory processes and community-organizing methods in doing this (Box 4.2). Later, CBDRR and CBDM became a regular program.

In CBDRR and CBDM, community organizing is the core method. Community organizing is the process of development from the people, by the people, and for the people. The steps and activities are community entry, community integration, social analysis, spotting and developing indigenous community leaders, core group building, recruitment of members, setting up the organization and working with other organizations for development (Manalili 1990). It is

a method which refers to the activities aimed at the grouping of people to struggle for their common needs and aspirations in a given locality. [Community organizing] processes involve the following activities, which may overlap and be repeated at a new level during the process of organizing: integration with the community, social investigation, problem/issue spotting, ground work, meeting, role play, mobilisation, evaluation, reflection and setting up of the organisation.

(Third World Studies Center 1990: 5–6)

Box 4.2 From development work to relief and rehabilitation and back

In the early 1990s, the Philippine Rural Reconstruction Program (PRRM) attempted to provide financial assistance and also to enhance self-reliance. When the great earthquake struck Central Luzon in July 1990, the municipality of Caranglan was isolated due to landslides. The earthquake loosened the rocks and the heavy rains eroded the mountainside along the highway, making it impassable and burying the houses and farms along the road. Transportation of food and other basic supplies was interrupted.

Initially, PRRM workers brought some relief goods to one community isolated by disaster. These workers asked for volunteers to take relief goods to another community. Afterwards, they went to the next upland community, distributed relief materials and asked for volunteers to get the goods from the base. This approach was systematized when the development workers set up a camp. Radio communication was set up with the isolated upland communities. Community-organizing techniques were adopted by socially integrating with the people. They called meetings to discuss the situation. A relief committee was formed that handled the relief operations.

While the relief operation was taking place, the community organizers did a rapid rural appraisal to determine the extent of the damage to the families and farms. They conducted Village Social Analysis (VSA) and had community meetings to evaluate other needs. They also mobilized volunteers in order to assess damage, including in remote areas. The VSA was very useful in determining what kind of goods should be given to the families. As a result, bigger families received more goods and those with children received milk. A list of priority families entitled to receive relief goods was also elaborated. The community meetings became very useful in clarifying issues and in resolving internal conflicts.

After a week of doing relief operations, the PRRM staff saw the need to go beyond relief and launched a more comprehensive program to prepare the communities for rehabilitation. They called this the Relief and Rehabilitation Program, which had four parts: (1) sustained relief distribution for three weeks – this was done through the active participation of the relief committees and meetings with the people; (2) disaster monitoring – this was done through a committee whose members were trained to do monitoring of damages and possible threats of more landslides and erosion; (3) establishment of evacuation centers for a number of families who had lost their houses and were living in dangerous areas where possible landslides might occur; (4) study of alternative sources of livelihood. Through the community meetings, the people were able to analyze their situation and the possible courses of action. Due to the massive destruction of the farms and the difficulty of transporting goods, some families considered relocating to other areas.

As a result of the meetings with the people, the PRRM did not promise that it could provide a relocation area. However, it facilitated establishing linkages with government agencies so that the communities would be able to know their plans. Other planned assistance included transport assistance, provision of soft loans, use of the logs carried by the flood for housing, relief provision and communal farming.

Reflecting on the experience, those involved realized that the people in the area could easily be mobilized. The same observation was true for support groups and individuals such as volunteers and donors of goods and funds. During this crises situation, local leaders also surfaced naturally. Also the PRRM workers learned a golden rule: *any agency offering assistance should work within the committee system and procedures should be agreed with the community.*

(Luna 2004a)

Site selection, community entry and integration

If CBDRR and CBDM are initiated by the residents in their own community, then there is no need for site selection (see Chapter 17). Organizing takes place in their community for DRR and DM. The residents are usually known to each other, have common interests and needs, though there could be conflicts as well. However, if CBDRR and CBDM are undertaken by an outside agency, be it a governmental or non-governmental entity, then it must choose a site that fits its own criteria, usually poor and vulnerable communities. Community integration is done by an organizer fielded in the area by establishing rapport with the residents, becoming familiar with the situation, and becoming like one of them. In times of emergency, site selection directs one to the community where the disaster is taking place (Luna 2004a).

Enhanced social investigation through participatory hazard, vulnerability and capacity analysis

In CBDRR and CBDM, the analysis of the community situation is done through socio-economic profiling, hazard analysis and PCVA and damage assessment.

- *Hazard analysis* looks at the various natural and human-induced threats that can cause disasters (see Chapter 2). Among the factors considered are the characteristics of the hazards, such as the frequency of occurrence, the magnitude, the intensity, scope or areas that can be affected, the duration when the hazard takes place, the onset or the time before the hazard occurs and the possible impact.

- *Vulnerability analysis* identifies the people, sectors or geographical areas that will be most likely affected by hazards and the possible impacts. It addresses various issues such as the physical, social, economic, political and environmental elements that are at risk and the factors that make these elements vulnerable.
- *Capacity analysis* focuses on awareness of the risk and the resources available to enable people to acquire skills, materials or tools that can reduce disaster impact. Among capacities are also local and traditional knowledge of hazards and of ways of protecting oneself, one's family, and assets. Participatory tools and techniques used in community development such as participatory rapid appraisal and participatory learning and action are adapted in undertaking capacity and resource analysis for CBDRR and CBDM. These tools determine the innate capacity of the person, the family and the community to prevent, mitigate, prepare and respond to disasters (Theis and Grady 1991; Luna and Falk 2003; Jayakaran 2001).
- *Damage assessment* is done immediately after a disaster event. An inventory of the human, physical, economic, social and environmental losses is done to determine the extent and quality of damages in the community. Damage assessment may also be conducted in a participatory manner (Heijmans and Victoria 2001).

The various tools for data gathering in a participatory rural appraisal, such as **mapping**, transect, historical timeline, and the like, can be used prior to any disaster event. However, during actual emergency, a more rapid way to assess the situation is done by locating and estimating the condition of people who are in danger, while simultaneously conducting rescue operations, relief distribution, evacuation and provision of medical and psychosocial services. In communities where there is an adequate assessment of the situation even before disaster takes place, the analysis during an emergency situation becomes easier. In fact, the situation can be forecast through contingency planning that can show different scenarios if the hazards occur (Luna 2004a).

In addition to more appropriate appreciation of the community situation, PCVA can have surprising positive, unintended outcomes (Box 4.3).

Leadership development and organization building

One basic principle in CBDRR and CBDM is developing the capacity of the people, organizations and the community. The people need to be equipped with leadership capabilities and skills such as hazards and risk mapping and monitoring, warning and communication, search and rescue operations, evacuation planning and management, mobilization for emergency response and the like.

CBDRR and CBDM are community centered but they do not exclude the need for support from the outside. However, this has to be done in an empowering way. The best way of doing this is by building mechanisms through which the people can participate. Establishing a core group of leaders and mobilizing community

---

Box 4.3 Harmonization in Radefasu, the Solomon Islands

Radefasu is a coastal village in the Solomon Islands. The village is comprised of two distinct groups, the Rade Tolo and the Rade Asi. Since the 1940s the relationship between the two groups has been affected by land disputes. Each group kept within its own boundaries at all times. The two groups continued to live and work in different ways until August 2004 when the Solomon Islands Red Cross (SIRC) decided to carry out a PCVA in Radefasu. The PCVA process allowed the two communities to come together and start talking to each other.

Rade Asi elders planned a weekend retreat to identify and refocus the roles and responsibilities of adults in the community. To help the community's young people develop in a positive manner, they decided to set a good example and became role models. The Rade Tolo community heard about the Rade Asi's initiative but, initially, it was not particularly interested in the project. However, during one of the PCVA meetings to discuss the drainage activities, which both communities had identified as essential, a representative of the Rade Tolo acknowledged the importance of community youth development and thanked the Rade Asi for having taken the initiative. He asked that the community as a whole should work together to develop their community and living standards, as well as to help their young people.

As a result of their efforts, the community began to work together. Community elders and youth, in particular, became closely involved in the PCVA activities, especially after a landowner gave the community his land for the drainage system. The PCVA process for Radefasu's youth was a landmark event. They have asked whether they can take part in the PCVA process when it is launched in nearby communities, and expressed a keen interest in developing a local Red Cross group in 2005.

(IFRC 2005)

---

members are ways of engaging people to participate. People's organizations can be established with committees tasked to work on disaster-related concerns. At the same time, these organizations can be linked together to establish networks and alliances that can provide mutual support and help strengthen each other in pursuing DRR and DM activities.

Before the enactment of a new law on DRR and DM in the Philippines, the villages or *barangay* had a Disaster Coordinating Council (DCC). However, findings from the field show that the DCCs are seldom organized in communities. If ever they are organized, this is just to comply with requirements and no orientation, training or action takes place. They are also passive and become active only when there are disasters or emergencies. It is not enough for local groups or

---

Box 4.4 Internationally conceived but locally engaged

The Program for Hydro-Meteorological Disaster Mitigation in Secondary Cities in Asia (PROMISE) focuses on the need to reduce the vulnerabilities to climate change and to minimize the destructive impacts of the hydro-meteorological hazards on vulnerable urban communities and economic structures through enhanced preparedness and mitigation. PROMISE-Bangladesh established 10 formal DRR and DM committees in 10 wards and 10 informal Volunteer/Change Agents (CA) groups. DRR and DM committees include the Ward Commissioner as the chairperson and other members included schoolteachers, NGO representatives, political leaders, religious leaders, the local elite and local people. This networking and partnering led to the formalization and recognition of the community-level DRR and DM by the higher authorities.

The lessons learned were that community-level capacity building, awareness creation, effective information dissemination and advocacy are effective tools in reducing the vulnerability to climate change impacts and strengthening DRR and DM processes at the local level. However, decentralization is needed to utilize these tools well. Therefore, community-level DRR and DM institutions are very important. The Memorandum of Understanding signed between the community and the City Government enhances trust between the two parties which results in smooth and easy coordination in achieving development and DRR and DM goals.

(Jayamanna 2008)

---

institutions that can be venues for people's participation to be organized. They have to be equipped for the tasks. External support that would help develop the capacities of the community groups in doing CBDRR and CBDM is essential for the latter's effectiveness and sustainability (Luna 2004a).

Support institutions such as NGOs, churches, academic institutions, businesses, and government agencies can facilitate community processes that will enable the people to participate. Even large and internationally conceived projects can adopt CBDRR and CBDM as guiding frameworks in establishing local institutions for DRR and DM, as shown in a case from Bangladesh (Box 4.4).

Mainstreaming CBDRR in development planning

The major shift in approach to DRR and DM worldwide that began to take hold in the 1990s has two aspects. So far, this chapter has discussed one of these: a focus on the community as a site for hazard and risk assessment and action to reduce risks and manage disasters. However, the other aspect of new thinking is equally important. DRR should be integrated into routine development planning. No longer are expenditures on DRR considered as 'competing' with resources for development. In fact, investment in DRR can boost development, and development investments – if done with disaster reduction also in mind – run less risk of being wasted because they are wiped out in the next event (Box 4.5).

Box 4.5 The disaster–development continuum in India

In 1999, a super-typhoon hit the State of Orissa in India, causing 10,000 deaths and damaging housing, livestock, crops, infrastructure and the environment. This prompted the government of Orissa to form an autonomous organization called the Orissa State Disaster Mitigation Authority (OSDMA). This organization was tasked to look after the reconstruction work and to develop a mitigation and preparedness strategy that would minimize future losses and destruction. The OSDMA recognized the primary role of the communities in confronting and responding immediately to any emergency. The program, though mainly initiated at the state level, focused on strengthening communities to combine disaster preparedness and mitigation work with development planning.

Following participatory assessment and hazard mapping, community contingency plans were developed in more than one thousand villages. DRR Committees at the Block, GP (principal village, Gram Panchayat) and village levels were formed and trained to organize and systematize disaster response at the local levels. Various Task Forces were also organized and trained to manage early warning, search and rescue operations, first aid, relief, medical and housing needs, damage assessment, and psychosocial counseling. The program was successful in putting disaster risk management on the agenda of the **local government** by integrating it into the development planning process and systems at the Block and GP levels.

The integration of CBDRR into development planning sensitized local government personnel to risk management and included mitigation measures identified in the process of formulating community contingency plans. These measures included the construction of schools which can also be used as cyclone shelters, the repair or installation of tube wells, the strengthening of weak embankments, the construction of facilities for storing nets and dry fish, and the identification of the appropriate technology for safer but affordable building construction. Non-structural measures undertaken were public awareness campaigns, training and registration of high-risk groups.

(Delica 2003a)

Disaster risk-sensitive community planning

In addition to the general goals of alleviating poverty, enhancing the growth and the welfare of the people, improving the environment, or increasing access and participation in the development process, there are planning goals and objectives that need to be set in CBDRR (Luna 2004a). The ultimate goal in DRR is the prevention and reduction of losses in all areas: physical, social, economic, environmental and other parts of community life. This entails reducing the vulnerabilities of the people and of the community and increasing their capacity. Community planning should include more specific goals such as increasing people's awareness of and skills in DRR, improving their access to resources and facilities that will enable them to prepare and respond effectively to threats and other hazards, developing community systems and procedures for DM, organizing them to ensure participation and systematic collective actions. Both structural and non-structural measures can be planned by the community for DRR and DM.

Among the structural measures are dykes and riprapping on the riverbanks to prevent erosion and flooding; building roads, bridges, hanging bridges, footpaths to ensure safe access and mobility; potable sources of water; safe evacuation centers; medical facilities; housing and resettlement. Non-structural measures for the community include hazards and risk mapping and monitoring; contingency planning; installing warning and communication systems; public awareness and information campaigns; training and organizing of volunteers and residents on various aspects of DRR and DM; drills and simulation exercises; evacuation planning and management; community land-use planning; integration of DRR in community development plans; and provision of adequate supplies and equipment appropriate to the hazards threatening the community.

More important than these measures are environmental protection and management initiatives that can prevent or mitigate disasters such as banning logging, reforestation, protecting the mangrove plantation, waste management, drainage clean-up, non-use of inorganic chemicals in agriculture, environmentally friendly methods in resource extraction in marine, forestry and quarries, and urban environment protection from pollution, congestion, industrial and transport disasters.

Similarly, development projects like livelihood, health services, land reforms and other services in both rural and urban communities address people's vulnerability and are therefore indispensable. What matters is the incorporation of a DRR perspective in these development projects and activities so that the adverse effects are identified and corresponding responses are planned out.

Mobilization, networking and advocacy

Disaster itself is an issue for community mobilization and advocacy. Among those directly hit by disasters, the people have to organize and mobilize to facilitate relief operations. In the evacuation center, the evacuees work for better services and faster resettlement. The content therefore of advocacy for DRR and DM includes the call for better environmental practice; new legislation that promotes proactive and community-based approaches to implementation of projects that can mitigate disasters; influencing the policies of local government and the national government to be more responsive to communities affected by disasters; resource generation for victims of disasters; mobilizing volunteer workers for disaster response; resisting development projects that pose danger and threat to people and the community; and exposing and confronting authorities and groups that are violating DRR and DM policies and principles. Communities and NGOs can be mobilized for these purposes. Linkages can be established among concerned entities to enhance greater coordination, collaboration and capacity to exert greater strength (Luna 2004a).

Evaluation, phasing out and follow-up

Evaluation in CBDRR and CBDM is inevitable for rational decision-making and in drawing lessons from the experience. The people have the capacity for evaluation and to sustain their work. Many community disaster-related activities focus on relief distribution. This is very relevant during the emergency phase but it has an end in the DRR and DM cycle. Similarly, evacuation is not meant as a permanent solution, but just as a temporary response to the situation. In both cases, phasing out does not mean leaving the community, but moving to another phase, that is towards rehabilitation and reconstruction. As the communities reach these stages, they are also being ushered into the area of development (Luna 2004a).

Issues and challenges in CBDRR and CBDM

The practice of CBDRR and CBDM is faced with several issues and challenges. CBDRR and CBDM are based on participation which is the means of empowering people and mobilizing communities collectively. However, attempts to encourage participation may lead to community fragmentation. This is illustrated by an NGO's attempt to undertake participatory management of an evacuation center that went wrong (Box 4.6).

One reason for the failure of participation is the lack of a thorough understanding of the community situation. Twigg (2004) explains the main challenges lie in not having this understanding. The communities are complex with different attributes and diverse needs and priorities that can create or worsen divisions in the community. There are power relationships among different groups which have varied levels of power. Social relations are not equal and the voices of the more vulnerable groups may not be heard. Organizationally, there could be limited community capacity in responding to the various tasks in CBDRR and CBDM. There is a need to address change as the communities and their needs and resources are always changing. There is a question about whether participatory approach is applicable in situations of social breakdown due to conflicts. The people are uprooted and live in dislocated communities without traditional authorities, kinship affiliation and reciprocity. Furthermore, there are external forces which can have decisive impacts on the community services and the assistance to which they are entitled (Twigg 2004: 197–121).

Box 4.6 Participation efforts that went wrong

The eruption of Mt. Pinatubo in 1991 in the Philippines caused the evacuation of thousands of families affected by lahar flows that destroyed and buried communities till 1995. One of the evacuation centers set up was the Sapang Maisac Evacuation Center (SMEC) in Mexico, Pampanga. Built in 1996 and supported by a faith-based non-governmental organization, the evacuation center was only 6 km away from the town proper. It had 18 bunkhouses. Each bunkhouse had ten units, each with a floor area of 1250 square feet (25x50 ft). If fully occupied, the SMEC could accommodate 180 families. At the height of the lahar threat, the SMEC was fully occupied. But due to the transfer to resettlement areas and non-occupancy of some families, the family occupants decreased. In July 1997, there were 120 families living in the SMEC.

The SMEC was known to be the model staging area for all the evacuation centers in Pampanga. A staging area was a temporary place for residents who had been evacuated while waiting for a final resettlement area where they could live permanently. The community was organized with an established system for decision-making, program planning, implementation, coordination and liaison work with outside agencies. The community was organized with a General Assembly (GA) composed of residents 18 years old and above. The GA set the general direction and defined the programs and **policies** of the organization. There was an Executive Committee composed of the leaders of the 18 bunkhouses. A presiding officer was elected on a quarterly and then on a monthly basis to give each bunk leader a chance to be the presiding officer. There were also five working committees composed of two representatives from each bunkhouse. The committees were the Committee of Finance, Ways and Means; the Committee on Health and Sanitation; the Committee on Livelihood, Education and Training; the Committee on Peace and Order; and the Committee on Youth, Culture and Sports. The organization was very active in managing the evacuation but there were also some conditions that triggered its downfall (Fernandez and Siojo 1997).

When the SMEC was formed, the original plan was to establish just one resettlement area for affected families. But this was not done when the NGO managing the evacuation center and the government agencies started to resettle the families in different areas and at different times. Most of the active and reliable leaders of SMEC were resettled, leaving the rest of the members in a state of emptiness and insecurity.

The evacuees were not interested in participating in the organization's activities and programs because of the organizational change. It was observed that the NGO organizers "turned out to be supervisors or commanding officers . . . in monitoring the activities and behaviour of the people" (Fernandez and Siojo 1997). The NGO emphasized moral values more than the economic needs of the evacuees. Policies were formulated without consulting the community leaders. There was an issue on the personal use of the Social Credit Fund by the chairperson of the livelihood committee, causing the people to become restless since their project proposals could not be funded. There was an apparent knowledge of the scam by the community organizer of the NGO, but without informing the organization. The scam led to a split among the residents staying at the SMEC.

Another disturbing situation was the reapplication rule of the NGO that required the evacuees to comply. Reapplications meant that the evacuees had to submit application papers to the NGO, asking the latter to allow the evacuees to stay. This move was seen by the evacuees as the agency's organizing strategy to oust evacuees who were delinquent and not sympathizers. The community leaders voiced their disapproval of the rule. They felt that this ignored what the organization stood for.

When the results of the reapplication rule came out in August, 1997, a number of residents were considered as having pending cases or were "not in good standing" based on certain criteria like not attending meetings regularly, being caught gambling, drinking or causing a public disturbance. By September, the NGO had sent out eviction notices to 21 families who had failed to come for a review of their cases. This caused another outrage in the SMEC, though 15 families who appealed were given a second chance to stay. After this experience, the people stated their decision that the community organizer of the NGO had to settle disputes first with them before taking them to the higher authority. They demanded that they should be informed and consulted first on rules being implemented in the SMEC. They also said that most of those who had been gambling were already senior and could no longer apply for jobs and had no livelihood opportunities.

The evacuation center was seen as a temporary community. It was a place where the people could find refuge when affected by lahar flooding. For those whose lives were totally devastated, it was a staging area before they could find a final resettlement. The people had three options available: (1) to return to their community if it was still livable; (2) to go to a final resettlement area; or (3) to continue waiting at the evacuation center, without any assurance of what changes would take place and prolonging their very unstable condition.

The people were also struggling against external issues confronting them such as unexpected resettlement schemes, non-payment of electric bills, new policies imposed without consultation, the fund scam, and lack of possible sources of income. At the same time, they were struggling internally. They felt neglected, deceived, and afraid of the future. This was true not only for the individual but for the whole community as well.

> The initial stage of the SMEC was considered an ideal state of participatory management of an evacuation center because people had high hopes that something could happen if they got involved. But when they found out that what they were looking forward to – a common resettlement area for all and a viable source of livelihood – was not falling in place but falling apart, the idealism of participatory management also started to disintegrate. Thus they were not interested, refused to participate and worse, were very much in personal conflict with the community workers.
>
> (Luna 2004a)

The heterogeneity of communities adds challenges because people in a community experience different degrees of vulnerability. There are vulnerable groups who may be affected by physical, cultural or social barriers that prevent them from accessing services; they may also tend to be excluded from the CBDRR and the CBDM.

Also the wider context of analysis must go beyond the community. Hazards that affect the community could come from several hundred kilometers away, and this has to be recognized by the community. For example, the floods that devastate communities could originate in the mountain ranges in other provinces, regions or countries. There is a spatial and organizational relationship with the higher and larger communities that has to be considered in action planning.

The political context and continuity raise other concerns. Community leadership is always linked with the leadership at the higher level of government bureaucracy. When the leaders change at the higher level, corresponding changes could also transpire at the village level. In the Philippines, election of public officials takes place every three years. Because of this, there are situations where community leaders who have been trained in DRR and DM are removed because new leaders have to be put in place as a consequence of patronage politics. In the communities affected by the 2004 flash flood in the province of Quezon, the local leaders were organized into *barangay* (village) Disaster Coordinating Councils and were trained in CBDRR and CBDM. In 2009, the author discovered that the communities which remained vulnerable to river flooding had new leaders but they did not have any training in DRR and DM.

In another case, a corporate foundation promoting social responsibility committed to providing services to the community changed its leadership and consequently the priorities of the organization. The committed funds promised for the community housing of the families affected by the flood were cancelled, causing further distress to the community (Luna 2009). The NGO facilitating the organizing work in the community was faced with the burden of finding new sources of funds to support the housing project that had initially been promised by the corporate foundation.

Conclusion

CBDRR and CBDM emerged from community development approaches in the period 1950–1990 to take their place as a central approach not only to DRR and DM, but also in routine development planning. In addition to their proven usefulness as a planning and community mobilization approach, they have another vital function. CBDRR and CBDM mobilize people and enable hope to survive. The greatest enemy that a person could encounter in a disaster may not be the hazard itself, but loss of hope and feelings of powerlessness. Losing one's hope because of the disaster could be the greatest loss. CBDRR and CBDM place people at the center. It is an empowering process to reduce risks and enable the person and the community to regain their identity and agency. Material losses can be replaced with the provision of resources, but a devastated self and community take more complex efforts and a longer time to repair. Participation by the people in CBDRR and CBDM has a healing power as the aggrieved victims of disasters express themselves through voices and actions, releasing deep-seated suffering and regaining energies that can be used to build resilience.

References

Abarquez, I. and Murshed, Z. (2004) *Community-Based Disaster Risk Management: Field Practitioners' Handbook*, Pathumthani: Asian Disaster Preparedness Center.

Bello, W. (1994) 'Clash of development models in the Asia-Pacific', in International Institute for Rural Reconstruction (ed.) *Making a Stand, Claiming the Future: A Sustainable People's Agenda for the 21st Century*, Proceedings of the Asia-Pacific NGO Conference for the World Summit for Social Development, Silang: International Institute for Rural Reconstruction, pp. 14–21.

Borlagdan, S.B. (1987) *Working with the People in the Upland: The Bulolakaw Social Forestry Experience*, Quezon City: Institute of Philippine Culture, Ateneo de Manila University Press.

Braid, R.F. (1993) *Sustainable Development Through Cooperatives*, Manila: Asian Institute of Journalism.

Delica, D. (2003a) 'Community-based disaster risk management: gaining ground in hazard-prone communities in Asia', *Philippine Sociological Review*, 51: 41–64.

—— (2003b) 'Challenges in CBDM in Asian and Philippine Context', in Philippine Disaster Management Forum, *Disaster Risk Reduction through Advocacy and Coalition Building*, Quezon City: Project Development and Monitoring Facility.

Fernandez, B.J. and Siojo, M.J. (1997) *Changing Times, Changing Needs: The Sapang Maisac Evaluation Center Experience*, Quezon City: University of the Philippines Diliman, College of Social Work and Community Development.

Ferrer, E., Polotan-de la Cruz, L. and Newkirk, G.F. (eds) (2001) *Hope Takes Root: Community-Based Coastal Resources Management Stories from Southeast Asia*, Quezon City: CBCRM Resource Center and Coastal Resources Research Network.

Flor, A.G., Guerrero, S.H., Kroske, H., Reuther, R. and Cardenas, M.L. (1993) *Public Participation in EIA: An Environmental Monitoring Manual*, Laguna: Environmental Management Bureau/MADECOR Environmental Management Systems, Inc.

Garcia, E., Macuja II, J. and Tolosa Jr, B. (eds) (1993) *Participation in Governance: The People's Right*, Quezon City: Ateneo de Manila University Press.

Hayami, Y., Quisumbing, M.A.R., and Adriano, L.S. (1990) *Towards an Alternative Land Reform Paradigm: A Philippine Perspective*, Quezon City: Ateneo de Manila University Press.

Heijmans, A. and Victoria, L. (2001) *Citizenry-Based and Development-Oriented Disaster Response: Experiences and Practices in Disaster Management of the Citizens' Disaster Response Network in the Philippines*, Quezon City: Center for Disaster Preparedness.

IFRC (2005) *Solomon Islands: From Risk Assessment to Community Actions*, Geneva: IFRC.

Jayakaran, R. (2001) *Carrying Out a Rapid Situation Analysis at the District Level for Community Capacity to Respond to Disasters (A Resource Manual)*, Manila: Asia Pacific Disaster Management Office/World Vision International.

Jayamanna, W. (2008) 'Reducing vulnerabilities to climate change impact and strengthening hydro-meteorological disaster risk mitigation in secondary cities in Asia', *Safer Cities*, 25: 1–12.

Korten, F.F. and Siy Jr, R.Y. (eds) (1989) *Transforming Bureaucracy: The Experience of the Philippine National Irrigation Administration*, Quezon City: Ateneo de Manila University Press.

Kuitenbrouwer, J.B.W. (1976) *Premises and Implications of a Unified Approach to Development Analysis and Planning*, Bangkok: Economic and Social Commission for Asia and the Pacific, United Nations.

Luna, E.M. (1999) 'Rethinking community development: indigenizing and regaining grounds', in A.M. Virginia (ed.) *The Philippine Social Sciences in the Life of the Nation: The History and Development of Social Science Disciplines in the Philippines*, Quezon City: Philippine Social Science Council, pp. 315–43.

—— (2000) 'A case study on the endogenous system of response to river flooding in Bula, Camarines sur: towards an appropriate and integrated development and disaster management planning (AIDMAP)', PhD dissertation, Quezon City: University of the Philippines Diliman.

—— (2004a) 'Lessons from areas affected by disasters: implications for fieldwork instruction program in community development', *CSWCD Development Journal*, 3: 49–69.

—— (2004b) 'Rising from the field: the concept and practice of community-based disaster risk management in the Philippines', in *Proceedings of the Third Disaster Management Practitioners' Workshop for Southeast Asia*, Bangkok, Asian Disaster Preparedness Center, 10–13 May, pp. 61–70.

—— (2006a) 'Power from within to overcome vulnerabilities: a Philippine case on the endogenous system of response to river flooding', *Science and Culture*, 72(1–2): 41–51.

—— (2006b) 'Community development in disaster risk reduction: Transforming vulnerabilities, empowering the vulnerable', paper presented at the Conference on Disaster Management through Regional Cooperation, Association of Southeast Asia Institutions of Higher Learning, University of Indonesia, Jakarta, 4–7 December.

—— (2009) *Community Development as an Approach to Reducing Risk among Flashflood Affected Families in Albay, Philippines*, Disaster Studies Working Paper 24, Aon Benfield, London: UCL Hazard Research Centre.

Luna, E.M. and Falk, K. (eds) (2003) *Guidelines for Implementing the Integrated Community Disaster Planning Model*, Manila: Philippines National Red Cross.

Luneta, M. and Molina, J.G. (2008) 'Community based early warning system and evacuation: planning, development and testing', *Safer Cities*, 20: 1–8.

Luz, J.M. and Montelibano, T.Y. (eds) (1993) *Corporations and Communities in a Developing Country*, Manila: Philippine Business for Social Progress and Bookmark.

Manalili, A.G. (1990) *Community Organizing for People's Empowerment*, Manila: Kapatiran-Kaunlaran Foundation.

Mercer, J. (2012) 'Knowledge and disaster risk reduction', in B. Wisner, JC Gaillard and I. Kelman (eds) *The Routledge Handbook of Hazards and Disaster Risk Reduction*, London: Routledge, pp. 97–108.

Office of Civil Defense (2007) *Strategic Plan to Integrate Community-based Disaster Risk Management to the Socio-economic Development Processes in the Philippines 2007–2011*, Quezon City: Office of the Civil Defense, Department of National Defense.

Osteria, T.S. and Okamura, J.Y. (eds) (1986) *Participatory Approaches to Development: Experiences in the Philippines*, Manila: De La Salle University Press.

Osteria, T.S., Ramos-Jimenez, P., Marinas, O.C. and Okamura, J.Y. (1988) *Community Participation in the Delivery of Basic Health Services*, Manila: De La Salle University Press.

OXFAM (2002) *Participatory Capacities and Vulnerabilities Assessment: Finding the Link Between Disasters and Development*, Quezon City: OXFAM.

—— (2009) *Rain Gauges in the Context of Community-based Disaster Early Warning Systems Case Studies for Four Cities*, Quezon City: OXFAM.

PhilDRRA (1997) *Making Agrarian Reform Work: Animating Peasant Organizations*, Quezon City: Philippine Partnership for the Development of Human Resources in Rural Areas.

Polson, R.A. (1964) 'Community development in The Philippines: observations and comments', in S.C. Espiritu and C.L. Hunt (eds) *Social Foundation of Community Development: Readings on the Philippines*, Manila: R.M. Garcia Publishing House.

Szymanski, A. (1981) *The Logic of Imperialism*, New York: Praeger Publishers.

Theis, J. and Grady, H.M. (1991) *Participatory Rapid Appraisal for Community Development*, London: International Institute for Environment and Development and Save the Children.

Third World Studies Center (1990) *The Language of Organizing: A Guidebook for Filipino Organizers*, Quezon City: Third World Studies Center, University of the Philippines Diliman.

Twigg, J. (2004) *Disaster Risk Reduction: Mitigation and Preparedness in Development and Emergency Planning*, Good Practice Review No. 9, London: Humanitarian Practice Network.

Uy, S.A. (2004) 'Nature and practice of community-based disaster risk management in Southeast Asia: Cambodia', in *Proceedings of the Third Disaster Management Practitioners' Workshop for Southeast Asia*, Bangkok, Asian Disaster Preparedness Center, 10–13 May, pp. 55–60.

Villarin, T.S. (1996) *People Empowerment: A Guide to NGO-PO Partnership with Local Government*, Quezon City: KAISAHAN.

Wisner, B. (2004) 'Assessment of capability and vulnerability', in G. Bankoff, G. Frerks and D. Hilhorst (eds) *Mapping Vulnerability, Disasters, Development and People*, London: Earthscan, pp. 183–93.

Wisner, B., Blaike, P., Cannon, T. and Davis, I. (2004) *At Risk: Natural Hazards, People's Vulnerability and Disasters*, 2nd edn, London: Routledge.

5 People-centred early warning

Juan-Carlos Villagrán de León

Lessons for practitioners

- Warning systems need to take both technical and social factors into account.
- **Knowledge** of **hazards**, vulnerabilities and capacities is all important.
- Both local knowledge and outside specialist knowledge are essential.
- Warnings must reach all those who need to be warned.
- Warning messages must be clear and specific.

Introduction

Early warning conveys critical information on potentially hazardous events to people and institutions so that actions can be taken to minimize loss and damage. These systems have allowed a growing number of societies to reduce the number of fatalities, injuries, and other losses in such events. However, as the 2004 Indian Ocean tsunami showed, there is still room for improvement in warning systems.

Early warning systems have been designed and implemented to address a variety of hydro-meteorological, geological and biological hazards. New technologies are also helping to improve early warning capacities. The use of satellite communications is now essential when it comes to intercontinental-range hazards such as tsunamis. Improved dissemination tools and the internet are now used to broadcast warnings and to conduct awareness campaigns. Improved modelling capacity allows experts to track the dynamics of such phenomena in a more precise fashion, leading to more precise forecasts of events in space and time. But as former US President Bill Clinton stated, in his role as special representative of the UN Secretary General for Asian tsunami recovery (PPEW 2006a: 9): 'We know that the most effective early warning takes more than scientifically advanced monitoring systems. All the sophisticated technology won't matter if we don't reach communities and people.'

In recent decades, Cuba has been cited as the textbook example when it comes to effective early warning in case of hurricanes (Wisner *et al.* 2005). Compared with other countries of the Caribbean and Central American regions, Cuban authorities have managed to reduce the number of fatalities dramatically when large hurricanes make landfall on their coasts. Relying on information generated through its network of weather instruments and through the regional efforts conducted by the World Meteorological Organization to track hurricanes heading this way, the Cuban Meteorological Institute disseminates warnings to government agencies and to the exposed population, so that evacuation to safe areas takes place in a timely fashion. Experts recognize that the Cuban success relies on the trust that the Cuban people have in these warnings, a decentralized system of neighbourhood committees, and the relatively high level of education and literacy among the Cuban population (ibid.). By contrast, the disaster triggered by Hurricane Katrina in New Orleans in 2005 could have been prevented, as it was later proved during Hurricane Gustav in 2008. The number of fatalities (more than a thousand) could have been reduced if people had been fully aware of the risks as this hurricane approached the city. While there was foreknowledge of the approach of Katrina, warning came late and was ambiguous, especially considering that many thousands of New Orleans' poor had no access to transportation for evacuation (Fussell 2006).

What these examples and many more suggest is that early warning is more than a scientific issue; it extends to the areas of policy and social behaviour. People in neighbourhoods and villages need to be active participants in early warning systems and not mere recipients of warning messages. This implies a new paradigm or approach that may be called people-centred early warning:

> The objective of people-centred early warning systems is to empower individuals and communities threatened by hazards to act in sufficient time and in an appropriate manner so as to reduce the possibility of personal injury, loss of life, damage to property and the environment and loss of livelihoods.
>
> (PPEW 2006b: 2)

Such systems are designed from the bottom up, ensuring that communities at risk become an integral part of the system (Villagrán de León 2003).

Early warning: basic notions

Early warning is a matter of providing people and institutions with timely information about the potential impacts of an imminent natural hazard such as a tsunami, a volcanic eruption or a tropical storm. In most countries, early warning is provided by scientific and technical agencies. For example, in the case of hydro-meteorological phenomena such as typhoons, hurricanes, storms and droughts, the service is provided by meteorological departments. In the case of volcanic eruptions, the service is usually provided by geological surveys or specialized agencies devoted to monitor active volcanoes. In typical early warning systems, different instruments are used by experts to track precursors (something that suggests a forthcoming occurrence of a hazardous event). When the forecast indicates that impacts are likely, a warning would be issued by the authorities via public media. However, under conditions of present knowledge, there may be false alarms. In addition, some communities at risk are not fully aware

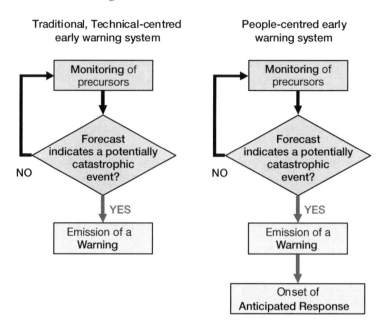

Figure 5.1 Types of early warning systems
Source: Villagrán de León (2006a, 2006b).

of the potential consequences they are facing or they have no clear predetermined actions they can take (as was the case with many of the poor and elderly in the face of Hurricane Katrina).

Hurricane Katrina in New Orleans has been mentioned as a case in which warnings issued days in advance by the US National Weather Service did not motivate many people to evacuate in time and did not cause the authorities to help those without means to self-evacuate. Similar examples come from Central America during Hurricane Mitch in 1998 and in Myanmar a decade later in 2008. These failures of warning suggest the need to move from a *technical-centred* to a *people-centred* approach to warning (Basher 2006; Villagrán de León 2003, 2006b). Figure 5.1 displays these two approaches.

The technical early warning system is designed from top to bottom and is focused on installing sensors in key locations to monitor precursors and other phenomena. Warnings are then disseminated through bulletins issued by the media. These systems clearly show that the main focus of the system is on issuing a warning of an event and not on the potential response to that warning. What communities and people at risk may do with that information is not a component of the system.

By contrast, people-centred early warning systems are designed from the bottom up, beginning with communities at risk, and ensure that *a local early warning plan* will guide them in the anticipated response once a warning has been issued. Such systems target **resources** to ensure that communities are well pre-pared to respond if a warning is issued and promote the use of indigenous and local knowledge when assessing the potential occurrence of an event whenever possible. People-centred early warning systems aim at forecasting impacts, rather than just events, and are tied to pre-established responses by the residents of a **community**. The term 'end-to-end' early warning is synonymous with this people-centred approach, as it promotes links among all elements of the early warning chain, particularly ensuring that communities at risk are connected to the system. While the language of technical-centred systems refers to the challenge of getting the message to local people as the 'last mile' issue; the people-centred system thinks of people as the 'first mile' (Kelman 2012).

There are four elements one needs to consider in the case of people-centred early warning:

- risk knowledge and awareness;
- monitoring and forecasting events;
- dissemination and communication;
- response to warnings.

When taken into consideration, these four elements allow the transformation of any technical early warning system into a people-centred system. Risk knowledge implies knowledge of the exposed groups and their location, so that warnings can reach them on time. In addition, it is equally important to ensure that when a warning is issued, the proper communication methods are used to guarantee that warnings reach all those persons exposed and in a language they can understand. It is also important to ensure that at this local level communities have the capability to respond to the warning so that losses can be minimized or avoided.

Risk knowledge and awareness

Both professionals and local communities have some knowledge and awareness of hazards, vulnerabilities and capacities to take action in response to warnings. But it is important to stress the difference between *knowledge for sustainable development* and *knowledge for early warning*. In the context of sustainable development, knowledge about hazards, vulnerabilities and capacities should lead to profound changes in the way communities and societies adapt to their environment (see Chapter 2). Knowledge concerning hazards should lead to the establishment of land-use norms and zoning ordinances; limiting where people can settle themselves and practise their **livelihoods** to avoid unnecessary exposure to hazards. It should also assist governments to identify and establish protective measures for some hazards, such as floods. Knowledge concerning **vulnerabilities** and capacities should allow all sectors of development to identify measures to reduce them. In the case of social vulnerability, forms of discrimination and exploitation would have to be addressed so that people have access to the necessary resources to protect themselves from hazards. In the case of physical vulnerability, this knowledge should lead to the establishment or improvement of building codes which should ensure that infrastructure suffers minimum damage in case of events (see Chapter 8). For example, ensuring the safety of schools and health facilities against multiple hazards has to be based on both specialized knowledge of the hazards, the building location, design and construction, and the local knowledge of hazards, use of the buildings and, above all, citizens' awareness that expresses a demand for infrastructure safety (see Chapters 6 and 11).

Knowledge for purposes of early warning is more limited. The concern is the specific place or area likely to be affected, the likely nature and magnitude of the physical hazard and its timing. In addition, if possible, knowledge about differential impacts of the hazard on less and more vulnerable groups and their assets should be sought through social science research and scenario building. Such knowledge should lead to the identification of procedures which must be implemented such as evacuation routes, search and rescue capacities, standard operating procedures, etc.

It could be concluded that while knowledge is essential for both sustainable development and for early warning, in the case of sustainable development, risk assessment aims to promote transformation of **underlying risk factors** in order to reduce the risk of *all potential harmful events*. In the case of early warning, knowledge focuses on *a single, particular event*, and ways to ensure through disaster preparedness that losses are minimized if it manifests itself. These two approaches should complement each other. For example, in the case of tsunamis, **hazard assessment** in the context of sustainable development should lead to the identification of measures either to reduce the exposure of communities to the hazard through land-use norms and zoning ordinances, or ways to minimize the impact of a tsunami through the erection of levees or barriers. In the case of early warning, hazard assessment should allow experts in collaboration with local residents to identify and demarcate evacuation routes and safe areas to be used as temporary shelters.

Risk assessment is a recent practice in disaster risk reduction in many countries, and thus the degree of advancement in regards to risk knowledge varies from country to country. In the survey of early warning systems conducted by the Platform for the Promotion of Early Warning (PPEW) in 2006, two critical issues were identified regarding this element (PPEW 2006b):

- In most countries hazards have been assessed more precisely than vulnerabilities.
- In many countries the degree of advancement concerning risk assessment varies from one type of hazard to another.

Such unevenness persists at the present time of writing, and, in addition, climate change and rapid urbanization add to the urgency of addressing both vulnerability and **capacity** across multiple hazards (PPEW 2010).

Another critical issue is the fact that there is no international consensus on a single definition for vulnerability, and yet there are multiple efforts to assess it

Table 5.1 Challenges: risk knowledge and awareness

There is a need to conduct vulnerability assessments for early warning in a more systematic fashion	In the context of early warning, there is a need to 'discover' hidden vulnerabilities such as the physical format in which important information is stored (paper and electronic files in the case of water-related hazards). For example, the 2004 tsunami revealed the vulnerability of paper documents such as land-titles, birth, marriage and death certificates held in municipal archives; critical information in terms of criminal records held in police stations; and credit vouchers held by vendors. Such information could easily have been saved, if proper early warning had included specific measures.
There is a need to standardize methodologies for risk assessment	It is imperative to advance on the standardization of methods to assess hazards, vulnerabilities, and risks, so that this knowledge can then be used to improve existing early warning capacities or to design new early warning systems.
There is a need to improve assessments for coupled hazards	For example, storms, hurricanes and typhoons provoke heavy rains leading to floods. Such rains can also lead to landslides but the connection between hurricanes and landslides is often neglected. It is important to highlight the connection between coupled hazards in the context of early warning.

(see Chapter 2) (Cardona 2004; Thywissen 2006; Villagrán de León 2006a). These challenges are highlighted in Table 5.1.

Monitoring and forecasting events

Monitoring of natural hazards or their precursors is usually conducted through multiple instruments (Saito *et al.* 2012). For example, networks of satellites and meteorological stations track the path and the characteristics of potentially damaging hurricanes in the Caribbean and eastern Pacific and typhoons or cyclones in the western Pacific and Indian Ocean. In the case of floods, arrays of weather stations, rain gauges and discharge gauges are used to monitor the dynamics of precipitation and river discharge to forecast floods in particular segments of rivers using hydrological models. In the case of tsunamis, arrays of seismometers, deep-ocean pressure sensors and tide gauges form the basis for forecasts when an underwater earthquake occurs.

Floods may be predicted fairly accurately, as there are several precursors that, when monitored in parallel, allow for precise forecasts. These include local weather conditions, the amount of rainfall which has accumulated in the ground, soil moisture and the level or discharge of rivers in the upper segments of river basins.

Despite many such advances in science and technology, there are some events which cannot be forecasted yet, such as powerful earthquakes, landslides and violent volcanic eruptions.

In the case of volcanic eruptions the situation is very complex, and therefore, forecasting an eruption is no easy task. This may lead to difficult social situations. As Hugo Yepez, Head of the Geophysical Institute of the National Polytechnic Institute in Ecuador, commented during the American Hemisphere Consultation on Early Warning Conference held in 2003, tremor activity may increase gradually. On any given day it is impossible for vulcanologists to forecast whether the tremor activity will continue to rise the following day, remain stable or begin to drop. The 1999 evacuation of more than 60,000 inhabitants of the town of Baños de Agua Santa, located at the foothills of Tungurahua volcano in Ecuador, is a case in point. The volcano did not produce the large eruption that was expected. People contracted illnesses in shelters; the education of children and livelihood activities were disrupted, and many people returned home despite continued warnings even when it meant breaching road blocks (Tobin and Whiteford 2002).

An important issue to consider in this context of monitoring and forecasting of potentially damaging events is the notion of indigenous, traditional or local knowledge (Mercer 2012). Gathered through systematic observations of changes in the environment and often combined with non-local elements, this knowledge is much used in rural areas of Africa, Asia, the Pacific, Latin America and the Caribbean. Traditional, indigenous and local knowledge for early warning are based on the systematic observation of changes in such characteristics as:

- the appearance of constellations, stars, and of the moon and its glow at certain times of the year;
- the behaviour of particular species of plants;
- the behaviour of particular insects or animals;
- the behaviour of local weather conditions (sea, atmosphere).

For example, the height of nests built by particular species of birds could be used as a precursor with respect to floods. As expected, if nests are built at a higher elevation, floods might be expected during that particular year.

Indigenous knowledge concerning precursors linked to tsunamis saved lives in Indonesia and Thailand in 2004 and in the Solomon Islands in 2007 (UNISDR 2007, 2008b). Indigenous groups understood the process of water receding at the coast of the ocean and in coastal lagoons following an earthquake as a warning of a tsunami, and they passed this knowledge down from generation to generation.

Much effort has gone into the identification, systematization and promotion of indigenous knowledge in various parts of the world (Mercer 2012; Wisner 2010). In Asia, Professor R. Shaw, working as a consultant to the United Nations International Strategy for Disaster Reduction (UNISDR), in a recent policy note stressed the need to mainstream indigenous knowledge in all sectors of development (UNISDR 2008a). He concluded that the key to promoting such use of

Table 5.2 Linking scientific knowledge and indigenous knowledge

Approach	Method	Comments
Identify root causes that lead to changes in the environment that are the basis of indigenous knowledge	Conduct scientific research to identify in the case of plants, animals, and the weather those root causes responsible for the changes in the environment (precursors) which are the basis of indigenous knowledge in order to establish networks of instruments capable of measuring these root causes	The presumption is that plants, animals, and the weather may be reacting to such root causes, which may be explained through scientific theories based on geology, hydrogeology, geochemistry, atmospheric sciences, etc.
Systematize indigenous knowledge through Western scientific methods	Systematic observations of precursors using scientific methods to establish the statistical behavior of these precursors as a basis to set monitoring and forecasting procedures	The objective would be to systematize precursors associated with indigenous knowledge to the degree that they gain the 'trust' of technical institutions

indigenous knowledge on a more global basis relies on the transferability of such knowledge, which will require efforts along the lines of researching, systematizing, documenting, and advocating such knowledge at this global level. The actual use of such knowledge also depends on the establishment of mutual trust and respect between outside authorities and affected communities (Wisner 2010).

A critical challenge is to overcome the gap that exists between local lay people and scientists when it comes to such knowledge for early warning purposes. A gap exists in how knowledge is generated and accepted (ibid.). In the scientific community, the formal peer-review process is essential to accept knowledge stemming from research. In contrast, indigenous knowledge does not require such a formal peer-review process, although informally, consensus about some elements of local knowledge is attained within and between generations. In an attempt to move forward, the present author has proposed two potential approaches to validate indigenous knowledge, which are presented in Table 5.2 (Villagrán de León 2005). Challenges to monitoring and forecasting are highlighted in Table 5.3.

Dissemination and communications of warnings

Once a forecast has been made concerning a potentially damaging event, a warning must be issued based on this forecast. It is important to stress the difference between a forecast and a warning.

A *forecast* presents information on a potentially catastrophic event in terms of its geographical location, the time at which it may occur and how long it will take to move away or to cease its release of energy. As such, it provides information

Table 5.3 Challenges: monitoring and forecasting

The need to improve capacities to forecast some hazards	As it has been mentioned, in the case of some hazards such as volcanic eruptions, additional research is needed to identify the set of precursors which may be needed to predict catastrophic events in a more precise fashion.
The need to revise forecasting procedures	It is important to have a feedback mechanism that allows the revision of forecasting procedures based on historic events, so that such forecasting procedures are improved using lessons learned from such events.
The need to widen the scope of forecasts for chained events	Sometimes an event triggers subsequent events. It is important to forecast these chained events as well. For example, landslides are usually triggered by torrential rainfall associated with hurricanes or storms. While Meteorological Offices usually forecast those hurricanes or storms, these offices rarely forecast the associated landslides which can provoke huge losses. An interesting chained event could be the failure of a levee, as happened in New Orleans. People may have been only aware of hurricane Katrina, but not of the possibility of levees failing.
The need to promote the sharing of knowledge concerning monitoring instruments and forecasting methods	It is important for international agencies to promote a more efficient interaction among agencies which conduct monitoring and forecasting of events, with the purpose of sharing experiences regarding the use of particular instrumentation for monitoring purposes, as well as to share lessons learned concerning forecasting methods employed in different countries of the world for the same type of phenomena.
The need to bridge the gap between scientific and indigenous knowledge	It is important to facilitate the establishment of programmes to ensure that these two sources of knowledge are better integrated to benefit from their use in the context of early warning systems.

on the event itself. Forecasts are usually made and reported by technical and scientific agencies based on the outcome of monitoring activities.

A *warning* should provide information, based on the forecast, on the *potential impact* in the affected geographical areas, the most probable time of occurrence *and instructions to reduce the impact through precise measures, including evacuation to safe areas*. These safe areas have to be predetermined as part of routine emergency management planning (Buckle 2012). The dissemination of a warning is usually made by a government agency. In some countries warnings may be issued by technical agencies such as the meteorological departments. In other countries, warnings are issued by Civil Defence or Civil Protection agencies or by local authorities, based on forecasts issued by technical agencies.

Once a warning has been issued by the appropriate authorities, it is often left up to the media and other networks to disseminate such warning to all communities at risk. As mentioned earlier, the efficiency of the early warning systems will be enhanced if warnings reach the target audience as quickly as possible. It is therefore important for early warning system operators to be up to date on advances in communication technologies, so as to incorporate emerging systems as soon as possible.

The other issue to consider in the context of warnings is related to the audience, which is composed of:

- the most vulnerable groups;
- authorities who need to order certain activities and who may have the power to stop routine operations at all levels if needed;
- civil defence, civil protection and other emergency response agencies (fire services, Search and Rescue Teams, the Red Cross, the Red Crescent, etc.).

Box 5.1 presents an example of the most vulnerable groups identified in the coastal city of Galle, Sri Lanka, and procedures for warning them.

It is essential that the information in the warning message be communicated in a clear language that is understood by those who will receive it. In addition, it is also important to use parallel channels of communication whenever possible to ensure that warnings reach the entire target audience and to reinforce the original warning message.

Box 5.1 Targeting vulnerable groups in Galle, Sri Lanka

The city of Galle, on the south-western coast of Sri Lanka, was heavily impacted by the 2004 tsunami. A survey of vulnerable groups and their location with respect to coastal hazard was employed to design a warning strategy within the city. Taking into consideration the notion that the local police department would be in charge of issuing tsunami warnings locally, a plan was designed to assist the police in reaching those places in coastal areas where three different types of vulnerable groups would be found and also where large concentrations of people would be found (Table 5.4).

Having identified the location of these sites with the use of a map, four parallel warning routes were established. Each warning route would lead a specific police team to some of these sites. However, when combined, the four warning routes encompassed 16 priority warning sites.

The plan was complemented with the identification of evacuation routes which should be employed by people to reach safe areas inland, and the role of the armed forces in supporting the evacuation of people to such safe areas. In addition, the plan also targeted the hotel sector, so that warnings would also reach tourists on beaches and in coastal areas (Villagrán de León 2008).

Table 5.4 Locations of three vulnerable social groups and places with many people before the 2004 tsunami

Children/Schools	Patients/Hospitals	Groups of women	Places with many people
Kannangara school	Mahamodera hospital	School of Nursing	Public bus stand, train station,
Dadalla school	Central hospital		Fish and vegetable markets
Suddharma college	Sanboddhi hospital		Main street, commercial areas
			Fishing marinas (3)
			District Secretary building, Municipal Council building

A comprehensive review of many relevant issues related to early warning systems was undertaken and presented by Mileti and Sorensen in 1990. According to these authors, it is important to understand how people receive and perceive warnings. There is a need to focus not only on issues related to the emission of such information but also on how such information is presented to individuals to ensure that they respond adequately to minimize impacts provoked by hazardous events.

Important issues to highlight in the context of the dissemination of warnings are:

- The need to ensure that warnings reach all those who need to be warned through the use of many communication channels.
- The need to ensure clarity and certainty in the messages ensuring that they are understood by the audience. Messages should not lead to uncertainties. The use of standardized messages could help improve the clarity and reduce uncertainties. It is important to ensure that messages are brief but clear, contain precise information on the places at risk and the types of impacts expected, as well as instructions on how to reduce losses.
- The use of different messages for different audiences according to their needs and responsibilities.

Challenges which can be highlighted at this time are presented in Table 5.5.

Response to warnings

Response to a warning, when properly planned, widely discussed and practised in advance, may minimize the impact of an event by reducing injuries and fatalities

Table 5.5 Challenges: dissemination and communication

The need to ensure that warnings reach those communities at risk	Every community may include particular vulnerable groups or places where vast numbers of people congregate. It is important to ensure that operators of early warning systems strive to ensure that warnings reach these vulnerable groups.
The need to work with the mass media	It is important for early warning system operators to establish contacts with the media and to ensure that they use the established format of the messages without deviation, in order to create a **culture** regarding the way in which warning messages are delivered to the population at risk.
The need to work with global news networks (CNN, BBC, etc.)	It is important to recognize the impact that international networks have in communicating warnings related to catastrophic events at global level. For example, people watching such news networks may not wait for an official warning to evacuate to safe areas. A particular example took place in New Zealand, where the BBC commented in its news network that as a consequence of an earthquake in the Pacific, the Regional Tsunami Warning Center had issued a warning. People in coastal areas evacuated to mountainous areas. Unfortunately, it took too long for the BBC to transmit the posterior cancellation message issued by this Regional Warning Center. This event demonstrated the massive power of international news networks in triggering responses from the population and thus the need to consider how to address this issue in every country.

and losses of critical assets. While an early warning is meant to minimize losses, the occurrence of the event may provoke unavoidable losses of many kinds. For example, a flood may inundate a rural area and damage or destroy crops. But while the loss of crops may be unavoidable, the loss of lives and other important assets such as tools and livestock is avoidable.

Experience shows that people may react to warnings when they believe that an impact is imminent and could have severe consequences. However, there are cases where people may not necessarily be aware of the degree of risk they are exposed to, and consequently they may not respond to warnings. People may also not understand warnings. Warnings may be issued in a format which may not be understood by those who need to respond. A case in point could be the 2004 Indian Ocean tsunami. The 'warning sign' manifested by the sea through its recession prior to the tsunami's landfall was misunderstood by many and only understood by a few. This underscores the importance of risk awareness and the importance of school curricula that include relevant information on hazards from early on (see Chapter 6).

Table 5.6 The anticipated response: steps required

Task	Comment
Elaboration of a warning scheme that reaches all vulnerable groups, based on their location	It is important to identify vulnerable groups and their geographic location in order to assess potential evacuation strategies. For example, in case of tsunamis, time might be too short and so, vertical evacuation may be a solution to keep in mind as an alternative to evacuation to safe areas far inland.
Elaboration of a plan (standard operating procedures) that outlines what tasks should be conducted if a warning is issued	The plan should contemplate what tasks should be conducted prior to an evacuation to a safe area, as well as which safe areas will be employed. If the early warning system is built to make use of different levels of warnings, it is important to make use of such benefits when planning tasks according to each level of warning, rather than just reacting to the highest possible level of warning.
	It is important to ensure the participation of vulnerable groups in the elaboration of the plan so that their needs and limitations are taken into consideration, leading to their empowerment so that they can take charge of the execution of a variety of activities.
	In addition, it is important to ensure that the plan is officially adopted so that it becomes part of the routine in all institutions involved in the operation of the system.
Evaluation and demarcation of evacuation routes to safe areas	Using hazard information and additional information (population dynamics during the day, on peak hours, and at night), identify and demarcate evacuation routes. These routes should be clearly identified with signs for such purpose. Safe areas and meeting points should also be demarcated with signs.
Coordination among government agencies to facilitate and ensure the evacuation of vulnerable groups to safe areas	Any emergency evacuation is chaotic by nature. However, through proper coordination, government agencies can support each other in assisting vulnerable groups to evacuate to safe areas through the evacuation routes.
Conduct simulations and drills	During the design stages, simulations help planners and vulnerable groups to identify weaknesses in evacuation procedures. Drills can also be used for such purposes. However, in most cases drills are used as awareness activities to ensure that vulnerable groups practise how they need to respond in case of warnings. It is important that drills should be conducted on a regular basis to maintain the social memory about hazards and the system.
Update as necessary	Advances in monitoring and forecasting capacities, as well as in the use of technology (information, communications), should be incorporated into the planning procedures to ensure that the benefits they offer can be maximized.

A critical issue is what responsibility community members have within early warning systems. For example, while government agencies may be able to provide transportation to safe areas and shelters, it is important to recognize that vulnerable groups also have a responsibility as well in such tasks – for example, neighbours helping transport elderly, ill or disabled neighbours (Alexander *et al.* 2012; Buckle 2012). A strategy to promote acceptance of shared responsibility for response to warnings is to ensure that the early warning system engages communities as partners in the design and operation of the warning and response system (see Chapter 4).

Table 5.6 presents a list of steps that need to be conducted in relation to the warning response phase. The warning response plan, which outlines the required responses to a warning, should include the following tasks:

- Ensuring an information flow in case of warnings.
- Activating mechanisms employed to issue and disseminate the warnings.
- Double checking the activation of mechanisms for conveying warnings to the target audience, especially vulnerable groups.
- Ensuring clarity about roles and responsibilities of all agencies and vulnerable groups in the different activities contemplated in the plan. In particular, the *Emergency Operation Centre*, which coordinates response activities (see Chapter 9).
- Activation of agencies that conduct response activities (police, search and rescue teams, fire service, Red Cross, Red Crescent, etc.).
- Mobilizing strategic resources and pre-positioning them where they may be needed to facilitate the evacuation of vulnerable groups to safe areas and care of people in shelters.
- Coordination and monitoring of evacuation, especially of vulnerable groups.
- Dissemination of an 'all-clear message' that signals the end of the alert. This is particularly useful in case of tsunamis, for example, which may last several hours.

Involving the community: community-operated early warning systems

Community-operated early warning systems have been established in Central America (Villagrán de León 2003), and in other regions of the world. Incorporating the notions of people-centred early warning, these systems have been set up to ensure that an anticipated response is conducted in communities which may be impacted by events such as floods, volcanic eruptions and forest fires. To this end, these systems are established within the hierarchical structures set up by the national disaster-reduction or civil protection agencies, which include emergency or disaster-reduction committees at provincial, municipal and local levels. All activities in relation to the various phases of early warning are conducted by members of the communities in a voluntary fashion and are supported by local authorities.

For example, in the case of floods, volunteers situated in the upper and middle segments of the basin monitor precursors such as rainfall and river level and transmit this information to communities at risk, where forecasting and anticipated response activities are conducted by municipal and local disaster-reduction committees. Simple technology such as markers on stones to gauge stream height and mobile phones are enough. Hydrological models developed beforehand allow warnings downstream when such messages are received by upstream community volunteers (IFRC 2006; Villagrán de León 2001, 2003).

Essential requirements when setting up such systems are:

- The use of technology that fits capacities and limitations of people in rural communities. To this end, simple rain gauges can replace sophisticated, telemetric, automatic rain gauges.
- The use of a voice-based communication network, such as an HF or VHF radio network or mobile phones to link those people who monitor weather conditions with local authorities and local emergency committees in communities at risk.
- Consideration of issues related to technical and operational sustainability. In most cases, these systems are set up by national disaster-reduction agencies or by outside non-governmental organizations. Such agencies may or may not provide resources and technical assistance to maintain the systems operational throughout the year.
- Drills and exercises to put in practice emergency plans developed by local and municipal emergency committees.

Policy issues and conclusion

As noted by PPEW (2006c), it is important to ensure that early warning activities are based on policies to promote their institutionalization, so that resources are available to operate these systems on a permanent basis. The institutionalization of the early warning system should ensure that:

- All institutions and organizations and stakeholders, especially the people at risk, need to be involved and become engaged in the various activities required to design it, implement it, and operate the warning system and response plan.
- All institutions and stakeholders involved become aware of their responsibilities in the operation of the system, thereby allocating resources for this purpose.
- A chain of command is established to coordinate the execution of all tasks contemplated in the operation of the systems.
- The authority and political responsibility concerning the emission of warnings are established by law.
- All required inter-institutional arrangements, including those spanning different levels (from international to local) are facilitated.

Unfortunately, these **policy** preconditions are not universally present. There are significant political dimensions to all aspects of disaster management, including warning systems (Mascarhenas and Wisner 2012). National governments may resist devolving sufficient resources to local governments to implement and maintain a people-centred warning system (GNDR 2009, 2011). At the scale of the urban neighbourhood and rural villages, age, gender, ethnic, religious and social class differences may make common effort towards development of a warning response difficult. Clearly, a people-centred warning approach is not a mere matter of technology, nor is it one of just finding the correct clear language and mode of communication. There are underlying socio-economic and political dynamics, part and parcel of what Wisner *et al.* (2004) call '**root causes**' of vulnerability that must also be addressed patiently through prolonged listening and community mobilization and lobbying at the national level.

Acknowledgement

Some parts of this chapter appeared in J-C Villagrán de León (2012) 'Early warning principles and systems', in B. Wisner, JC Gaillard and I. Kelman (eds) *The Routledge Handbook of Hazards and Disaster Risk Reduction*, London: Routledge, pp. 481–92.

References

Alexander, D., Gaillard, JC and Wisner, B. (2012) 'Disability and disaster', in B. Wisner, JC Gaillard and I. Kelman (eds) *The Routledge Handbook of Hazards and Disaster Risk Reduction*, London: Routledge, pp. 413–24.

Basher, R. (2006) 'Global early warning systems for natural hazards: systematic and people-centred', *Philosophical Transactions of the Royal Society A*, 364 (1845): 2167–82. Available at: http://rsta.royalsocietypublishing.org/content/364/1845/2167.full (accessed 13 March 2013).

Buckle, P. (2012) 'Preparedness, warning and evacuation', in B. Wisner, JC Gaillard and I. Kelman (eds) *The Routledge Handbook of Hazards and Disaster Risk Reduction*, London: Routledge, pp. 493–504.

Cardona, O.D. (2004) 'The need for rethinking the concepts of vulnerability and risk from a holistic perspective: a necessary review and criticism for effective risk management', in G. Bankoff, G. Frerks, and D. Hilhorst (eds) *Mapping Vulnerability: Disasters, Development, and People*, London: Earthscan, pp. 37–51.

Fussell, E. (2006) *Leaving New Orleans: Social Stratification, Networks, and Hurricane Evacuation*, New York: Social Science Research Council. Available at: http://understandingkatrina.ssrc.org/Fussell/ (accessed 13 March 2013).

GNDR (2009) *Clouds but Little Rain: Views from the Frontline 2009*, London: GNDR. Available at: http://www.globalnetwork-dr.org/images/documents/VFL%20archive/reports09/vflfullreport0609.pdf (accessed 13 March 2013).

—— (2011) *If We Do Not Join Hands: Views from the Frontline 2011*, Teddington: GNDR. Available at: http://www.globalnetwork-dr.org/views-from-the-frontline/voices-from-the-frontline-2011 (accessed 13 March 2013).

IFRC (2006) *Red Cross Red Crescent Good Practices in Early Warning*, Geneva: IFRC. Available at: http://www.ifrc.org/Global/Case%20studies/Disasters/cs-earlywarning.pdf (accessed 13 March 2013).

Kelman, I. (2012) 'First mile of warning systems', in B. Wisner, JC Gaillard and I. Kelman (eds) *The Routledge Handbook of Hazards and Disaster Risk Reduction*, London: Routledge, box, p. 483.

Mascarhenas, A. and Wisner, B. (2012) 'Politics: power and disaster', in B. Wisner, JC Gaillard and I. Kelman (eds) *The Routledge Handbook of Hazards and Disaster Risk Reduction*, London: Routledge, pp. 48–60.

Mercer, J. (2012) 'Knowledge and disaster risk reduction', in B. Wisner, JC Gaillard and I. Kelman (eds) *The Routledge Handbook of Hazards and Disaster Risk Reduction*, London: Routledge, pp. 97–108.

Mileti, D.S. and Sorensen, J.H. (1990) *Communication of Emergency Public Warnings: A Social Science Perspective and State-of-the-Art Assessment*, ORNL-6609, Oak Ridge, TN: Oak Ridge National Laboratory.

PPEW (2006a) *Conclusions EWC3*, Geneva: PPEW/UNISDR. Available at: http://www.unisdr.org/files/606_10041.pdf (accessed 13 March 2013).

—— (2006b) *Global Survey of Early Warning Systems: An Assessment of Capacities, Gaps, and Opportunities Towards Building a Comprehensive Global Early Warning System for All Natural Hazards*, Geneva: PPEW/ UNISDR. Available at: http://www.unisdr. org/we/inform/publications/3612 (accessed 13 March 2013).

—— (2006c) *Developing Early Warning Systems: A Checklist*, Geneva: PPEW/UNISDR. Available at: http://www.unisdr.org/we/inform/publications/608 (accessed 13 March 2013).

—— (2010) *Upcoming Challenges in Early Warning*. Accessible: http://www.prevention web.net/files/15689_ewsincontextofccandurbanization.pdf (accessed 13 March 2013).

Saito, K., J. Strachan, T. Fewtrell, N. Rosser, S. Jenkins, A. Slingsby, and K. Haynes. 2012. Tools for Identifying Hazards. Chapter 17, pp. 191–203 in B. Wisner, JC Gaillard and I. Kelman (eds.), *Handbook of Hazards and Disaster Risk Reduction*, Routledge, Abingdon, UK.

Thywissen, K. (2006) *Components of Risk: A Comparative Glossary*, UNU-EHS Publication Series No. 2/ 2006, Bonn: UNU-EHS.

Tobin, G. and Whiteford, L. (2002) 'Community resilience and volcano hazard', *Disasters*, 26(1): 28–48.

UNISDR (2007) *Lessons for a Safer Future: Drawing on the Experience of the Indian Ocean Tsunami Disaster*, Geneva: UNISDR. Available at: http://www.unisdr.org/2006/ppew/tsunami/pdf/lesson-for-a-safer-future.pdf (accessed 13 March 2013).

—— (2008a) *Indigenous Knowledge*, Policy Note. Geneva: UNISDR. Available at: http://www.preventionweb.net/files/8853_IKPolicyNote.pdf (accessed 13 March 2013).

—— (2008b) *Indigenous Knowledge for Disaster Risk Reduction: Good Practices and Lessons Learned from Experiences in the Asia-Pacific Region*, UNISDR. Available at: http://www.unisdr.org/we/inform/publications/3646 (accessed 13 March 2013).

Villagrán de León, J. (2001) *Community-Operated Early Warning Systems in Central America*, ISDR Informs, 4, Latin America and the Caribbean, Geneva: UNISDR. Available at: http://www.eird.org/eng/revista/No4_2001/pagina11.htm (accessed 13 March 2013).

—— (2003) *Sistemas de Alerta Temprana para Emergencias de Inundaciones en Centro América*, Guatemala City: CEPREDENAC. Available at: http://www.crid.or.cr/digitalizacion/pdf/spa/doc14297/doc14297.htm (accessed 13 March 2013).

—— (2005) 'Precursores indígenas en el contexto de sistemas de alerta temprana de Guatemala', in *HEI-ILO Research Programme on Strengthening Employment in Response to Crises; Volume III: Strengthening Crisis Prevention Through Early Warning Systems*, Geneva: ILO. Available at: http://www.ruig-gian.org/ressources/Warner_Volume_3_Final.pdf?ID=64&FILE=/ressources/Warner_Volume_3_Final.pdf (accessed 1 October 2012).

—— (2006a) *Vulnerability: A Conceptual and Methodological Review*, UNU-EHS Publication Series No. 4/ 2006, Bonn: UNU-EHS.

—— (2006b) 'Support for Sri Lanka from the United Nations University', *Disaster Reduction in Asia and the Pacific: ISDR Informs*, 2: 61–5, Bangkok: UNISDR. Accessible: http://www.unisdr.org/files/8569_InformAsia3%5B1%5D.pdf (accessed 13 March 2013).

—— (2008) *Rapid Assessment of Potential Impacts of a Tsunami: Lessons Learned from the Port of Galle in Sri Lanka*, UNU-EHS Publication Series No. 9/ 2008. Bonn: UNU-EHS.

Wisner, B. (2010) 'Climate change and cultural diversity', *International Social Science Journal*, 61 (199): 131–40.

Wisner, B., Blaikie, P., Cannon, T. and Davis, I. (2004) *At Risk: Natural Hazards, People's Vulnerability and Disasters*, 2nd edn, London: Routledge.

Wisner, B., Lavell, A., Ruiz, V. and Meyreles, L. (2005) *Run Tell Your Neighbour: Early Warning in the 2004 Caribbean Hurricane Season*, World Disasters Report 2005, Geneva: IFRC.

6   Disaster education in schools

Rajib Shaw, Yukiko Takeuchi and Koichi Shiwaku

Lessons for practitioners

- School disaster education should go beyond the school boundary and should include family and community education to make decisive proactive actions.
- School disaster education should be participatory, action oriented and should not be restricted to classroom lectures.
- Teachers can play the role of key change agents in school disaster education, and therefore, proper teacher training is an essential component.
- No amount of disaster education can help if the school buildings themselves are not safe.

Introduction

When one talks about mainstreaming disaster risk reduction into development practices, much emphasis has been given to national and local development policies and plans. Development plans are important, but the real mainstreaming begins in education. Education is the key to development. Disaster reduction is ultimately linked to human behaviour. National and **local government** planning, civil society **participation**, interventions of donors and international agencies are all important to create an enabling atmosphere. However, within that enabling atmosphere, it is of the utmost importance to generate activities at the individual, family and **community** levels. For this, education is the first and foremost vehicle.

The UN's global framework for disaster reduction focuses on education (both formal and informal), public awareness, strengthening networks and promoting dialogue and cooperation among disaster experts, technical and scientific specialists, planners and other stakeholders (UNISDR 2005). There are many disaster risk reduction (DRR) training programmes in different areas. However, there is still a lack of formal education in DRR at the undergraduate and graduate levels (Wisner 2006) and still not enough DRR content in primary and secondary education.

The importance of disaster education has been recognized by global and regional authorities. Education for Disaster Risk Reduction (EDRR) as part of DRR has to be inherent within Education for Sustainable Development (ESD) and to support the frameworks of ESD in three important ways (DESD Conference 2009):

1 Education for DRR is interdisciplinary. Therefore, important consideration is given to the impacts on (and relationship between) society, the environment, economy and **culture**.

2 Education for DRR promotes critical thinking, problem solving and other social and emotional life skills that are essential to the empowerment of stakeholder groups threatened or affected by disasters.

3 Education for DRR supports the Millennium Development Goals. Without considering DRR in development planning, all efforts, including decades of development initiatives, could be destroyed in seconds.

A recent review shows some progress in achieving these overall goals, but still a long way to go (Selby and Kagawa 2011). Within this broad context this chapter will focus on the key challenges of school disaster education using as an example survey results from schoolchildren of Japan. The chapter will also argue for the importance of linking school education with family and community education, and engaging students in a more proactive partnership with the neighbourhood. The chapter will provide some examples of 'activity-based' school education with the participation of larger stakeholders in the society. The chapter also discusses the role of schoolteachers as change agents of school education. The chapter's final topic is school protection.

Japan is considered one of the world's most earthquake-prone countries. Major earthquakes of magnitude greater than seven occur once in every five to ten years somewhere in Japan. The Great Hanshin Awaji Earthquake (popularly known as the Kobe Earthquake) in 1995, took the lives of more than 6400 people, besides injuring several thousands, damaging more than 250,000 houses and causing economic loss of more than seven trillion Japanese Yen (US$71.1 billion)[1] within the city of Kobe itself. This earthquake was a severe blow to Japanese society, and afterwards many changes were observed in the social, economic and educational fields. Two major changes after the earthquake were: (1) an increase in voluntary activities; and (2) the involvement of the community in the decision-making process (Nakagawa 2003; Shaw and Goda 2004). Several other major earthquakes occurred in western and northern parts of Japan in 2000, 2001 and 2003, following the Kobe earthquake and 2011 saw the triple disaster involving seismic damage, a tsunami and the nuclear meltdown associated with The Great East Japan Earthquake (magnitude 9.0). An important educational question is: does the frequent occurrence of earthquakes in Japan enhance people's perception of and awareness of earthquake preparedness?

The importance of education and training at the school and community level has been emphasized and re-emphasized several times by different authors (Andrews 1998; Arya 1993; Frew 2002; Kuroiwa 1993; Radu 1993). It is widely acknowledged that the school plays an important role in raising awareness among students, teachers and parents (Shaw and Kobayashi 2001). Examples from both developed and developing countries provide numerous best practices for successful school earthquake safety initiatives (Dixit *et al.* 2002). In Japan, school disaster education is considered to have begun as long ago as the 1980s (Kaji 1993). School earthquake education in Japan has two components: first, to provide correct **knowledge** to the students about earthquake disasters – their causes and effects; and, second, to provide them with practical training on how to protect themselves. This type of education is more intense in the elementary schools, and lessons are provided in a simplified and easy-to-remember manner (ibid.). However, only after the 1983 tsunami in Akita prefecture in northern Japan, which killed 13 elementary schoolchildren, did awareness grow of the need for the education of teachers about their roles as the disaster managers in the schools. The board of education launched a new curriculum for teachers on evacuation guidelines, emergency information systems and human resource management. This was found to be effective during the Kobe earthquake, where schools played a crucial role as a shelter and evacuation area.

Participatory school education

Participatory learning

Yamori (2006) states that it is necessary for disaster education in the future to focus on the process of restructuring 'communities of practice', and not just the transfer of knowledge and skills between individuals. That is, it should be an important goal of education or learning to establish a community in which the teacher and the learner can 'participate' together. For example, in schools, it is useful to involve students, teachers or the school system itself with network experts, organizations or groups to work together on disaster prevention. One such learning tool will be 'town watching' or 'neighbourhood watching'.

Town watching

Town watching is a participatory technique used in community or neighbourhood planning in the context of a larger administrative unit (such as a municipality or city) in order for residents to recognize problems as a group and put forward solutions together. The problem-solving process is guided by at least one expert or professional trained in one or more aspects of planning (Ogawa *et al.* 2005). Town watching, which has been developed as a technique practised by Japanese urban planners since the 1970s, has become popular as a participatory tool in *machizukuri* (Setagaya Machizukuri Center 2003). '*Machizukuri*' has been translated as 'community planning' by Evans (2003), and as 'town making' or participatory community building by Yamada (2001). '*Machi*' means town, district, community and '*zukuri*' means making or building. The origins of *machizukuri* can be traced to its development as a movement associated with organized citizen actions to fight pollution in the 1960s in Japan; local authorities needed to adapt to include consultation with the citizens. Lately, *machizukuri* in some localities has developed into partnerships (Yoshimura 2002). In recent years, the *machizukuri* movement has emerged from Japanese planning practice with a predominant focus on urban design that encourages citizen involvement. Concerns in *machizukuri* such as access to public roads, open space, land use, etc. are included and taken into account by town watching. The use of town watching has been extended to deal with disaster and safety-related physical issues such as safe or unsafe places and evacuation routes; we call this 'disaster town watching'.

Relevance of town/mountain watching in Saijo City

At the time of the typhoons 21 and 23 in 2004, the mountainous area of Saijo City was particularly badly damaged (Shaw *et al.* 2008). The condition of the land and concentrated heavy rain were major factors, but there were other reasons concerning the numbers of the elderly population in the region. Many of the elderly had difficulty in evacuating and needed the help of younger people. Little awareness of disaster prevention was also a problem. According to research by OYO Corporation (2005), a significant number of people did not evacuate at the time of the typhoon. The same problem was faced in the plains area below.

The areas in the plains are urban in nature, and there are many young people there. Therefore, it is necessary to make connections and produce a 'disaster education network' (Figure 6.1) between the plains area and the mountainous area, in order to help elderly people in the latter in case of a disaster. Driftwood was stuck under bridge piers and caused the plains area to flood. Thus, events in the mountainous area have consequences in the plains below. Residents in both areas must be aware of the interrelated effects of disasters in the mountains and plains areas. For these reasons, mountain watching was proposed to be implemented in Saijo City. Mountain watching is just like town watching and it is conducted in the mountainous area. The main target was children, and also residents in the mountain areas, teachers, municipal officials and forest workers were involved. The working field was a school in the upper catchment of a river. Participants

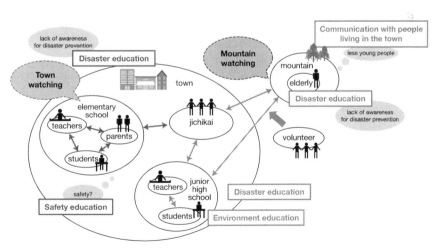

Figure 6.1 Comprehensive disaster education network through town watching and mountain watching in Saijo, Shikoku in Japan

visited the site damaged by the typhoon in 2004 and heard the story from people who had been affected.

At the same time, town watching was implemented in the plains area. Students and others walked around the school zone and looked for dangerous places, and useful facilities in case of disaster, which they did not normally notice otherwise in their daily life. At first, town watching was implemented in five elementary schools and mountain watching was implemented in three junior high schools as part of the disaster education programme – an activity for 12-year-old students.

Experiencing learning

A similar exercise was conducted with schools in Vietnam, India, and Malaysia with the same age groups. In the case of Vietnam and India, town watching (for India, it was coastal watching, focusing on the coastal areas) was combined with experimental laboratory activities (Figure 6.2) to explain **hazards** and other concepts (like the importance of forest management in flood risk reduction, vulnerable areas like meandering, the origin of tsunamis and the importance of coastal vegetation as buffer zones, etc.). These were demonstrative examples, where the students could experience the **root causes** of hazards and vulnerabilities. This type of experimental learning, coupled with town watching (or neighbourhood watching) was found to be a productive education process, which can be facilitated as a part of school education.

Impact evaluation of town watching

How effective is 'town watching'? A questionnaire survey was conducted to evaluate the impact of town/mountain watching (Yoshida 2007). The targets were students, teachers, municipal officers, parents, mountain residents and forest workers. The questionnaire survey was conducted both before going into the field and after the whole process. Figure 6.3 presents the impact of the town watching on the schoolchildren.

Figure 6.2 Experiencing learning in Vietnam (left) showing the impact of forests on flood reduction, and in India (right) showing the impacts of mangroves in tsunami and coastal hazard protection

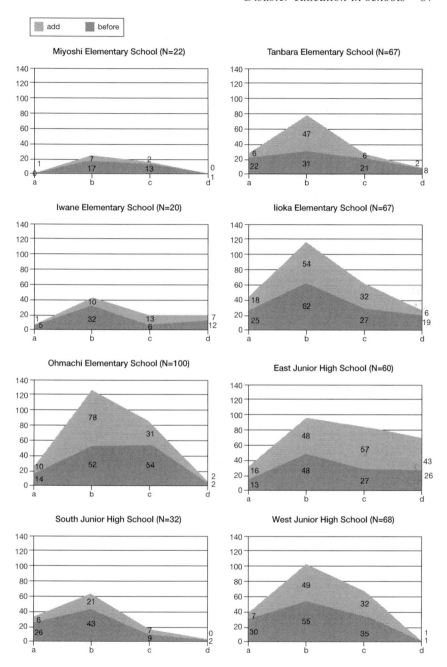

Figure 6.3 Impacts of town watching on schoolchildren. The shaded part is the
additional knowledge base due to town watching (lower shade is before the
town watching, and upper shade is after town watching, the vertical axis
stands for the number of students surveyed and the horizontal axis represents
four evaluation criteria: a): about the hazard, b): impact on infrastructure, c):
impact on assets, and d): impacts on people).

School education beyond school boundaries

Teaching about disasters in schools may be effective, but questions arise: What about pre-disaster preparedness? How effective is the education in the school for actual implementation of pre-disaster preparedness measures?

From the experiences of the Kobe earthquake, it was observed that many people were rescued by their friends, families and neighbours, particularly in the places where the community ties were strong (Shaw and Goda 2004). Also, in the neighbourhoods which had strong social networks, reconstruction and rehabilitation were smoother and faster, with better collective decision making among the communities and better cooperation between the communities and the local government. Education is one of the key tools for building social networks and a 'culture of prevention'.

A survey of high school students (15–16 years old) in Japan was done to revisit the direction of disaster education and awareness, and to discover how the earthquake experiences and disaster education affect awareness and behaviour. Five prefectures were selected for the survey: Aichi, Hyogo, Osaka, Shizuoka and Wakayama. Two of these prefectures, Hyogo and Osaka, had experienced damage due to the Kobe earthquake, while Aichi, Shizuoka and Wakayama were expecting the big so-called Tokai earthquake, forecast by seismologists. In total, 12 schools were selected for the survey and the number of students surveyed was 1065. The survey results show that while almost 70–80 per cent of the students understand disaster risk, and almost 80 per cent of the students have undertaken risk reduction education in schools, only 20–30 per cent of them have *actually taken* pre-disaster preparedness and prevention measures. Thus, there is a large gap between knowledge and action, and this is a key challenge for school disaster education (Shaw *et al.* 2004).

Shaw *et al.* (2004) offer a model of disaster knowledge, awareness and behaviour. They identify a sequence of stages: 'knowing', 'realizing', 'deepening', 'decision' and 'action'. Knowledge comes from two sources: experience and education (EE). Experience here denotes not only experiences of damaging earthquakes, but general experience of earthquakes. Education has four parts: school, family, community and self-education. School education is divided into two parts: education from teachers (S), and proactive education with participation of teachers and students (ST). Family education (F) originates from parents and other family members. Community education (C) is related to education in the neighbourhood, community organizations, NGO activities, research workers and voluntary activities, etc. Self-education (Se) is acquired from books, the internet, newspapers, TV and other sources through the students' own initiative (Figure 6.4). All these lead to 'knowing' about earthquakes and their impacts. The next step after 'knowing' is 'realizing' which denotes perceiving real, concrete, local hazard as opposed to theoretical knowledge. After 'realizing', comes 'deepening', which is divided into two parts: 'deepening' A (which is considered as the wish to deepen knowledge), and 'deepening' B (which is considered as actual deepening). The next step is 'decision', which is the wish to take action and disseminate knowledge,

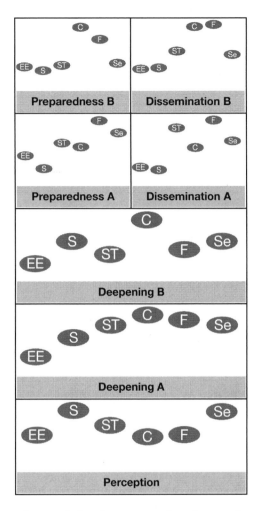

Figure 6.4 Impacts of types of education on perception of preparedness

denoted as 'preparedness' A and 'dissemination' A respectively. 'Action' comes after it, which is linked to 'preparedness' B and 'dissemination' B.

Looking at Figure 6.4, it is notable that while earthquake experience (EE) and school education (S) are important to develop perception of earthquake risk, active school education (ST) and community (C) and family education (F) play a more crucial role in developing the wish and interest (A) in deepening knowledge. Self-education is also an equally important factor in this aspect. However, actual deepening of knowledge is observed through intensive community education. Experience and school education play a relatively smaller role in this regard. This is possibly attributed to enhancing perception and deepening through active participation of different types of community activities in the neighbourhood. In contrast, when the wish for preparedness is concerned, family education is the most influential factor, followed by self-education. For actual preparedness, it is the community and family education, which are most important. This is attributed to the importance of the family and the neighbourhood level of preparedness, which is developed mainly through family and community education. The wish to disseminate experience is enhanced by active school education (ST) and family education, while actual dissemination is promoted by community and family education. In both cases, the school education's (S) role is not as prominent.

Thus, two important aspects came out of this survey as the general challenges of school education: (1) how to reduce the gap between knowledge and practice in school students; and (2) how to enhance disaster education in communities (since school education only enhances perception, but for actual preparedness, family and community education is important.

Teachers as a key agent of change

Teachers can be key change agents. However, in many cases, schoolteachers are either not equipped with proper disaster information (as their teaching guides) or they are too occupied with their regular teaching loads (Shiwaku 2007; Shiwaku and Shaw 2008; Wisner 2006). Shiwaku *et al.* (2006) conducted a survey in Kathmandu, Nepal, to understand the state of disaster education in schools and the needs of teachers. Some 130 teachers of 8th, 9th and 10th grades (students aged 14–17 years) were interviewed. Teachers of science and environment and related subjects (health, population and environment) were specifically selected. Table 6.1 gives details of the teachers involved in the study. Three types of schools were targeted: public, private and SESP (SESP stands for School Earthquake Safety Program, which was conducted by the National Society for Earthquake Technology (NSET), an NGO dedicated to earthquake safety in Nepal). The research showed that all teachers in the SESP and more than 95 per cent of teachers in private schools were implementing disaster education as opposed to 80 per cent in public schools. Thus most teachers in Nepal were implementing disaster education to some extent. Teachers used both formal and informal teaching methods.

In Nepal, curriculum-based (or 'formal') education was based on textbooks. Topics addressed in Nepal included floods, landslides, epidemics and environmental issues. Meanwhile, earthquakes and windstorms received less attention. It is thought that this gap is caused by the occurrence of disasters in Nepal. Floods, landslides, epidemics and land degradation are hazards that occur often or which are related to **livelihood**. Earthquake and windstorm are hazards that do not occur as often as floods or landslides.

Most teachers in all types of school thought the current curriculum for disaster education was not sufficient. Many teachers suggested that the curriculum was a key barrier to effective implementation. Therefore, teachers thought the curriculum was the most important problem and did not think disaster education was necessary for their curriculum education. To promote disaster education in school, 100 per cent of SESP teachers reported the need for curriculum development; 78 per cent

Table 6.1 Number of teachers surveyed and their categorization

Subject	SESP	Government	Private	Total
Science	3	18	17	38
Environment	4	13	26	43
Social Studies	2	15	23	40
Others	1	5	3	9
Total	10	51	69	130

Notes: SESP: government schools where SESP was conducted. Government: government schools where SESP has not been conducted. Private: private schools. Others: teachers' subject is not one of the three subjects above or teachers are in charge of several subjects.

of teachers in government and private schools also recognized this need for curriculum development. The second most frequent method of improving disaster education suggested by teachers was teacher training. In his review that launched the UN's campaign for 'safe schools', Wisner (2006) also pointed to teacher training and curriculum development as pillars of effective education.

Protecting schools

One of the tragic ironies of disaster education is that many of the school buildings in the world are unsafe (see Chapter 8). Many schools have been destroyed by earthquakes, buried in landslides or washed away by tsunamis. Every few years schoolchildren in Africa are electrocuted in thunderstorms. More frequently schools burn down. Safer schools depend on better design, location decisions made in awareness of local hazards, good structural maintenance and the retrofitting or rebuilding of grossly unsafe structures (GFDRR and INEE 2009). This requires political will that begins with the sort of community networks forged in part by the cycle of disaster education that begins with knowledge and ends in action (Figure 6.4).

Safe school facilities, disaster reduction and disaster management and planning in schools are the three fundamentals of 'safety in education' (UNESCO-UNICEF 2011). The last mentioned will take the form of planning for emergency action by staff and students (Petal 2009; Wisner 2006), including evacuation, making sure staff and older students know first aid and stockpiling of first-aid kits, and, as in the examples of 'town watching' earlier, a thorough study of the school and its surroundings in order to detect hazards.

Conclusion

Education alone cannot solve the challenges of disaster reduction and cannot motivate a person to take action for **mitigation** activities. However, school

Table 6.2 Impacts of listening, watching, doing and talking on disaster education

Different schools surveyed	Listen				Watch				Do										Talk	
	S1	S2	S3	S4	S5	S6	S7	S8	S9	S10	S11	S12	S13	S14	S15	S16	S17	S18	S19	S20
Perception					○														○	
Deepening A								○								○			○	○
Deepening B								○								○	○	○		○
Preparedness A																			○	○
Preparedness B																			○	○
Dissemination A																○	○		○	○
Dissemination B																		○	○	○

Note: The left column corresponds to the education model used in the study. The circle means that there is an impact.

education is useful for the very important first step, which is providing knowledge and activating students' interest. School education also has different elements: listening, visual, experience and conversation. Table 6.2 shows the different degree of effect of these different components of school education from knowing to behaviour. Conversation with friends and teachers has a very positive impact on different levels of awareness. While listening to lectures only creates knowledge, its actual usage can be applied properly though visual aids, experiencing and participating in conversations with other students. Family, community and self-learning, coupled with school education can lead a person along the gradual path of knowledge to perception of concrete, local hazards, leading to specific action.

Numerous studies are in accord with the findings in Japan. In the US, Frew (2002) found public awareness of hazards to be responsive to social marketing, a customized approach that is based on the individual characteristics of a specific target audience. Dixit *et al.* (2002) have shown a practical example of social marketing raising public awareness through Nepal's School Earthquake Safety Program, outside the regular school curriculum. They considered the school to be a unique element within the community, and they argued that the role of education should not be confined within the school itself, but should be extended to family and community. Fisek *et al.* (2002), in their studies in Turkey, described how earthquake mitigation is not only a financial matter but perception and awareness also play an important role. Suwa (2006) pointed out that disaster education is related to various subjects and that disaster-related topics can be found in any subject.

At the time of writing, most of the educational efforts directed towards the public and children have neither been systematically conceived nor tested, nor has their impact been scientifically evaluated (Petal 2009). Disaster risk reduction education is not yet an integral part of disaster risk management **policy**, planning and implementation. Often scientific and technical experts have taken on the task of developing educational material with very little evidence of cross-disciplinary input from public health, communications, marketing and education professionals with experience in allied efforts. It is time now to begin to give substance to the terms 'public awareness' and 'disaster risk reduction education', to lay out some of the 'dos and don'ts' including some that have already been identified above, to display the range of methods that are open to teachers and to discuss how we might identify promising practices. It is also vital to evaluate the impacts of different approaches to disaster reduction and scale them up to the level needed to achieve a tipping point in establishing a culture of safety. A new cadre of researchers and research support will be needed to achieve this goal (Shaw *et al.* 2008).

The goal of education is to change people's behaviour (Nathe 2000). Awareness about **risks** and dangers needs to start in early education, even before the ability to address them, but can become part of growing civic and professional responsibilities as people mature (UNISDR 2005).

Acknowledgements

This chapter is a composite of several studies over a period of years by the three co-authors. We would like to acknowledge the help and cooperation of individual schools (their teachers and students) and respective local governments for their support and cooperation.

Note

1   Yen/US$ conversion as of 16 January 1995 from http://research.stlouisfed.org/ fred2/data/EXJPUS.txt.

References

Andrews, J. (1998) Southern California Earthquake Center Outreach Report 1998: Public Awareness, Education and Knowledge Transfer Programs and Fiscal Year 1998 Activities. Available at: http://www.scec.org/research/98research/ 98andrews.pdf (accessed 27 June 2012).

Arya, A. (1993) 'Training and drills for the general public in emergency response to a major earthquake', in *Training and Education for Improving Earthquake Disaster Management in Developing Countries*, UNCRD Meeting Report Series no. 57: pp. 103–14.

DESD Conference (2009) Background document for the WCESD workshop on Education for Sustainable Development and Disaster Risk Reduction: Building Disaster-Resilient Societies, Bonn, Germany.

Dixit, A., Nakarmi, M., Pradhanang, S., Basnet, S., Pandey, B., Bothara, J., Pokharel, K., Upadyay, B., Guragain, R., Tucker, B. and Samant, L. (2002) 'Public awareness and social marketing: experiences of KVERMP', paper presented at the Regional Workshop on Best Practices in Disaster Management, Bangkok, pp. 394–400.

Evans, N. (2003) 'Discourses of urban community and community planning: a comparison between Britain and Japan', *Sheffield Online Papers in Social Research*. Available at: http://www.shef.ac.uk/polopoly_fs/1.71434!/file/evans.pdf (accessed 14 April 2012).

Fisek, G., Yeniceri, N., Muderrisoglu, S. and Ozkarar, G. (2002) 'Risk perception and attitudes towards mitigation', paper presented at the IIASA-DPRI meeting on Integrated Risk Management, Luxemburg.

Frew, S. (2002) 'Public awareness and social marketing', paper presented at the Regional Workshop on Best Practices in Disaster Management, Bangkok, UNESCO, Thailand, pp. 381–93.

GFDRR (Global Facility for Disaster Risk Reduction) and INEE (International Network for Emergency Education) (2009) *Guidance Notes on Safe Schools*, Washington, DC and New York: GFDRR/World Bank and INEE Secretariat. Available at: http://gfdrr.org/ docs/Guidance_Notes_Safe_Schools.pdf (accessed 12 March 2013).

Kaji, H. (1993) 'School education for earthquake disasters: Japanese experiences', in *Training and Education for Improving Earthquake Disaster Management in Developing Countries*, UNCRD Meeting Report Series, 57: 115–20.

Kuroiwa, J. (1993) 'Peru's national educational program for disaster prevention and mitigation (PNEPDPM)', in *Training and Education for Improving Earthquake Disaster Management in Developing Countries*, UNCRD Meeting Report Series 57: 95–102.

Nakagawa, Y. (2003) 'Disaster and development: applying social capital in disaster recovery', unpublished Master's thesis, Kobe University, Japan.

Nathe, S. (2000) 'Public education for earthquake hazard', *Natural Hazards Review*, 1(4): 191–6.

Ogawa, Y., Fernandez, A. and Yoshimura, T. (2005) 'Town watching as a tool for citizen participation in developing countries: application in disaster training', *International Journal of Mass Emergencies and Disasters*, 23(2): 5–36.

OYO (2005) *Questionnaires and DIG conducted by OYO Corporation*, Saijo City: OYO.

Petal, M. (2009) 'Disaster risk reduction education', in R. Shaw and R. Krishnamurthy, (eds) *Disaster Management: Global Challenges and Local Solutions*, Hyderabad: University Press, pp. 285–304.

Radu, C. (1993) 'Necessity of training and education in an earthquake-prone country', in *Training and Education for Improving Earthquake Disaster Management in Developing Countries*, UNCRD Meeting Report Series 57: 15–33.

Selby, D. and Kagawa, F. (2011) *Disaster Risk Reduction in School Curricula: Case Studies from Thirty Countries*, Paris and New York: UNESCO and UNICEF. Available at: http://unesdoc.unesco.org/images/0021/002170/217036e.pdf (accessed 12 March 2013).

Setagaya Machizukuri Center (2003) *Tool Box of Participatory Design*, Tokyo: Setagaya Machizukuri Center.

Shaw, R. and Goda, K. (2004) 'From disaster to sustainable civil society: the Kobe experience', *Disasters*, 28(19): 16–40.

Shaw, R. and Kobayashi, M. (2001) 'The role of schools in creating earthquake-safer environment', paper presented at the OECD Workshop, Thessaloniki, Greece.

Shaw, R., Shiwaku, K., Kobayashi, H. and Kobayashi, M. (2004) 'Linking experience, knowledge, perception and earthquake preparedness', *Disaster Prevention and Management,* 13(1): 39–49.

Shaw, R., Takeuchi, Y. and Rouhban, B. (2008) 'Education, capacity building and public awareness for disaster reduction', in K. Sassa and P. Canuti (eds) *Landslide Disaster Risk Reduction*, Berlin: Springer, pp. 99–116.

Shiwaku, K. (2007) 'Towards innovation in school disaster education: case research in Kathmandu, Nepal', unpublished doctorate thesis, Kyoto University, Japan.

Shiwaku, K. and Shaw, R. (2008) 'Proactive co-learning: a new paradigm in disaster education', *Disaster Prevention and Management*, 17(2): 183–98.

Shiwaku, K., Shaw, R., Kandel, R.C., Shreshtra, S. R., and Dixit, A. (2006) 'Promotion of disaster education in Nepal: role of teachers as change agents', *International Journal of Mass Emergencies and Disasters,* 24(3): 403–20.

Suwa, S. (2006) 'New perspective of disaster education by making use of the lessons of Kobe Earthquake', *Journal of Natural Disaster Science*, 24(4): 356–63 (in Japanese).

UNESCO-UNICEF (2011) *DRR in Education*, Paris and New York: UNESCO and UNICEF. Available at: http://unesdoc.unesco.org/images/0021/002139/213925e.pdf (accessed 12 March 2013).

UNISDR (2005) *Hyogo Framework for Action for Effective Disaster Risk Reduction,* Geneva: UNISDR. Available at: http://www.unisdr.org/we/coordinate/hfa (accessed 12 March 2013).

Wisner, B. (2006) *Let Our Children Teach Us! A Review of the Role of Education and Knowledge in Disaster Risk Reduction,* Report for UNISDR and ActionAid. Available at: http://www.unisdr.org/2005/task-force/working%20groups/knowledge-education/docs/Let-our-Children-Teach-Us.pdf (accessed 24 March 2013).

Yamada, M. (2001) 'A philosophy for community building', *Aichi Voice*, 14: 3–7 (in Japanese).

Yamori, K. (2006) 'Frontier of disaster education', *Natural Disaster Science*, 24(4): 343–86.

Yoshida, Y. (2007) 'Study on effective and sustainable community disaster education through town watching in Saijo City', unpublished master's thesis, Kyoto University.

Yoshimura, T. (2002) 'Machi-zukuri: new challenge in Japanese urban planning', paper presented to the Thirtieth International Course in Regional Development Planning, 16 May–26 June 2002, Nagoya: United Nations Centre for Regional Development.

7 Many Strong Voices for climate change education

Examples from Belize and Timor-Leste

Ilan Kelman, Jessica Mercer and Marianne Karlsson

Lessons for practitioners

- To best address climate change for people struggling with day-to-day existence, connect climate change to current concerns in order to seek **livelihood** changes that will be viable, irrespective of short-term and long-term futures.
- Education should not be one-way, but instead should be about education through cooperation, so that people can set and create their own pathways by combining their own knowledge and concerns with those being brought in from outside.
- Climate change should not be isolated, but should be placed within other disaster, development, and livelihoods challenges.
- Climate change should not distract from other disaster, development, and livelihoods challenges.

Introduction

People from Small Island Developing States (SIDS; http://www.sidsnet.org) know that climate change will severely affect them and realise that they have plenty to offer from their own experience and expertise, but they are also willing to learn from others to improve their knowledge and actions (Byrne and Inniss 2002; Kelman and West 2009; Lewis 1999, 2009; Nunn and Mimura 1997). That entails embracing 'education' in a wide sense: sharing stories, exchanging information, and combining knowledge forms, so that the parties involved are simultaneously teachers and learners. The lessons and approaches from numerous international initiatives on education are embraced, from declaring education as a fundamental human right (UN 1948) to education in the context of development (Freire 1970) to the contemporary 'Education for All' campaign (UNESCO 2004; http://www. unesco.org/education/efa/ed_for_all/background/jomtien_declaration.shtml) and the ongoing United Nations Decade of Education for Sustainable Development 2005–2014 (UNESCO 2005).

Many projects covering education for sustainable development in the context of disasters and **hazards**, including the hazard of climate change, have already been implemented on SIDS. Examples are community-based education for ecosystem-based adaptation in Jamaica (UNEP 2010), disaster risk reduction in PNG (Mercer *et al.* 2009), and education for village-based coastal management in Samoa (Daly *et al.* 2010). This chapter describes work in two other SIDS, Belize and Timor-Leste, drawing on and linking the educational approaches from two programmes: Many Strong Voices (MSV) and Risk Reduction Education for Disasters (Risk RED).

MSV (http://www.manystrongvoices.org; CICERO and UNEP/GRID-Arendal 2008; Kelman 2010) was set up at the request of SIDS and Arctic peoples to bring them together to deal with climate change within wider development and sustainability contexts. Their focus is to use MSV as a space to educate themselves on their own terms by sharing stories, participating in scientific research, and ensuring that their voices are heard at venues such as international climate change negotiations (Crump and Kelman 2009).

Risk RED (http://www.riskred.org; Petal *et al.* 2008) aims to increase the effectiveness and impact of disaster risk reduction education, which incorporates climate change, since climate change is one form of hazard. The approach is to use whichever educational techniques are appropriate to the context in order to bridge gaps between specific ideas and specific audiences, such as different knowledge forms; the content of education material and its presentation and design; and pure scientific research and on-the-ground application.

Both programmes are based on the long history of educational approaches in the context of development challenges (e.g. Freire 1970; UNESCO 2004). They have particularly targeted the most vulnerable and marginalised communities to ensure that education reaches those with the fewest options and opportunities. SIDS peoples often fall within that category and have been taking action for themselves to increase the opportunities for themselves. That is particularly illustrated by Belize and East Timor.

Belize: fishermen and education

In Belize, MSV worked with two rural communities, Sarteneja and Monkey River, to understand perceived and actual environmental changes as well as other challenges to local livelihoods. The aim is to use broad forms of education to support them in dealing with the difficulties that they face.

Projected climate change impacts in Belize are similar to most SIDS: sea-level rise is likely to affect the coastal lowlands, especially in the northern part of the country (McSweeney *et al.* 2008). In terms of Atlantic hurricanes, it appears as if frequency is likely to decrease but when a hurricane forms, it is likely to be more intense than before (Knutson *et al.* 2010). Impacts also include ocean acidification and higher sea temperatures leading to changing marine life composition and coral bleaching. This constitutes a significant threat as the country depends heavily on the Belize Barrier Reef for two of its major livelihood-generating activities:

tourism and fisheries. Fisheries resources are almost exclusively exploited within the coral reef, which supports stocks of the commercially important species: spiny lobster, queen conch, and fin-fish (Gillet 2003). Similarly to other small-scale fisheries in other SIDS, there is currently insufficient information on how climate change may impact different fish stocks in Belize (Badjeck *et al.* 2010; Gillet and Myvette 2008).

In addition to climate change, the reef system faces numerous pressures. The reef's health has deteriorated over the past three decades due to a combination of overfishing, coastal development, agricultural run-off, disease, and coral bleaching. Included among initiatives designed to support the reef system is a network of Marine Protected Areas (MPAs) covering 13 per cent of Belize's coastal waters; a recent fishing ban on grassers such as parrot fish; and a coral nursery cultivating species that are known to withstand increased sea temperatures (Cho 2005; Healthy Reefs 2010).

Sarteneja and Monkey River both depend on fishing for their livelihoods. Fifty interviews with fishermen, government officials, and representatives from conservation and other interested organisations were used to understand perceptions of the problems and solutions. While observed changes in the climate were an important component of the interviews, the main objective was to understand these groups' needs, interests, and suggestions for dealing with climate change in the context of their livelihoods. One element that emerged was that the communities have long experience with development and conservation programmes, some of which were perceived to be detrimental to the communities, leading the villagers to distrust external organisations. This suggests that when education about climate change is initiated, trust must be carefully considered and built up to ensure that any education and suggested actions are done on the communities' own terms through their own decisions.

According to a survey in Belize, 57 per cent of the respondents in coastal rural areas had insufficient **knowledge** about the impacts and causes of climate change (Ek and Lima 2005). Similarly, the fishermen interviewed here displayed limited knowledge about climate change as externally defined and constructed. Yet many of the fishermen had observed changes in the climate. Key changes were described as increasing numbers of hot days, irregular rainfall patterns, and unpredictable weather in seasons previously deemed stable. Changes in weather and climate were attributed to natural causes or, in some cases, to 'an act of God' (focusing on Christian interpretations); however, some informants also mentioned global warming as a potential cause. A challenge emerges in whether or not education about climate change, as externally defined and constructed, should be implemented and would be useful for improving fishing livelihoods.

Within that context, unfavourable weather conditions including strong winds, waves, and poor visibility were stated as constituting a major **risk** to the fishermen's livelihoods – and lives. The seaworthiness of the small fishing boats used in Belize has been questioned, in particular with regards to changing storm regimes (Gillet and Myvette 2008). The fishermen's concerns were linked to the indirect impacts of storms: loss of income during periods when they were forced to be in the harbour, rather than directly considering their own safety and risk of equipment loss. As an entry point to communication and education on wider climate change concerns, the fishermen's starting point was clear: livelihoods.

The fishermen are also being directly affected by increases in fuel costs and fluctuations in the national and global economy. For example, during the current economic downturn, tourism has decreased in Belize, leading more people to turn to fishing with higher levels of exploitation as a consequence (Hagan 2011). As people in these communities think about their future livelihoods, they might need training and awareness-raising regarding their future under climate change, with expectations of even higher fuel costs as well as increased travel costs for tourists.

Nonetheless, the interviews indicated that decreases in lobster and conch stocks are the fishermen's principal ongoing concern. Conch and lobster production is reported to have peaked in the mid-1980s and has since remained relatively stable (Villanueva 2010). Huitric (2005) argues that the catch statistics mask increasing numbers of fishermen as well as extended fishing areas and augmented fishing efforts, all resulting in overexploitation. Habitat destruction of mangroves and dredging of coastal areas directly impact fish recruitment. All these issues are enmeshed in the fishermen's responses, burying climate change among these immediate concerns based on past knowledge rather than considering future possibilities.

While environmental legislation in Belize is extensive, it has demonstrated limited success in safeguarding the sustainability of marine ecosystems (Cho 2005; Gillet 2003). Education to improve the situation is important, but it is also complicated because the issue is about making suggestions that can help despite the current status of monitoring and enforcement. In particular, fishermen often expressed distrust of management tools such as MPAs which were perceived to restrict fishermen from their fishing grounds while bringing few benefits to the communities. The concern is the imposition of top-down approaches with consultation practices that, in reality, mean that communities have limited influence on decisions. In effect, authorities and organisations could be educated on working with communities for appropriate consultation approaches.

The fishermen have extensive knowledge of climate and the dynamics of marine ecosystems that should be included in any attempts to provide them with more information about climate change and actions to deal with it. The solution is from Risk RED in terms of connecting climate change to current concerns in order to seek livelihood changes that will be viable irrespective of short-term and long-term futures. Additionally, the education should not be one-way. The fishermen need more knowledge regarding the future under climate change, but external people need more knowledge regarding the fishermen's interests, experiences, and contributions towards managing marine ecosystems in such a way that will provide livelihood opportunities. As with MSV, this is not about the external education of the fishermen, but instead is about education through cooperation, so that they can set and create their own pathways by combining their own knowledge and concerns with those being brought in from outside – in the context of climate change and other development and livelihood challenges.

Timor-Leste: national strategies and education

The second case study is Timor-Leste, for which the focus here is top-down strategies to deal with climate change and the self-education processes at the national level that are being enacted to do that. As a relatively new independent state, Timor-Leste is still in the process of building its policies and institutional structures for climate change, which includes educating and building the **capacity** of the staff and departments involved. In Timor-Leste's government, the understanding of climate change impacts, vulnerabilities, **mitigation**, and adaptation on the country's development is increasing. Yet gaps in **resources**, capacities, and data, as well as in education mechanisms, are impeding the potential for climate change challenges to be incorporated into national and subnational development planning (Norton and Waterman 2008). Timor-Leste provides a good case study for MSV in terms of understanding the contexts of a new SIDS grappling with independence as well as climate change among its development challenges.

Specific climate change impacts on Timor-Leste are not fully known (Kirono 2010; Wasson 2001). Historical climate and weather data are not available; monitoring systems to provide a consistent baseline do not exist; models for downscaled projections are not available; and the necessary baseline data, such as bathymetry and topography for sea-level rise, need to be collected.

Recognising the gaps and seeking to educate themselves to fill them, these questions are being asked and national governance structures are being created. The National Directorate of Meteorology and Geophysics (NDMG) has placed a high priority on expanding climate data collection, monitoring, and analysis. NDMG is working with the Pacific Climate Change Science Program (PCCSP) to re-establish a meteorological network, to undergo professional education for the topic, and to recover, digitize and analyse climate data collected under the Portuguese and Indonesian administration periods (Da Silva and Moniz 2010).

Meanwhile, responsibility for climate change adaptation in Timor-Leste currently resides in the Secretariat for Environment within the Ministry of Economy and Development. At the national level, two main initiatives stand out with respect to climate change adaptation. First, on 8 January 2007, Timor-Leste signed the United Nations Framework Convention on Climate Change (UNFCCC) under which it is required to develop and submit a National Communication Document. The process of developing the National Communication Document is currently underway led by the United Nations Development Programme (UNDP 2009). Second, as a Least Developed Country (LDC) within the UNFCCC, Timor-Leste has produced a National Adaptation Programme for Action (NAPA) in which the Ministry for Social Solidarity and the National Disaster Management Directorate (NDMD) have been key players. Few staff involved had experience in these topics or processes, leading to intensive self-education regarding climate change – effectively learning by doing.

That led to some aspects that could have been improved. For example, the NAPA was produced with limited consultation at the district or local levels. Only five out of the 13 districts were consulted in the process and there was no in-depth study of the historical (e.g. Lape and Chin-Yung 2008) and present experiences of climate variability, trends, and change in Timor-Leste. As such, the national-led NAPA process produced limited subnational education regarding climate change and its potential impacts (OXFAM 2011).

Regarding climate change mitigation, on 14 October 2008, Timor-Leste ratified its accession to the UNFCCC's Kyoto Protocol which came into force in the country on 12 January 2009. Yet Timor-Leste is aggressively pursuing its fossil fuel reserves, hoping to extract and sell oil and gas to generate income for development and nation-building (Steele 2002) irrespective of the climate change consequences. The situation here might not be lack of education. Instead, it might be emerging from an informed choice to balance different needs: climate change mitigation compared to the need for immediate, domestic funds for development.

Overall, climate change is a new (even if growing) concern in Timor-Leste, but more education and capacity building are required for the staff tasked with developing laws, regulations, policies, and plans. Further education and capacity are needed to ensure that climate change-related laws, regulations, policies, and plans are monitored and enforced. MSV can help with that, drawing on experience from other SIDS to see what would and would not be transferable to Timor-Leste. Applying Risk RED's techniques would ensure that all needed audiences would be reached through appropriate consultation, that different knowledge forms would be combined, and that any application is based on the best available science. In particular, a balance is needed to ensure that all aspects of climate change are addressed – mitigation and adaptation – while enabling Timor-Leste to pursue its legitimate self-directed development as a new state.

For example, forests play a key role in climate change mitigation and adaptation (for more information on forests and climate change in Timor-Leste, see Godinho *et al.* 2003). Despite the banning of large-scale logging in 2000 and smallholder logging in 2008, logging continues on a minor scale, supported by widespread practices of slash-and-burn agriculture plus using wood for fuel. Given the geology and steep terrain in Timor-Leste, loss of forest cover is a major contributory factor to worsening floods and landslides, the effects of which in turn could be exacerbated by climate change with, for example, fewer but more intense rainfall events contributing to increased hazard impacts (Kirono 2010).

Deforestation has been identified by some as the major environmental issue in Timor-Leste (Sandlund *et al.* 2001). Lack of education regarding deforestation's impacts combined with lack of alternative livelihoods means that tackling deforestation on the ground is challenging. From a national perspective, there are currently major discrepancies in estimates of forest distribution, cover, and degradation. No forest inventory system exists, although one is currently being developed. Without such systems alongside monitoring of other natural resources in Timor-Leste, it is difficult to introduce subsequent laws, regulations, and education approaches regarding forests and climate change, because: (1) it will not be evidence-based to obtain **community** buy-in and for monitoring and enforcing regulations; and (2) the impacts, positive or negative, of forestry initiatives on other sectors and wider livelihoods cannot be known.

In parallel to climate change discussion, Timor-Leste is addressing disaster risk reduction with similar gaps in education and capacity. Most disaster-related work occurs in isolation from the climate change work, even though climate change is one hazard among many that Timor-Leste faces. Others include volcanic ash, tsunamis, and landslides. As MSV's and Risk RED's work demonstrates, educating about hazards including climate change can be linked directly to daily activities supporting livelihood, ensuring that extreme and long-term trends are addressed in a manner that does not detract from day-to-day development.

In fact, the policies and actions suggested for climate change adaptation have also long been suggested and tested for wider disaster risk reduction. Simultaneously, many initiatives for climate change mitigation, such as preserving forests, should be considered anyway for disaster risk reduction, such as flood and landslide prevention. Little need exists to separate climate change work and disaster risk reduction (see also Shaw *et al.* 2010a, 2010b). As per Risk RED's approach, climate change adaptation could be enfolded into disaster risk reduction so that any education and action to build capacity are not separated, but work together.

Conclusion

The two case studies show remarkable contrasts, yet are nicely complementary. Using different regions, balancing local and national concerns, and demonstrating top-down and bottom-up approaches illustrate what can be achieved for climate change education on SIDS. The SIDS context for both countries, as with MSV, shows the importance of sharing experiences with each other and with the rest of the world. The common overarching lesson to emerge is that climate change is important, but it must be viewed in wider contexts.

On-the-ground, day-to-day and year-to-year livelihood changes and challenges are of far higher concern than the decade-to-decade influences of climate change. But climate change will certainly have severe livelihood impacts in the future in Belize and Timor-Leste, meaning that adjustments need to start now in order to create a better future under climate change. In particular, natural resources – most notably from coastal or marine environments – represent the basis for the livelihoods for many SIDS peoples, including in these two case studies. Climate change is projected to significantly affect these resources, adding to the sustainability challenges that the people already face regarding their natural resource-based livelihoods.

To ensure the sustainable continuation of these livelihoods under climate change, it is necessary to use education as an exchange process to link long-term and short-term approaches at the local level, so that short-term endeavours support long-term needs. That would be achieved through consulting those involved in local livelihood-related decisions for mutual education and advice exchange. Meanwhile, at the national level, lessons for climate change are already well known from many other sectors, but especially from disaster risk reduction. No need exists to separate climate change from its wider contexts.

Both Risk RED and MSV are about such connections – among topics, among peoples, and among scales so that, as part of climate change education, the local consultations inform and are informed by regional, national, and international processes. Local knowledge can and should provide rich input into dealing with climate change in its wider contexts, but local knowledge cannot be the only input. Instead, it needs to be linked with other knowledge forms and scales as part of educating and being educated regarding climate change action.

Ultimately, many concerns other than climate change exist, but climate change must remain prominent in order to construct a sustainable future by supporting livelihoods now. The fundamental lesson from the differences and similarities of Belize and Timor-Leste is the same, matching science and action from other SIDS and around the world (Gaillard 2010; Kelman 2010; Mercer 2010; Shaw *et al.* 2010a, 2010b). This lesson is that climate change education is about connecting climate change to other concerns that people face so that climate change is placed into wider development and sustainability contexts.

References

Badjeck, M.C., Allison, E., Halls, A. and Dulvy, N. (2010) 'Impacts of climate variability and change on fishery-based livelihoods', *Marine Policy*, 34(3): 375–83.

Byrne, J. and Inniss, V. (2002) 'Island sustainability and sustainable development in the context of climate change', in H-H.M. Hsiao, C.-H. Liu and H-M. Tsai (eds) *Sustainable Development for Island Societies: Taiwan and the World*, Taipei: Asia-Pacific Research Program, pp. 2–29.

Cho, L. (2005) 'Marine protected areas: a tool for integrated coastal management in Belize', *Ocean and Coastal Management*, 48 (111–12): 932–47.

CICERO and UNEP/GRID-Arendal (2008) *Many Strong Voices: Outline for an Assessment Project Design*. CICERO Report 2008:05, Oslo: CICERO (Center for International Climate and Environmental Research – Oslo).

Crump, J. and Kelman, I. (2009) 'Many strong voices from Arctic and island peoples', in UNESCO (ed.) *Climate Change and Arctic Sustainable Development*, Paris: UNESCO (United Nations Educational, Scientific and Cultural Organization), pp. 284-95.

Daly, M., Poutasi, N., Nelson, F. and Kohlhase, J. (2010) 'Reducing the climate vulnerability of coastal communities in Samoa', *Journal for International Development*, 22(2): 256–81.

Da Silva, S. and Moniz, T.F. (2010) *Climate, Climate Variability and Change of Timor-Leste*, Timor-Leste: Pacific Climate Change Science Program.

Ek, E. and Lima, R. (2005) *Belize Climate Change Survey*, Belmopan: Caribbean Community Climate Change Centre.

Freire, P. (1970) *Pedagogy of the Oppressed*, trans. M.B. Ramos, New York: Seabury Press.

Gaillard, JC (2010) 'Vulnerability, capacity and resilience: perspectives for climate and development policy', *Journal of International Development*, 22(2): 218–32.

Gillet, V. (2003) 'The fisheries of Belize', *Fisheries Centre Research Reports*, 11(6).

Gillet, V. and Myvette, G. (2008) *Vulnerability Assessment and Adaptability of the Fisheries and Aquaculture Industries to Climate Change*, Belmopan: Ministry of Natural Resources.

Godinho, L., Nacuray, E., Cardinoza, M.M. and Lasco, R.D. (2003) 'Climate change mitigation through carbon sequestration: the forest ecosystems of Timor-Leste', in *Proceedings from the 1st National Workshop on Climate Change, 19th November 2003*, Dili, Timor-Leste.

Hagan, A. (2011) *Effectiveness of Different Levels of Management on Three Marine Protected Areas: A Case Study from Belize, Central America*, Placencia, Belize: Southern Environmental Association (SEA).

Healthy Reefs (2010) *Report Card for the Mesoamerican Reef*, Belize City: Healthy Reefs.

Huitric, M. (2005) 'Lobster and conch fisheries of Belize: a history of sequential exploitation', *Ecology and Society*, 10(1):21. Available at: http://www.ecologyandsociety.org/vol10/iss1/art21.

Kelman, I. (2010) 'Policy arena: introduction to climate, disasters and international development', *Journal of International Development*, 22(2): 208–17.

Kelman, I. and West, J. (2009) 'Climate change and Small Island Developing States: a critical review', *Ecological and Environmental Anthropology*, 5(1): 1–16.

Kirono, D. (2010) *Climate Change in Timor-Leste: A Brief Overview on Future Climate Projections*, Canberra: CSIRO.

Knutson, T.R., Mcbride, J.L., Chan, J., Kerry, E., Holland, G., Landsea, C., Held, I., Kossin, J.P., Srivastava, A.K. and Sugi, M. (2010) 'Tropical cyclones and climate change', *Nature Geoscience*, 3 (3): 157–63.

Lape, P.V. and Chin-Yung, C. (2008) 'Fortification as a human response to late Holocene climate change in East Timor', *Archaeology in Oceania*, 43(1): 11–21.

Lewis, J. (1999) *Development in Disaster-prone Places: Studies of Vulnerability*, London: Intermediate Technology Publications.

—— (2009) 'An island characteristic: derivative vulnerabilities to indigenous and exogenous hazards', *Shima: The International Journal of Research into Island Cultures*, 3(1): 3–15.

McSweeney, C., New, M. and Lizcano, G. (2008) *Belize: The UNDP Climate Change Country Profiles*, Oxford: School of Geography and the Environment, University of Oxford.

Mercer, J. (2010) 'Disaster risk reduction or climate change adaptation? Are we reinventing the wheel?' *Journal of International Development*, 22(2): 247–64.

Mercer, J., Kelman, I., Suchet-Pearson, S. and Lloyd, K. (2009) 'Integrating indigenous and scientific knowledge bases for disaster risk reduction in Papua New Guinea', *Geografiska Annaler: Series B, Human Geography*, 91(2): 157–83.

Norton, J. and Waterman, P. (2008) *Reducing the Risk of Disasters and Climate Variability in the Pacific Islands: Timor-Leste Country Assessment,* Washington, DC: World Bank.

Nunn, P.D. and Mimura, N. (1997) 'Vulnerability of South Pacific island nations to sea-level rise', *Journal of Coastal Research*, 24: 133–51.

OXFAM (2011) 'Climate change impacts upon communities in Timor-Leste', unpublished research, OXFAM, Timor-Leste.

Petal, M., Green, R., Kelman, I., Shaw, R. and Dixit, A. (2008) 'Community-based construction for disaster risk reduction', in L. Bosher (ed.) *Hazards and the Built Environment: Attaining Built-in Resilience*, Abingdon: Taylor & Francis, pp. 191–217.

Sandlund, O.T., Bryceson, I., de Carvalho, D., Rio, N., da Silva, J. and Silva, M.I. (2001) *Assessing Environmental Needs and Priorities in East Timor: Issues and Priorities*, Dili, Timor-Leste: UNDP.

Shaw, R., Pulhin, J.M. and Pereira, J.J. (eds) (2010a) *Climate Change Adaptation and Disaster Risk Reduction: An Asian Perspective. Community, Environment and Disaster Risk Management*, Bingley: Emerald Group Publishing Limited.

—— (eds) (2010b) *Climate Change Adaptation and Disaster Risk Reduction: Issues and Challenges. Community, Environment and Disaster Risk Management*, Bingley: Emerald Group Publishing Limited.

Steele, J. (2002) 'Nation building in East Timor', *World Policy Journal*, 19(2): 76–87.

UN (1948) *Universal Declaration of Human Rights*, New York: UN.

UNDP (2009) *Project Document: Initial National Communication under the UN Framework Convention on Climate Change for Timor-Leste*, Timor-Leste: UNDP.

UNEP (2010) *Risk and Vulnerability Assessment Methodology Development Project (RiVAMP), Linking Ecosystems to Risk and Vulnerability Reduction: The Case of Jamaica, Results of the Pilot Assessment*, Geneva: United Nations Environment Program.

UNESCO (2004) *Education for All (EFA): Global Monitoring Report 2003/2004*, Paris: UNESCO.

—— (2005) *UN Decade of Education for Sustainable Development, 2005–2014*, Paris: UNESCO.

Villanueva, J. (2010) *Fisheries Statistical Report 2010*, Belmopan: Belize Fisheries Department, Ministry of Agriculture and Fisheries.

Wasson, M. (2001) 'East Timor and climate change: security and sustainable development', in R. Anderson and C. Deutsch (eds) *Sustainable Development and the Environment in East Timor*, Melbourne: Cleveland Press, pp. 38–41.

8 Managing infrastructure, environment and disaster risk

Ana Maria Cruz

Lessons for practitioners

- **Knowledge** exists to protect buildings and lifelines from **hazard** impacts.
- Communities must demand that such knowledge is applied.
- Communities must be vigilant that building codes are implemented.
- Natural and technological hazards may combine in surprising ways.
- Planning that involves communities, engineers and political leaders is vital to anticipate such 'surprises'.

Introduction

All over the world urban and rural dwellers depend on infrastructure – roads, bridges, electricity, water, drainage and sanitation systems, health facilities and schools, to name but a few. Recent damage and losses to infrastructure systems triggered by natural hazards, technological accidents and acts of terrorism have prompted governments to re-evaluate current practices for the protection of infrastructure systems. Particularly, there is concern about the cascading effects on other infrastructure systems and on society when one infrastructure system is disrupted. In areas where many people depend on one or a few infrastructure systems (e.g., the only bridge across a large river providing access to a remote village; a transformer station and power lines providing electricity to a small town), the results could be devastating. Industrial, warehousing, storage, port and rail infrastructure vital to the economic life of cities, regions and even nations have also been affected by recent disasters. Damage to ports can have severe economic impact on a region, as occurred following the Kobe earthquake, cutting Kobe off from the rest of Japan and the outside world (Cataldo 1995).

The following events serve as examples of what can happen when natural hazards affect infrastructure systems:

- The March 2011 Tohoku earthquake and tsunami in Japan destroyed 45,700 buildings and damaged 144,300 more in dozens of cities, towns and villages, according to the National Police Agency of Japan (2012). Damage to the Fukushima Dai Ichi nuclear power complex and resulting radioactive contamination has made many more whole towns and villages uninhabitable and put farms, shops, factories and workshops out of use.

- The 2010 earthquake in Haiti did enormous damage to the capital city, Port-au-Prince and the surrounding area (Madabhushi *et al.* 2013). Two years later, some 515,000 people were still living in tents with minimal sanitation infrastructure (Booth 2012). Indeed, destruction of an already deficient water and sanitation system in Haiti provided the ideal conditions for the spread of cholera that killed 4500 people, made almost 300,000 people sick, and continues to cause infections and deaths in Haiti (United Nations 2011).

- Hurricanes Katrina and Rita in 2005 caused extensive damage to the oil and gas production infrastructure both onshore and offshore in the Gulf of Mexico. More than 163 platforms and hundreds of kilometers of pipelines needed to transport the oil and gas from the platforms to the mainland were destroyed or severely damaged (Cruz and Krausmann 2008). Damage onshore resulted in impassable roads, little or no communication systems available, complete loss of power, limited personnel available, and no place to provide boarding and lodging for workers and responders, making recovery slow (Cruz and Krausmann 2009).

- In September 2003, at 3:01 a.m., high winds knocked down a spruce fir tree onto the Matten-Lavorgo power line in Brunnen, Switzerland, cutting electrical power on a line supplying Italy with 1320 MW. Within 19 minutes Italy was plunged into a complete blackout affecting hospitals, transportation systems, water distribution systems, communication systems and everything that depends on electrical power. According to the Director of the Italian Civil Protection Department (DiGennaro 2004), hospitals, trains and communications were the most affected.

- From December 1999 to March 2000, the highest rainfall rate since 1951 was recorded in Mozambique, triggering the worst flooding ever recorded in the southern and central parts of the country. The flooding affected about 30 per cent of the Mozambican population, displacing 491,000 people. Road and railways and other infrastructures were destroyed, resulting in economic losses estimated to have totalled US$600 million (Matsimbe 2003).

- In 1964, a large earthquake of magnitude 7.5 triggered a 4-metre tsunami in Niigata, Japan. The earthquake initially caused fires in five storage tanks and hundreds of oil spills at two oil refineries in Niigata harbour (Iwabuchi *et al.* 2006). When the tsunami hit the already earthquake-stricken facilities, additional damage to storage tanks and plant processing equipment occurred and spread the fire throughout the two plants. The ignited crude oil from the refineries was then carried by the flood waters into residential areas and resulted in the destruction of 286 houses by fire (Akatsuka and Kobayashi 2008; Iwabuchi *et al.* 2006).

These events highlight the need to evaluate and plan for threats involving the impact of natural hazards on infrastructure systems that can result in potentially devastating impacts on people and their **livelihoods**.

Risk reduction options for the protection of infrastructure systems

Infrastructure systems are often located in areas subject to natural hazards, and thus may be at **risk** of damage or disruption if appropriate measures are not taken to prevent or prepare for such events. In this chapter we are particularly concerned with infrastructure systems that are critical to the well-being of a **community** or to society, and infrastructure systems and facilities that are considered essential such as hospitals, emergency operation centres, fire and police stations, evacuation shelters, electrical power distribution systems, communication systems, transportation systems, and water distribution and sewage collection systems. Wastewater treatment plants and certain industrial facilities that handle large quantities of hazardous materials deserve special attention due to the potential for hazardous material releases, if they are severely impacted by a natural hazard, and the additional threat to nearby residents.

In general, most infrastructure systems and essential facilities are composed of a combination of buildings and lifelines. The vulnerability of buildings and lifelines will vary for each type of hazard, as well as the risk reduction measures available for their protection.

Buildings

Buildings may be affected by earthquakes, tsunamis, floods, high winds, and landslides and soil problems, among other hazards. Buildings are complex combinations of the foundation and structure, and the plumbing, electrical, heating, ventilation, air conditioning, and ancillary systems which may suffer damage when one or a combination of these systems fails (Heaney *et al.* 2000). Building structures house office use and administrative functions related to the operation of a critical infrastructure system as well as storing materials, and housing equipment. Control rooms are generally housed in building structures and may require a special design to ensure that they are operational following a major disaster. Damage or collapse of buildings may result in human casualties or major upsets to an infrastructure system. For example, following the Gujarat earthquake in India in January 2001, water distribution systems were affected when water pump buildings collapsed, damaging electrical controls and emergency generators (Eidinger 2001). Schools and health facilities as well as the buildings that house vital functions such as police and fire services also deserve special care in their location, design, construction and maintenance (see Chapter 9).

Earthquakes and buildings

Large earthquakes pose one of the greatest threats to buildings. The adoption of appropriate seismic building codes for new structures and the retrofitting of older buildings to updated seismic building codes can help minimize loss of life and property during earthquakes. Most countries subject to earthquake hazards have adopted modern seismic building codes. However, only wealthier countries have been successful in implementing them. One example is Turkey which had adopted modern building codes since 1975, and had updated and strengthened them in 1998 prior to the 1999 Kocaeli earthquake. Nonetheless, the extensive damage to residential buildings (more than 215,000) and the hazardous material releases from industrial plants during the earthquake were attributed to poor decisions, lack of clear housing and land-use policies and lack of oversight of building regulations (USGS 2000; Cruz 2003).

Tsunamis and buildings

Buildings located on coastal areas subject to tsunami hazards may be vulnerable to tsunami wave impact and flooding. Site conditions in the run-up zone will determine the depth of tsunami inundation, water flow velocities, the presence of breaking wave or bore conditions, debris load, and warning time, and can vary greatly from site to site (NTHMP 2001; Yeh *et al.* 2005). The vulnerability of buildings to tsunami loads will depend on several factors including number of floors, the presence of open ground floors with movable objects, building materials, age and design, and the building's surroundings such as the presence of barriers (Dominey-Howes and Papathoma 2007).

The National Tsunami Hazard Mitigation Program (NTHMP 2013) in the United States recommends four basic techniques that can be applied to buildings and other infrastructure to reduce tsunami risk, including:

- *Avoiding development in inundation areas*: This is of course the most effective **mitigation** strategy but not always possible, particularly for existing buildings.
- *Slowing techniques*: These include the use of specially designed forests, ditches, slopes, and berms which can slow and strain debris from waves.
- *Steering techniques*: Used to guide the tsunamis away from vulnerable structures and people by placing structures, walls and ditches and using paved surfaces that create a low-friction path for water to follow.
- *Blocking techniques* that consist of building hardened structures such as breakwalls and other rigid constructions that can block the force of the waves.

There are no tsunami-specific building codes (Cruz *et al.* 2009). Current structural designs to protect buildings in tsunami-prone regions are generally based on loadings due to riverine floods and storm waves. They provide little guidance for loads specifically induced by tsunami effects on coastal structures (Yeh *et al.* 2005). Resent research concerning the performance of buildings and structures impacted by the 2011 Great East Japan tsunami will provide important lessons for improved tsunami risk reduction (Suppasri *et al.* 2012).

Floods and buildings

Flood loads are similar to tsunami loads and include the impact of the mass of water, additional energy from breaking waves, the buoyant or 'lifting' and hence weakening effect on structural elements and the force of impact with floating debris (Yeh *et al.* 2005). Buildings located in river basins and near large water bodies may be subject to flood loads. As with tsunamis, flood protection measures include avoiding building in flood-prone areas, particularly on the flood plains that are, on average, inundated once or more in a hundred years, waterproofing buildings, and the use of slowing, steering and blocking techniques discussed above. Elevation of buildings or important building components above the 100-year flood contour level can protect building functionality and contents. The United States Army Corps of Engineers (USACE) has done extensive work in flood mitigation control and has produced a comprehensive review of floodproofing techniques (USACE 1997).

Most wealthier nations (e.g. the United States, Germany, Italy, Spain, France, Japan) as well as many developing countries (e.g. Mexico, Colombia) limit or prohibit development in the 100-year flood plain. However, the law generally applies to new construction. Thus, existing buildings located within the 100-year flood plains are not protected. Furthermore, political pressure and **corruption** sometimes result in the authorization of building permits or illegal development in flood-prone areas (Santander 2010; Sierra 2005).

High winds and buildings

Building structures may be subject to wind damage, particularly storm-induced winds, hurricane winds and tornadoes. Engineering design codes are used to ensure that buildings and structures are constructed to withstand particular wind speeds depending on the characteristics of each region. In the United States, the American Society of Civil Engineers (ASCE) provides guidelines for the design and calculation of wind loads in the design standard ASCE 7, 'Minimum Design Loads for Buildings and Other Structures' (Cruz 2007). ASCE 7 requires design for the highest wind experienced on average once or more in 50 years (50-year wind) with an importance factor for critical infrastructures and industrial facilities containing hazardous materials. This results in the equivalent of a 500-year wind speed for these priority structures (Cruz *et al.* 2001; Steinberg 2004).

It is important to note that very often wind damage to building structures is due to failure of roofing materials, doors and windows. These failures, which are often less expensive to prevent or mitigate, lead to weather penetration and damage (Heaney *et al.* 2000).

Landslides and other soil problems and buildings

Landslides and other soil problems often accompany other natural hazards such as earthquakes, floods, hurricanes and volcanic eruptions. The Wenchuan earthquake in Sichuan Province, China, in 2008 triggered 5117 landslides, 3575 rock falls, 358 debris flows and the creation of 34 barrier lakes formed by partial blockage of a river (Shi 2008). Barrier lakes, when the blockage shifts, may cause flooding downstream. Such geological failures were responsible for the destruction of infrastructure systems, industrial plants, and roads and bridges in the Wenchuan event. Hurricane Mitch in Central America in 1998 triggered hundreds of landslides which were responsible for damage to buildings and the majority of fatalities (Spiker and Gori 2003).

As with other natural hazards, landslide hazard reduction includes both structural and non-structural prevention and mitigation measures. Structural measures include construction of earth-retaining walls, construction of surface water drainage systems, slope surface protection such as seeding ground covering plants in a slurry containing plant nutrients and compost (hydro-seeding), spraying concrete on slopes and constructing reinforced concrete grids, and re-compaction of fill slopes (Kwong *et al.* 2004).

Lifeline systems

Natural hazards have the potential to disrupt lifeline systems. Lifelines and infrastructure systems were seriously affected by liquefaction and strong ground shaking during the 1999 Kocaeli earthquake in Turkey, resulting in disruption and damage to roads, bridges and port facilities, power distribution systems, communications systems and water distribution systems (Tang 2000).

Damage to lifeline systems can delay or impede emergency response activities. For example, loss of water due to multiple pipeline breaks delayed the emergency response to several of the gas-caused fires following the Northridge earthquake (City Administrative Officer 1994); and the loss of water and power outages following the Kocaeli earthquake hampered the emergency response to the earthquake-triggered hazardous materials releases (Steinberg and Cruz 2004).

Bridges and roadways

Liquefaction, ground settlement and slope instability can cause extensive damage to bridges, elevated highways and roadways during earthquakes. Transportation systems, including highways, bridges and roads suffered damage during the Kocaeli earthquake. Typical damage included pavement openings, ground heaving, fissures, displacement, settlement and road buckling due to compression damage (EQE 1999; Tang 2000). In addition, the large amount of debris from damaged buildings and an increased amount of traffic as rescue efforts and other traffic converging to the affected area overwhelmed the region's road network. Extensive damage to transportation routes was also reported following the Kobe earthquake, which destroyed the city's main highway, several railroad tracks and much of its port (Dawkins 1995).

The structural integrity and performance of bridges and roadways can be improved with proper design and materials (Cruz 2007; Erdik 1998). Tunnels, although expensive, usually prove to be cost-effective in the long term to avoid landslide hazard in transportation routes with slope problems (Bhasin *et al.* 2001). Spiker and Gori (2003) observe the need to establish standardized codes for excavation, construction and grading in landslide-prone areas.

Ports and marine terminals

Ports and marine terminals are affected by earthquakes and tsunamis, and lique-faction and soil problems during earthquakes (Erdik 1998; Tang 2000). Ground shaking, settlement, and lateral displacement caused damage to port facilities in Izmit Bay following the Kocaeli earthquake (Tang 2000). To illustrate, ground subsidence and/or submarine slides caused the loss of 200 metres of pier at the AKSA chemical company in Yalova on the south shore of Izmit Bay (Steinberg and Cruz 2004). Liquefaction and permanent ground deformation devastated the Port of Kobe, Japan, damaging more than 90 per cent of the port's moorings (Erdik 1998).

Ports and marine terminals are susceptible to hurricane winds and storm surge (Hanstrum and Holland 1992). Several ports in Central America were severely affected by Hurricane Georges in 1998 (Beam *et al.* 1999), while the Port of New Orleans was brought to a complete stop following Hurricane Katrina (Cashell and Labonte 2005). Protection of ports and harbours from wave action and storm surge may include natural or manufactured breakwaters and surge barriers.

The American Society of Civil Engineers' Ports and Harbors Committee has developed planning and design guidelines for small harbours (Sorensen *et al.* 1992). The International Navigation Association has published the *Seismic Design Guidelines for Port Structures* (PIANC 2001). These guidelines address the limita-tions present in conventional design, and establish the framework for a design strategy based on seismic response and performance requirements. The provisions reflect the diverse nature of port facilities throughout the world, where the required functions of port structures, economic and social environment, and seismic activities may differ from region to region (PIANC 2001).

Underground pipelines

Underground pipelines can be affected by earthquakes, poor ground conditions, liquefaction, flooding, storm surge, erosion and landslides. Earthquakes and flooding have caused extensive damage to gas, water, sewage, wastewater and oil pipelines (ATC 1991). Damage to gas and oil pipelines can result in secondary hazards such as gas leaks, fires and explosions (Lau *et al.* 1995). Lindell and Perry (1997) reported nine petroleum pipeline ruptures during the Northridge earthquake. The authors estimated that more than 230,000 gallons of oil were spilled from multiple breaks on the ARCO Four Corner's line. The spills caused property damage and an injury in connection with one spill when leaking crude oil was ignited. Venancio *et al.* (2003) reported on the effects of the 2000–2001 floods in Mondego, Portugal. The large water flow due to overflowing of dams and several levee breaks exposed an underground gas pipeline, posing a major threat to nearby villages and the city of Coimbra.

Damage to water distribution lines can leave people without drinking water for long periods of time (see Chapter 11). Following the Gujarat earthquake, damage to water pumping stations and transmission lines left people without drinking water supply. Restoration of potable water supply via a pipeline took 4–6 months to restore (Eidinger 2001). Cyclone Aila in May 2009 damaged the little potable water distribution systems available in Sajnekhali, West Bengal. The high storm surge overtopped levees, killing many people and livestock, while causing salt water intrusion into drinking water reservoirs, leaving victims without any source of water (based on author's visit to the region in December 2009).

Loss of water can also hamper or impede response to fires triggered by the primary hazard event. Erdik (1998) reports over 2000 water pipeline breaks during the Kobe earthquake, having a negative effect on firefighting capabilities. Steinberg and Cruz (2004) reported that damage to the main water pipeline, which provided service to several industrial facilities in Korfez, severely hampered emergency response to the multiple earthquake-triggered fires at Turkey's largest oil refinery following the Kocaeli earthquake.

Protection measures to reduce pipeline (as well as other lifeline) vulnerability to natural hazards include avoiding areas close to active faults or in areas susceptible to liquefaction, landslides, flooding or other natural hazards, the use of proper materials and following international standards for design and construction. Detailed guidelines on lifeline protection are available from ASCE's Technical Council on Lifeline Earthquake Engineering (see, for example, ASCE 2009; Schiff and Buckle 1995).

Electrical power systems

Electrical power is highly susceptible to natural hazards. Damage to power systems can severely hamper emergency response capabilities. Earthquakes, storms and high winds can knock down electrical power lines. Power outages have been reported during most major hurricanes. Often electrical power is shut down as a preventive measure before the arrival of hurricane strength winds, and remains so until crews verify the integrity of electrical power lines and poles after the storm. Damage to electrical power systems during hurricanes is often caused by water penetration into power stations and toppling transformers and electrical power lines and posts.

Most major earthquakes have resulted in electrical power outages of varying lengths. The most vulnerable components during earthquakes include generators and transformers, with damage often occurring due to improperly anchored equipment (Erdik 1998). Indirect damage to electrical power lines and poles caused by building collapse can also be extensive, as was documented by Tang (2000) following the Kocaeli earthquake.

Communication systems

Communication systems are also highly susceptible to natural hazard impacts. Most often communication systems fail during earthquakes due to poor seismic protection of backup power systems. During the Kocaeli earthquake (Tang 2000), communication systems suffered due to failure or lack of protection and mitigation measures including:

- toppled batteries due to lack of anchoring bolts, straps or chains;
- air conditioning failure due to structural collapse of walls on equipment;
- electronic equipment damage because it was not designed to withstand strong ground motion.

Damage to several communication towers and unavailability of backup power affected both landlines and wireless networks following the Padang, Sumatra, earthquake in September 2009 leaving the region without communications for at least six hours (Tang 2000).

Protection and mitigation measures for communication systems include the adoption of appropriate building codes to ensure buildings can withstand the forces of the natural hazard, the use of anchoring mechanisms for electronic equipment, batteries and backup generators, and the raising above 100-year/500-year flood levels and floodproofing of sensitive equipment.

Industrial facilities, water and wastewater treatment plants

Natural hazards can cause extensive damage to industrial facilities and disrupt water and wastewater treatment plants. Damage to storage tanks and plant processing equipment may result in accidental releases of hazardous materials. Of particular concern are large water treatment plants because they generally store high volumes of chlorine gas for water treatment. Hazardous materials releases triggered by natural hazards can occur in any place where natural hazards and hazards from industrial activities and the handling of large quantities of hazardous materials are both present. Hundreds of hazardous materials releases triggered by natural hazards occur every year in the United States (Sengul *et al.* 2012) and elsewhere, as evidenced by the following examples.

- During the August 2002 floods in the Czech Republic, 40 tons of chlorine were released from the Spolana Chemical Works company in Neratovice, north of Prague (European Commission 2002). The chlorine release forced authorities to declare an emergency and warn the local population to stay inside their homes and to keep doors and windows closed.
- In Japan, the 8.0 magnitude Tokachi-oki earthquake in 2003 caused severe damage to infrastructure and triggered a major fire in the oil storage facilities of an oil refinery. Structural damage to 45 tanks at the refinery was reported (Kurita 2004).
- Van Dijk (2008) reported on hazardous materials being released during the December 2004 Indian Ocean tsunami in the city of Banda Aceh, including oil spills and release of other materials from two depots of fertilizer and pesticides.
- More than two hundred hazardous materials releases from fixed industrial facilities were triggered by Hurricane Katrina in 2005. One of the largest releases occurred from the Murphy Oil refinery in St. Bernard Parish, where

a storage tank was ruptured, releasing more than 25,000 barrels of oil, affecting 1,800 homes (EPA 2006).

- Krausmann *et al.* (2010) reported releases of ammonia and other hazardous materials with possible effects on nearby residents following the Wenchuan earthquake in China on 12 May 2008.

- Krausmann and Cruz (2013) reported numerous hazardous materials releases following the magnitude 9.0 earthquake and tsunami on 11 March 2011 off the Pacific coast of Tohoku in Japan. The TV images of raging fires at an oil refinery in Chiba Prefecture was just one example. In this case, the earthquake forces initiated a chain of events that resulted in multiple fires and explosions which completely destroyed 17 liquefied petroleum gas (LPG) storage tanks, and caused damage both onsite and offsite of the refinery.

Industrial facilities and water and wastewater treatment plants can be protected against natural hazards through the adoption of design standards that account for natural hazard loads (e.g. wind, seismic, flood, and tsunami) on buildings, with steel support structures for processing equipment and storage tanks (ASCE 2011; Cruz and Okada 2008; NTHMP 2001).

Infrastructure interdependencies and disaster planning

Recent disasters point out the need to better understand infrastructure failure interdependencies and their societal significance. One of the major concerns is the threat that the inherent interdependencies of critical infrastructures can lead to cascading failures which cross boundaries between both technological and social structures (NIPP 2006; O'Rourke 2007, Santella *et al.* 2009). To illustrate, Menoni (2001) analyzed the interactions and couple effects induced by the Kobe earthquake on the various systems such as lifelines, industrial facilities, hospitals and emergency response facilities, residential buildings and people. The author showed how the earthquake-induced secondary hazards in each of these systems (e.g. gas leakages, toxic releases, toxic release from hospital) led to effects in other subsystems such as the economic, emergency services and social system. Menoni noted the need to incorporate both parameters of the physical environment such as lifelines and building stock as well as organizational, social and systemic factors into the analysis.

Because of the complex and interlinked nature of infrastructure systems, models of these systems and their interdependencies have been proposed, including the Critical Infrastructure Protection Decision Support System (CIPDSS) developed through collaboration between Los Alamos, Sandia, and Argonne National Laboratories, sponsored by the Science and Technology Directorate of the U.S. Department of Homeland Security (DHS) (Santella *et al.* 2009). The University of British Columbia in Canada runs a project entitled 'Analyzing Infrastructures for Disaster-Resilient Communities'. The main aim of the project is to develop and disseminate knowledge that is needed to prioritize investments for fostering disaster-resilient infrastructures, and thus, more disaster-resilient communities.

The European Community has set out guidelines for the identification and designation of European Critical Infrastructure and the assessment of the need to improve their protection. These guidelines are non-binding.

Conclusion

The human and economic, financial and environmental cost of damage to infrastructure can be very high. Knock-on effects and cascades of failures are also common because of the interdependence of infrastructural systems. This chapter has discussed the vulnerabilities of different infrastructure systems to various types of natural hazards and the possible risk reduction measures that can be taken to protect them.

The adoption of building codes and standards, and building code enforcement, an important measure in infrastructure protection, has been fairly successful in the wealthier nations with professional engineers and builders, well-trained inspectors, and well-educated users (Petal *et al.* 2008). Nonetheless, as the examples of the Great East Japan earthquake and tsunami, Hurricane Katrina and the Tokai and Niigata floods above show, there have been failures even in the rich world. Petal *et al.* (2008, pp. 193–94) write:

> Building code enforcement as a strategy is more likely to succeed where there is social demand for safe construction, there are educational resources for builders to know about and implement the standards, the financial resources to meet these standards; and a large well trained and adequately paid cadre of licensed professionals, technical and enforcement, with a manageable caseload, who are able to respond rapidly to problems.

Petal *et al.* (2008) point out that generally these conditions are absent in the majority of less affluent countries, making the need for a comprehensive community-based approach even more imperative.

Large-scale engineering approaches to protection of infrastructure from natural hazards has a mixed record and must be considered carefully from social and environmental points of view – where displacement of people or ecological disruption are side effects – and not just from an economic cost-benefit perspective.

While structural mitigation measures have helped communities to reduce the risk from natural and technological hazards, in some cases, they have placed communities at risk from unforeseen threats (Cruz 2007). Consider the large and costly engineering flood control projects involving the construction of levees and floodwalls during the first half of the twentieth century in the United States after the passing of the Flood Control Act in 1934. These infrastructures did not protect the citizens from major disasters, particularly Hurricanes Betsy and Camille in 1965 and 1969, respectively. Indeed, engineered flood control measures alone, particularly structural mitigation measures, can disrupt or destroy the natural environment, be extremely costly, and create a sense of false security (Godschalk *et al.*1999).

The Hurricane Katrina disaster, 50 years later, proved just this. The levee system, an engineered structural mitigation measure, had created a 'false' sense of security, placing the entire community at risk of flooding (Cruz 2003). The City of New Orleans had little protection against storms (Fischetti 1999). It sits in a bowl below sea level protected by a levee system that was not designed to resist storms higher than category 3 (which were possible and had occurred in the past), and because of human activities in the region there had been further sinking of the city and environmental degradation and shrinking of the Mississippi Delta which served as a buffer zone against hurricane impacts (Cruz 2003).

Similar problems were documented in Japan. Ikeda *et al.* (2008) write that two major flood disasters in Japan, the 2000 Tokai flood and the 2004 Niigata/Fukui flood, resulted from the construction of large-scale control infrastructure projects that failed. During both events, the authors explain, unexpected flow rates, far beyond the design scale of the river protection measures, provoked large breaks of levees downstream in urban areas, which in turn resulted in catastrophic damage to unprepared people and assets. The authors also note that these flood control projects resulted in river degradation, biodiversity reduction, shrinking of the habitats of aquatic fauna and flora, degradation of water quality, and changing of the water–soil cycles.

Clearly, then, risk reduction and effective disaster management require all stakeholders, not just professional planners and the owners/managers of these systems to engage together in contingency planning and also vigilance to make sure that building codes and regulations are followed. A comprehensive approach to infrastructure protection should be adopted in order to integrate structural and non-structural measures. It would strengthen the **capacity** of local communities to make their own informed disaster risk management choices, and promote the **participation** of all stakeholders, in particular community groups, non-governmental organizations (NGOs) and municipal governments, in all stages of disaster risk management (Ikeda *et al.* 2008).

Acknowledgement

Some material in this chapter appeared earlier in A.M. Cruz (2012) 'Protection of infrastructure', in B. Wisner, JC Gaillard and I. Kelman (eds) *The Routledge Handbook of Hazards and Disaster Risk Reduction*, London: Routledge, pp. 676–86.

References

Akatsuka, H. and Kobayashi, H. (2008) *Fire of Petroleum Tank, etc. by Niigata Earthquake*, Failure Knowledge Database, Japan Science and Technology Agency. Available at: http://shippai.jst.go.jp/en/Detail?fn=0&id=CB1012035&kw=Environment (accessed 1 April 2008).

ASCE (2009) 'TCLEE 2009: Lifeline earthquake engineering in a multihazard environment', ASCE Technical Council on Lifeline Earthquake Engineering Conference, Oakland, CA, 28 June–1 July.

—— (2011) *Guidelines for Seismic Evaluation and Design of Petrochemical Facilities*, Task Committee on Seismic Evaluation and Design, ASCE Publishers.

ATC (1991) *Seismic Vulnerability and Impact of Disruption of Lifelines in the Conterminous United States. Report ATC-25*, Redwood City, CA: Applied Technology Council.

Beam, A.R., de Caceres, L. and Moroney Jr., M.J. (1999) 'Restoration of maritime navigation systems in Central American Ports', *Oceans Conference Record (IEEE)*, 3: 13–17.

Bhasin, R., Grimstad, E., Larsen, J.O., Dhawan, A.K., Singh, R., Verma, S.K. and Venkatachalam, K. (2001) 'Landslide hazards and mitigation measures at Gangtok, Sikkim Himalaya', *Engineering Geology*, 64 (4): 351–68.

Booth, W. (2012) 'Two years after the earthquake, Haiti is trying to clear tent cities', *The Washington Post with Foreign Policy. World News*, February 20. Available at: http://www.washingtonpost.com/world/clearing-earthquake-camps-in-haiti-is-not-pretty/2012/01/27/glQAnxzNOR_story.html (accessed 9 October 2012).

Cashell, B.W. and Labonte, M. (2005) *The Macroeconomic Effects of Hurricane Katrina. CRS Report for Congress. Order Code RS22260, September 13.* Available at: http://fpc.state.gov/documents/organization/53572.pdf (accessed 23 January 2010).

Cataldo, A. (1995) 'Japan industry weighing Kobe earthquake impact: infrastructure damage may pose problem', *Electronic News*, 41(2049), Jan, 23: 2.

City Administrative Officer (1994) *City of Los Angeles Northridge Earthquake After-Action Report,* report presented to the Emergency Operations Board, City of Los Angeles, CA, June 3.

Cruz, A. (2003) 'Joint natural and technological disasters: assessment of natural disaster impacts on industrial facilities in highly urbanized areas', dissertation, Tulane University, New Orleans, LA.

—— (2007) 'Engineering contribution to the field of emergency management', in D. McEntire (ed.) *Disciplines, Disasters and Emergency Management*, Springfield, IL: Charles C. Thomas Publisher, Ltd.

Cruz, A. and Krausmann, E. (2008) 'Damage to offshore oil and gas facilities following Hurricanes Katrina and Rita: an overview', *Journal of Loss Prevention in the Process Industries,* 21(6): 620–6.

—— (2009) 'Hazardous-materials releases from offshore oil and gas facilities and emergency response following Hurricanes Katrina and Rita', *Journal of Loss Prevention in the Process Industries*, 22(1): 59–65.

Cruz, A., Krausmann, E. and Franquello, G. (2009) 'Analysis of tsunami impact scenarios at an oil refinery', *Natural Hazards*, 58(1): 141–62.

Cruz, A. and Okada, N. (2008) 'Consideration of natural hazards in the design and risk management of chemical industrial facilities', *Natural Hazards*, 44(2): 213–27.

Cruz, A., Steinberg, L. and Luna, R. (2001) 'Identifying hurricane-induced hazardous material release scenarios in a petroleum refinery', *Natural Hazards Review*, 2(4): 203–10.

Dawkins, W. (1995) 'Corporate Japan shakes in after-shock of quake: some companies' losses from the Kobe tragedy may prove competitors' gains', *Financial Times*, 24 Feb., p. 30.

DiGennaro, M. (2004) 'The black-out of September 28, 2003', in A.L. Vetere-Arellano, A.M. Cruz, J.P. Nordvik and F. Pisano (eds) *Proceedings: NEDIES Workshop Analysis of Natech (Natural Hazard Triggering Technological Disaster) Disaster Management. Report EUR 21054 EN*, Ispra, Italy: European Commission, DG Joint Research Centre.

Dominey-Howes, D. and Papathoma, M. (2007) 'Validating a tsunami vulnerability assessment model (the PTVA Model) using field data from the 2004 Indian Ocean Tsunami', *Natural Hazards,* 40(1): 113–36.

Eidinger, J.M. (2001) *The Gujarat (Kutch) India Earthquake of January 26, 2001: Lifeline Performance,* Technical Council on Lifeline Earthquake Engineering. Monograph No. 19, April 2001.

EPA (2006) *Murphy Oil USA Refinery Spill, Chalmette & Meraux, LA,* United States Environmental Protection Agency (US EPA), Region 6, Response and Prevention Branch Oil Team, May. Available at: http://www.epa.gov/oem/docs/oil/fss/fss06/franklin_2.pdf (accessed 10 July 2007)

EQE (1999) *An EQE Briefing, Izmit, Turkey Earthquake of August 17, 1999 (M7.4).* Oakland, CA: EQE International.

Erdik, M. (1998) 'Seismic vulnerability of megacities', in E. Booth (ed.) *Seismic Design Practice into the Next Century: Research and Application,* Rotterdam: Balkema.

European Commission (2002) 'Floods in Czech Republic', *Information Sheet No. 5, 19 August,* Brussels: Directorate General Environment, Civil Protection Unit.

Fischetti, M. (1999) 'Drowning New Orleans', *Scientific American,* 285(4): 76–85.

Godschalk, D.R., Beatley, T., Berke, P., Brower, D.J. and Kaiser, E.J. (1999) *Natural Hazard Mitigation: Recasting Disaster Policy and Planning,* Washington, DC: Island Press.

Hanstrum, B.N. and Holland, G.J. (1992) 'Effects on ports and harbours of tropical cyclone storm surges: a case study at Port Hedland, Western Australia', *National Conference Publication, Institution of Engineers,* 82(8): 201–3.

Heaney, J.P., Petarka, J. and Wright, L.T. (2000) 'Research needs for engineering aspects of natural disasters', *Journal of Infrastructure Systems,* 6(1): 4–14.

Ikeda, S., Sato, T. and Fukuzono, T. (2008) 'Towards an integrated management framework for emerging disaster risks in Japan', *Natural Hazards,* 44 (2): 267–80.

Iwabuchi, Y., Koshimura, S. and Imamura, F. (2006) 'Study on oil spread caused by the 1964 Niigata earthquake tsunami', *Journal of Disaster Research,* 1(1): 157–68.

Krausmann, E. and Cruz, A.M. (2013) 'Impact of the 11 March, 2011, Great East Japan earthquake and tsunami on the chemical industry', *Natural Hazards,* 67(2): 811–28.

Krausmann, E., Cruz, A.M. and Affeltranger, B. (2010) 'The impact of the 12 May 2008 Wenchuan earthquake on industrial facilities', *Journal of Loss Prevention in the Process Industries,* 23 (2): 242–8.

Kurita, T. (2004) 'Observation of the recent earthquake damage in Japan', in A.L. Vetere-Arellano, A.M. Cruz, J.P. Nordvik and F. Pisano (eds) *Proceedings: NEDIES Workshop Analysis of Natech (Natural Hazard Triggering Technological Disaster) Disaster Management. Report EUR 21054 EN,* Ispra, Italy: European Commission, DG Joint Research Centre.

Kwong, A.K.L., Wang, M., Lee, C.F. and Law, K.T. (2004) 'A review of landslide problems and mitigation measures in Chongqing and Hong Kong: similarities and differences', *Engineering Geology,* 76: 27–39.

Lau, D.L., Tang, A. and Pierre, J.R. (1995) 'Performance of lifelines during the 1994 Northridge earthquake', *Canadian Journal of Civil Engineering,* 22(2): 438–51.

Lindell, M.K. and Perry, R.W. (1997) 'Hazardous materials releases in the Northridge earthquake: implications for seismic risk assessment', *Risk Analysis,* 17(2): 147–56.

Madabhushi, S.P.G., Saito, K., Booth, E.D. (2013) 'EEFIT mission to Haiti following the 12th January 2010 earthquake', *Bulletin of Earthquake Engineering,* 11(1): 35–68.

Matsimbe, Z. (2003) 'Assessing the role of local institutions in reducing the vulnerability of at-risk communities in Búzi, Central Mozambique', DiMP, University of Cape Town. Available at: ftp://ftp.fao.org/docrep/fao/007/ae079e/ae079e00.pdf (accessed 9 September 2008).

Menoni, S. (2001) 'Chains of damages and failures in a metropolitan environment: some observations on the Kobe earthquake in 1995', *Journal of Hazardous Materials*, 86 (1–3): 101–19.

National Police Agency of Japan (2012) *Damage Situation and Police Countermeasures Associated with 2011 Tohoku District off the Pacific Ocean Earthquake*, Emergency Disaster Countermeasures Headquarters, NPA, October 3 2012. Available at: http://www.npa.go.jp/archive/keibi/biki/higaijokyo_e.pdf (accessed 14 March 2013).

NIPP (2006) *Introduction*. Available at: http://www.dhs.gov/xprevprot/programs/editorial_0827.shtm (accessed 15 September 2008).

NTHMP (2001) *Designing for Tsunamis – Seven Principles for Planning and Designing for Tsunami Hazards*, Washington, DC: NTHMP.

—— (2013) *Tsunami Ready*, Washington, DC: NTHMP. Available at: http://www.tsunamiready.noaa.gov/ (accessed 14 March 2013).

O'Rourke, T.D. (2007) 'Critical infrastructure, interdependencies and resilience', *The Bridge*, 37(1): 22–9.

Petal, M., Green, R., Kelman, I., Shaw, R. and Dixit, A. (2008) 'Community-based construction for disaster risk reduction', in L. Bosher (ed.) *Hazards in the Built Environment: Attaining Build-in Resilience,* London: Routledge.

PIANC (2001) *Seismic Design Guidelines for Port Structures*. Working Group No. 34 of the Maritime Navigation Commission, International Navigation Association, Lisse, Belgium: A.A. Balkema Publishers.

Santander, I. (2010) *350 Mil Personas del Sur Viven en Zonas Inundables. Coatzacoalcos.* Agencia Imagen del Golfo, 6 February. Available at: http://www.imagendelgolfo.com.mx/resumen.php?id=154331 (accessed 11 February 2010).

Santella, N., Steinberg, L.J. and Parks, K. (2009) 'Decision making for extreme events: modeling critical infrastructure interdependencies to aid mitigation and response planning', *Review of Policy Research*, 26(4): 409–22.

Schiff, A.J. and Buckle, I.G. (eds) (1995) 'Critical issues and state-of-the-art in lifeline earthquake engineering', in *Proceedings of the Session Held in Conjunction with the ASCE National Convention in San Diego, California*, October, 1995.

Sengul, H., Santella, N., Steinberg, L.J. and Cruz, A.M. (2012) 'Occurrence of hazardous material releases due to natural hazards in the U.S.', *Disasters,* 36(4): 723–43.

Shi, P. (2008) 'China Wenchuan earthquake disaster (May 12, 2008) and its loss assessment', presentation at the 8th IIASA-DPRI Conference on Integrated Disaster Risk Management, Induno-Olona, Varese, Italy, 1–2 September.

Sierra, J. (2005) *Sesenta municipios valencianos permiten que se construya en zonas inundables*. Available at: http://www.levante-emv.com/comunitat-valenciana/2906/sesenta-municipios-valencianos-permiten-construya-zonas-inundables/134340.html (accessed 25 January 2010).

Sorensen, P.H., Wortley, C.A., Hunt, F.G., Tobiasson, B.O., Childs, K.M. and Forster, C.G. (1992) 'Planning and design guidelines for small craft harbors', paper presented at Ports'92, 20–22 July, Seattle, WA.

Spiker, E.C. and Gori, P.L. (2003) 'National landslides hazards mitigation strategy: a framework for loss reduction', *US Geological Survey Circular*, 1244: 1–54.

Steinberg, L.J. (2004) 'Natechs in the United States: experience, safeguards, and gaps', in A.L. Vetere-Arellano, A.M. Cruz, J.P. Nordvik and F. Pisano (eds) *Proceedings: NEDIES Workshop Analysis of Natech (Natural Hazard Triggering Technological Disaster) Disaster Management. Report EUR 21054 EN*, Ispra, Italy: European Commission, DG Joint Research Centre.

Steinberg, L.J. and Cruz, A.M. (2004) 'When natural and technological disasters collide: lessons from the Turkey earthquake of August 17, 1999', *Natural Hazards Review*, 5(3): 121–30.

Suppasri, A., Mas, E., Charvet, I., Gunasekera, R., Imai, K., Fukutani, Y., Abe, Y. and Imamura, F. (2013) 'Building damage characteristics based on surveyed data and fragility curves of the 2011 Great East Japan tsunami', *Natural Hazards*, 66(2): 319–41.

Tang, A.K. (ed.) (2000) *Izmit (Kocaeli), Earthquake, Earthquake of August 17, 1999 Including Duzce Earthquake of November 12, 1999: Lifeline Performance*, Monograph No. 17, Virginia: Technical Council on Lifeline Earthquake Engineering, ASCE.

United Nations (UN) (2011) 'Final Report of the Independent Panel of Experts on the Cholera Outbreak in Haiti', New York: United Nations. Available at: http://www.un.org/News/dh/infocus/haiti/UN-cholera-report-final.pdf (accessed 8 January 2012).

USACE (1997) *Flood Proofing Techniques, Programs, and References*, prepared by Dewberry and Davis with French & Associates, LTD., Washington, DC: US Army Corps of Engineers National Flood Proofing Committee.

USGS (2000) *Implications for earthquake risk reduction in the United States from the Kocaeli, Turkey, earthquake of August 17, 1999: U.S. Geological Survey Circular 1193*, United States: Geological Survey, United States Government Printing Office.

Van Dijk, S. (2008) *Environmental Impact Assessment: Tsunami Indonesia*, United Nations, Office for the Coordination of Humanitarian Affairs, Banda Aceh, Aceh, Indonesia. Available at: http://humanitarianinfo.org/sumatra/reference/assessments/doc/other/report_def_draft_send_2601.pdf (accessed 5 March 2008).

Venancio, C., Pires, P. and Mendes, C. (2003) 'Natech risk management in Portugal', in A.L. Vetere-Arellano, A.M. Cruz, J.P. Nordvik and F. Pisano (eds) *Proceedings: NEDIES Workshop Analysis of Natech (Natural Hazard Triggering Technological Disaster) Disaster Management , Report EUR 21054 EN*, Ispra, Italy: DG Joint Research Centre, European Commission.

Yeh, H., Robertson, I. and Preuss, J. (2005) *Development of Design Guidelines for Structures that Serve as Tsunami Vertical Evacuation Sites*, Washington State, Department of Natural Resources, Washington, Division of Geology and Earth Resources, Open File Report 2005-4, November.

Part II

Response and recovery

9 Emergency and disaster planning

David Alexander

> In preparing for battle, I have always found that plans are useless, but planning is indispensable.
>
> Dwight D. Eisenhower

Lessons for practitioners

- Emergency planning should be an ongoing process rather than an end in itself.
- Scenario-based planning is a flexible means of exploring a range of possible future situations and assessing the response needs that could be associated with them.
- Emergency plans need to be integrated between levels of government, jurisdictions and services: this should ensure that all responsibilities are assigned and all main tasks will be covered.

Emergency planning is a relatively new discipline. The world community is gradually becoming aware of the need for disaster and contingency plans at many scales and in diverse sectors and jurisdictions. However, it has been slow to acknowledge the need for consensus on the objectives, content and methodology of such plans. As a contribution to the standardisation of goals and methods, this chapter examines the rationale of emergency planning and considers the principles that underlie it. First, it considers how to define an emergency plan and delineate the concept and rationale. Next, it discusses the use of scenarios as a basis for rational planning. After that, it discusses the connections between emergency planning and other disciplines, notably urban and regional planning. The importance of establishing connections between plans is emphasised. Finally, this chapter discusses some of the issues and challenges that the emergency planner must face in the present century.

In both socio-economic and geographical terms, **risk** is unevenly distributed (Adams 1995). Because of the prevalence of strong imbalances in **vulnerability**, disaster risk is particularly skewed. On the one hand, this stems from lack of choice among poor and disadvantaged people, while on the other it reflects an increasing propensity to take risks by increasing the range of occupations and fixed capital in hazardous areas (Birkmann 2006). Disaster planning is one of the potential means of redressing the balance towards a more equitable distribution of risk (Waugh and Tierney 2007). However, the ability to prepare for adverse events is only one part of a range of structural and non-structural techniques that should be employed to reduce, redistribute or transfer risks in favour of a safer world. Structural measures include anti-seismic building techniques and the construction of barriers against floods or explosions. Non-structural measures embrace restrictions on land use in hazardous places and forms of emergency preparedness such as disaster planning. As the next section shows, planning should be considered as much a process as an end in itself, especially as it is a perpetual task that must respond to constant changes in **hazards**, society and emergency organisation. However, first, it is necessary to define what is meant by the process and the product.

What is emergency planning and what is an emergency plan?

A crisis or emergency can be defined as a situation of enhanced risk in which abnormal conditions prevail, to the probable detriment of people and their assets (Perry 2005). Such events vary from unusual incidents to major catastrophes. Emergency plans are required in order to effectively manage events that exceed the threshold at which it becomes impossible to respond using normal everyday **resources**, and changes must be made in procedures, availability and working conditions. Because of the tendency of disasters to evolve and thus slowly reveal their size and characteristics, in the heat of the moment it is not always apparent that an event is large enough to require special actions, such as declaration of a state of emergency, activation of a disaster plan and emergency call-up of personnel.

Although many attempts have been made to impose rigorous and quantitative definitions on terms such as 'disaster' and 'catastrophe', none has so far been fully successful (Perry and Quarantelli 2005). The uniqueness of each new event and the complexity and multiplicity of contributing factors conspire to invalidate across-the-board demarcations. Nevertheless, as Table 9.1 demonstrates, there is a distinction between incidents, disasters and catastrophes, which are adverse events of different sizes (Tierney 2008).

Emergencies are thus events which bring society to crisis point by revealing its vulnerabilities and putting people and things imminently at risk. In organisational terms, they must be dealt with using procedures, protocols and plans (Alexander 2002). Contingencies and needs that cannot be foreseen and thus met with these instruments must be tackled by improvising a response. Although some people regard improvisation as a source of resilience because it stimulates human creativity, it is usually equated with inefficiency, largely because too much effort must be devoted to learning on the job, and too little to devising remedies to the crisis. Hence, improvisation is permissible only insofar as needs cannot reasonably be anticipated. If they can be foreseen, they should be prepared for in advance, as a crisis is the worst time to extemporise actions. Nevertheless, as all emergencies are to some extent different from each other, every crisis will involve some improvisation and it is thus a natural aspect of the response (Webb 2004).

Table 9.1 Functional differences between different sizes of event

	Incidents	Major incidents	Disasters	Catastrophes
Size of impact	Very localised	Fully or partially localised	Widespread and severe	Extremely large in the physical and social sphere
Size of response	Local resources used	Mainly local resources used, with some mutual assistance from nearby areas	Intergovernmental, multi-agency, multi-jurisdictional response needed	Major national and international resources and coordination are required
Plans and procedures activated	Standard operating procedures used	Standard operating procedures used; emergency plans may be activated	Disaster or emergency plans activated	Disaster or emergency plans activated, but huge challenges may overwhelm them
Impact on response resources needed for response	Local resources will probably be sufficient	Local resources and some outside resources needed	Extensive damage to resources in disaster area; major inter-regional transfers of resources	Local and regional emergency response systems paralysed and in need of much outside help
Involvement of public in response	Public generally not involved in response	Public largely not involved in response	Public extensively involved in response	Public overwhelmingly involved in response
Challenges to post-event recovery	No significant challenges to recovery	Few challenges to recovery processes	Major challenges to recovery from disaster	Massive challenges and significant long-term effects

Source: Partly after Tierney (2008).

It is important to distinguish between procedures and protocols, on the one hand, and emergency plans, on the other. The difference is similar to that which exists between the sheet music read by individual players in an orchestra and the combined score used by the conductor. Procedures can be defined as standard operating methodologies known in advance to their users. Where these are held in common between different organisations, they may be termed protocols, as is the case for the *modus operandi* of inter-agency communications. Emergency plans are the orchestration of procedures. A plan should not, for example, tell firemen how to extinguish fires or policemen how to direct the traffic, but it should ensure that they are able to do such jobs under crisis conditions. Emergency plans are therefore needed when multiple agencies respond to events, and when exceptional circumstances make it impossible to do so without major changes in the way organisations operate and cooperate with one another (Devitt and Borodzicz 2008).

It is important to note that there are several levels of emergency planning. Most of this chapter refers to permanent plans, which need to be drawn up and maintained. If they are to remain valid, plans of this kind must be living documents. They require to be revised, disseminated and exercised on a repetitive, perhaps cyclical, basis. Any lapse in this process, and the elements of the plan risk becoming out of date. New forms of organisation, changes in the geography of the area it covers, substitution of personnel, growth and renewal of the emergency response system, and changes in telephone numbers and email addresses are examples of vital ingredients that may become out of date if they are not monitored and incorporated into the plan in a timely manner.

However, the permanent plan is simply an instrument that should stimulate shorter-term preparedness when a crisis occurs. At this point, emergency planning is needed at the strategic, tactical and operational levels. In synthesis, strategic command involves ensuring that resources are procured and available for use without delay (Choi 2008). Tactical command signifies making sure that the resources are distributed to where they are needed, and operational command uses the resources in the field to ameliorate conditions. In a major event, there should be strategic, tactical and operational command units, established within the compass of the permanent emergency plan (Minciardi *et al.* 2009). They should be looking forward in order to anticipate developments and devise solutions, not merely to pressing immediate difficulties, but also to any problems that can be foreseen as developing in the near future. All plans should be guided by a set of policies, which form the upper stratum of the planning process and determine its general direction and overall objectives (Burling and Hyde 1997). Funding for emergency planning and response is usually determined at the stage of **policy** formulation and in line with the policies adopted.

Planning for recovery and reconstruction is usually considered to be a separate process to emergency planning, although it is inevitably intertwined with the latter (Wamsler 2006). While conventional **wisdom** once suggested that recovery planning should begin at the end of the emergency phase, after the first responders had been stood down, it is more efficient to set up a recovery planning unit as soon as is reasonably practicable, which may even be immediately after the start of the crisis. In a well-regulated society with sufficient resources, recovery may begin very rapidly, as many different systems need to be restored or put back in place as soon as possible (Sullivan 2003).

Over time, emergency planning thus involves a nested hierarchy of processes that are permanent (i.e. ongoing), and temporary in the strategic, tactical and operational spheres (Figure 9.1). Not only are recovery and reconstruction planning parallel processes, but so is business continuity planning (Figure 9.2). As this is applicable to both the private and the public sector, it should be distinguished from emergency planning. The latter is required to ensure that the demands created by the emergency can be met, for example, for evacuation, firefighting and damage limitation. Business continuity planning is designed to ensure that normal activities can be continued, despite the interruption caused by a crisis or disaster. Failure to make contingency plans for this may worsen the emergency response as well as leading to service interruptions. This is especially true where personnel and resources must be diverted from normal duties in order to tackle the emergency. The business continuity plan should indicate how the shortfall is to be made good during the crisis period and thereafter (Lindstedt 2008).

Clearly, emergency planning is an integrative process (Towfighi 1991). It must use protocols to mesh together different organisations and jurisdictions, and plans to foresee and predispose organisational and resource needs. This process of orchestration needs to be based on an assessment of needs that is as good as possible. This is why scenario modelling is a vital basis of the process.

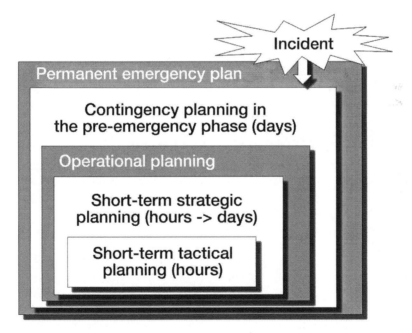

Figure 9.1 Permanent (ongoing) and temporary (contingent) emergency planning

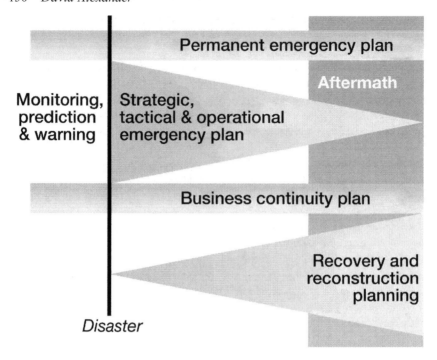

Figure 9.2 Time phases and salience of different kinds of planning

The importance of scenario-based planning

Modern emergency plans are generic instruments that should be applicable to all hazards. This means that they are valid for both anticipated events, such as flooding on a flood plain or earthquakes in a known seismic zone, and exceptional events, such as the crash of a jet aircraft onto a residential area. Emergency responders should rely on generic procedures and processes to tackle unforeseeable events, but the plan should address foreseeable hazards specifically. It is not usually appropriate to have separate plans for each hazard, especially as there may be interaction between events (for example, earthquakes may cause floods, landslides or snow avalanches as well as direct damage). Hence a general purpose emergency plan should include chapters that outline the specific provisions for each type of hazard that is endemic to the area it covers. These can be considered as akin to the branches on a tree, in which the trunk, or stem, is the set of generic provisions that will be activated in any kind of emergency (Alexander 2002).

In the context of emergency planning, a scenario is a detailed answer to the question 'what if . . .?' Although there will be aspects of the next emergency that cannot be foreseen, many aspects can. Scenario modelling can be considered as a science, that rationally explores the implications of events, and an art, which necessitates the carefully controlled use of fantasy and imagination. It can best be accomplished using a simple form of General Systems Theory (Von Bertalanffy and Sutherland 1974), based on inputs, transformations and outputs. In the scenario, physical hazards act upon vulnerabilities in the human socio-economic system to produce impacts. The scenario should be extended to responses and thus should indicate what resources and forms of organisation are needed to bring relief. Most hazards require multiple scenarios in order to cope with aggregate patterns of human activity (the times of day when people move around and occupy particular spaces) and different sizes, intensities or locations of hazard. Most scenarios are based on past events, but it is best to use an amalgam of elements rather than assume that the next event will be an exact replica of the last one.

The importance of scenarios to emergency planning lies in the need to foresee contingencies and prepare for them. A scenario should be treated as a dynamic exploration of future events which considers how vulnerability will be mobilised by the impact of events (Alexander 2000). Scenarios can be constructed for most recurrent or common events, including natural and technological hazards. Even human error can be factored into a scenario. Engineers are well acquainted with this through their use of fault trees in industrial processes, which consider the consequences of equipment failure and wrong decisions by operators (Kletz 1999).

Despite its utility for most risks, acts of terrorism are difficult to plan for using scenario analysis. This is because the range of options open to terrorists is infinitely variable and human inventiveness can be employed to create new ways of wreaking havoc and causing destruction or loss of life. Nevertheless, most terrorist outrages are relatively conventional and follow something of a pattern. Moreover, in some cases, intelligence can be used to ascertain what the terrorists are planning to do next and they can then be outwitted or forestalled. However, there remains a lingering fear that chemical, biological, nuclear or radiological terrorism could suddenly introduce entirely new scenarios of attack, which current plans are ill-equipped to deal with (Tofani and Bartolozzi 2008). Even the use of relatively simple implements, box-cutting knives, to hijack commercial aircraft and fly them into strategically important buildings in the USA on 11 September 2001 represented a form of innovation that pointed to the inventiveness of the terrorists involved, their high degree of organisation and the difficulty of anticipating such behaviour by constructing scenarios in advance of the attacks.

Another problem with scenario methods is the question of what size of event to plan for. If one assumes a maximum impact and plans accordingly, then lesser events can presumably be dealt with by scaling down resources. The main problems therefore lie with events that are significantly larger than those anticipated in the plan. Most experts in the field would agree that it makes no sense to prepare for events that have inordinately long recurrence intervals and thus a very low probability of occurrence. However, the last ten years have seen a revision of this attitude in the light of new data on the magnitude-frequency relationships of natural hazards and gloomier thinking about the propensity of technology and terrorists to cause disaster.

Nevertheless, the question of what size of event to plan for remains unsolved. The assumption that natural hazards follow normal distributions (i.e. a bell-shaped curve with slim tails representing very improbable high- and low-magnitude events) was disproved in the 1960s (Hewitt 1970). The occurrence of large natural hazards may not be particularly constrained by frequencies, and, in any case, some of the meteorological hazards are likely to be enhanced by climate change. Hence, there has been a re-evaluation of the propensity for very large events to occur. Unfortunately, it has so far not been matched by a willingness to devote resources to emergency preparedness for such events, especially as their probability of occurrence during the lifetime of existing political administrations remains exceedingly low.

Despite the widespread lack of belief in the need to plan for extremely large events, several kinds of them have the potential to change the risk – and the emergency response –landscape rapidly and radically. Pandemic influenza could be one of these, with rapid diffusion, easy contamination, repeated waves of infection, shortage of vaccines and complex but profound non-medical effects (Cinti 2005). Many of these aspects can be foreseen, but not all experts agree that pandemic flu is a likely prospect, despite the relentless 30- to 40-year cycle of large epidemics in the past. Earthquakes in places like Tehran, Istanbul and Tokyo have the potential to cause extremely large death tolls, perhaps in the millions; volcanic eruptions could occur of a size that would severely affect world climate and threaten the food chain. Finally, if severe radioactive contamination were to affect a major urban centre it could cause impacts on health, life, communication and commerce that would be virtually permanent. These are all scenarios that are well known but so far have been largely disconnected from the detailed processes of emergency planning.

Finally, scenario construction must somehow get to grips with the role of secondary hazards, interactions between hazards, collateral vulnerabilities and coincidences. It may be bad form to discuss the last of these, as by definition they should defy prediction, but it is surprising how strong the role of coincidence is in, for example, transportation crashes – almost to the extent that it can be planned for. Besides that, much needs to be learnt about anticipating the unexpected. Lateral thinking is badly needed. For example, it is common to overlook the plight of prisoners in disasters, yet when flood surges descend on prisons, as happened in Hurricane Katrina in the southern USA in August 2005, prisoners should neither be spontaneously released nor abandoned to drown. Studies of the plight of prisoners in New Orleans after Hurricane Katrina revealed severe and unjustifiable violations of their rights (ACLU 2006), yet their needs should have been anticipated, given that the hurricane had been foretold accurately by impact scenarios that were constructed months or years before it arrived in the Gulf of Mexico (Laska 2004).

In synthesis, scenario modelling as a basis for emergency planning must face up to the magnitude-frequency problem and decide on the maximum size of event that should be planned for. This will inevitably involve assessing the available resources and simply planning to commit them, if necessary in an all-out manner. Whatever size of event is considered, the scenario should enjoy the benefits of lateral thinking that actively searches for unusual connections and consequences.

Indeed, the whole emergency planning exercise is largely about making connections, and that includes those with other forms of planning.

The connection with urban and regional planning

There is a substantial parallel between the processes of planning for emergencies and for the disposition of urban and regional development (Wamsler 2006). Both require background research on the physiography, demography, economics, culture and social aspects of the areas that they cover. Given the functional roles of administrative units (municipalities, counties, regions, etc.), they may well cover the same territory. In both cases, the problems to be solved are largely geographical – a question of where impacts occur and where resources need to be. In fact, as geography develops the ability to 'read' the human and physical landscape, as well as the skills of creating synthesis, geographers may make some of the best urban and emergency planners. The tragedy is that relatively few places in the world have instituted formal connections between the two disciplines (Britton and Lindsay 1995).

The essence of emergency planning is that it should be able to match needs with resources. This is both a spatial and a temporal problem. Timeliness is obviously essential in a crisis situation, but so is the ability to know where impacts are likely to occur, or have their worst effects, to maintain streams of information on them, and to move resources promptly to where they are most in demand. Emergency planning is thus a means of solving a version of the classical supply and demand graph of economics (demand for and supply of emergency assistance) in space and time (Russell 1970).

In this context, some of the links with urban and regional planning are very evident. The first is the delineation of areas of hazard: the streets around plants that manufacture dangerous goods, the approaches to airport runways, flood plains, seismic zones, and so on. These are both the areas in which emergency responders can expect to work and zones in which permanent planning restrictions can be imposed in favour of public safety and security. Second, emergency plans will need to designate routes and places – the 'paths' and 'nodes' of Lynch's cognitive mapping exercise (Lynch 1960). These include evacuation corridors, evacuee reception centres, refuge areas, assembly areas, centres for stockpiling and distributing resources and places to set up posts for mobile command, first aid and triage. These are seldom incorporated into urban or regional plans, which is a pity. In some cases there are particular emergency requirements which are the preserve of urban planning. For example, in Tehran, a city of more than 12 million inhabitants that sooner or later will experience a devastating magnitude 7 earthquake, there are important questions regarding the width of roads and streets and restrictions on access for the emergency services, especially when the way is partially blocked by rubble (Hosseini *et al.* 2009). Urban planning ordinances could contribute significantly to the search for a solution.

As both disciplines are essentially based on spatial science, it is not surprising that they have been revolutionised by the use of geographic information systems

(GIS). The ability to present information in layers and structure it in flexible and interactive ways has vastly increased the potential of cartography for resolving problems of how to match resources with emergency needs. The current challenges are, not only to connect this process to urban and regional planning, perhaps through the combined use of GIS, but also to provide cartographical representations that respond to changing needs and information flows during a crisis (Dubois *et al.* 2006).

Integration of plans

As the previous section has shown, emergency planning is essentially an integrative process which is about finding, establishing and developing connections. In a disaster or catastrophe, scores of different agencies may participate and they need to have clearly defined roles, competencies and means of communication. Although an emergency plan should be administered, preferably by a person who is qualified in this discipline, from a single place, which will probably be an emergency operations centre, planning should be a collaborative process. It thus requires a committee approach. A good example is the London Emergency Services Liaison Panel, which meets regularly and is composed of representatives of the emergency services, local governments and other pertinent services and both produces and oversees the development of plans and procedural manuals (LESLP 2007).

Plans need to integrate forces in terms of providing connections between geographical, organisational, functional and hierarchical divisions. Effectively, this pulls the planner in four different directions (Figure 9.3). However, the success of the plan depends on creating the right balance between division and integration (i.e. linkages) in each of the four dimensions.

As with any collaborative work, strong leadership and a good division of roles and competencies are the keys to success. It is also clear that the value of an emergency plan is critically dependent on the command structures that will implement it when a crisis arises (Buck *et al.* 2006). Command systems will depend on the available infrastructure (communications facilities and operations centres), the legislative framework (which organisations are enabled to do what), and relations between organisations. There is a spectrum of possible modes of organisation that extends from a full command-and-control model based on strategic, tactical and operational commands, to a fully distributed collaborative model based on common support functions (telecommunications, logistics, shelter, and so on). Generally, information technology has tended to flatten the chain of command and facilitate collaboration at the expense of control, largely through sharing information and instructions. One function of the emergency plan is to articulate the command structure and ensure that it matches the needs generated by the emergency. Clearly, it must also remain robust and functional under any foreseeable crisis conditions.

In principle, no emergency responder should be without a role and the plan should ensure that tasks are distributed appropriately and fully. With larger emergencies, the question of mutual aid becomes increasingly important, as particular

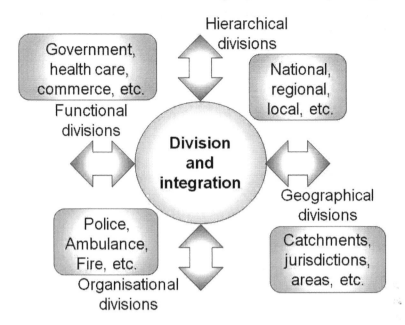

Figure 9.3 Division and integration of emergency plans in four dimensions

jurisdictions find that their own resources become insufficient, or that they are adequate to tackle the emergency but not ongoing normal tasks. No provider of mutual aid would want to find that his or her resources are committed outside the normal area if this is left without adequate coverage. Nor is it acceptable to be faced with a large and unexpected bill for the costs of intervention. Hence a significant part of emergency planning should involve settling questions of bilateral or multilateral assistance, as well as determining the roles of different levels of government and organisation in favour of a unified command. Not surprisingly, most emergency plans include flow charts of competencies and spheres of responsibility.

A previous section of this chapter described the emergency planner's unresolved dilemma of what size of event to plan for. It is clear that not all events can be the subject of a detailed plan. The authors of such documents will have to accept that if an event of truly exceptional power and size were to occur, the plan might instantly become redundant. This is one of the pitfalls of the profession, although such occurrences are thankfully rare. However, it is always possible that *force majeure* may require plans to be abandoned. Yet even in such cases, the planning process, as General Eisenhower noted, will have proved useful and instructive.

The final point about integration is that plans should form a nested hierarchy. In principle, no place on earth is without hazards, and no jurisdiction should be without a plan to tackle them. Hence, emergency plans will be needed for municipalities, intermediate levels of public administration (counties, provinces,

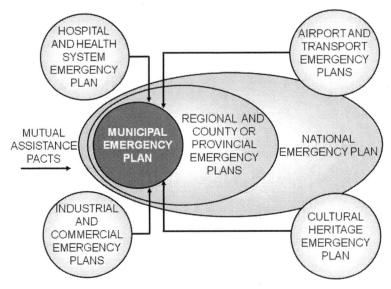

Figure 9.4 A nested hierarchy of emergency plans centred around the municipal level

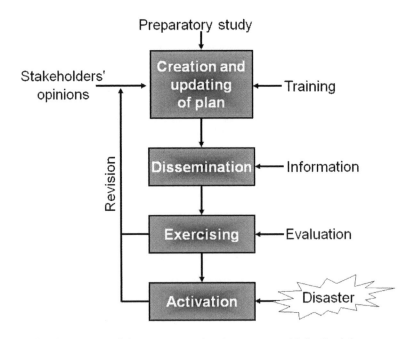

Figure 9.5 A summary of the emergency planning process, with feedback loops

regions, etc.), national governments and some international bodies. They will also be needed for particular sectors: tourism, cultural heritage protection, educational establishments, commercial and industrial premises, ports and airports, health centres, and so on (Figure 9.4). It is clearly a significant challenge to ensure, not merely that all such plans exist, but also that they are compatible with one another. Fortunately, in most cases, it is simply a matter of making a comparative reading of plans to search for evident inconsistencies in their provisions. The process is greatly facilitated if there are strong national guidelines that clearly assign competencies and responsibilities. It goes without saying that the many different stakeholders in a plan must be aware of their roles, as discussed in the next section.

A vital part of integration is communication, which in the context of emergencies and disasters is a multifaceted process (De Silva *et al.* 2005). It is obviously vital before disaster (for warning, readiness and mobilisation), during the event for coordinated emergency action, and afterwards for effective recovery. It is also important during the creation and development of emergency plans. Indeed, planning should be a democratic process in which the views of stakeholders are listened to, their concerns are addressed and as far as possible their needs are incorporated (Figure 9.5). The communication needs to be a two-way or multilateral process and the plan must be sensitive to its needs. Inability to communicate or act on important information is one of the main reasons for the failure of emergency plans and responses.

Conclusion: emergency planning for the twenty-first century

The flattening of the chain of command caused by increasing use of information and communications technology is part of a general process of demilitarisation of emergency response, which in most cases is a sign of its developing maturity (Figure 9.6). Military assistance in civilian disasters can be extremely valuable, but questions of self-reliance and democratic response require the civilian response to predominate and military aid to be relegated to specialist help and assistance in the case of impacts that overwhelm the civil responders, although there are obvious exceptions which may be linked to counterterrorism and public order problems (Arbuthnot 2008).

The relationship between civil society and institutions is at the heart of the emergency planning question (Özerdem and Jacoby 2006). Indeed, in many countries (Italy, Germany and Australia, for example), emergency response would have little meaning without the presence of large numbers of volunteers drawn directly from civil society. The challenge of the present century is to consolidate the relationship and transfer a portion of risk management from authorities and experts to the general public: the disaster risk reduction problem is simply too large to be borne by the former alone. It requires the public to assume more responsibility for managing its own risks. Hence there will be an imperative in emergency planning to ensure that it is properly inclusive of the public. Indeed, there has been a tendency to plan somewhat exclusively for institutions and emergency services, rather than for the beneficiaries. The need for a reorientation was highlighted on

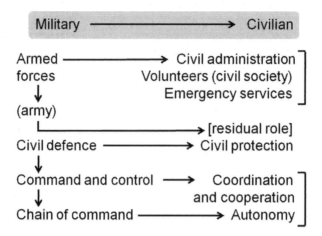

Figure 9.6 The demilitarisation of civil protection

the basis of a mass of convincing evidence related to the London bombings of 7 July 2005 (London Assembly 2006).

In as much as prediction is possible in a rapidly changing world, it can fairly be stated that emergency planning will increase in scope, salience and professionalism. Nevertheless, it may take a major event to shake the world of officialdom out of its torpor and boost the field to prominence. Meanwhile, the work of bodies such as the International Association of Emergency Managers (IAEM) and the UK Emergency Planning Society (EPS) is vital in preparing the ground and furthering the cause. As the emergency manager is the professional 'figure of reference', the question of his or her role is pertinent to emergency planning, which must be based on command structures and organisational links.

In many countries, there is a duality between the emergency manager as a professional figure and the 'lead agency', which may have its own managers. A lead agency is the organisation on which the major burden of coordinating emergency actions devolves. For example, in the United Kingdom, where emergencies are considered to be first and foremost a public order problem, it is the police; in Italy, where technical rescue is predominant, it is the fire brigades, while in Iran, where mass casualties are feared on a vast scale, it is probably the national Red Crescent Society, although some would argue that it is the Revolutionary Guards, who represent authority. In contrast, emergency planning may be centred on public administration bodies, which have a rather more passive role in emergency response. Hence, the emergency manager may essentially be a manager of resources, and rather less so of emergency actions (Gillespie 1991). If this is the case, the plan must articulate this feature in a manner with which all participants can be comfortable.

In the first decade of the twenty-first century three issues have begun to dominate the debate on emergency preparedness. The first is the changing and increasing impact of terrorism, the second is the potential for a major international disease pandemic, and the third is the huge scope of vulnerabilities to enhanced meteorological events, particularly the impact of very large hurricanes upon densely populated coastlines. At the same time other large disasters, such as major earthquakes, tsunamis and volcanic eruptions, have not lost prominence. All of these issues challenge the emergency planner. The tasks of creating, maintaining, disseminating, updating and improving plans will become increasingly sophisticated and require more and more training and expertise.

Emergencies and disasters are dominated by uncertainty. To an increasing extent so is the world as a whole. The emergency planner is essentially a person who is searching for certainty in an ocean of vagueness, ambiguity and inconclusiveness. Hence, emergency planning is seldom a precise process: it is a blunt instrument. However, it is nonetheless essential. The planner must assume a political role in convincing the representatives of the people that it is essential, not merely prudent, to think about adverse events even when they are not happening. As disasters have obvious negative connotations, reducing their risks is seldom a vote winner, unless the population has an unusual preoccupation with the risks in question. Nevertheless, the emergency planner must soldier on through the long winters of scarce funding and lukewarm support. On some fateful day when disaster strikes, the fruits of his or her labours will suddenly become apparent.

References

ACLU (2006) *Abandoned and Abused: Orleans Parish Prisoners in the Wake of Hurricane Katrina*. National Prisons Project, Washington, DC: American Civil Liberties Union.

Adams, J. (1995) *Risk: The Policy Implications of Risk Compensations and Plural Rationalities,* London: UCL Press.

Alexander, D.E. (2000) 'Scenario methodology for teaching principles of emergency management', *Disaster Prevention and Management,* 9(2): 89–97.

—— (2002) *Principles of Emergency Planning and Management*, New York: Oxford University Press.

Arbuthnot, K. (2008) 'A command gap? A practitioner's analysis of the value of comparisons between the UK's military and emergency services' command and control models in the context of UK resilience operations', *Journal of Contingencies and Crisis Management,* 16(4): 186–94.

Birkmann, J. (ed.) (2006) *Measuring Vulnerability to Natural Hazards: Towards Disaster Resilient Societies*, Tokyo: United Nations University Press.

Britton, N.R. and Lindsay, J. (1995) 'Integrated city planning and emergency preparedness: some of the reasons why', *International Journal of Mass Emergencies and Disasters,* 13(1): 67–92.

Buck, D.A., Trainor, J.E. and Aguirre, B.E. (2006) 'A critical evaluation of the Incident Command System and NIMS', *Journal of Homeland Security and Emergency Management,* 3(3): 1–27.

Burling, W.K. and Hyde, A.E. (1997) 'Disaster preparedness planning: policy and leadership issues', *Disaster Prevention and Management,* 6(4): 234–44.

Choi, S.O. (2008) 'Emergency management: implications from a strategic management perspective', *Journal of Homeland Security and Emergency Management,* 5(1): 1–21.

Cinti, S. (2005) 'Pandemic influenza: are we ready?', *Disaster Management and Response*, 3(4): 61–7.

De Silva, T., Chikersal, J., Snoad, N., Woodworth, B., Ghafy, C. and Catterall, M. (2005) 'Panel 2.18: logistics, information technology (IT), and telecommunications in crisis management', *Prehospital and Disaster Medicine*, 20(6): 464–7.

Devitt, K.R. and Borodzicz, E.P. (2008) 'Interwoven leadership: the missing link in multi-agency major incident response', *Journal of Contingencies and Crisis Management*, 16(4): 208–16.

Dubois, G., Pebesma, E.J. and Bossew, P. (2006) 'Automatic mapping in emergency: a geostatistical perspective', *International Journal of Emergency Management*, 4(3): 455–67.

Gillespie, D.F. (1991) 'Coordinating community resources', in T.E. Drabek and G.J. Hoetmer (eds) *Emergency Management: Principles and Practice for Local Government*, Washington, DC: International City Management Association, pp. 55–78.

Hewitt, K. (1970) 'Probabilistic approaches to discrete natural events: a review and theoretical discussion', *Economic Geography Supplement*, 46(2): 332–49.

Hosseini, K.A., Jafari, M.K., Hosseini, M., Mansouri, B. and Hosseinioon, S. (2009) 'Development of urban planning guidelines for improving emergency response capacities in seismic areas of Iran', *Disasters* 33(4): 645–64.

Kletz, T. (1999) *Hazop and Hazan: Identifying and Assessing Process Industry Hazards*, 4th edn, London: Institute of Chemical Engineering.

Laska, S. (2004) 'What if Hurricane Ivan had not missed New Orleans? Disasters Waiting to Happen Series No. 6', *Natural Hazards Observer*, 29(2): 5–6.

LESLP (2007) *Major Incident Procedure Manual*, 7th edn, London: London Emergency Services Liaison Panel, HMSO.

Lindstedt, D. (2008) 'Grounding the discipline of business continuity planning: what needs to be done to take it forward?', *Journal of Business Continuity and Emergency Planning*, 2(2): 197–205.

London Assembly (2006) *Report of the 7 July Review Committee, Vol. 1.*; *Vol. 2. Views and Information from organisations*; *Vol. 3. Views and Information from Individuals*, London: Greater London Assembly.

Lynch, K. (1960) *The Image of the City*, Cambridge, MA: MIT Press.

Minciardi, R., Sacile, R. and Trasforini, E. (2009) 'Resource allocation in integrated pre-operational and operational management of natural hazards', *Risk Analysis*, 29(1): 62–75.

Özerdem, A. and Jacoby, T. (2006) *Disaster Management and Civil Society: Earthquake Relief in Japan, Turkey and India*, International Library of Postwar Reconstruction and Development no. 1, London: I.B. Tauris.

Perry, R.W. (2005) 'Disasters, definitions and theory construction', in R.W. Perry and E.L. Quarantelli (eds) *What is a Disaster? New Answers to Old Questions*, Philadelphia, PA: Xlibris Press, pp. 284–99.

Perry, R.W. and Quarantelli E.L. (eds) (2005) *What is a Disaster? New Answers to Old Questions*, Philadelphia, PA: Xlibris Press.

Russell, C.S. (1970) 'Losses from natural hazards', *Land Economics*, 46 (4): 383–93.

Sullivan, M. (2003) 'Integrated recovery management: a new way of looking at a delicate process', *Australian Journal of Emergency Management*, 18(2): 4–27.

Tierney, K. (2008) 'Hurricane Katrina: catastrophic impacts and alarming lessons', in J.M. Quigley and L.M. Rosenthal (eds) *Risking House and Home: Disasters, Cities, Public Policy*, Berkeley, CA: Institute of Governmental Studies, Berkeley Public Policy Press, pp. 119–36.

Tofani, A. and Bartolozzi, M. (2008) 'Ranking nuclear and radiological terrorism scenarios: the Italian case', *Risk Analysis*, 28(5): 1431–44.

Towfighi, P. (1991) 'Integrated planning for natural and technological disasters', in A. Kreimer and M. Munasinghe (eds) *Managing Natural Disasters and the Environment*, Washington, DC: Environment Department, World Bank, pp. 106–10.

Von Bertalanffy, L. and Sutherland, J.W. (1974) 'General Systems Theory: foundations, developments, applications', *IEEE Transactions on Systems, Man and Cybernetics*, 4(6): 592.

Wamsler, C. (2006) 'Mainstreaming risk reduction in urban planning and housing: a challenge for international aid organisations', *Disasters*, 30(2): 171–7.

Waugh Jr., W.L. and Tierney, K. (2007) *Emergency Management: Principles and Practice for Local Government*, 2nd edn, Washington, DC: ICMA Press, International City Management Association.

Webb, G. (2004) 'Role improvising during crisis situations', *International Journal of Emergency Management*, 2(1–2): 47–61.

10 Common myths and misconceptions in disaster management

Alejandro López-Carresi

Lessons for practitioners

- When public officials deal with myths, they must carefully address their inconsistencies but also acknowledge the fears in which they are rooted.
- All statements disproving myths should be backed with solid scientific data.
- When dispelling myths in disaster response, do not highlight only the problem and the actions to be avoided, but also provide practical solutions to deal with them and actions to be taken.
- Address disaster myths with a more comprehensive approach, beyond emergency response.

Introduction

A chimera is a mythical monster, a legendary creature made up of different animal parts, including both real species and imaginary ones. It is usually portrayed as a three-headed monster – with the heads of a lion, a goat and a dragon – with a feline body and large wings. Those who focus on the lion, the goat or the wings will argue that such animals do exist. Those looking at the dragon's head or the creature as a whole will counter-argue that such animal is no more than a legend. In a sense, both are right – and wrong – it just depends on what the focus of your attention is.

The debate on the issue of disaster myths and misconceptions has been a recurrent issue among scholars, practitioners and other actors involved in disaster management. Most myths contain bits of reality, pieces of proven facts, but distorted by fears, twisted logic and wrapped in ignorance.

The Pan American Health Organization provides a list of myths and misconceptions that has been widely used (PAHO 2000) (Box 10.1).
Alexander's (2007) survey of disaster management students in Italy and the US illustrates how deeply rooted and persistent some of these wrong assumptions are.

While the role of the media in the perpetuation of myths cannot be denied, journalists frequently look for confirmation or support for their articles after major disasters. Unfortunately it is quite easy for them to find 'experts' who will confirm myths or provide the gloomiest forecasts or the most alarmist statements.

Box 10.1 Myths and misconceptions
(adapted from PAHO 2000)

A: General issues

Myth: Disasters are truly exceptional events.
Reality: They are a normal part of daily life and in very many cases are repetitive events.

Myth: Disasters kill people without respect for social class or economic status.
Reality: The poor and marginalized are more at risk of death than are rich people or the middle classes.

Myth: Technology will save the world from disaster.
Reality: The problem of disasters is largely a social one. Technological resources are poorly distributed and often ineffectively used. In addition, technology is a potential source of vulnerability as well as a means of reducing it.

B: Morbidity and mortality

Myth: Earthquakes are commonly responsible for very high death tolls.
Reality: Collapsing buildings are responsible for the majority of deaths in seismic disasters. Whereas it is not possible to stop earthquakes, it is possible to construct anti-seismic buildings and to organize human activities in such a way as to minimize the risk of death. In addition, the majority of earthquakes do not cause high death tolls.

Myth: People can survive for many days when trapped under the rubble of a collapsed building.
Reality: The vast majority of people brought out alive from the rubble are saved within 24 or perhaps even 12 hours of impact.

Myth: Disease epidemics are an almost inevitable result of the disruption and poor health caused by major disasters.
Reality: Generally, the level of epidemiological surveillance and health care in the disaster area is sufficient to stop any possible disease epidemic from occurring. However, the rate of diagnosis of diseases may increase as a result of improved health care.

Myth: Unburied dead bodies constitute a health hazard.
Reality: Not even advanced decomposition causes a significant health hazard. Hasty burial demoralizes survivors and upsets arrangements for death certification, funeral rites, and, where needed, autopsy.

C: Social behaviour

Myth: When disaster strikes, panic is a common reaction.

Reality: Most people behave rationally in disaster. While panic is not to be ruled out entirely, it is of such limited importance that some leading disaster sociologists regard it as insignificant or unlikely.

Myth: People will flee in large numbers from a disaster area.

Reality: Usually, there is a 'convergence reaction' and the area fills up with people. Few of the survivors will leave and even obligatory evacuations will be short-lived.

Myth: After disaster has struck, survivors tend to be dazed and apathetic.

Reality: Survivors rapidly start reconstruction. Activism is much more common than fatalism (this is the so-called 'therapeutic community'). Even in the worst scenarios, only 15–30 per cent of survivors show passive or dazed reactions.

Myth: Looting is a common and serious problem after disasters.

Reality: Looting is rare and limited in scope. It mainly occurs when there are strong preconditions, as when a **community** already is deeply divided.

Myth: Disasters cause a great deal of chaos and cannot possibly be managed systematically.

Reality: There are excellent theoretical models of how disasters function and how to manage them. After 75 years of research in the field, the general elements of disaster are well known, and they tend to repeat themselves from one disaster to the next.

Myth: Disasters usually give rise to widespread, spontaneous manifestations of antisocial behaviour.

Reality: Generally, they are characterized by great social solidarity, generosity and self-sacrifice, perhaps even heroism.

D: Assistance

Myth: Any kind of aid and relief is useful after disaster, providing it is supplied quickly enough.

Reality: Hasty and ill-considered relief initiatives tend to create chaos. Only certain types of assistance, goods, and services will be required. Not all useful resources that existed in the area before the disaster will be destroyed. Donation of unusable materials or manpower consumes resources of organization and accommodation that could more profitably be used to reduce the toll of the disaster.

Myth: In order to manage a disaster well, it is necessary to accept all forms of aid that are offered.

Reality: It is better to limit acceptance of donations to goods and services that are actually needed in the disaster area.

Myth: One should donate used clothes to the survivors of disasters.

Reality: This often leads to accumulations of huge quantities of useless garments that survivors cannot or will not wear.

Myth: Great quantities and assortments of medicines should be sent to disaster areas.

Reality: The only medicines that are needed are those used to treat specific pathologies, have not reached their sell-by date, can be properly conserved in the disaster area, and can be properly identified in terms of their pharmacological constituents. Any other medicines are not only useless, but potentially dangerous.

Myth: Companies, corporations, associations and governments are always very generous when invited to send aid and relief to disaster areas.

Reality: They may be, but, in the past, disaster areas have been used as dumping grounds for outdated medicines, obsolete equipment, and unusable goods, all under the cloak of apparent generosity.

Myth: There is usually a shortage of resources when disaster occurs and this prevents them from being managed effectively.

Reality: The shortage, if it occurs, is almost always very temporary. There is more of a problem in deploying resources well and using them efficiently than in acquiring them. Often, there is also a problem of coping with a superabundance of certain types of resources.

Chaos, antisocial behaviour and epidemic outbreaks are words commonly found in their statements.

This chapter will focus on two of the most widespread myths: **risks** of epidemics and looting. There are two reasons to focus our attention in these myths. First, they seem to prevail with undiminished strength across decades despite attempts to eliminate them. Second, they have some special characteristics that make them slightly different from other misconceptions. Some other misconceptions involve assumptions about the positive outcome of ill-considered acts, for example, that any and all kinds of donations are useful, or that moving disaster survivors to temporary settlements will help the recovery process. By contrast, misconceptions about disease and looting are based on the belief that something terrible will happen and actions must be taken to avoid it: dead bodies must be quickly buried to prevent epidemics; law enforcement must be deployed to prevent looting. A detailed description of what actually happens in disasters, regarding these two myths, is essential in trying to debunk them.

Disasters, epidemics and disease

Shortly after nearly every disaster the news headlines alert people to the risk of major epidemics of communicable diseases. For example, after the 2004 Asia tsunami, the World Health Organization stated that a second wave of deaths was to be expected, that disease and epidemics may cause as many casualties as the tsunami itself (a widely published view in the media and commented on by de Ville de Goyet, 2007). The forecasted disease mortality and epidemics failed to materialize.

Consequences of the epidemics myth

Myths associated with health and diseases have several negative consequences. The unfounded fear of epidemics has triggered many massive vaccination campaigns. Many vaccines commonly used in these campaigns, such as tetanus or typhus, are multi-dose, and subsequent shots are frequently missed. This might increase a false sense of security and lead to neglecting effective disease control measures, like appropriate water and sanitation. WHO does not recommend massive vaccination campaigns, since its effectiveness is yet to be proved and devotes a great number of workers and **resources** which could be applied elsewhere (PAHO 2000).

The hasty disposal of human remains causes psychological and legal problems. It leaves the surviving relatives without the chance of developing culturally accepted funerals and grieving for the dead properly (Thieren and Guitteau 2000). The lack of registration of the deceased means no death certificate is issued. All the financial assets and properties of the deceased cannot be claimed by otherwise rightful heirs. They may not obtain any public aid they may be entitled to; bank accounts cannot be accessed; properties cannot be sold; life insurance the deceased may have cannot be claimed. The situation may be even worse for widows in some countries, where a male spouse's permission is still requested for some arrangements such as loans. There are very few exceptions to this pattern of quick mass burials. After the 2004 Indian Ocean tsunami, mass burials were initiated but quickly stopped and bodies exhumed. All human remains were properly identified in an unprecedented forensics operation supported by Western governments (Morgan *et al.* 2006), unwilling to deal with the legal problems described above. Finally, mass burials displace resources like heavy machinery and workers, most needed in the immediate aftermath of the disaster.

Dead bodies and epidemics

One of the reasons why myths persist is that there are elements of truth embedded in the misconception. Dead bodies *can* transmit a number of diseases for a limited period of time (Morgan 2004), but those diseases must be already present in the host *before* death takes place. It is impossible for a dead body to transmit any communicable disease which was not present when the person was alive. Cholera or tuberculosis, or any other infectious disease, does not spontaneously appear in non-infected corpses. The health risks of dead bodies resulting from natural **hazards** are very few, since the immediate cause of death is trauma, not infectious disease.

There are some other health risks associated with cadavers. Pathogens may enter the human body through contact with body fluids, through the respiratory or oral route. A dead body with blood-borne viruses (HIV or Hepatitis B, for example) could infect a living person in case of direct contact with body fluids, open wounds or contact with needles or protruding bones. While the latter may happen almost exclusively to pathologists or other professionals who perform autopsies, the former could result from a careless manipulation of bodies by people conducting search and rescue. In a disaster setting, both possibilities seem rather remote.

Infection by oral route could result from bodies polluting drinking water sources, but it is unlikely people would drink from water contaminated in this way. The possibility of body fluids from buried corpses percolating the soil and contaminating groundwater is a theoretical possibility, but it appears to be remote (ibid.).

Finally, transmission of airborne diseases from dead bodies could only happen if individuals have contact with residual air in the lungs or with fluids from chest cavity tissues putrefaction, expelled during careless manipulation.

Even if an individual is in contact with pathogens in any way described above, the probability of acquiring a disease is low (ibid.) since most pathogens die with the host after the cooling of the body.

Regarding dead bodies not affected by previous diseases, the health risks are confined to those linked to natural putrefaction. Death triggers a well-known decomposing process, which involves the growth of common microorganisms (Conly and Johnston 2005). The typical bacteria found in a decaying body are part of the human body's natural flora and will only cause disease to a living person in the case of a massive transmission of microorganisms. In the case of an unlikely contamination from a cadaver, this infection would produce gastroenteritis – common diarrhoea with occasional vomiting – rarely life-threatening in healthy individuals.

There are only a few diseases transmitted by previously infected bodies capable of triggering the most feared epidemics, such as cholera or certain haemorrhagic fevers. However, there seems to be a simplification process in many people's minds: a 'leap' which eliminates the logical chain, ignores essential elements and retains only the impression caused by portions of the first and last factors (Figure 10.1).

It is true that under extremely rare circumstances, most of them found in previous centuries, some diseases may be transmitted from dead bodies and contribute to the spread of epidemics (e.g. cholera). There have been moments in history in which corpses posed a risk to the living. The plague epidemic of 1347–50, known as the Black Death, killed millions in Europe (Duncan and Scott

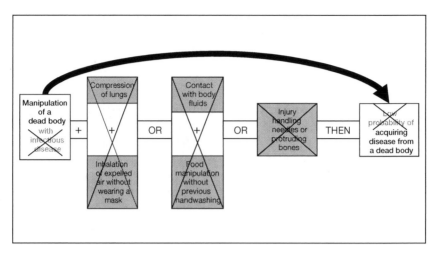

Figure 10.1 Simplification or 'leaping' process understanding risk from a dead body with a communicable illness

2005). Approaching deceased people was indeed hazardous, although the risk was not originated by the cadaver *per se*. The disease was caused by bacteria, *Yersinia pestis*, usually found in rats. It was transmitted by fleas which had bitten infected rats and jumped on to humans, biting them afterwards, and spreading the disease. When the human host dies and cools, fleas jump from the cadaver to the nearest living being when they feel the proximity of a warm organism, thus infecting the new host and spreading the disease. The actual route of transmission was not understood at the time (Figure 10.2), but the risk of approaching the dead was quite clear to survivors. It cannot be said that the fear was unfounded despite the fact that dead bodies themselves were harmless.

The prevalence of this fear in a current disaster setting is somehow puzzling, since the process that made some bodies dangerous in the Middle Age is almost

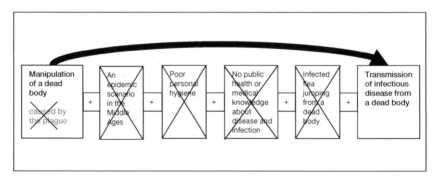

Figure 10.2 Simplification or 'leaping' process understanding risk from a dead body with a communicable illness in plague epidemics in the Middle Ages

impossible to be reproduced in today's disasters. The precautions to handle corpses are universal hygiene measures (PAHO 2004), enough to prevent any contamination from dead bodies.

Epidemics after disaster

As rare as they may be, it is still worth commenting on the occasional outbreaks of disease after disasters caused by natural hazards. According to the Centers for Disease Control and Prevention (CDC), an epidemic is the occurrence of more cases of disease than expected in a given area or among a specific group of people over a particular period of time. Only three out of more than 600 geophysical disasters recorded worldwide from 1984 to 2004 experienced epidemic outbreaks: measles after the Pinatubo eruption in Philippines in 1991, coccidioidomycosis (a fungal infection caused by inhalation of spores) after an earthquake in California in 1994, and malaria after earthquake and heavy rains in Costa Rica in 1991 (Floret *et al.* 2006). The measles epidemic after the evacuation of the population settled near Mount Pinatubo affected mostly the Aeta tribe, virtually isolated in the slopes of the volcano and never subjected to previous vaccination (Magpantay *et al.* 1992). The crowded shelters, the presence of vulnerable groups and the deteriorated sanitary conditions set the scenario for the outbreak. This particular situation shows that epidemics after disasters are a possibility when certain conditions appear, but gross generalization must be avoided. Health surveillance measures must be in place in order to undertake specific actions if certain risk factors appear such as overcrowded camps with extended permanence, poor health and sanitation and vulnerable groups. However, decision-makers should keep in mind that the convergence of these factors after disasters is very rare and that massive and indiscriminate actions to prevent unfounded health risks are not recommended. Still, the perception of high risk of epidemics remains and the exceptions are far more vividly remembered than the norm, no matter how remotely related to the disasters they may be. The cholera outbreak in Haiti in October 2012 is instructive. Although perceptually linked with the devastating earthquake of January 2010, it started ten months after the seism, in a distant area unaffected by the tremor. It is clear that the epidemic was the product of an external input and pre-existing sanitary conditions and not related with the earthquake (Piarroux *et al.* 2011).

Refugee or Internally Displaced People (IDP) camps in armed conflict scenarios or when displaced people can be counted by tens of thousands have a higher risk of disease outbreaks than collective shelters or camps after non-conflict disasters (CDC 1998; Djeddah *et al.* 1988; Kamugisha *et al.* 2003; Shultz *et al.* 2009; Sorensen and Dissler 1988; Toole and Waldman 1997). Although the risk of major disease outbreaks is lower than in refugee camps, health-care provision, and especially appropriate sanitation facilities must be in place in shelters after all disasters (Wisner and Adams 2002).

Disease after disaster

The overrated risk of major epidemics after disasters does not imply that all health concerns in disaster response are irrelevant (see Chapter 11) (Figure 10.3). Frequently, local health services are affected or destroyed, interrupting the provision of adequate community care. Apart from immediate trauma injuries, there are many other health problems (Noji 1997; PAHO 2000): interruption of regular vaccinations programs or poorly treated trauma injuries resulting in delayed health problems that eventually affect the working **capacity** of adults (Wisner 2002).

But what worries many decision-makers in the immediate aftermath of disasters are not long-term health effects. Their main concern is the risk of epidemics of communicable diseases. Some of the infectious diseases that have the potential to trigger an outbreak are, in fact, present after disasters. But very rarely the most feared diseases are registered, such as cholera. Common diseases are far more frequent and rarely in epidemic proportions.

Acute diarrhoea

Acute diarrhoea in most disasters is usually the result of drinking from contaminated sources of water. An increase of diarrhoea has been frequently reported after disasters (Kondo *et al.* 2002; Lai *et al.* 2000). In those cases where there are pre-disaster records, studies do not suggest increased mortality by this cause compared to pre-disaster levels (Schwartz *et al.* 2006: 1072).

For most healthy adults, common diarrhoea is not deadly, although young and elderly patients are more vulnerable. Still, the appearance of diarrhoea cases after

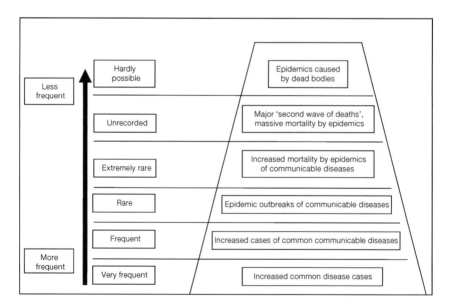

Figure 10.3 Likelihood of epidemics and disease after disasters

disasters triggers the alarm of epidemics of infectious diseases such as cholera or dysentery, even in the Gulf coast of the US after Hurricane Katrina, despite the fact that those diseases have been absent from the area for a long time. All patients with cholera or dysentery suffer from acute diarrhoea, but *not all patients with acute diarrhoea suffer from cholera or dysentery*.

Respiratory diseases

Acute respiratory infections are also occasionally found among disaster survivors in cold climates (Lai *et al.* 2000), usually following destruction of homes which leave survivors with less protection from the natural environment. Besides, it is an easily person-to-person transmitted infection. Most patients develop minor problems, such as upper respiratory tract infections. Less frequently there are cases of pneumonia, a more serious condition (Matsuoka *et al.* 2000; Tanaka *et al.* 1999) but not among the most contagious.

Vector-borne diseases

After an earthquake in Costa Rica and subsequent heavy rains, an increase in malaria cases was detected (Saenz *et al.* 1995). It seems logical to expect cases since more people sleep unprotected after the destruction of their homes. The additional factor of rains increases mosquito breeding spots. Yet there is currently little evidence that a deadly outbreak of malaria will cause 'a second wave of deaths'.

Conclusions on epidemics

A factor affecting the perception of a higher disease rate is the increased number of medical examinations. More medical workers attending more patients will detect more diseases. Despite the frequent statements by foreign medical workers responding to disasters, it is quite difficult for people from outside the community to establish whether the detected cases constitute an epidemic. The lack of crucial data about the number of previous cases of the detected disease prevents any comparison and the determination of the trend as increasing or decreasing.

Health and disease after disasters are a major issue, and undoubtedly some illnesses do increase and public health deteriorates. But the presence of infectious diseases mentioned earlier does not justify unfounded fears of major epidemics. The diseases and health problems mentioned above are real, and should be taken care of in appropriate time and manner. But the chimera of almost inevitable epidemics spreading death and disease is a myth, not a reality.

Looting and social disorder

In past centuries, there were frequent rumours following disasters of savage looters caught severing fingers or ears from dead bodies to get the jewellery. Examples of written stories containing these kinds of actions were found in the press after the Johnstown flood of 1889, the Ohio floods of 1913, the Galveston hurricane of 1900 or the earthquake in San Francisco in 1906 (Gray and Wilson 1984). The imprint of violent criminals waiting to jump over disaster-affected cities is still widely spread. In this vision, hordes of vandals, once-law-abiding citizens, spread uncontrolled among rubble and debris, looting whatever is left after the impact of a geophysical hazard. Far away from the mentioned US examples and many decades after, this perception seems to have found its way among the rubble of the 2009 earthquake in Italy. The expected but never materialized looters were called *sciacalli* (jackals) (*El Mundo* 2009), reminiscent of legendary past stories of bloodthirsty criminals.

That seems to be the most expected social behaviour as portrayed in numerous movies, feared by many decision-makers and deeply rooted in the minds of the majority of people. According to this view, looting is frequent after disasters and preventative measures must be taken immediately. This perception is based on the idea that disasters change societies and communities, triggering negative actions and antisocial collective behaviour. Quarantelli (1994) invokes R.L. Stevenson's novel, *Dr. Jekyll and Mr. Hyde*. The prevalent fear is that after disasters, respected and law-abiding citizens mutate into destructive monsters and commit crimes. But the reality is that looting is the exception and not the norm (Auf der Heide 2004; Fischer 1998) and when it happens, it follows different patterns than looting during riots and civil unrest crisis. Prosocial and adaptive behaviour in communities (see Chapter 4) and the willingness to help others is generally the collective reaction to be expected (Dynes and Tierney 1994).

Still, fear of looting among survivors and decision-makers is prevalent, reinforced by the media. The overstated risk of looting and the presumption that almost everyone is a potential looter have real negative consequences in disasters. Diversion of law enforcement resources from relief operations to prevent expected looting hinders disaster response operations. In the 2009 Italy earthquake, police forces were deployed throughout the affected Abruzzo region, and even the government expressed their intention to call in the Army, if needed, since they expected an incursion of the feared looters (*El Mundo* 2009), a typical example of how the media tend to exaggerate their reports on disasters and in particularly about looting (Goltz 1984). After the dramatic headline saying that looting had already started and the citation within the main text of an alleged civil protection source stating that looters 'came from all over Italy', the number of arrested people on suspicion of looting was two, only to be later released after proving that they owned the allegedly stolen money they had on them. That reduces the reported number of looters in this article to zero, clearly contradicting the article headline, the dramatic statements in the text and the idea that the Armed Forces are necessary to contain a non-existent invasion of 'jackals', an idea which implies that the situation is so out of control that the police are not enough to preserve law and order and contain looters. After Hurricane Katrina in New Orleans, lifesaving operations were suspended to concentrate emergency responders on arresting looters, only to find out some time later that reports were severely exaggerated (Tierney and Bevc 2007: 43).

This fear of looters also makes many people ignore evacuation orders before the impact of forecasted natural hazards, typically in hurricanes (Fischer 1998; Auf der Heide 2004: 347).

Here again we may face a distorted reality, tiny bits of truth misreported and quickly magnified to unreal proportions. As with the myths about disease and disaster, it is possible to distinguish, in the case of collective behaviour, between the lion's head, the real part, and the chimera, the imaginary monster.

Looting vs. appropriation

A distinction should be made between looting and taking essential items for survival. While looting may be considered the illicit taking of non-essential items with the sole purpose of obtaining personal profit, many researchers use the term 'appropriation' when the goods taken are used to cover basic needs, such as the need for food, water and shelter (Quarantelli 1994). Taking non-essential goods, like electronic devices, or luxury items, is clearly a crime. But taking survival items should not fall under the label of antisocial behaviour. These actions are not driven by greed or personal profit. In fact, in some occasions, some of those essential items are shared with other survivors in need. Such appropriation is not uncommon. After an earthquake in Peru in 2007 (*El País* 2007), and also after the devastating earthquake in Haiti in 2010 (Whittell 2010), relief supplies were taken by force by desperate survivors from trucks, warehouses or collapsed stores. The sluggish reaction of the authorities, combined with mistrust of the population in fair distribution, seem to have triggered such actions.

However, most of these events were perceived and reported by media, law enforcement or casual observers as examples of social disorder, violent behaviour and looting. People taking relief goods from trucks is a powerful picture and, if observed without attention to context, it reinforces the preconceived idea about looting.

Looting vs. salvaging

In San Francisco, after the 1906 earthquake and fire, an executive order was issued by the authorities: looters will be shot on the scene without warning or questioning. This drastic measure added more deaths to the earthquake toll. Allegedly, many of them were not looters but survivors searching for usable items among the rubble of their own homes (Meyer 1977: 40; Steinberg 2000). Similar stories were found in the written press after other disasters. Nowadays, it is easy to find pictures in the media of people sifting through the debris, collecting any recyclable or usable items, not from inhabited houses, but from piles of rubble. Unfortunately, those actions are frequently interpreted as acts of pillage and looting.

Looting vs. rumours of looting

Little change in the frequency of rumours about looting has been observed over several decades. After a tornado in Arkansas, in 1952, a random sample of people among the affected population were asked whether they had lost any property by looting. Only 9 per cent said they *thought* some property had been taken by looters; one-third of those were not sure if their property was lost after looting or buried under the debris or taken away by the wind. Most articles were declared to have a reduced value. However, 58 per cent of the interviewees said they heard other people's properties had been looted. The researchers could verify only two cases of valuables being stolen (Quarantelli and Dynes 1972). Again, time does not seem to affect the acceptance of rumours as truths. Constable (2008) found most press stories of looting after Hurricane Katrina in New Orleans to be mainly second-hand accounts. The expectation of massive looting seems to upgrade any suspicious action or mere rumours to confirmed fact; deeply rooted fears and emotions take over reason and critical thinking.

Actual looting

When actual looting occurs in disasters, it is commonly performed by people from outside the community, frequently by people usually involved in criminal activities, individually or in small groups, taking advantage of the sudden opportunity (Quarantelli 1994, 2007). Complaints of looting by the security forces who should be protecting the abandoned houses are not unheard of, although difficult to prove, for obvious reasons. By contrast, looting in riots and situations of civil unrest is enacted by law-abiding people from the community, in a collective manner and openly undertaken with wide social support. Table 10.1 and Figure 10.4 differentiate some such actions.

Most of those who loot and steal after disasters also do it before disasters. The disaster itself does not act as a social transformer that triggers deep changes or significantly increases in antisocial behaviour. Still, the actual extent of crime in disasters remains difficult to determine. After disasters it is frequent to find reports in the media about arrests of alleged looters, which may lead one to think that crime in the area is on the rise. Only a detailed comparison of that data with figures of crime before the disaster would support a judgment on whether figures are above or below routine daily crime rates in that **locality**. In fact, some studies suggest that crime rates tend to decline after a disaster (Auf der Heide 2004: 363; Tierney and Bevc 2007).

Table 10.1 Looting in disasters versus riots/civil unrest

Disasters	Riots /civil unrest
Law-abiding people from the community	Non-local residents involved in criminal activities
Individual actions or by small groups	Collective action
Undertaken openly with social support	Undertaken covertly with social rejection
Sites chosen randomly	Sites selected and targeted

Source: Based on studies by Quarantelli and Dynes (1968) and Quarantelli (1994; 2007).

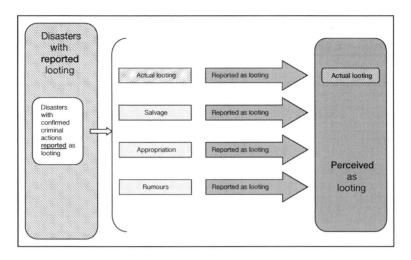

Figure 10.4 Perceived looting vs. actual looting

A detailed series of field interviews by disaster researchers were performed in New Orleans, after the post-Hurricane Katrina reports of massive looting (Rodríguez *et al.* 2006). Their findings do not deny that looting took place but certainly challenge the idea of massive, widespread antisocial behaviour and indiscriminate looting. They found numerous examples of rumours accepted as truths, unconfirmed statements and decisions based on vague allegations. A detailed examination of those arrested on alleged charges of looting showed interesting results. According to the estimations of a police officer in charge of a temporary jail for alleged looters, 75 per cent of arrested people had taken essential life-saving items. The majority of the remaining 25 per cent who took luxury items already had criminal records (Barsky *et al.* 2006).

Conclusions on looting

In summary, while detailed observation of disasters and the vast majority of the scientific literature indicate that widespread looting and social disorder are a myth and actual looting is truly exceptional, with some exceptions (Frailing 2007), the number of disasters with actual looting and the precise extent of it, as reduced as it may be, remain unclear. In the same volume of post-Katrina studies (Brunsma *et al.* 2007), there are different opinions. Some authors believe that looting after Katrina Hurricane was rampant (Frailing and Harper 2007) while others support that it was gravely exaggerated (Dynes and Rodríguez 2007; Tierney and Bevc 2007) and that the crime level was lower than during non-disaster periods.

The result is rumours of pillage accepted as facts, people taking essential items or trying to recover some usable items among the rubble will be mixed with any exceptional isolated antisocial actions. The ingredients, real or imagined, will be merged into an exaggerated perception of looting. Tiny bits of truth distorted and embedded in a large misconception; a little goat's head transformed into an imaginary monster.

Conclusion and recommendations

Disaster research has produced rigorous works analysing the actual extent of myths and solid evidence against widespread misconceptions. And, although much of the research on disaster myths was undertaken decades ago, it is still applicable today. However, regarding recommendations to address the problem, there is still a gap. Complex problems do not benefit from simplistic solutions, so probably a multifaceted approach may be the best option.

First, education about disasters for the public, the media and above all, the practitioners. It should contribute significantly to offer a more realistic picture of disasters and increase the critical analysis of distorted information. Part of education is working on messages. Paraphrasing Drabek (1986), rather than statements like 'do not worry about epidemics because they are very infrequent' or 'leave your house without fear because looting is very rare', we should try to offer a clear explanation of true facts while addressing people's concerns. Alternatives could be:

> Although we are aware of the public concerns about outbreaks, there has not been any epidemic of infectious disease after any earthquake over the last 40 years, and we do not have any reasons to believe that this is going to be an exception. Nevertheless, we have all measures in place to respond if that is the case, as unlikely as it may be.

Or:

> Despite the widespread concerns about looting, our experience and that of many others too tell us that the perception is bigger than the real problem and that criminal acts are isolated and very rare. However, plans have been developed in case we have to deal with some isolated cases.

Second, better organized relief operations would contribute to reducing social problems caused by unsatisfied basic needs (Fischer 2006), such as the cases seen in post-Hurricane Katrina New Orleans in 2005 and post-earthquake Haiti in 2010. The aim should be to promote a **culture** of safety and prevention (Wisner *et al.* 2004: 372) and to address disaster issues with a more comprehensive approach, beyond emergency response. That will also contribute to the fight against myths.

Finally, affected people should be included as far as possible in planning and decision-making so that they have a say in preparedness planning and do not feel like passive recipients of policies and planning. This too will contribute to facilitate relief actions since local people will be partners in this work. Thus, some of the stress and tension that might lead to appropriation will be reduced.

The struggle to debunk myths was initiated long time ago and this fight will not be won in the short term. But we should not give up because the final objective of this fight, strictly speaking, is not to dispel myths but to reduce suffering caused by inappropriate actions based on fears and misconceptions. At the end of the day, to reduce human suffering is the ultimate goal of disaster management.

References

Alexander, D.E. (2007) 'Misconception as a barrier to teaching about disasters', *Prehospital Disaster Medicine*, 22(2): 95–103.

Auf der Heide, E. (2004) 'Common misconceptions about disasters: panic, the disaster syndrome, and looting', in M. O'Leary (ed.) *The First 72 hours: A Community Approach to Disaster Preparedness*, Lincoln, NB: iUniverse Publishing.

Barsky, L., Trainor, J. and Torres, M. (2006) *Disaster Realities in the Aftermath of Hurricane Katrina: Revisiting the Looting Myth*, Natural Hazards Center Quick Response Report Number 184, Boulder CO: Natural Hazards Center, University of Colorado at Boulder.

Brunsma, D.L., Overfelt, D. and Picou, J.S. (eds) (2007) *The Sociology of Katrina: Perspectives on a Modern Catastrophe*, Lanham, MD: Rowman & Littlefield.

CDC (1998) 'Cholera outbreak among Rwandan refugees, Democratic Republic of Congo, April 1997', *Morbidity and Mortality Weekly Report*, 47(19): 389–91.

Conly, J.M. and Johnston, B.L. (2005) 'Natural disasters, corpses and the risk of infectious diseases', *The Canadian Journal of Infectious Diseases & Medical Microbiology*, 16(5): 269–70.

Constable, M. (2008) 'Disaster mythology: looting in New Orleans', *Disaster Prevention and Management*, 17(4): 526–35.

De Ville de Goyet, C. (2007) 'Myths, the ultimate survivors in disasters', *Prehospital Disaster Medicine*, 22 (2): 104–5.

Djeddah, C., Miozzo, A., Di Gennaro, M., Rosmini, F., Martino, P. and Pasquini, P. (1988) 'An outbreak of cholera in a refugee camp in Africa', *European Journal of Epidemiology*, 4(2): 227–30.

Drabek, T.E. (1986) *Human System Responses to Disaster*, Heidelberg: Springer-Verlag.

Duncan, C.J. and Scott, S. (2005) 'What caused the Black Death?', *Postgrad Med Journal*, 81 (955): 315–20.

Dynes, R. and Quarantelli, E.L. (1968) 'What looting in civil disturbances really means', *Transaction*, 5 (6): 9-14.

Dynes, R.R. and Rodríguez, H. (2007) 'Finding and framing Katrina: the social construction of disaster', in D.L. Brunsma, D. Overfelt, and J.S. Picou (eds) *The Sociology of Katrina: Perspectives on a Modern Catastrophe,* Lanham, MD: Rowman & Littlefield.

Dynes, R.R. and Tierney, K.J. (eds) (1994) *Disasters, Collective Behavior, and Social Organization*, Newark: University of Delaware Press.

El Mundo, Online Edition (2009) 'Tras el Seísmo, los "Chacales"'. Available at: http://www.elmundo.es/elmundo/2009/04/08/internacional/1239207965.html (accessed 14 October 2009).

El País, Online edition (2007) 'El Gobierno peruano redobla la seguridad para frenar los saqueos ante la llegada de la ayuda internacional'. Available at: http://www.elpais.com/articulo/internacional/Gobierno/peruano/redobla/seguridad/frenar/saqueos/llegada/ayuda/internacional/elpepuint/20070818elpepuint_1/Tes (accessed 25 October 2009).

Fischer III, H.W. (1998) *Behavioral Response to Disaster: Fact Versus Fiction and its Perpetuation*, 2nd edn, Lanham, MD: University Press of America.

—— (2006) 'Disaster myths and their implications for disaster planning', *Natural Hazards Observer*, 31(1): 6–7.

Floret, N., Viel, J.F., Mauni, F., Hoen, B. and Piarroux, R. (2006) 'Negligible risk for epidemics after geophysical disasters', *Emerging Infectious Diseases Journal*, 12(4): 543–8.

Frailing, K. (2007) 'The myth of a disaster myth: potential looting should be part of disaster plans', *Natural Hazards Observer*, 31(4): 3–4.

Frailing, K. and Harper, D.W. (2007) 'Crime and hurricanes in New Orleans', in D.L. Brunsma, D. Overfelt and J.S. Picou (eds) *The Sociology of Katrina: Perspectives on a Modern Catastrophe*, Lanham, MD: Rowman & Littlefield.

Goltz, J.D. (1984) 'Are the news media responsible for the disaster myths? A content analysis of emergency response imagery', *International Journal of Mass Emergencies and Disasters*, 2 (3): 345–68.

Gray, J. and Wilson, E. (1984) *Looting in Disasters: A General Profile of Victimization*, Working Paper 71, Columbus, OH: The Ohio State University Disaster Research Center.

Kamugisha, C., Cairns, K.L. and Akim, C. (2003) 'An outbreak of measles in Tanzanian refugee camps', *The Journal of Infectious Diseases*, 187 (1): 558–62.

Kondo, H., Seo, N., Yasuda, T., Hasizume, M., Koido, Y., Ninomiya, N. and Yamamoto, Y. (2002) 'Post-flood-infectious diseases in Mozambique', *Prehospital Disaster Med*, 17(3): 126–33.

Lai, S.W., Liu, C.S., Li, C.I., Tan, C.K., Ng, K.C., Lai, M.M. and Lin, C.C. (2000) 'Post-earthquake illness and disease after the Chi-Chi earthquake', *European Journal of Internal Medicine*, 11(6): 353–4.

Magpantay, R.L., Abellanosa, I.P., White, M.E., and Dayrit, M.M. (1992) 'Measles among Aetas in evacuation centers after volcanic eruption', Abstracts, International Scientific Conference on Mt. Pinatubo, 27–31 May 1992, Manila: Department of Foreign Affairs.

Matsuoka, T., Yoshioka, T., Oda, J., Tanaka, H., Kuwagata, Y., Sugimoto, H. and Sugimoto, T. (2000) 'The impact of a catastrophic earthquake on morbidity rates for various illnesses', *Public Health*, 114(4): 249–53.

Meyer, L.L. (1977) *California Quake,* Nashville, TN: Sherbourne Press.

Morgan, O. (2004) 'Infectious disease risks from dead bodies following natural disasters', *Revista Panamericana de Salud Pública/Pan American Journal of Public Health*, 15(5): 307–12.

Morgan, O.W., Sribanditmongkol, P., Perera, C., Sulasmi, Y., Van Alphen, D., *et al.* (2006) 'Mass fatality management following the South Asian Tsunami disaster: case studies in Thailand, Indonesia, and Sri Lanka', *PLoS Med*, 3(6): e195. doi:10.1371/journal.pmed. 0030195. Available at: http://www.plosmedicine.org/article/info%3Adoi%2F10.1371 %2Fjournal.pmed.0030195 (accessed January 2013).

Noji, E. (ed.) (1997) *The Public Health Consequences of Disasters*, New York: Oxford University Press.

PAHO (2000) *Natural Disasters: Protecting the Public's Health*, Scientific Publication 575, Washington, DC: Pan American Health Organization.

—— (2004) *Management of Dead Bodies in Disaster Situations. Disaster Manuals and Guidelines on Disaster Series, No. 5*, Washington, DC: Pan American Health Organization.

Piarroux, R., Barrals, R., Faucher, B., Haus, R., Piarroux, M. and Gaudart, J. (2011) 'Understanding the cholera epidemic, Haiti', *Emerging Infectious Diseases*, 17(7): 1161–7.

Quarantelli, E.L. (1994) *Looting and Antisocial Behavior in Disasters*, Preliminary Paper 205, Newark: Disaster Research Center, University of Delaware.

—— (2007) 'The myth and the realities: keeping the "looting" myth in perspective', *Natural Hazards Observer*, 31(4): 2–3.

Quarantelli, E.L. and Dynes, R.R. (1972) 'When disaster strikes (it isn't much like what you have heard and read about)', *Psychology Today*, 5 (9): 66–70.

Rodríguez, H., Trainor, J. and Quarantelli, E.L. (2006) 'Rising to the challenges of a catastrophe: the emergent and pro-social behavior following Hurricane Katrina', *Annals of the American Academy of Political and Social Science*, 604 (1): 82–101.

Saenz, R., Bissel, R.A., and Paniagua, F. (1995) 'Post-disaster malaria in Costa Rica', *Prehospital Disaster Medicine*, 10 (3): 154–60.

Schwartz, B.S., Harris, J.B., Khan, A.I., Larocque, R.C., Sack, D.A., Malek, M.A., Faruque, A.S., Qadri, F., Calderwood, S.B., Luby, S.P. and Ryan, E.T. (2006) 'Diarrheal epidemics in Dhaka, Bangladesh, during three consecutive floods: 1988, 1998, and 2004', *The American Journal of Tropical Medicine and Hygiene*; 74(6): 1067–73.

Shultz, A., Omollo, J.O., Burke, H., Qassim, M., Ochieng, J.B., Weinberg, M., Feikin, D.R. and Breiman, R.F. (2009) 'Cholera outbreak in Kenyan refugee camp: risk factors for illness and importance of sanitation', *The American Journal of Tropical Medicine and Hygiene*, 80(4): 640–5.

Sorensen, E. and Dissler, K. (1988) 'Practical experience with the management of a cholera outbreak in a refugee camp in Eastern Sudan, 1985', *Disasters*, 12(3): 274–81.

Steinberg, T. (2000) *Acts of God: The Unnatural History of Disaster in America*, Oxford: Oxford University Press.

Tanaka, H., Oda, J., Iwai, A., Kuwagata, Y., Matsuoka, T., Takaoka, M., Kishi, M., Morimoto, F., Ishikawa, K., Mizushima, Y., Nakata, Y., Yamamura, H., Hiraide, A., Shimazu, T. and Yoshioka, T. (1999) 'Morbidity and mortality of hospitalized patients after the 1995 Hanshin-Awaji earthquake', *The American Journal of Emergency Medicine*, 17(2): 186–91.

Thieren, M. and Guitteau, R., (2000) 'Identifying cadavers following disasters: why?', *Disasters: Preparedness and Mitigation in the Americas*, 80: 12. Online. Available: http://www.paho.org/disasters/newsletter/index.php?option=com_docman&task=doc_view&Itemid=&gid=39&lang=en (accessed 25 January 2010).

Tierney, K. and Bevc, C. (2007) 'Disaster as war: militarism and the social construction of disaster in New Orleans', in D.L. Brunsma, D. Overfelt and J.S. Picou (eds) *The Sociology of Katrina: Perspectives on a Modern Catastrophe*, Lanham, MD: Rowman & Littlefield.

Toole, M.J. and Waldman R.J. (1997) 'The public health aspects of complex emergencies and refugee situations', *Annual Review of Public Health*, 18: 283–312.

Whittell, G. (2010) 'No food, no buildings, no money, no hope . . . and not even a rumour of aid', *The Times*. Available at: http://www.timesonline.co.uk/tol/news/world/us_and_americas/article6993136.ece (accessed 25 January 2010).

Wisner, B. (2002) 'Disability and disaster: victimhood and agency in earthquake risk reduction', in C. Rodriguez and E. Rovai (eds) *Earthquakes*, New York: Routledge.

Wisner, B. and Adams, J. (2002) *Environmental Health in Emergencies and Disasters: A Practical Guide*, Geneva: World Health Organization.

Wisner, B., Blaikie, P., Cannon, T. and Davis, I. (2004) *At Risk: Natural Hazards, People's Vulnerability and Disasters*, 2nd edn, London: Routledge.

11 Health aspects of disaster management

Joachim Kreysler

Lessons for practitioners

- Chronically poor and isolated people as well as millions of migrant labourers in cities are subject to spiral of poor living conditions and diet, ill health and exposure to **hazards**, all reinforcing one another.
- Many tools are available for building capacity to break this vicious cycle.
- Partnership with affected populations is necessary to implement both health improvements and preparedness for the health consequences of hazard events.
- Reproductive health care in emergencies has been a neglected area.
- Neglected tropical diseases have a huge impact on **livelihoods**, well-being and the ability of people to invest in disaster reduction measures.

Introduction

Health in context: globalisation, rapid change and conflict

Worldwide, the numbers of disasters are on the increase, and as a consequence, health outcomes and health security are in crisis (WHO 2007a). Furthermore, deterioration in both people's baseline health status and the condition of health care is likely to increase the health burden of disaster. An aging population in many countries and an associated increase in the prevalence of degenerative disease and special needs, the HIV-AIDS pandemic, deterioration of nutrition in some populations, increase of diabetes all shift the health 'normal' upon which the impact of disaster and displacement are overlain (Wisner *et al.* 2004).

Economic globalisation also interacts with both health and disaster. Accelerated economic growth is strongest in coastal areas on all continents, and has encouraged rapidly increasing voluntary and forced migration for many reasons to mega-agglomerations. As a rule, new migrants live in substandard housing, often in hazardous areas in overcrowded conditions, while governments focused on economic growth continue to ignore environmental concerns in sprawling cities (Pelling and Wisner 2009). These include deforestation, unregulated, unsafe housing and a proliferation of sealed-surface roads, which have a major impact on microclimates. Since the engine of economic growth is cheap labour in weakly regulated manufacturing industries, large public health concerns for the workforce are the consequences, often multiplied through potentially hazardous conditions of work involving toxic substances which can also affect residential areas. In fast-growing industrial areas the complex nature of **risks** of these industrial hazards are often insufficiently appreciated by local authorities (ibid.).

Current global prospects indicate increased numbers of violent conflicts, accompanied by displacement, disability and loss of livelihoods. With increasingly destructive weapons, the human cost in health will steeply increase during conflicts (Perrin 1996), while the protection of civilians has become a dangerous task. Marginalisation in drawn-out often undeclared wars carries its own specific load of health burden and negative social consequences. With this prospect in mind, major emphasis must be given to health during rehabilitation in post-conflict and the restoration of appropriate health services.

The 9/11 attack in the USA changed the understanding of disaster in relationship with health and its implications for management in emergencies. While concerns such as management of refugee camps or disease threats for large numbers of displaced people persist and are even increasing (e.g. post-earthquake cholera in Haiti), one of the key issues raised by 9/11 is 'health-security' also in affluent, urban zones. This new focus is on health and safety concerns posed by terrorism and pandemic diseases. The sending of letters poisoned with anthrax in the US heightened attention to bioterrorism. Bioterrorism is a threat now taken on board by global strategists across the globe (GHSI 2005). In addition, advances in real-time monitoring and information technology have completely overhauled not only the approach to disaster health management but also the means to control strategy and long-term vision. The field of complex health emergencies has become larger. The Global Outbreak Alert and Response Network (GOARN) by the World Health Organization (WHO) (http://www.who.int/csr/outbreaknetwork/en/), WHO's Health Action in Crises (HAC) department (http://www.who.int/hac/en/) and the Pan American Health Organization (PAHO) focus on disaster planning (http://new.paho.org/disasters/index.php?option=com_frontpage&Itemid=1) are only three outstanding examples.

The response by the global health system

Until the beginning of the 1990s, public health operations and the general promotion of 'tropical disease' research had been widely perceived as the main focus of global public health. It was given high priority in the World Health Organization (WHO) as the designated UN agency mandated to set health standards and to promote 'physical, mental and social health', as stated in the WHO Constitution. This view was shared by a group of well-defined international institutions and the Red Cross–Red Crescent system. However, there have been significant changes since. The AIDS Pandemic (recognised in about 1984–85) mobilised civil society, particularly in the Western Hemisphere on a large scale and encouraged the health industry (particularly pharmaceutical producers) to become involved. When it was realised that AIDS-related diseases (such as tuberculosis) were re-emerging on a large scale, private foundations (such as Carter and Bill and Melinda Gates) began to engage in public health. In this constellation, the notion of 'public–private partnerships' (PPP) was conceived and systematically explored around 1990. Ethical and legal implications of health governance in a changing world came to the forefront of the shifting global health agenda. This led to a fundamental revision of international health regulations.

As a result, global health **policy** and governance are increasingly shared by a broad international and private group of public health promoters, and the monopolistic role of WHO as international standard setter has been increasingly eroded. The resulting international health policy landscape in the twenty-first century is now populated by initiatives that have emerged from the broadened range of health policy stakeholders such as large foundations. These are called Global Emergency Health Initiatives (GEHI) – also called Private–Public Partnerships in Emergencies (PPPiE). In order to improve the performance of these recent initiatives, certain essential functions of prevention and control must be agreed upon. The core functions in this system transcend the sovereignty of any one nation-state (Jamison *et al.*1998) and can be summarised as:

- *promotion of international public goods in health*, e.g. research and development; documentation, training, etc.;
- *surveillance and control of international priorities*, e.g. environmental risks and spread of pathogens;
- *development and application of standards*, e.g. health facility safety and functionality in disasters, minimum standards of health protection in disaster such as Sphere standards (Sphere 2011).

Despite all this activity, some reflections on the current global health situation have led to the conclusion that worldwide health management is a disaster in itself. Garrett (2007) cites the following to justify such a claim:

- Negative biomedical statistical trends, e.g. static maternal mortality; resurgent tuberculosis; little progress in immunisation coverage in some countries; high malaria morbidity and mortality rates despite Global Fund inputs.
- Poor functioning of social welfare systems.
- Privatisation of health in a neo-liberal era.
- Disastrous effects of globalisation, e.g. poor living conditions and health of migrant labour, trafficking of women and children, rising food prices, adulterated and counterfeit pharmaceuticals.
- Underachievement of the Millennium Development Goals, e.g. poorest achievement in areas of maternal mortality, global food security rates and chronic malnutrition.

The food price crisis of 2007/8 had a huge impact on numbers of people at risk in any natural and complex emergency (UN/SCN 2009). The lessons drawn from the Niger crisis in 2005 had given advance warning and eventually helped to refocus on nutrition in the development agenda. Despite dissenting voices (Franke and Chasin 1980; Meillassoux 1973; Wisner 1988), earlier famines and massive epidemics of malnutrition were understood as linked exclusively to natural hazard events such as drought and flood. However, more recently the role of social, economic and political factors has been recognised (Wisner *et al.* 2004). This made it easier to identify at-risk groups early on and prospectively. Innovation in the social science approach to food crisis ran parallel with acceleration in technological development (e.g. lipid-based foods used as supplement carriers for nutritional rehabilitation) as well as innovation in community-based rehabilitation techniques and logistics (MSF 2007). The combination of social and technological approaches has saved many lives.

Health management in disasters 'à la carte': the essential menu

As result of the increasing number, size and severity of humanitarian crises during the 1990s, a large number guides and textbooks were produced in order to rationalise the practice of 'health in disasters'. A good summary of relevant websites and resources can be found in the Health Services chapter of *Forced Migration on Line* (Refugee Studies Centre 2009) and in the review by Keim and Abrahams (2012). Within the limitations of this chapter only some essential approaches are highlighted, looking mainly at 'Why?' and 'How to?' questions.

Health system preparedness

In 2007, the WHO undertook a global survey assessing national health sector emergency preparedness and response. As a consequence, the WHO developed a six-year strategy for developing capacities in the health sector and in communities. While major emergencies are often unpredictable, much can be done to prevent and mitigate their effects as well as to strengthen the response capacity of communities at risk. As the lead agency for addressing the health aspects of emergency preparedness and response, the WHO developed a strategy to help mitigate the effects of crises, coordinate the response and thus save lives and reduce suffering (WHO 2007a).

Many countries have not yet developed mass casualty management plans, and communities are too often left alone to develop preparedness and response plans. Building capacity at the **community** level to develop emergency management plans for mass casualty incidents requires strong involvement by health authorities at all levels, especially the national level, as well as support from other sectors. In September 2006, the WHO held a global consultation on mass casualty management (Cooper 2006) that explored these issues.

There are now minimum standards of preparedness in WHO country offices. All aspects of eventual emergencies and crises need to be covered by a preparedness plan to be activated immediately once the government and the UN Country Team declare a state of emergency. Specific plans include health preparedness and response to chemical and nuclear incidents and emergencies and include the development of a national plan for action.

Finally, the WHO has been active since 2008 in a worldwide effort to promote and facilitate the protection of health facilities (hospitals, health centres, dispensaries) from hazards such as earthquake and high winds. This involves inspections of facilities and their sites and possible investment in retrofitting them, as well as careful selection of new sites, hazard-aware design, and scrupulous inspection of construction practices (WHO 2010) (see Chapter 8 in this volume).

Minimum health standards: the Sphere Project

The Sphere Project originated in 1995 as a response to the Rwanda refugee crisis and the tragic cholera outbreak in Goma, Zaire (Epidemiology Group 1995). When public health response in emergencies is poorly designed, coordinated and executed, a large number of preventable deaths will occur (Salama *et al.* 2004). The growing number of humanitarian agencies in Zaire (now the Democratic Republic of Congo) at that time, each with its own mission, strategies and systems of accountability, further complicated efforts to ensure the quality and precision of humanitarian assistance. The evidence base underlying humanitarian action was at best sketchy in that period, with few established 'best practices' and no generally agreed standards.

Against this background, a broad crosssection of NGOs committed to collaborate on a process, initiated by the International Federation of Red Cross and Red Crescent Societies (IFRC) that would promote the quality and accountability of disaster response. The resulting Sphere standards and their associated indicators represent perhaps the most significant development in the theory and practice of humanitarian health assistance in the past few decades (Sphere 2011: 287–337). For the first time, disaster-affected populations, humanitarian agencies, governments and donors could refer to established standards of service that have been generally accepted as 'industry norms'. However, Sphere is more than a collection of technical standards. The basic philosophy of the Sphere approach (the Humanitarian Charter), developed in consultation with all actors working on a new disaster ethics in the 1990s, has contributed to the Global Health Initiatives mentioned earlier.

Through the Humanitarian Charter that represents the cornerstone of the *Handbook*, Sphere also strongly asserts the universal right of individuals to humanitarian assistance; the charter itself is derived from several bodies of international law (Carmault and Haeni Dale 2012) and is based on a number of core principles:

- All possible steps must be taken to minimise suffering in disasters and emergencies.
- A distinction between combatants and non-combatants must be maintained, as well as the principle of non-refoulement (commitment not to returning refugees to places where their lives would be in danger).

- Disaster-affected people have a right to life with dignity and a right to health.
- The accountability of states and humanitarian agencies needs to be improved.

Sphere represents a unique voluntary initiative, triggering new initiatives to global health governance and reflecting the collective will and shared experience of a broad array of humanitarian actors. Partners include international and national non-governmental organisations, the IFRC, United Nations agencies, donor agencies, host governments, and representatives from affected populations. After the production and testing the initial *Handbook*, a small project team developed the 'Minimum Standards' over the years, based in the IFRC. Since its inception, the Sphere process has endeavoured to be inclusive, transparent, and globally representative. Support services are available to all interested parties (http://www.sphereproject.org/).

Box 11.1 Sphere guiding principles and strategic objectives

The guiding principles for the Sphere project are based on:

- international humanitarian law, human rights and refugee law;
- the Code of Conduct: Principles of Conduct for the IFRC Movement and NGOs in Disaster Response Programmes.

There are five strategic objectives:

1 To improve the commitment to and effective use of Sphere by all actors involved in humanitarian action.
2 To strengthen the diversity and regional balance of organisations in the governance and implementation of Sphere.
3 To develop and nurture a cadre of people who are able to use Sphere effectively.
4 To coordinate and interact with other humanitarian activities, and work together when that complements Sphere's aim.
5 To make Sphere widely understood and increase its impact.

Public health and environmental health in disasters

A number of resources exist to guide planning and practice in the areas of public and environmental health in disasters. Johns Hopkins University and the International Red Cross/Red Crescent have produced a guide called *Public Health Guide in Emergencies* (Johns Hopkins and IFRC 2008). The second edition of this volume is an action-oriented book to help implementers manage emergencies on a solid footing. It provides scientific guidance in practical terms toward the solution of the many technical and management issues that challenge health workers in disasters associated with a variety of triggers: technology failure, natural hazard and conflict. All phases of disasters from prevention to recovery are covered. The analysis of *health systems and infrastructure* closely follows the Sphere standards. Emphasis is given to support for local health services, which often are inadequate to meet needs in an emergency. Capacity building is therefore a major objective in prioritising health services and includes the essential tasks:

- development of capacity to conduct an initial assessment;
- identification of the major causes of morbidity and mortality;
- use of evidence-based intervention to address major causes of morbidity and mortality;
- development of a health information system to identify epidemics and guide changes needed in interventions.

All four tasks require specific skills, which are applied through standard protocols, which in turn are clearly quantifiable. The degree of health system competence determines the efficacy and efficiency of disaster response outcomes.

Perhaps one of the most important developments in emergency management (see Chapter 9) has been that of the Incident Command System (ICS) (Johns Hopkins and IFRC 2008; López-Carresi 2012). This is particularly important in low-income countries that typically have a heavily centralised hierarchy, where implementation of command from the site of the incident can greatly improve responsiveness. The ICS is a vertical command structure that plans, controls and coordinates an effective emergency response among all the agencies involved in a disaster. It is designed to organise all the vital **resources** for allocation to the affected population. The ICS is composed of five major components (Ciottone 2006):

- Coordination
- Operations
- Planning
- Logistics
- Finance.

The ICS and the corresponding Hospital Emergency Incident Command System (HEICS) are not yet used as disaster management tools worldwide and even less so in low-income countries. However, ICS and HEICS are progressively being introduced and incorporated in disaster preparedness plans.

The role of water and sanitation in emergencies and disasters

Most epidemic diseases in disaster situations are related to the disruption of safe water supplies, destruction of housing and the sanitation infrastructure. There are now widely agreed basic standards and there is ample evidence that the use of these measures is very effective in emergencies affecting large populations. Relief workers need competence to identify and quantify problems of water supply, sanitation and the hygienic situation of affected populations in an emergency

(Wisner and Adams 2003). Likewise, basic know-how in the installation of control measures for environmental health problems is a necessary competence of any relief team. The assessment and prediction of long-term problems in this realm are a core activity of assessment in order to optimise not only health outcomes but also social cohesion in the rehabilitation phase. The Sphere standards mentioned earlier also cover water and sanitation.

Few emergencies leave people displaced for only a short time. Since emergencies result in stress, fatigue and other ailments apart from injuries, unsanitary living conditions such as substandard sanitation, inadequate water supplies and poor hygiene, make disaster-affected people particularly vulnerable to disease and increased stress. In this respect, **households** headed by children, people scattered among the host community, and those without **access** to the administrative focus of relief assistance are of high priority, but are often overlooked, since relief efforts concentrate on the 'classic' vulnerable groups (children, pregnant and lactating women, and old people) (OXFAM 1999).

Water-, sanitation- and hygiene-related diseases are controllable and preventable. Most death and morbidity due to diarrhoeas, together with other preventable diseases, including acute respiratory infection, measles, malaria and malnutrition, must be classified as excessive since they are caused by inadequate prevention (WHO 2005). These are the most common causes of death in any emergency. Risk factors are known and are present in most waterborne, water-washed, water-based, food-borne and vector-borne illnesses. The greatest killers are diarrhoeas and upper respiratory infections, especially in children.

The full **participation** of disaster-affected communities in the planning, establishment and control of sanitation and hygiene measures is essential in the control of preventable infectious diseases. In most case studies that have been evaluated, the positive role of community volunteers has been emphasised (Davis and Lambert 2002).

Epidemiological assessments and surveillance in emergencies and disasters

Epidemiology is a fundamental tool in emergency management (CDC 2012; OFDA 2004). Disasters triggered by natural hazards, including those further complicated by conflict and/or breakdown of techno-social systems, are often followed by disease as a secondary hazard. Also, epidemic disease may have disastrous consequences in its own right (Dibben 2012). Planning and priority setting are possible using rates, ratios and event counting. Outbreak investigations and surveys are the basic methods to determine needs and measure changes of health management requirements. Control of communicable diseases is an ongoing process analysed with epidemiological methods; likewise, the assessment of risk and the prediction of future **vulnerability** require probability assessments. The management of certain diseases, such as malaria, tuberculosis, meningitis and diarrhoeas are hard to control in normal circumstances and require constant epidemiological vigilance in emergencies.

Relief workers need training in the collection and basic analysis of reliable findings in order to improve essential health care in emergency response; however, applied epidemiology is also used to determine the long-term requirements of affected communities. Basic needs in the disaster preparedness phase include village **mapping**, identification and counting of special vulnerable groups who are at high risk from disease. These skills are highly valuable for communities far beyond any given emergency, since they increase the ownership of decision-making in communities.

The following *overall epidemiological objectives* in all emergencies must include:

- *identification* of priority health needs during and after a disaster;
- *measuring* extent and severity of disease in affected communities;
- *determining* the cause of disease and risk to different populations by age, etc.
- *prioritisation* of health interventions as a result of initial assessment;
- *surveillance* of disease trends during disaster response;
- *measurement* of efficiency and impact of disease control programmes;
- *inventory* of damage and destruction in the health infrastructure including loss of health workers.

Practical experience (e.g. conflict displacement in Darfur; Sri Lanka's post-tsunami situation; Haiti post-earthquake) have simplified and standardised epidemiological methods in the areas of Rapid Needs Assessment (RNA), demographic studies, the estimation of death rate, incidence and prevalence[1] of disease, and nutrition and immunisation status of affected populations (CDC 2012).

Public health surveillance in the recovery phase of disasters in many countries is now a routine activity of the health sector and has a positive impact on the quality and precision of routinely collected health statistics (WHO/GOARN 2009). As a consequence, prediction of epidemic outbreaks has become easier, so that early and seasonal resource deployment in crisis regions has often become a routine activity (e.g. health planning for the annual Islamic pilgrimage to Saudi Arabia).

Main constraints in epidemiologic assessments are still due to the poor understanding of epidemiologic principles and measurement techniques by many health staff. Medical training in many countries does not include public health issues in sufficient depth and emergency response is often perceived as a clinical subject. Also, because of the unpredictability of disasters, in most countries, disaster response is entrusted to the civil defence, the military or non-governmental institutions (e.g. the Red Cross/Red Crescent). The consequence is a large turnover of staff with inadequate routine experience.

In many countries insufficient resources are allocated to the processing of information, often leading to wrong estimates of population size and consequent erroneous resource allocations. Since survey samples might not represent all of the affected population, it becomes difficult to investigate long-term needs and to develop exit strategies for the disaster response. In conflict situations there is often lack of support for the assessment of needs for the internally displaced, particularly when governments are part of the conflict (Wisner 2012). Since the original mandate of UNHCR does not cover internally displaced persons (IDPs), the situation may deteriorate further.

Participatory epidemiology has become an important technique in the estimation of post-emergency populations, when reliable information from census or registration is lacking (Catley *et al.* 2011; Jost *et al.* 2007). With a group of individual members representing all affected population groups, boundaries and important landmarks of affected zones are mapped, and progressively settlements and estimated numbers of affected people are included. These semi-quantitative estimates have proven surprisingly accurate, particularly in conflict-affected emergencies, when strategic consideration by the conflict parties might make official information unavailable.

Judging the quality of mortality surveillance data is crucial for planning specific public health measures over time, and it should therefore be entrusted to members of the assessment team with considerable experience. The calculations of crude mortality rates (CMR) and under-five mortality rates (U5MR) are very sensitive to the number used to estimate the population size (denominator). A reliable estimate is therefore crucial for eventual interventions, particularly since in small populations CMR and U5MR might 'jump' over time (Checchi and Roberts 2005).

Reproductive health care in emergencies and disasters

Until recently, reproductive health care in emergencies had been a neglected area of relief work, when it was not realised that poor care in this area is a significant cause of death and disease, particularly among refugee populations living in camps, and displaced persons. The following statistics underline the importance of reproductive health care:

- 75 per cent of most refugee populations are women and children, including about 30 per cent who are adolescents;
- 25 per cent are in the reproductive stage of their lives, at 15–45 years old;
- 20 per cent of women of reproductive age (15–45), including refugees and the internally displaced, are pregnant;
- more than 200 million women who want to limit or space their pregnancies lack the means to do so effectively;
- in developing countries, women's risk of dying from pregnancy and childbirth is 1 in 48. Additionally, it is estimated that every year more than 50 million women experience pregnancy-related complications, many of which result in long-term illness or disability (White Ribbon Alliance for Safe Motherhood 2006).

The introduction of the Minimum Initial Services Package (MISP) (Box 11.2) has enormously increased the efficiency of a comprehensive response in reproductive

---

Box 11.2 The Minimum Initial Services Package for reproductive health in emergencies

The Minimum Initial Services Package (MISP) (see: Sphere Project 2011) should always focus on four priorities:

1   Safe motherhood (antenatal care, delivery care, and postpartum care).
2   Family planning.
3   Prevention and care of sexually transmitted infections (STI) and HIV/AIDS.
4   Prevention from and response to sexual and gender-based violence.

The MISP for reproductive health is a coordinated set of priority activities designed to do the following:

• Prevent and manage the consequences of sexual violence.
• Reduce HIV transmission.
• Prevent excess maternal and neonatal mortality and morbidity.
• Plan for comprehensive reproductive health services in the early days and weeks of an emergency.

---

health during the initial phase of an emergency involving large number of people (refugees, IDPs), mostly composed of women and children (RHRC 2012).

The *Field Manual* by the IAWG (Inter-agency Working Group on Reproductive Health in Crises) (IAWG 2010) is an excellent source of information for reproductive health service delivery in crises.

As highlighted in the MISP objectives and activities, four core reproductive health services are required in all emergencies:

Family planning

•   Contraceptives available on demand, if possible.
•   Sustainable access to a range of contraceptive methods.
•   Staff training.
•   Community information, education and communication.

Avoiding sexual and gender-based violence (GBV)

•   Setting up systems to prevent sexual violence.
•   Health services available to survivors of sexual violence.
•   Staff training in sexual violence prevention and response systems.
•   Medical, psychological and legal care for survivors.
•   Prevention of all forms of GBV, including domestic violence, forced/early marriage, female genital cutting, and trafficking.

Safe motherhood

- Clean delivery kits.
- Midwife delivery kits.
- Referral systems for obstetric emergencies.
- Antenatal care.
- Postnatal care.
- Training of traditional birth attendants and midwives.

Avoiding STI/HIV/AIDS

- Access to free condoms.
- Adherence to universal precautions.
- Safe blood transfusions.
- Identification and management of sexually transmitted infections (STIs).
- Raising awareness of prevention and treatment services for STIs/HIV.
- Procurement of antibiotics and other relevant drugs as appropriate.
- Care, support, and treatment for people living with HIV/AIDS.
- Provision of community information, education and communication.

Global public health risks in the twenty-first century

A sea change in the approach to health security

In 1951, the WHO issued the first legally binding health regulations with the aim of preventing the international spread of six diseases: cholera, plague, relapsing fever, smallpox, typhus and yellow fever. Since then, the situation has changed through the effects of globalisation, population growth and migration, as well as incursion into formerly non-settled areas, rapid urbanisation, innovative and intensive farming methods, environmental degradation and the misuse of antibiotics, which has disrupted the equilibrium of the microbial world.

The global disease situation at the beginning of the third millennium is highly unstable, with new diseases emerging at an unprecedented rate. The high capacity of international air travel – nearly two billion per year (IATA 2010) – provides infectious organisms as well as their vectors the opportunity for rapid spread of disease. Climate change is likely to change disease vector habitats and patterns of human disease. Also the worldwide industrialisation of food production, processing and marketing can change a local disease outbreak into a potentially international threat. At the same time, the resistance of microbes to antibiotics is growing at a faster rate than the emergence of new infectious microbial strains.

Priority discussion of global health has turned, since the less complex decade of the 1950s, to how to protect the world from pandemics and new diseases, the health consequences of conflict, bioterrorism and the secondary health consequences of natural hazards events. The tools for this collective defence include the revised International Health Regulations (IHR) (WHO 2007b). These are an international legal instrument designed to achieve maximum security against the international spread of disease. They also aim to reduce the international impact of public health emergencies. The IHR expand the focus of defence from a few infectious diseases to include 'any emergency with international repercussions for health', including the outbreak of emerging and epidemic-prone disease, food-borne disease, disasters following natural hazards and chemical or radio-nuclear events, whether accidental or caused deliberately. The IHRs provide a strategy of proactive risk management and move away from the traditional focus on passive controls at border crossings. Recognising the importance of rapid response, the new regulations require that member states report potential public health emergencies to the WHO within 24 hours after they have identified and assessed them. The new regulations also allow the WHO to consider unofficial 'reports from sources other than notifications or consultations'.

For many developing countries, early detection and reporting of a public health emergency may be of little benefit if the country lacks the capacity to control the outbreak in its early stage. Early reporting could also trigger the rapid closure of international borders to travel and trade, which could be devastating to their economy. Furthermore, investment in surveillance infrastructure, also required by the regulations, may divert scarce resources away from areas of public health that have greater need, such as the treatment and control of tuberculosis, malaria and HIV/AIDS (Calain 2007). Efforts to control influenza worldwide in the 2000s revealed tensions that might undermine the IHRs. This is due to the economic concerns of low-income countries. Current arrangements were partly responsible for Indonesia's decision in 2008 to withhold virus samples from the WHO (Fidler 2008).

On the other side of the world, in the USA, the proposed Global Pathogen Surveillance Act (GPSA) would make the provision of financial assistance to poorer countries to develop the capacity to detect and respond to public health threats conditional on permitting investigation of outbreaks by the US Centers for Disease Control and Prevention and the WHO, and on the transfer of surveillance data (Mitka 2006). The US Department of Defense's Global Emerging Infections Surveillance and Response System (GEIS) is a network of overseas centres that independently conducts global infection disease surveillance (Culpepper and Kelley 2002).

Neglected Tropical Diseases (NTD)

Over one billion people are affected by one or more NTDs. They are called *neglected* because these diseases persist exclusively in the poorest and the most marginalised communities, and have been largely forgotten elsewhere. There are 20 diseases and conditions currently listed as NDTs (WHO 2012), and most can be prevented and eliminated. They thrive in places with unsafe water, poor sanitation and limited access to basic health care. They cause severe pain and life-long disabilities, and thus erode productivity and livelihood security. In addition, these patients and their families are less able to engage in activities and make investment that make their homes and livelihoods safer from natural hazards such as floods and storms. Their capacity to adapt to climate change is reduced and they are more vulnerable to natural extreme events (Wisner *et al.* 2012) (see Chapter 2). These diseases are less visible and have therefore low priority in complex emergencies occurring in low-income populations in remote rural areas, urban slums or conflict zones. They affect people with little political voice. Some NTDs can be tackled with simple and affordable diagnostic tools which cost as little as 4 US cents per test. The rest require skilled health workers and hospitalisation.

The economic impact of NTDs is staggering. The case of river blindness (onchocerciasis) shows the scale of NTDs on food security and economic prosperity. Over 25 million hectares of fertile land in West Africa were resettled for crop growing and cattle-raising after an effective prevention strategy and treatment was found and systematically applied in the affected countries (WHO 2002). There are other success stories in the management of complex chronic health emergencies in the past 20 years. For example, 116 of 122 endemic countries have eliminated leprosy as a public health problem since the introduction of multi-drug therapy in 1985, and 14.5 million people have been cured of leprosy (Shaikh 2011).

NTDs are now high on the international health and disaster prevention agendas. The successes achieved to date prove that the interventions are technically feasible, immediate, visibly powerful and highly cost effective. They demonstrate that programmes to tackle NTDs can be rapidly scaled up to prevent future economic disasters.

Conclusion

In the past few decades, increasing numbers of emergencies and disasters disproportionately have burdened the health systems in low-income and middle-income countries. Pandemics and re-emerging diseases have contributed to the disaster-caused disease burden. For instance, half the world's population is at risk of contracting malaria and about one million out of an estimated 250 million people with malaria died of the disease in 2006 (WHO 2008). Since 2000, several Global Initiatives for Emergency Health (GIEH) have resulted in a concerted response to such challenges. GIEHs have capitalised on the urgency that has been generated by the media, but also by the adoption of the Millennium Development Goals (United Nations 2000). GIEHs show the increased involvement of the private (NGO) sector, philanthropic trusts and civil society in health care.

GIEHs have rapidly become an essential part of the established international health emergency framework and have been used to leverage substantial additional financial and technical resources for targeted health interventions in emergencies. Additional resources on a large scale have been provided for emergency health systems in low-income countries, but the effects of these increased resources have not been evaluated. The involvement of new groups of people (notably civil society organisations) in this debate has garnered the political will of donors and led to an increased focus on social justice.

Decades of neglect and insufficient investment have weakened health systems in most developing countries (United Nations General Assembly 2001). Structural adjustment policies, that were designed to improve the stability of fragile econ-omies, have led to cuts in public spending and the maldevelopment of effective health disaster management. Moreover, the globalisation of labour markets accelerated during the 1990s, increasing the emigration of health workers from the countries that had invested in their training.

Although new resources, new partners, the technical capacity and the political commitment were generally welcomed, critics soon began to argue that increased efforts to meet minimum standards in disaster preparedness and response with selective interventions were exacerbating the burden on already fragile health systems. While the positive effects of GIEHs are unquestionable, they are limited by the weaknesses of country systems, such as inadequate infrastructure, shortages of trained health workers, the interruption in the procurement and supply of health products, insufficient health information and poor governance (Atun *et al.* 2008; Bill and Melinda Gates Foundation and McKinsey and Company 2005; WHO 2009; WHO, UNAIDS and UNICEF 2008). The resulting tensions have contributed to a long-standing debate about the interplay of disease-specific pro-grammes or selected health interventions versus integrated health systems in emergencies. These problems need to be addressed urgently as it is likely that climate change and continuing violent conflict will increase even further the demands on the emergency health care sector.

Note

1   *Incidence* refers to the number of new cases of disease during a set period of time; while *prevalence* is the total number of people suffering from the disease during that time period.

References

Atun, R., Bennett, S. and Duran, A. (2008) 'When do vertical (stand-alone) programs have a place in health systems?', Health Systems and Policy Analysis Policy Brief, Copen-hagen: WHO/EURO.

Bill and Melinda Gates Foundation and McKinsey and Company (2005) 'Global health partnerships: assessing country consequences', paper presented at High-Level Forum on the Health MDGs, Paris, Nov. 14–15.

Calain, P. (2007) 'Exploring the international arena of global public health surveillance', *Health Policy Planning*, 22(1): 2–12.

Carmault, J. and Haeni Dale, C. (2012) 'Human rights and disaster', in B. Wisner, JC Gaillard and I. Kelman (eds) *The Routledge Handbook of Hazards and Disaster Risk Reduction*, London: Routledge, pp. 61–70.

Catley, A., Alders, R. and Wood, J. (2011) 'Participatory epidemiology: approaches, methods, experiences', *The Veterinary Journal*, 191(2): 151–60. Available at: http://origem.info/FIC/pdf/catley_participatory_epidemiology_Vet_J_2011.pdf (accessed 15 March 2012).

CDC (US Centers for Disease Control and Prevention) (2012) *Health Surveillance after a Disaster*, Atlanta: CDC. Available at: http://www.cdc.gov/nceh/hsb/disaster/surveillance.htm (accessed 15 March 2013).

Checchi, F. and Roberts, L. (2005) *Interpreting and Using Mortality Data in Humanitarian Emergencies: A Primer for Non-epidemiologists*, Humanitarian Practice Network Paper 52, London: Overseas Development Institute. Available at: http://www.odihpn.org/documents/networkpaper052.pdf (accessed 15 March 2013).

Ciottone, G. (2006) *Disaster Medicine*, Boston: Mosby.

Cooper, D. (2006) *Mass Casualty Management in Disasters: Executive Summary*, Geneva: WHO. Available at: http://www.who.int/hac/events/experts2006/D_Cooper_Mass_casualth_disasters.pdf (accessed 15 March 2013).

Culpepper, R. and Kelley, P. (2002) 'DoD-Global emerging infectious surveillance and response system', *Navy Medicine*, 93: 10–14.

Davis, J. and Lambert, R. (2002) *Engineering in Emergencies: A Practical Guide for Relief Workers*, 2nd edn, London: Intermediate Technology Development Group.

Dibben, C. (2012) 'Human epidemic', in B. Wisner, JC Gaillard and I. Kelman (eds) *The Routledge Handbook of Hazards and Disaster Risk Reduction*, London: Routledge, pp. 361–71.

Epidemiology Group (1995) 'Public health impact of Rwandan refugee crisis: What happened in Goma, Zaire in July, 1994?', *The Lancet*, 245 (8946): 339–44.

Fidler, D. (2008) 'Influenza virus samples, international law and global health diplomacy', *Emerging Infectious Diseases*, 14 (1): 88–94.

Franke, R. and Chasin, B. (1980) *Seeds of Famine*, Montclair, NJ: Allenheld, Osmun.

Garrett, L. (2007) 'The challenge of global health', *Foreign Affairs*, January–February. Available at: http://www.foreignaffairs.com/articles/62268/laurie-garrett/the-challenge-of-global-health (accessed 15 March 2013).

GHSI (2005) 'Strengthening pandemic influenza preparedness and response', World Health Assembly Technical Briefing, Geneva: WHO and GHSI.

IATA (2010) *Fact Sheets*. Available at: http://www.iata.org/pressroom/facts_figures/fact_sheets/pages/iata.aspx (accessed 15 March 2013).

IAWG (2010) *Inter-agency Field Manual on Reproductive Health in Humanitarian Settings*, Geneva: IAWG. Available at: http://www.iawg.net/resources/field_manual.html (accessed 15 March 2013).

Jamison, D., Frenk, J. and Knaul, F. (1998) 'International collective action in health: objectives, functions, and rationale', *The Lancet*, 351 (9101): 514–17.

Johns Hopkins and IFRC (2008) *Public Health Guide in Emergencies*, 2nd edn, Baltimore, MD and Geneva: Bloomfield School of Public Health, Johns Hopkins University and International Federation of Red Cross and Red Crescent Societies. Available at: http://www.jhsph.edu/research/centers-and-institutes/center-for-refugee-and-disaster-response/publications_tools/publications/_CRDR_ICRC_Public_Health_Guide_Book/Forward.pdf (accessed 15 March 2013).

Jost, C., Mariner, J., Roeder, P., Sawitri, E. and Macgregor-Skinner, G. (2007) 'Participatory epidemiology in disease surveillance and research', *Review of Science and Technology*, 26(3): 537–47. Available at: http://www.oie.int/doc/ged/D4693.PDF (accessed 15 March 2013).

Keim, M. and Abrahams, J. (2012) 'Health and disaster', in B. Wisner, JC Gaillard and I. Kelman (eds) *The Routledge Handbook of Hazards and Disaster Risk Reduction*, London: Routledge, pp. 530–42.

López-Carresi, A. (2012) 'Emergency management principles', in B. Wisner, JC Gaillard and I. Kelman (eds) *The Routledge Handbook of Hazards and Disaster Risk Reduction*, London: Routledge, pp. 505–17.

Meillassoux, C. (1973) *Qui se nourrit de la famine en Afrique?*, Paris: Gallimard.

Mitka, M. (2006) 'Global pathogen surveillance', *Journal American Medical Association*, 295 (6): 617.

MSF (Médecins sans Frontières – Niger) (2007) *Une catastrophe si naturelle*, Paris: Karthala.

OFDA (2004) *Field Operations Guide for Disaster Assessment and Response*, Washington, DC: USAID.

OXFAM (1999) *Water Supply and Sanitation in Emergencies*, London: Oxfam.

Pelling, M. and Wisner, B. (eds) (2009) *Disaster Risk Reduction: Cases from Urban Africa*, London: Earthscan.

Perrin, P. (1996) *Handbook on War and Public Health*, Geneva: International Committee of the Red Cross.

Refugee Studies Centre (2009) *Forced Migration on Line: Health Services*, Oxford: Refugee Studies Centre. Available at: http://www.forcedmigration.org/sphere/health.htm (accessed 15 March 2013).

RHRC (2012) *Reproductive Health in Emergencies*, New York: RHRC. Available at: http://www.rhrc.org/resources/index.cfm?sector=er (accessed 15 March 2013).

Salama, P., Spiegel, P., Talley, L. and Waldman, R. (2004) 'Lessons learned from complex emergencies over past decade', *The Lancet*, 264 (9447): 1801–13.

Shaikh, A. (2011) *Four NTD Successes You Should Know About. End the Neglect*, Global Network for Neglected Tropical Diseases. Available at: http://endtheneglect.org/2011/09/four-ntd-successes-you-should-know-about/ (accessed 15 March 2013).

Sphere Project (2011) *Humanitarian Charter and Minimum Standards in Humanitarian Response*, 3rd edn, Geneva: Sphere Project. Available at: http://www.sphereproject.org/handbook/ (accessed 15 March 2013).

United Nations (2000) *United Nations Millennium Declaration*, New York: United Nations.

United Nations General Assembly (2001) *Declaration of Commitment on HIV/AIDS*, New York: United Nations.

UN/SCN (2009) 'Landscape analysis on countries' readiness to accelerate action in nutrition', *SCN News*, 37. Available at: http://www.unscn.org/layout/modules/resources/files/scnnews37.pdf (accessed 15 March 2013).

White Ribbon Alliance for Safe Motherhood (2006) *Fact Sheet: General Information on Safe Motherhood*, Washington, DC: White Ribbon Alliance.

WHO (2002) 'River Blindness campaign ends, West Africans return to fertile farmlands', *Media Center*. Available at: http://www.who.int/mediacentre/news/releases/pr93/en/ (accessed 15 March 2013).

—— (2005) *Communicable Disease Control in Emergencies: A Field Manual*, Geneva: WHO.

—— (2007a) *Risk Reduction and Emergency Preparedness: WHO Six-Year Strategy for the Health Sector and Community Capacity Development*, Geneva: WHO. Available at: http://www.who.int/hac/techguidance/preparedness/emergency_preparedness_eng.pdf (accessed 15 March 2013).

—— (2007b) *World Health Report 2007: A Safer Future. Global Public Health Security in the 21st Century*, Geneva: WHO.

—— (2008) *World Malaria Report*, Geneva: WHO.

—— (2009) *Global Tuberculosis Control 2009: Epidemiology, Strategy, Financing*, Geneva: WHO.

—— (2010) *Hospitals Safe from Disasters*, Geneva: WHO. Available at: http://www.safe hospitals.info/ (accessed 15 March 2013).

—— (2012) *Neglected Tropical Diseases*, Geneva: WHO. Available at: http://www.who.int/neglected_diseases/diseases/en/ (accessed 15 March 2013).

WHO/GOARN (2009) *Global Outbreak Alert and Response Network (GOARN)*, Geneva: WHO/Center for Biosecurity.

WHO, UNAIDS and UNICEF (2008) *Towards Universal Access: Scaling Up Priority HIV/AIDS Interventions in the Health Sector: Progress Report*, Geneva: WHO, UNAIDS and UNICEF.

Wisner, B. (1988) *Power and Need in Africa*, London: Earthscan.

—— (2012) 'Violent conflict, natural hazards and disaster', in B. Wisner, JC Gaillard and I. Kelman (eds) *The Routledge Handbook of Hazards and Disaster Risk Reduction*, London: Routledge, pp. 71–82.

Wisner, B. and Adams, J. (2003) *Guidelines for Health and Environment in Emergencies and Disasters*, Geneva: WHO, UNHCR & IFRC. Available at: http://whqlibdoc.who.int/publications/2002/9241545410_eng.pdf (accessed 15 March 2013).

Wisner, B., Blaikie, P., Cannon, T. and Davis, I. (2004) *At Risk: Natural Hazards, People's Vulnerability and Disasters*, 2nd edn, London: Routledge.

Wisner, B., Gaillard, JC and Kelman, I. (eds) (2012) *The Routledge Handbook of Hazard and Disaster Risk Reduction*, London: Routledge.

12 Disaster insurance for the poor

Mihir Bhatt, Tommy Reynolds and Mehul Pandya

Lessons for practitioners

- There is demand for micro-insurance among the poor.
- Yet pro-poor financial risk transfer initiatives combined with risk reduction measures remain rare.
- Convergence of efforts on the part of researchers, policymakers, donors and risk management practitioners along with affected communities is necessary to move micro-insurance into the mainstream.
- To be viable, risk transfer products need to be appropriately designed and piloting and up-scaling is a long process that requires dedicated local institutions.
- In order to expand awareness of the positive and negative aspects of insurance, agencies working with large groups of children in poor countries should explore options for commercial micro-insurance coverage for partner children and their schools.

Introduction

Due to the combination of high exposure to natural **hazards** and high **vulnerability**, South Asia experiences significant losses to disasters perennially. One study estimates that more than 90 per cent of the Indian population does not benefit from any kind of social protection (ILO 2005: 1). Despite high and steady growth in India, the cycle of disasters and vulnerability deprives many millions of the improvements in living standards that might have accompanied such growth (see Chapter 16).

Economic losses in South Asia

Each year, India suffers disaster losses totalling just under US$1 billion, according to a World Bank study (Lester and Gurenko 2003: 1). On average, direct disaster losses amount to 2 per cent of India's gross domestic product and up to 12 per cent of central government revenues. These estimates do not fully include losses incurred by informal sector businesses and workers, which constitute a major proportion of the economy in India. The Calamity Relief Fund of the Government of India on average spends US$286 million annually towards providing relief for those affected by disasters. Over the past 35 years, India has suffered direct losses of US$30 billion; losses are also increasing: US$9 billion in direct losses were suffered between 1996 and 2000 alone (Lester and Gurenko 2003: 5).

Risk transfer and sharing in Asia-Pacific

The poor in South Asia and elsewhere face the greatest difficulties recovering from disasters (see Chapter 16). Their small but important assets are often not secured, and their financial risks are not spread across insurance markets. These assets are at the heart of their **livelihood** strategies, and their loss makes recovery very difficult (see Chapter 2). According to Munich Re, the proportion of disaster losses in 2005 covered by insurance were 51 and 30 per cent for the Americas and Europe, respectively (Munich Re 2005: 9). Over the same period, only 5 per cent of losses faced in Asian countries were covered by insurance. Moreover, even within Asia, it is mostly the wealthy who purchase and use insurance. In recent years, however, there are signs of change. Insurance penetration grew from 1.93 per cent in 1998–1999 to 3.5 per cent in 2006[1] and life micro-insurance is estimated to reach nearly 14 million individuals in the region (Sinha and Sagar 2009: 16–71).

The region accounts for a large proportion of worldwide fatalities from natural hazard events. In the words of the UN Economic Commission for Asia and the Pacific (ESCAP 2012, p. x):

> In 2011, the Asian and Pacific region paid a huge human toll as a result of natural disasters. In East and North-East Asia almost 21 thousand people died due to natural disasters. In 2011, more than 170 million people in Asia and the Pacific were affected by natural disasters. South-East Asia was particularly hard hit by natural disasters. In 2011 alone, 14.3 million people in South-East Asia were affected by natural disasters.
>
> Of the world's total, in 2011, Asia and the Pacific included 83% of those affected by natural disasters, 81% of deaths due to natural disasters, and 80% of economic damage from natural disasters.

A study by the United Nations Development Programme (UNDP) on the demand for micro-insurance in India projects that the market size could include up to 70 per cent of those earning between one to two US dollars per day (UNDP 2007: 2). Social programmes that extend micro-insurance **access** to poor **households** are emerging as potentially viable mechanisms to minimise the financial exposure of the poor to disasters. But high-risk households are often not aware of the benefits that simple insurance can provide. Viable micro-insurance products must be affordable and available to informed customers.

India recently became one of the first countries to introduce micro-insurance regulations, creating incentives for regulated insurance companies to service traditionally under-serviced segments of the population (rural and poor households).

Although exact numbers are not known, it is expected that these regulations have encouraged further investment and penetration, especially around weather-indexed insurance products which sold over 650,000 policies in 2008 in Rajasthan state alone (Barrett *et al.* 2007: 6). The Government of India has introduced the National Agricultural Insurance Scheme (NAIS) to provide insurance coverage and financial support to farmers in the event of a crop failure due to natural hazards, pest attacks and crop diseases. Moreover, accelerated regulatory changes are taking place and more are to come to invite a greater role for private and foreign investments in the insurance sector. Although these disaster insurance facilities are available in the agricultural sector, mainstreaming risk transfer mechanisms for housing and other business products remains a challenge (GOI 2002).

Risk transfer has also been gaining international attention, which can assist domestic insurers with reinsurance and in refining global best practices in the emerging field of micro-insurance (Table 12.1). The 2009 Global Assessment Report on Disaster Risk Reduction listed the development of local insurance markets as a key issue in the Report's '20-point Plan to Reduce Risk' (UNISDR 2009: 6).

In order to support the growing demand for an evidence base on the impact of micro-insurance from donors, in 2009, AIDMI, in partnership with ProVention Consortium and the International Institute for Applied Systems Analysis (IIASA) led a regional study in South Asia covering five organisations offering disaster micro-insurance from Bangladesh, Sri Lanka and India. A total of 1640 disaster micro-insurance clients and 531 non-insured clients were surveyed and consulted (Chakrabarti *et al.* 2005; ProVention *et al.* n.d.).

Overall, the results of this study showed interest in and willingness to pay for disaster micro-insurance programs in South Asia. The products are reaching poor clients, many who are below the poverty line, highly indebted and employ limited

Table 12.1 Financing modes

Level	Savings	Credit	Investment	Insurance
Poor households	Micro-finance			Micro-insurance
Small businesses				
Middle-income households				
Community			Social funds	
National				Catastrophe Pools
Regional/ International				

Source: O'Donnell (2009: 2).

coping mechanisms after disasters. However, some challenges in claim processing, delay of payments and inadequate total coverage were reported.

The study concluded that the key seems to be awareness and information. The study signalled high demand for disaster micro-insurance after non-insured clients had been given information showing the relevance and pricing of such products as well as the power of organisations to reach more clients simply through outreach. An overwhelming majority (80 per cent) of clients felt that disaster micro-insurance should be promoted to others while only a minority (2.3 per cent) thought it should not.

Micro-finance: forerunner of micro-insurance

In India, micro-finance has made an impressive journey from micro-savings to microcredit and then to a wider range of financial services such as micro-insurance, micro-enterprise development, micro-remittances, and so on. Micro-credit refers to very small loans for unsalaried borrowers with little or no collateral, provided by legally registered institutions (Micro Finance Gateway 2013).

Micro-finance started with Ela Bhatt of the Self Employed Women's Association (SEWA) Bank in 1970s and it preceded the better-known Grameen Bank, pioneered by Professor Mohammed Yunus in Bangladesh by a year. SEWA Bank was the first micro-finance institution in India (Voice of Bharat 2013). In 1973, to address their lack of **access** to financial services, the members of SEWA decided to found 'a bank of their own'. Four thousand women contributed share capital to establish the Mahila SEWA Co-operative Bank (MercyCorps 2006). The microcredit movement in India and Bangladesh in the early 1980s successfully demonstrated that the poor in the informal economy can borrow, save and repay. This ushered in a number of public and private organisations in India with similar programmes and approaches. After a decade-long experimentation and expansion of microcredit services, many organisations recognised that the poor need a full range of micro-finance services to escape **poverty** and **risk**.

This realisation led to development of number of other micro-finance products. Development of micro-insurance products in the disaster and climate change context can be attributed to many but primarily two main reasons.

First, from the client perspective, though micro-savings and microcredit are considered more appropriate in some contexts (where the financial markets, especially the insurance sector, are underdeveloped), they cannot compensate or cover all the losses. Also, borrowing money to recover from disaster losses can be riskier and can potentially result in a debt trap. Indeed, the history of micro-finance is mixed, and there has been some critique of such pitfalls (Ashraf 2011; Karim 2011). Second, from the perspective of the micro-finance institutions (MFIs), a sudden rise in demand for savings withdrawals and emergency loans from those affected by disaster can lead to a short-term liquidity crisis. Additionally, lack of insurance can lead to increased number of defaulters on micro-loans, and in extreme cases MFIs may have to restructure their existing loan portfolios. Thus, an appropriate and viable micro-insurance option can be of great

Table 12.2 Examples of micro-insurance schemes

No.	Scheme
1	National Health Insurance Scheme (Rashtriya Swasthya Bima Yojana - RSBY), India, Government of India, http://www.rsby.gov.in/about_rsby.html
2	Horn of Africa Risk Transfer for Adaptation, Ethiopia, Oxfam America, Swiss Re, http://www.oxfamamerica.org/publications/horn-of-africa-risk-transfer-for-adaptation-harita-quarterly-report-october-20112013december-2011
3	Max Vijay – a life insurance product of Max New York Life Insurance Company in India, http://www.maxvijay.com/products_rajat.aspx
4	Kilimo Salama a weather index-based scheme, Kenya, UAP Insurance and the Syngenta Foundation for Sustainable Agriculture (SFSA), http://www.global-economic-symposium.org/knowledgebase/the-global-environment/meeting-the-rising-global-demand-for-food/implementations/kilimo-salama
5	Housing Insurance, India, GSDMA, http://reliefweb.int/sites/reliefweb.int/files/resources/A8E4E438D6A45E78C12572DE00486DB2-Full_Report.pdf
6	Crop insurance, India, Basix, http://www.basixindia.com/index.php?option=com_content&task=view&id=97&Itemid=113
7	Crop insurance, Sri Lanka, Yasiru, http://www.munichre-foundation.org/dms/MRS/Documents/2007_Microinsurance_conference_documents/MIC2007_WG9_Presentation_SunilSilva.pdf
8	Savings scheme with disaster coverage, Bangladesh, Proshika, http://www.proshika.org/report.html
9	Crop insurance, India, SEWA, http://www.sewainsurance.org/default.asp?ild=2749

use to both clients and MFIs. Overall, this can reduce dependency on external aid following a disaster.

Although the usefulness of micro-finance in the smoothing of socio-economic shocks has long been claimed by the micro-finance community, it is a relatively new topic for the disaster reduction community. In 2008, there were only 22 products marketed under the micro-insurance category in India. Also, coverage of insurance products in India was limited to geographical regions that already had better micro-finance coverage. Table 12.2 shows how different financing modes are used in practice to facilitate management of risk.

Case study of the *Afat Vimo* scheme

The development of Afat Vimo

In the course of work on disasters over a number of years, the All India Disaster Mitigation Institute (AIDMI) found that the poor are repeatedly affected by disaster. One study of the impact of drought on income poverty suggested that the proportion of Indian households in the poverty trap for three to five years jumps from 5.5 per cent to 14.8 per cent when the households face frequent small-scale losses (UNISDR 2009: 8).

This accumulated experienced by AIDMI crystallised during the 18 months following the 2001 Gujarat earthquake. Attending that disaster, AIDMI found that the majority of relief beneficiaries were still exposed to significant disaster-induced financial losses. Relief assistance was not enough to allow them to recover their livelihood assets. A 2002 survey in Gujarat revealed that access to insurance was correlated with sustainable economic recovery among those affected by the earthquake (AIDMI 2002). Yet the survey found that only 2 per cent of those they surveyed had insurance of any kind.

Based on this finding, AIDMI designed a micro-insurance scheme to augment their ongoing Livelihood Relief Fund activities. The resultant scheme was the product of discussions and negotiations with insurance providers who were interested in supplying low-premium insurance policies to poor clients. Two regulated Indian insurers currently underwrite the *Afat Vimo* disaster insurance scheme. The Life Insurance Corporation of India covers life aspects, and the United India Insurance Company provides general coverage.

Afat Vimo: a product for the poor

Afat Vimo is a version of micro-insurance designed for poor households in disaster-prone areas. It protects people from the impacts of hazards on their assets by providing predetermined cash payouts in the aftermath of a disaster. This is done in return for monthly premiums, which are paid to the insurance companies through AIDMI. By bundling several hazards into one contract, premiums paid for better understood hazards further reduce the rates of less predictable ones such as earthquakes. Otherwise, people would be less willing to pay insurance against the less-understood hazards.

While rigorous scientific assessments of the impact of micro-insurance are not yet available (Micro Insurance Network 2009; Radermacher *et al.* 2009: 2), current experience suggests that micro-insurance may increase access to finance after shocks, thus strengthening coping and reducing the likelihood of disastrous long-term consequences on livelihoods and household welfare. Insurance payouts also provide greater discretion to households and small businesses in pursuing coping and recovery strategies.

The scheme covers damages or losses in a very wide range of natural hazards including earthquakes, floods, cyclones, being struck by lightning, landslides (with 19 types of hazard in total). The product was first sold in April 2004 and now covers over 3,700 pioneering policyholders. Though the number is small for India, it is sufficient to start finding out how such ideas can and will operate on the ground. *Afat Vimo* is offered as a single package with an annual premium of around US$4.50 (including administrative charges) and a total potential benefit of US$1,560 across the various components of the coverage. All clients receive the same level of coverage. Table 12.3 provides an overview of the *Afat Vimo* scheme.

Table 12.3 Afat Vimo overview

Aspect/Coverage	Characteristic
Maximum liability for accidental loss of life	Rs. 20,000 ($416)
Maximum liability for damage to house	Rs. 10,000 ($208)
Maximum liability for damage to house contents	Rs. 10,000 ($208)
Maximum liability for stock-in-trade	Rs. 10,000 ($208)
Maximum liability for personal accident	Rs. 25,000 ($520)
Total Coverage	Rs. 75,000 ($1,560)
Annual premium amount	Rs. 220 ($4.50)

Afat Vimo has been developed and remains a product for the working poor. Actuarial calculations are assessed by the underwriting insurance company for the policyholder group, instead of individuals or households, based on the client profile. Typical policyholders have the following characteristics:

- low-income (average annual income between US$370 and US$410);
- average assets worth US$450;
- average monthly savings balance between US$5 to US$10;
- engaged in micro-enterprises in the unorganised sector or as labourers.

Current clients include:

- small business owners (e.g. those with small grocery, confectionaries or snack stalls, etc.);
- small vendors (e.g. those with handcarts selling vegetables, fruits, plastic utensils, etc.);
- home-based workers (e.g. those operating sewing machines, preparing ready-made clothes or weaving products);
- landless labourers (e.g. construction workers and small-scale plumbers, carpenters or barbers).

The poor families targeted are under-reached by mainstream insurance, especially the labourers and micro-enterprise owners. *Afat Vimo* is making progress in bringing together insurance providers and livelihood recovery support in times of disaster.

The operating system

Afat Vimo is a partner-agent micro-insurance model, where poor communities and commercial and public insurance companies have cooperated. The role of AIDMI in the *Afat Vimo* scheme is that of both facilitator and intermediary. At present, AIDMI does not serve as an agent or collect a commission.

The scheme is promoted in areas where AIDMI has ongoing **community** development work and field teams discuss insurance concepts with local households. The *Afat Vimo* team compiles a list of potential candidates for the scheme based on their registered demands. Once the insurance companies have designed operational policies and premiums have been set, AIDMI reconfirms the beneficiaries on the list and ensures that all of the requisite information has been collated and passed to the insurance companies. Policyholders' details are stored in a database kept by AIDMI. Once this is complete, AIDMI pays the premiums to the insurance companies on behalf of the beneficiaries, ensuring immediate coverage. Subsequently, the *Afat Vimo* team begins to collect the premiums from the beneficiaries. The process is effective but time consuming and costly, especially when renewal is optional (Figure 12.1).

If and when disaster strikes, the beneficiary immediately informs the *Afat Vimo* team of the occurrence, and the team responds quickly to process claim (see the case study in Box 12.1). AIDMI assists beneficiaries in filing claims. Since many of the *Afat Vimo* beneficiaries are illiterate or have poor literacy skills, they require such assistance. The need to build this general capability among policyholders is recognised. Therefore, training is provided to help policyholders understand

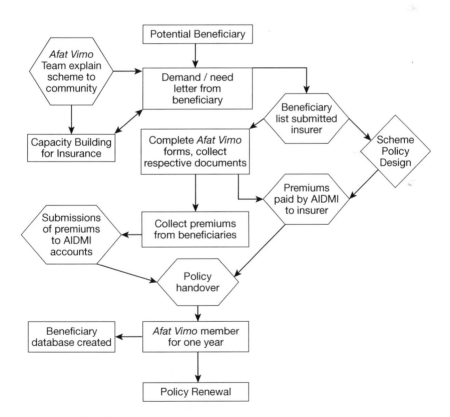

Figure 12.1 The *Afat Vimo* process

exactly how they can best use the policy. The *Afat Vimo* product is currently promoted by a local membership-based organisation called the Chamber of Commerce and Industry for Small Businesses (CCISB) that is a network of small-scale entrepreneurs. CCISB leverages interest in *Afat Vimo* through its close relations across many poor households.

Box 12.1 A young man in the Kajlinagar slum area, Bhuj

This young man was 22 years old when the earthquake hit Bhuj in 2001, destroying his confectionary cabin and its contents, so he sought financial assistance. He received a new cabin and stock worth Rs 8,721 to restart his business. He learned about *Afat Vimo* from the AIDMI team, but at first he did not understand the benefits. He did not see how he could benefit from an insurance policy, which would cost him Rs 135 per annum* when he only earned Rs 50–60 per day. The team explained that it was a one-time payment for coverage that lasted one year. He saw that if he paid a premium of Rs 135, it would give him life and non-life coverage of Rs 95,000. He agreed that it was advantageous and took out a contract.

Unfortunately, he fell seriously ill with jaundice, therefore, he was unable to continue working and so could not afford the necessary medication. He later died from jaundice. He was the only member of his family earning, and his sudden death was a disaster for his elderly parents. However, his parents were aware that he was insured, and immediately informed AIDMI, the intermediary, of his death. AIDMI initiated the claim process with the insurance company, and a payment was made to his parents for Rs 20,000. On receipt of the cheque, his parents explained that although nothing could replace their son or compensate for the personal loss that they had suffered, the cheque was vital for their economic survival. His younger brother said that they deposited Rs 15,000 in the bank for future medical needs, and had used the rest to purchase stock for the confectionary stall. The brother has now taken over the business and is supporting the family.

Note: *The premium and liabilities noted in examples provided are based on rates from prior years and may not match rates provided in Table 12.3.

Feedback from beneficiaries, who have made claims under the *Afat Vimo* policy, has been very positive and encouraging. To date, more than 300 claims have been made to insurance companies. Since the scheme began in 2004, 260 of these claims have been successfully settled, giving a combined payout of US$37,380. Forty-eight claims have been made for loss of life, 52 were for personal accidents (some resulting in fatalities, others causing loss of earnings), six for house fires and 154 for damage to property and contents as a result of monsoon flooding and hazards.

Discussion

Like many forms of micro-insurance, *Afat Vimo* offers several advantages. It is a transparent means of providing compensation against damage. It decreases the need for humanitarian aid. Additionally, micro-insurance offers those affected by disaster a more dignified means to cope with disasters than relying on the generosity of donors after disaster strikes (Mechler *et al.* 2006).

The growth of *Afat Vimo* can be attributed to its affordable premium. This puts insurance within the reach of those who otherwise would not be able to access conventional insurance services. Similarly, the policy has had a great deal of success in the prompt settlement of claims, which has translated into client satis-faction and a good relationship with the insurance companies. It has also contrib-uted to the good policy renewal rate which currently stands at 76 per cent. *Afat Vimo* policyholders are now found across several districts in Gujarat, as well as in Tamil Nadu and Pondicherry in South India.

A particular strength of the *Afat Vimo* scheme is the unified policy design. Under *Afat Vimo*, both life and non-life coverage are brought together under one client product. According to a recent study by the International Labour Office (2005: 7), 45 per cent of micro-insurance schemes in India cover only a single hazard. Only 16 per cent of schemes cover three hazards, making *Afat Vimo* one of the most comprehensive products in India. This not only makes the policy more attractive to clients, but also makes investment in the policy more efficient in economic terms. Another feature of *Afat Vimo* that sets it apart from other micro-insurance policies is the extensive range of eventualities covered under the policy. To combine micro-mitigation with micro-insurance, community **capacity** building and involvement in *Afat Vimo*, including training on insurance concepts and claim administration, has provided more stability and viability.

Afat Vimo promotes learning across insurance companies, authorities, donor communities and NGOs to facilitate the convergence of micro-finance tools and disaster risk reduction strategies. The *Afat Vimo* scheme represents an innovative approach to risk identification, pooling and transfer, which recognises the fact that the majority of poor disaster victims have limited, or no access to risk transfer schemes or programmes.

From the perspective of safer education and education about safety, *Afat Vimo* facilitates an insurance scheme for students and staff members of schools. The insurance is not limited to school hours; it is valid 24 hours a day, 7 days a week, 365 days a year. The insurance premium is around 0.40 US$ per year per insured person and the total policy amount is around US$500. The scheme is reaching out to schools located in poor and disaster-affected areas of different states of India. So far, more than 50,000 students and teachers are covered under the policy. The insurance of school students and teachers is under Child's Right to Safer Schools Campaign.

Afat Vimo is working on a scheme to make closer links with DRR and CCA by encouraging clients individually and in groups to take steps to reduce risk against existing hazards especially in coastal areas. The scheme is important for climate change adaptation in coastal areas.

Though fraud is one of the most common challenges for the micro-insurance sector, so far *Afat Vimo* has experienced very few incidents of false claims. Defaulting on premium payments is another challenge. The retrospective collection of premium payments from clients can be seen as a threat to the long-term sustainability of the *Afat Vimo* scheme. In terms of long-term sustainability, this means that unless the clients meet the full operating costs, perhaps covered by a commission, estimated to add 50 per cent more burden on the client, the scheme is not financially self-sustaining. In addition, there are a number of reasons why beneficiaries do not renew their policies. Migration and the inability to pay are believed to be factors. When exploring the impact of the *Afat Vimo* scheme in disaster-affected areas, Wipf (2008: 22) concluded:

> *Afat Vimo* has a lot of potential. It helped to empower poor people who are left out of other social security systems. The success of *Afat Vimo* can also be seen by the high renewal rates. Additionally, *Afat Vimo* serves as a model for other micro-insurance schemes. It has inspired other NGOs in Sri Lanka and Iran which intend to initiate similar schemes. Besides the potentials, *Afat Vimo* also has a lot of challenges. As AIDMI is a relatively small NGO, with 30 to 40 employees, and *Afat Vimo* is only one of several programs, its capacities are limited. An expansion by the membership of *Afat Vimo* would also mean a sustainable increase in operating costs, at least in the beginning. Because *Afat Vimo* is a pilot project, a lot of resources are demanded and it is more difficult to gain the support of the government or of international institutions.

Conclusion

The process of developing and administering *Afat Vimo* offers many lessons for up-scaling the product and for sharing with other risk transfer stakeholders.

1   Demand exists for disaster micro-insurance but it is not yet clear if potential clients are willing to pay a premium that covers all administrative costs without direct or indirect subsidies.
2   Pro-poor financial risk transfer initiatives combined with risk reduction measures such as *Afat Vimo* remain rare in the South Asian region. The 2007/08 floods in Bihar provided an opportunity for local institutions to extend access to community risk transfer services by discussing insurance concepts with disaster-affected households. It is possible that other disaster recoveries will result in new attention being paid to insurance.
3   Convergence of efforts on the part of researchers, policymakers, donors and risk management practitioners along with affected communities is necessary to move micro-insurance into the mainstream. Generating awareness and building the commitment to initiate micro-insurance cost money, time and effort.
4   To be viable, risk transfer products need to be appropriately designed and piloting and up-scaling are a long process that requires dedicated local

institutions. This needs planning, awareness building and long-term commitment. Pilot initiatives in micro-insurance should be based on medium- and long-term financial plans that emphasise financial viability. A minimum of a three- or five-year horizon for such a plan may help ensure that actions are taken to cover administrative costs in the product model. Options for collecting a commission to offset administration costs should be investigated.

5   Micro-finance organisations and civil society partners may consider bundling existing credit or other financial services with micro-insurance to hedge default risk and extend risk transfer to wider groups of the poor.

6   In order to expand awareness of the positive and negative aspects of insurance, agencies working with large groups of children in poor countries should explore options for commercial micro-insurance coverage for partner children and their schools (see Chapter 6).

Note

1   Insurance penetration is expressed as premiums paid as a percentage of Gross National Income (Micro Insurance Academy 2009).

References

AIDMI (2002) *Community Survey: Gujarat Earthquake 2001*, Ahmedabad and Geneva: AIDMI and ProVention Consortium.

Ashraf, M. (2011) *Microfinance or Debt Trap: Case for Yunus' Grameen Bank in Bangladesh: Income Impact of Grameen Bank on the Rural Poor in Bangladesh*, Saarbrücken: Lap Lambert.

Barrett, C., Barnett, B., Carter, M., Chantarat, S., Hansen, J., Mude, A., Osgood, D., Skees, J., Turvey, C. and Ward, M. (2007) *Index Microinsurance: An Innovative Tool for Risk and Disaster Management Insurance for Climate Risk Management & Poverty Reduction: Topics for Debate*, Palisades, NY: Columbia University, Earth Institute, International Institute for Climate and Society. Available at: http://portal.iri.columbia.edu/portal/server.pt/gateway/PTARGS_0_2_4714_0_0_18/Climate%20and%20Society%20Issue%20Number%202.pdf (accessed 25 March 2013).

Chakrabarti, P.G.D., Kull, D. and Bhatt, M.R. (eds) (2005) *International Workshop on Disaster Risk Mitigation: Potential for Micro-finance for Tsunami Recovery*. Available at: http://www.unisdr.org/2005/campaign/events/iddr-india-workshop.pdf (accessed 25 March 2013).

ESCAP (2012) *Statistical Yearbook for Asia and the Pacific*, Bangkok: ESCAP. Available at: http://www.unescap.org/stat/data/syb2012/did-you-know.asp (accessed 25 March 2013).

GOI (2002) *Tenth Five Year Plan 2002–2007*, New Delhi: GOI.

ILO (2005) *India: An Inventory of Microinsurance Schemes*, Geneva: ILO.

Karim, L. (2011) *Microfinance and Its Discontents: Women in Debt in Bangladesh*, Minneapolis: University of Minnesota Press.

Lester, R. and Gurenko, E. (2003) *India: Financing Rapid Onset Natural Disasters in India: A Risk Management Approach*, World Bank Report No. 26844-IN, New York: World Bank.

Mechler, R., Linnerooth-Bayer, J. and Peppiatt, D. (2006) *Microinsurance for Natural Disaster Risks in Developing Countries: Benefits, Limitations and Viability*, Geneva: ProVention Consortium and IIASA.

MercyCorps (2006) *Global Envision: Exploring Market-Driven Solutions to Poverty, History of Microfinance*, Cambridge, MA: MercyCorps. Available at: http://global envision.org/library/4/1051/ (accessed 25 March 2013).

Micro Finance Gateway (2013) *Home Page*, Washington, DC: CGAP/ Micro Finance Gateway. Available at: http://www.microfinancegateway.org/p/site/m/template.rc/1.26. 1226 (accessed 25 March 2013).

Micro Insurance Academy (2009) *Glossary*. Available at: http://www.microinsurance academy.org/glossary (accessed 25 March 2013).

Micro Insurance Network (2009) *Impact Assessment Working Group*. Luxembourg: Microinsurance network. Available at: http://www.microinsurancenetwork.org/working group4.php (accessed 25 March 2013).

Munich Re (2005) *Annual Review: Natural Catastrophes 2005*, Munich: Munich Re.

O'Donnell, I. (2009) *Global Assessment Report: Practice Review on Innovations in Finance for Disaster Risk Management*, Geneva: ProVention Consortium. Available at: http:// www.preventionweb.net/english/hyogo/gar/background-papers/documents/Chap6/Pro Vention-Risk-financing-practice-review.pdf (accessed 27 March 2013).

ProVention, AIDMI and IIASA (n.d.) *Impact Assessment of Disaster Micro-insurance for Pro-Poor Risk Management: Evidence from South Asia*. Available at: http://www.iiasa. ac.at/Publications/Documents/XO-11-059.pdf (accessed 25 March 2013).

Radermacher, R., Ashok, S., Zabel, K. and Dror, I. (2009) *What Do We Know about the Impact of Microinsurance?*, New Delhi: Micro Insurance Academy.

Sinha, S. and Sagar, S. (2009) *Making Insurance Markets Work for the Poor: Microinsurance Policy, Regulation and Supervision: India Case Study*, Ottawa: IDRC (International Development Research Centre) and CGAP.

UNDP (2007) *Building Security for the Poor: Potential and Prospects for Microinsurance in India*, Colombo: UNDP.

UNISDR (2009) *Global Assessment Report on Disaster Risk Reduction: Risk and Poverty in a Changing Climate*, Geneva: UNISDR.

Voice of Bharat (2013) *Microfinance: India: Voice of Bharat*. Available at: http://www. voiceofbharat.org/microfinance/index.asp (accessed 25 March 2013).

Wipf, C. (2008) 'The impact of AIDMI's microinsurance scheme Afat Vimo in disaster affected areas: a compilation of case studies', unpublished report, Ahmedabad: AIDMI.

13 Post-disaster recovery planning

Introductory notes on its challenges and potentials

Camillo Boano

Lessons for practitioners

- Governments and donors need to be realistic about what is achievable in the short and longer term. Ideally, a comprehensive reconstruction strategy should combine with development planning and address the long-term issues related to disaster reduction.
- Interventions are enhanced and far more responsive to the needs of the affected population through the adoption of a rights-based approach.
- A balanced position on recovery, combining a community-based, enabler approach plus a technology-based provider approach is better able to take account of contextual variations in societies and events.
- Appropriate integration of hardware (physical and material interventions) and software (regulation, local capacities, contacts) can improve interventions in the complex phases of relief and reconstruction.
- While reconstruction of damaged infrastructure is critical, it is inadequate unless local vulnerabilities are identified and effective ways of reducing them are available.

Introduction

Post-disaster reconstruction is a complex process. It deals with the underlying vulnerabilities of the society affected, the stress and pressures that connote its aftermath, and the hopes, challenges and potentials of the future ahead.

Such complexity takes place in different domains. In its political and institutional dimension, multiple actors are involved with often conflicting agendas and visions. In a spatial dimension, massive needs for physical reconstruction of damaged structures, provision of new housing for the affected population, and the conservation and restoration of heritage building challenge a faster response but also open up opportunities for incorporating preventive measures in relation to the occurrence of future possible disasters. In the societal arena, restitutions, compensation, resettlement, loss and death, as well as the erosion of **livelihoods** and security potentially trigger social cohesion and stability or increase social fragmentation.

Though located in the broader discipline of disaster studies and disaster management, this chapter deliberately uses housing and spatial/physical recon-struction as a prominent and specific theme able to illustrate, from a political economy perspective, tensions and challenges of post-disaster recovery.

Response and recovery frameworks

For the purposes of exploring these issues further and examining the ingredients of disaster recovery strategies in more detail, it is useful to look at the frameworks that have been used to describe the stages in response to disasters at the **community** level.

Moe and Pathranarakul (2006) make explicit that disaster management includes five generic phases: prediction, warning, emergency relief, rehabilitation, and reconstruction. They suggest, in line with Alexander (2000), that rehabilitation and reconstruction are two separate phases.

The emergency *relief phase* includes the provision of assistance or intervention during or immediately after a disaster to meet the life preservation and basic needs of affected people. It can be of immediate, short-term or protracted duration. The latter has proved to be problematic and subject to harsh criticism, in partic-ular, underlining **risks** of dependency (Collier 1999; Harrell-Bond 1986, 1999; Lautze and Hammock 1996; Lensink and White 1999) and in the Linking Relief, Rehabilitation and Development debate (LRRD) (Buchanan-Smith and Fabbri 2005; Harmer and Macrae 2004; Zetter 1995). *Rehabilitation* consists of decisions and actions taken after a disaster with a view to restoring or improving the pre-disaster living conditions of the stricken community while encouraging and facilitating the necessary adjustments to reduce disaster risk. *Reconstruction* refers to the rebuilding of damaged living conditions of the stricken community with the aim of long-term economic, environmental and social sustainability (Moe *et al.* 2007: 789).

As noted by Skotte (2004: 2) relief agents – as providers – 'act as an external force with a limited, yet crucial goal: that of saving lives and alleviating suffering'. However, external resources are channelled, using Albala-Bertrand's words (2000: 217), via:

> ad hoc, unpatterned, unguaranteed or irregular processes which are expressed in actions, measures and policies that may formally fill gaps left by in-built responses, bypass endogenous channels, shift initiatives away from regular actors or superimpose alternative structures. This normally implies private and public interventions that go beyond in-built actions, and international assistance and aid, to go beyond existing guarantees.

This superimposition does not happen in a vacuum, but happens in a socially defined context. There are also internal responses in place in the aftermath of a

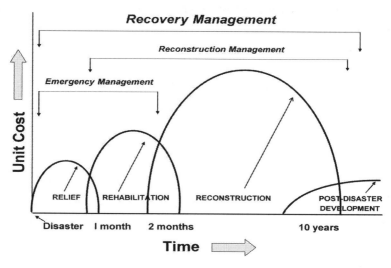

Figure 13.1 Davis's Disaster Cycle
Source: Adapted from Alexander (2000).

disaster. External and internal responses can be linked together and strengthen each other or can clash; failing to improve the situation and disabling the movement towards recovery or development.

Davis (2011), based on Alexander (2000), suggests that the three fundamental stages of post-disaster emergency relief, rehabilitation and reconstruction need to be conceived as all part of recovery management (Figure 13.1). This suggestion emerged from a critique of the so-called *disaster cycle* widely adopted internationally. Although it has the virtue of clearly making evident sequences and relationships before or after a disaster, in practice, it artificially represents a too strict and inflexible reality that happens on the ground. Moreover, the complexity created by multiple stakeholders with different agendas, mandates and attitudes that participate in the different phases of the cycle, makes coordination and the transition of the phases blurred and difficult (see Chapters 14, 15 and 16).

UN agencies have more recently begun to promote the concept of 'transition recovery' for the period during which relief activities have ended, but recovery is yet to begin. One example is in Aceh where, one year after the Indian Ocean tsunami of 2004, large-scale housing reconstruction had yet to begin and 67,000 people remained in temporary barracks or rotting tents (Arnold 2006). While people waited for permanent housing, a programme instituted in the first months of 2006 focused on ensuring that all internally displaced persons (IDPs) had suitable transitional housing. Although the concept of transition recovery is useful for agency planning purposes, the design of new phases reflects the failure of aid agencies to provide adequate support to disaster recovery – just as the very need for disaster reconstruction assistance reflects the failures of development.

In fact, all of these phases are artificial terms. A World Bank (2004) case studies collection concluded that recovery operations converge with the development process and that many communities live in a permanent state of recovery because 'temporary relief' has become a permanent coping strategy. In many countries, 'temporary housing' often becomes permanent housing for the poor and, due to poor timing and construction standards, the cycle of vulnerability continues (Boano 2007; Kreimer 1980; Wilford 2008).

Recovery projects themselves are often too short to address the projected length of recovery. Real-time recovery from a significant disaster can take five years or more. However, donors often have their own timetable which commonly ranges from one to three years. For example, US relief for Honduras following Hurricane Mitch towards the end of 1998 had to be spent by December 2001. Six years later, field assessments revealed that hundreds of people still remained in temporary shelters (Arnold 2006).

In this regard, governments and donors need to be realistic about what can be achieved in the short and longer terms. There is certainly a tendency to take advantage of the brief window of opportunity that these situations provide to incorporate numerous disaster prevention components into emergency operations. An ideal and comprehensive reconstruction strategy should merge with development planning and address the long-term issues related to disaster reduction. However, emergency recovery projects need to take into account the weakened administrative **capacity** that disasters bring, while exploiting the opportunity to strengthen risk management capacity. Emergency operations should focus on urgent reconstruction priorities.

Developmental considerations contribute to all aspects of the disaster management cycle. One of the main goals of disaster management, and one of its strongest links with development, is the promotion of sustainable livelihoods and their protection and recovery during disasters and emergencies. Where this goal is achieved, people have a greater capacity to deal with disasters and their recovery is more rapid and long-lasting. In a development-oriented disaster management approach, the objectives are to reduce **hazards**, prevent disasters and prepare for emergencies. Therefore, developmental considerations should be represented strongly in the **mitigation** and preparedness phases of the disaster management cycle. Inappropriate development processes can lead to increased vulnerability to disasters and loss of preparedness for emergency situations.

Recovery and reconstruction: housing and the built environment

Although there is general agreement that post-disaster reconstruction is a complex issue with several dimensions to be considered, there is an implicit assumption that approaches towards reconstruction are decided by funding agencies and implemented through a linear process based on consensus around needs, priorities and fixed implementation mechanisms. Often, such processes are implemented by governments in a bureaucratic and centralised manner or managed by newly created governmental bodies that emerge in the wake of the event, fully nourished by political tensions and expectations. Such complexity often leads to 'reconstruction discontents', a recurrent pessimism in disaster studies evidenced since the 1970s by Cuny (1978), through the 1990s by Aysan (1991) and more recently by Sanderson and Sharma (2008: 185).

Pessimism based on such experiences is visible when dealing with housing reconstruction especially. Because it is conceived as a basic need and fundamental right, and compounded by high visibility, housing tends to get a prominent role in the reconstruction and recovery debate. However, this opens up the risk of simply reducing reconstruction to physical housing reconstruction.

Such a debate is being reinvigorated by a growing body of literature that recognises the poor outcome of reconstruction projects within different clusters of studies. For example, on poor technological solutions (Duyne Barenstein and Pittet 2007; Lloyd-Jones 2006; Sanderson and Sharma 2008; Twigg 2006); on poor participatory approaches (Davidson *et al.* 2007; El-Masri and Kellett 2001; Lizarralde 2002); on conflictive reconstruction policies (Boano 2009; Boano and Hunter 2012); on resettlement and social disruption (Badri *et al.* 2006; Menoni and Pesaro 2008); on poor consideration of land tenure issues and land management (Keivani and Werna 2001; LeGrand 2004); on the poor incorporation of disaster risk reduction elements (Hamza and Zetter 1998; Wamsler 2006a, 2006b); on the poor recognition of the sociocultural context (Boen and Jigyasu 2005) and the reproduction of vulnerabilities (Birkman and Fernando 2008; Ingram *et al.* 2006).

Although from a conceptual point of view considerable progress has been made since Ian Davis's publication in 1987 of *Shelter after Disasters*, both in emergency shelter and in post-disaster settlement and reconstruction, in practice it appears that, in post-disaster reconstruction, we are 'condemned to repeat' (Davis 2011; Terry 2002).

Assistance after major disasters has become more international with massive flows of aid, both from government and private donors; this is mainly channelled through INGOs (Telford and Cosgrave 2007), becoming a globalized industry (Alexander 2006). At the **policy** level, a greater institutionalization of shelter and housing issues has emerged as a major trend thanks to specialized centres (e.g. Sheltercentre) and platforms (e.g. ProVention Consortium; International Recovery Platform), with a further increase in humanitarian reform and the adoption of the cluster strategy (ODI 2005; UN/OCHA 2005). In such circles, since the UNDRO guidelines, the central issue of *continuum*, from shelter to housing, has been reinforced and crystallized around the recent term *transitional* (Corsellis and Vitale 2005; ShelterCentre/UNOCHA 2008) which is used to stress the importance of recovery as consistent and with continuity through pre-disaster preparedness and planning as an exercise of strategic significance. This is an approach consistent with the classic disaster literature, especially Davis's (1978: 33) comment that 'shelter must be considered as a process, not as an object', which follows from Turner's maxim (1972: 148): 'housing as a verb'.

Despite the rich literature and the increasing experiences and lessons learned, especially emerging after the 2004 tsunami, international actors in the field are still in search of a coherent identity and off-the-shelf package designs. The following selected list is indicative of this trend:

- UN-HABITAT (2007) published *Anchoring Homes: UN-HABITAT's People's Process in Aceh and Nias after the Tsunami*, which covers the operations of the UN agency and focuses on the social impact of housing.
- UNEP (2008) issued *After the Tsunami: Sustainable Building Guidelines for South-East Asia* which focuses on the technical aspects of buildings and infrastructure.
- The Shelter Centre/UNOCHA recently published a field edition of *Transitional Settlement and Reconstruction After Natural Disasters* (Corsellis and Vitale 2008).
- ARUP International produced *Lessons from Aceh* (Da Silva 2009), commissioned by DEC members.
- The World Bank has completed a Manual on Housing and Community reconstruction to be drawn from the different experiences of the World Bank around the world (Jha *et al.* 2010).
- Practical Action published *After Disaster: Can Housing Reconstruction Bring development?* (Lyon *et al.* 2010).
- A special issue on shelter after disaster in the academic journal *Environmental Hazards* (Volume 10, Issue 3–4, 2011).

Recovery risks and misconceptions

There is a growing volume of literature on appropriate measures to ensure disaster resilience and recovery. The World Bank (2001) suggests that recovery programmes should follow principles such as: revival of the economy; empowering individuals and communities; private sector participation; and decentralization and equity. OED (2005), in a tsunami experience revision, makes explicit that the reconstruction of damaged infrastructure is imperative but insufficient in itself unless local vulnerabilities are identified and ways of reducing them effectively using financial incentives, revision of land-use patterns and management, and updating of building codes and practices are also offered.

Participatory mechanisms and community involvement are being recognised as critical to the process of post-disaster reconstruction (El-Masri and Kellett 2001; Lizarralde 2002; Skotte 2004) although, as Davidson *et al.* (2007) and Steinberg (2007) suggest, difficulties remain in agreeing the meaning of participation, and in defining the community (often seen as a 'monolithic entity' rather than a complex one).

Community **participation** is a **resource** that can be employed effectively at different scales and in different forms: in urban management and disaster recovery, spreading decision-making among local organisations and encouraging community involvement in the development of policies and future growth strategies; in funding reconstruction activities to address social vulnerability and avoid exclusions, build community empowerment and a gender-sensitive approach; in implementing a reconstruction management strategy at the policy and practice levels based on community partnerships with national, regional and local level public and private entities; and in designing and implementing technical solutions that may include self-help, the use of traditional building materials, progressively developed, core housing strategies and high-density, low-rise solutions to build-back-better (see Chapter 4).

The literature on post-disaster recovery is considerable and the lessons learned are freely available. However, too often, the lessons are not learned and common misconceptions about recovery and reconstruction prevail. The small space available here renders it impossible to present it all, but the following list summarises (in no specific order) some widespread myths and fallacies:

- *Recovery should be approached reactively.* This results from the combined pressure of political leaders, media demands, and donor agency staff under pressure from their headquarters, who are under pressure, in turn, from their own constituencies and from disaster survivors.
- *Recovery does not need to be especially participatory* because the community is a 'victim' and therefore unable to engage in its own reconstruction.
- *Recovery is a smooth process if implemented by a newly created state organisation* informed by external and international **knowledge** and financed by external donors.
- *Recovery is conceived as housing reconstruction and physical rehabilitation* of assets destroyed by the disaster, thus requiring a technical focus on urgent shelter delivery, with houses constructed irrespective of location, planning regulations, land tenure and the socio-economic status of people.
- *Participation mechanisms in recovery are conceived as cost-reduction strategies*, especially in physical and housing reconstruction at the local level; they do not require policy definition and support from other levels of government.
- *Agency-driven reconstruction is faster and more cost effective than owner-driven reconstruction* that needs highly committed staff, extra costs to create enabling mechanisms at local levels and time to be implemented.

It follows that if reconstruction and recovery are based on such erroneous values, then their practice will be equally ill informed. Too often reconstruction and recovery are:

- *Implemented reactively*, aiming to reproduce the status quo before the event rather than addressing the underlying vulnerabilities and risks that generated the disaster.
- *Implemented through reforms and changes* without taking into consideration post-disaster social and economic shock, nor the desires and needs of the affected population.

- *Conceived through a top-down process of implementation* as a window of opportunity to make effective and structural changes at different policy levels.
- *Conceived technocratically* because community participation is believed to delay the reconstruction process, and directly managed funds can appear to be obstacles to appropriate management without formal accounting and accountability skills.
- *Implemented technocratically* because risk mitigation becomes the only criterion in framing the reconstruction approach at the expense of feasibility, cultural, comfort and environmental considerations.
- *Conceived and planned as standard designs* that might not respond to local cultural, social and economic specificity but ensure speed, visibility and effectiveness.

A way forward: towards an equitable and just recovery

It is important to remember that inadequate housing or shortages constitute a severe problem for many societies, not merely those formally affected by disaster. Statistics explicitly illustrate a certain disconnect between programmes addressing post-disaster housing and the normal production of housing for low-income communities (Lyon *et al.* 2010). This implies that apart from emergencies, relief agencies rarely pay attention to the way in which housing is delivered, often assuming that developing countries have no experience in low-cost social housing schemes, no finance mechanisms, nor that they sometimes possess a profoundly rich and established informal housing sector.

Acknowledging a greater wealth of challenges facing the broad topic of post-disaster recovery, this brief assemblage has sought to reveal what are considered to be fundamental elements affecting the methodology and delivery of housing. These issues further suggest the need for a critical rethinking of post-disaster; one stressing the importance of reflective learning and promoting consciously people-centred processes.

Current practice is predicated on short-term emergency provision and a narrowly conceived 'bricks and mortar' output model. Reconstruction is driven by a top-down 'implementation push' approach to project delivery. The sector is characterised by a limited array of technical solutions, often designed by expatriate professionals – male-dominated in terms of concepts and personnel – with little understanding of local vernacular styles of shelter and building technologies and implemented with minimal participation by the disaster-affected populations. The fragmented institutional framework compounds these shortcomings and the political imperatives of rehousing disaster-affected populations as rapidly as possible make evident the need to 'get things done', in which only limited attention is devoted to vital constituency desires and the aspirations of local people.

Unlearned lessons are embedded in the 'we can fix it' attitude of recovery, played out at both national and international levels and reinforced by the relative strength and breadth of views that are held by government officials who are ultimately responsible for directing and overseeing a successful recovery process.

A fundamental step in re-approaching sustainable and reconstruction-only programmes may be taken by means of a *pluralistic artisanal approach* guiding strategic planning in establishing the balance between short-term and long-term outcomes in the relief and reconstruction complex.

Conceptual premises

(1) Recovery and reconstruction must be imagined, practised and institutionalised through a rights-based approach.

Ideally, a rights-based approach guarantees **access** to opportunities, compensation and choices as an individual and as a community. Disaster situations are periods of rapid social transformation where the rights of affected vulnerable populations are most under threat. The growth of rights-based approaches to humanitarian intervention, explored earlier by Slim (2000), has specific resonance for recovery. Indeed, Hurwits and colleagues (2005: 8) have demonstrated how a rights-based agenda, to enable those displaced in conflicts and natural disasters to repossess and return to their homes, is one of the most important developments in recent recovery efforts and is acknowledged at the international level (Leckie 2005; UNHCR 2005a).

By adopting rights-based approaches, interventions will be enhanced and far more responsive to the needs of the affected populations. The modalities of this approach should involve not only the protection of rights such as gender equality, freedom of movement, reducing vulnerability and meeting utilitarian needs such as the preservation of dignity and privacy, but also the active representation and involvement of affected populations in all levels of decision-making about reconstruction and resettlement including, for example, principles for design and layout; the production and construction of space and place both in displaced and return settings; and land rights, especially in repatriation or resettlement. For more on rights-based approaches, see Camp Management Project (2004); Corsellis and Vitale (2005); IFRC (1994); Sphere Project (2011); UNHCR (1999, 2005b); Van Dyke and Waldman (2004); Zetter and Boano (2007).

(2) Democracy and equity are fundamental preconditions for the creation of a recovery space.

Democracy and equity allow for self-expression and the reduction of inequalities. Recovery plans should not only right the wrongs caused by the disaster but also address the structures of inequalities that produce and reproduce vulnerabilities. In line with the debate as to whether reconstruction differs significantly from development, it is more helpful if reconstruction is viewed as the essential first step in the total development process after a disaster. In other words, reconstruction for development is about restoring the whole fabric of a society, by reconnecting and rebuilding what has broken down. At such reduced levels of vulnerability, creation of a resilient society would be a critical element in a just reconstruction plan.

Design for post-disaster reconstruction is far more complex than has been generally acknowledged to date, despite many decades of experience. It involves both the planning of material things and the resolution of competing social interests in a complex process of mediation and negotiation. Walls and joists are arrayed so that a building stands up; but owners and occupants must also be able to see a space that suits their needs. Thus, the design process is simultaneously the representation of an artefact in physical form, the creation of social and cultural and symbolic resources, and also the result of a negotiative/facilitative process. Such an approach fundamentally reconceives the role of the 'technical aid worker'. They are not, in Roy's pointed phrase, the 'innocent professionals' (Roy 2006: 21) but are involved in a process which requires them to reflect upon what they produce in the context of often conflictual struggles over development.

(3) Institutional design and the functioning dimensions of recovery are crucial for the effective and democratic content of reconstruction practices.

Reconstruction initiatives may also have important governance effects. The nature and scale of reconstruction programmes imply institutional and governmental engagement on a potentially significant scale. Procedures and institutional bodies have to be developed to oversee programmes, distribute resources, monitor the implementation and verify effectiveness. Institutions are not merely containers of political intent but rather mediate, in a fundamental sense, how interaction between diverse agendas and actors is channelled. This awareness brings into view the importance of dynamics and **cultures** of both state and non-state actors and especially the relationship between market pressures and civil society.

The management of the recovery and reconstruction process following a major disaster presents a colossal and often unprecedented challenge to any country, especially for those with limited or no prior experience of major disasters. However, where there has been detailed pre-disaster recovery planning that includes governance and institutional factors, more effective recovery will certainly follow. Governments may decide to manage reconstruction using their existing line ministries or departments or they may create a dedicated organisation for the task. Either option has its merits as well as inherent problems. If existing departments are used, then it will be essential to strengthen them to deal with an unprecedented scale and range of urgent tasks. Similarly, if a new, dedicated body is formed, it is essential that it works with existing line departments and does not duplicate their activities. When such a body is formulated, it is necessary to decide its future role when reconstruction is complete. In some cases the same organisation manages the immediate relief process as well as the longer-term recovery process; while in other cases the disaster management body will confine its actions to immediate post-disaster needs to be replaced by a disaster recovery organisation or by planning and management through existing governmental structures.

(4) The drivers of recovery and reconstruction must be located at the individual and community level, balancing centralised decisions that ensure equity in reconstruction and decentralised adaptation.

A balance between the two extreme paradigms of using post-disaster reconstruction strategies is envisaged as a general rule in order to encompass contextual variations: a community-based approach (accompanied by the so-called *enabler* policy and a central programme of self-help) and a technology-based approach (accompanied by a *provider* policy).

Mechanisms are needed in the design of recovery institutions that facilitate decision-making between the communities and the authorities that provide financial, human and material resources. Community-driven reconstruction employed by the World Bank (2009) and by UN-HABITAT in war reconstruction in Afghanistan, and tsunami reconstruction in Aceh (BAPPENAS 2005) is based on the idea that communities have the right to drive their own reconstruction and are best placed to do so (Barakat 2003; McBride and D'Onofrio 2008). Similarly, owner-driven reconstruction was developed in the aftermath of the 1999 earthquake in Turkey and widely adopted in 2001 in the Gujarat reconstruction (Duyne Barenstein 2008) and more recently in Sri Lanka (Boano 2007, 2009). With such an approach, people who lost their shelter are given assistance in cash and/or kind to repair or rebuild their house by themselves. In order to be effective, this approach needs to be embedded in a number of enabling mechanisms such as technical guidance, training of masons and homeowners, building codes and guidelines, a regulatory framework to regulate the price and facilitate access to building materials and a disbursement of the financial assistance in instalments.

Systematic framework

Conceptually grounded, systems thinking aims to explore, discover and navigate the territory of the relief and reconstruction complex (Boano 2007). Such an approach generates a more meaningful understanding of the link between disaster and development and overcomes the disconnection between policy intentions and outcomes.

This systemic four-dimension model is based on:

- *Processes*: this element focuses on all 'flows' of activities and dynamics undertaken in a specific time and space; processes are seen as all elements describing the territorial dimension as the product of material and social practices. At this level, territory (home/place dynamics) can play a fundamental role in which actors, economic interests, government institutions and aid agencies arrange their relationships stressing the role of proximity, sense of place and identity, and promoting collective local actions.
- *Structures*: this element focuses on norms and rules, attitudes and forms of involvement in a specific time and space; structures are seen as a set of systems which offer a perspective on negotiation/facilitation processes and localised

action and projects. Structures are not simplified 'coordination mechanisms' but discursive and practical elements which foster a process-oriented focus on higher objectives of reconstruction and recovery as development or re-development, not sacrificed to short-term priorities.

- *Meanings*: this element refers to ways in which definitions are articulated in order to understand and explain housing in ways that go beyond 'bricks and mortar' to include cultural and economic aspects.

- *Knowledge*: this element refers to functional knowledge – a body of systematic skills and attitudes (individual and organisational) applied to reconstruction which simultaneously produce an artefact in physical form and result from a negotiation/facilitation process. By contrast, instrumental knowledge is a body of skills focused on strengthening the initiatives of people themselves – those who remain and returnees. People are not passive and dependent victims but active survivors and stakeholders whose coping capacities in reconstructing their lives are frequently underestimated (see Chapter 2). This kind of knowledge is concerned with how to empower people at the grass-roots level to mobilise their own recovery and development objectives. It replicates the bottom-up characteristics of participation in the artisanal tradition.

From this perspective, the appropriate and balanced integration of hardware (physical and material interventions) and software (regulation, local capacities, contacts) can improve the impact of intervention in the complex phases of relief and reconstruction, and better improve the links between an emergency phase and a development one. International actors should balance a technology-based approach, mainly focused on the hardware dimensions, as providers of services, employment and projects, with a community-based approach, as enablers or facilitators. This conceptual framework requires dynamic organisations in which professionals should adjust their conventional authoritarian role and assume the role of 'facilitator', shifting from 'directing and imposing' to 'enabling and empowering'.

Figure 13.2 represents this conceptual framework. The symbolic outline conceives of post-disaster responses as the integration of four critical components. These components must be continuously articulated through time – three broad time periods of post-disaster recovery are identified – but the four critical components have differential importance at different phases: this is represented by the relative sizes of the symbols.

The critical components are:

- *The institutional*: this is the dynamic arena of policy and governance. Essential here is the need to draw up new or revised approaches to ensure far better institutional coordination of all the stakeholders involved in the design and delivery of post-disaster programmes. At the same time, intervention processes should safeguard the rights of returnees, those who are resettled and communities who remain, by ensuring they have critical inputs into the design and development of housing policies and approaches, and in rebuilding the

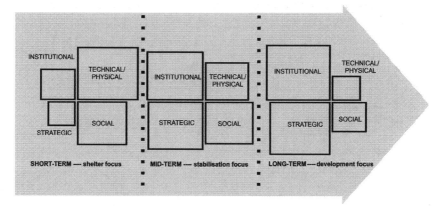

Figure 13.2 Programmatic and strategic element of recovery
Source: Adapted from Boano (2007).

various capacities for their implementation. In this arena, it is fundamental not to undermine the policy parameters such as location, standards and planning regulations, and to ensure that housing projects provide security of title and tenure, and secure transparency in the implementation.

- *The social*: this is related to the interface between individuals, communities and societies. This component is crucial to understanding the intersections between the physical artefact of the house and the social dimension of households, community and **locality**. Attention is given to strengthening local capacities and ensuring participation in setting reconstruction priorities. A high and continuous degree of user participation is fundamental as an empowering mechanism in order to avoid dependency, marginalisation and institutionalised domination of the tasks of reconstruction.
- *The technical/physical*: this is related to the physical aspect of reconstruction. This component is crucial to understanding all technical issues from building materials to construction mechanisms. Attention is dedicated to the use of local construction skills and materials, allowing for better maintenance and greater sustainability, enabling incremental upgrading and expansion. In addition, it embraces the use of traditional construction techniques which allow the involvement of owners, local builders and small contractors in the construction process, maximising the local economic value of the reconstruction programme. Moreover, attention should be dedicated to the intersection with different programme arenas, such as community strategies and livelihoods, and different spatial and operational scales, from field-level projects to national recovery and development strategies.
- *The strategic:* this component is related to recovery as a strategic resource and economic multiplier. Fundamental is the fact that reconstruction should directly support and link into economic objectives and policies, at local and regional levels, in regenerating building materials industries and factories

prefabricating housing components, and in re-establishing construction labour markets which generate income to support the livelihood needs of local populations. Conceiving of housing and physical assets strategically is thus fundamental in adopting a wider livelihoods approach in the reconstruction.

Thus, this integrated and multidimensional model is an attempt to move from a relief-based approach to a balanced asset approach. Assuming that relief and development occur both simultaneously and as a continuum, Figure 13.2 shows not distinct and sequential phases, but three different operational extensions (short-term, mid-term and long-term) but where different dimensions may have a different priority (objectives, focus, resources, etc.). However, they always coexist and cohere with others.

Conclusion

In a recent book on design and activism the authors consider that:

> Architecture and urban planning professions are undergoing a major transformation that is both proactive and reactive: proactive as a search for roles with greater relevance, and reactive as a response to the humanitarian and environmental crises facing the world.
>
> (Bell and Wakeford 2008: 8)

The issue of post-disaster housing in the present chapter has considered its essence as the 'most contradictory practice' (Dovey 1999). A perennial tension between the optimistic sense of creative innovation identified with the architects' engagement in the articulation of dreams (imagining and constructing a better future) and the conservative stream from the fundamental inertia of built form to 'fix' and 'stabilise' the world (Boano and Hunter 2012).

The originality of this revised approach lies in the fact that no matter how such processes are labelled, packaged and implemented, the themes of housing, post-disaster practices and participation need to converse with each other explicitly because they are embedded in a potentially transformative process of change. This requires a conceptual and policy shift towards a renewed anthropocentric recovery practice.

Despite the negative tone of much post-disaster literature cited here, some experiences and examples could be considered positive in their intentions and effective in their outcomes. For example: UpLink's work in Aceh (World Habitat Awards 2007); or the works of the Hunnar Shaala Foundation in Aceh (Hunnar Shaala Foundation 2010); and different owner-driven initiatives in Gujarat (Duyne Barenstein and Pittet 2007).

Disasters can risk reducing the checks and balances imposed on a government's power, resulting in the already dominant sociopolitical power in a space becoming 'hyper-dominant'. The lack of rational procedure and rigorous critique to arrive at such immediate tactics is often defended by the dominant power with reference to the existence of a 'state of emergency' (which ironically the government itself declares) that warrants new rules. The resultant *tabula rasa* planning policy mirrors the blank slate of the destroyed post-disaster city and landscape. Whenever the time period for action is significantly reduced, as it is in post-disaster situations, and the policy gap is filled with quickly devised plans, the procedural power balance tips away from the general populace or affected people. Simply put, there is less time for the participatory process to take root and thrive, and since this process is often highly contested, it requires time to build the momentum necessary to enact meaningful change (Boano and Hunter 2012).

The intensity of a disaster and the limited window of opportunity that immediately follows must be addressed from multiple angles concurrently to reconstruct the livelihoods and spatial networks of an affected area. Writing off the spatial element as something separate and unrelated severely limits the transformative potential of reconstruction and rehabilitation in the post-disaster context. Architecture as a discipline and practice will continue to be at risk as long as it fails to subject itself to critical self-reflection; to distance itself from the obsession with the object; and to recognise its dependency on outside forces and influences. Rethinking the limits of the discipline through the inclusion of others in the practice, could be especially significant in reattaching its worth to post-disaster reconstruction.

References

Albala-Bertrand, J.M. (2000) 'Responses to complex humanitarian emergencies and natural disasters: an analytical comparison', *Third World Quarterly*, 21(2): 215–27.

Alexander, D.E. (2000) *Confronting Catastrophe: New Perspectives on Natural Disasters*, Harpenden: Terra Publishing/New York: Oxford University Press.

—— (2006) 'Globalization of disaster: trends, problems and dilemmas', *Journal of International Affairs*, 59(2): 1–22.

Arnold, M. (2006) 'Disaster reconstruction and risk management for poverty reduction', *Journal of International Affairs*, 59(2): 261–79.

Aysan, Y. (1991) 'Disaster and the small dwelling: Conference held at the Disaster Management Centre, Oxford Polytechnic, 2–5 September 1990', *Disasters*, 15(1): 77–81.

Badri, S.A., Asgary, A., Eftekhari, A.R. and Levy, J. (2006) 'Post-disaster resettlement, development and change: a case study of the 1990 Manjil earthquake in Iran', *Disasters*, 30(4): 451–68.

BAPPENAS (2005) *Indonesia: Notes on Reconstruction*. The consultative group on Indonesia. Available at: http://www.e-aceh-nias.org/upload/09082006090602.pdf (accessed 21 March 2013)

Barakat, S. (2003) *Housing Reconstruction after Conflict and Disaster*, Network Paper 43, London: ODI.

Bell, B. and Wakeford, K. (eds) (2008) *Expanding Architecture: Design as Activism*, New York: Metropolis Books.

Birkman, J. and Fernando, N. (2008) 'Measuring revealed and emergent vulnerabilities of coastal communities to tsunami in Sri Lanka', *Disasters*, 32(1): 82–105.

Boano, C. (2007) 'Dynamics of linking reconstruction and development in housing and settlements for forced migrants in post disaster situations', unpublished thesis, Oxford Brookes University.

—— (2009) 'Housing anxiety, paradoxical spaces and multiple geographies of post tsunami housing intervention in Sri Lanka', *Disasters*, 33(4): 762–85.

Boano, C. and Hunter, W. (2012) 'Architecture at risk (?): The ambivalent nature of post-disaster practice', *Architectoni.ca*, 1: 1–13. Available at: http://ccaasmag.org/arch_v1-1.php (accessed 22 March 2013).

Boen, T. and Jigyasu, R. (2005) *Cultural Considerations for Post Disaster Reconstruction Post-Tsunami Challenges*. Available at: http://www.adpc.net/irc06/2005/4-6/TBindo1.pdf. (accessed 22 March 2013).

Buchanan-Smith, M. and Fabbri, P. (2005) *Links Between Relief, Rehabilitation and Development in the Tsunami Response: A Review of the Debate*, Tsunami Evaluation Coalition, ALNAP. Available at: http://www.alnap.org/pool/files/lrrd-review-debate.pdf (accessed 22 March 2013)

Camp Management Project (2004) *Camp Management Toolkit*. Oslo: Norwegian Refugee Council. Available at: http://103220.c.telecomputing.no/publisher/arch/_img/9069531.pdf (accessed 22 March 2013).

Collier, P. (1999) 'Aid "dependency": a critique', *Journal of African Economies*, 8(4): 528–45.

Corsellis, T. and Vitale, A. (2005) *Transitional Settlement Displaced Populations*, Oxford: OXFAM, University of Cambridge-Shelterproject.

—— (2008) *Transitional Settlement and Reconstruction after Natural Disasters, Field Edition*, Shelter Centre, Department for International Development and United Nations Office for the Coordination of Humanitarian Affairs. Available at: http://www.alnap.org/pool/files/transitionalsettlementandreconstructionafternaturaldisasters.pdf (accessed 22 March 2013).

Cuny, F.C. (1978) 'Disasters and the small dwelling: the state of the art', *Disasters*, 2(2/3): 118–24.

Da Silva, J. (2009) *Lessons from Aceh: Key Considerations in Post Disasters Reconstruction*, Rugby: Practical Action.

Davidson, C., Dikmen, N., Johnson, C., Lizarralde, G. and Sliwinski, A. (2007) 'Truths and myths about community participation in post-disaster housing projects', *Habitat International*, 31 (1): 100–15.

Davis, I. (1978) *Shelter After Disaster*, Headington: Oxford Polytechnic Press.

—— (2011) 'What have we learned from 40 years' experience of Disaster Shelter?', *Environmental Hazards*, 10(3–4): 193–212.

Dovey, K. (1999) *Framing Places: Mediating Power in Built Form*, London: Routledge.

Duyne Barenstein, J. (2008) 'From Gujarat to Tamil Nadu: Owner-driven vs. contractor-driven housing reconstruction in India', paper presented at I-Rec conference Building Resilience: Achieving Effective Post-disaster Reconstruction. Available at: http://shelter centre.org/sites/default/files/IREC_OwnerDrivenVsContractorDrivenHousingReconstruction.pdf (accessed 29 August 2013).

Duyne Barenstein, J. and Pittet, D. (2007) 'Post-disaster housing reconstruction: current trends and sustainable alternatives for tsunami-affected communities in coastal Tamil Nadu', *Point Sud*, 8(5–8).

El-Masri, M. and Kellett, P. (2001) 'Post-war reconstruction: participatory approaches to rebuilding the damaged villages of Lebanon, a case study of al-Burjain', *Habitat International*, 25 (4): 535–57.

Environmental Hazards (2011) Special Issue: Shelter After Disaster, ed. J. Burnell and D. Sanderson 10(3–4): 189–345.

Harmer, A. and Macrae, J. (2004) *Beyond the Continuum: The Changing Role of Aid Policy in Protracted Crises*, HPG Report 18, London: Overseas Development Institute.

Hamza, M. and Zetter, R. (1998) 'Structural adjustment, urban systems, and disaster vulnerability in developing countries', *Cities*, 15(4): 291–9.

Harrell-Bond, B. (1986) *Imposing Aid: Emergency Assistance to Refugees*, Oxford: Oxford University Press.

—— (1999) 'The experience of refugees as recipients of aid', in A. Ager (ed.) *Refugees: Contemporary Perspectives on the Experience of Forced Migration*, New York: Cassell.

Hunnar Shaala Foundation (2010) 'Post-Tsunami community-led reconstruction in Banda Aceh'. Available at: http://hunnar.org/aceh.htm.

Hurwits, A., Studdard, K. and Williams, R. (2005) *Housing, Land, Property and Conflict Management: Identifying Policy Options for Rule of Law Programming*, International Peace Academy Security-Development Nexus Program Report. Available at: http://2001-2009.state.gov/documents/organization/98035.pdf (accessed 22 March 2013).

IFRC (1994) *Code of Conduct*, Geneva: International Federation of Red Cross and Red Crescent Societies.

Ingram, J.C., Franco, G., Khazai, B. and Rumbaitis del Rio, C. (2006) 'Policy aftershocks following disasters: balancing short-term relief with long-term vulnerability reduction, under review', *Environmental Science and Policy*, 9(7–8): 607–13.

Jha, A.K., Duyne Barenstein, J., Phelps, P.M., Pittet, D. and Sena, S. (2010) *Safer Homes, Stronger Communities: A Handbook for Reconstructing after Natural Disasters*, Washington, DC: World Bank. Available at: http://www.housingreconstruction.org/housing/toc (accessed 22 March 2013).

Keivani, R. and Werna, E. (2001) 'Refocusing the housing debate in developing countries from a pluralist perspective', *Habitat International*, 25(2): 191–208.

Kreimer, A. (1980) 'Low-income housing under "normal" and post disaster situations: some basic continuities', *Habitat International*, 4(3): 273–83.

Lautze, S. and Hammock, J. (1996) *Coping with Crisis, Coping with Aid: Capacity Building, Coping Mechanisms and Dependency, Linking Relief and Development*, Boston, MA: Feinstein International Famine Center, Tufts University.

Leckie, S. (2005) 'Housing, land and property rights in post conflict societies: proposal for a new United Nations institutional and policy framework', Geneva: UNHCR. Available at: http://www.unhcr.org/refworld/pdfid/425689fa4.pdf (accessed 22 March 2013).

LeGrand, L.M. (2004) 'Land title and tenure issues in transitional shelter relief programmes', paper prepared for Shelter Project Meeting in Geneva, November 4–5.

Lensink, R. and White, H. (1999) *Aid Dependence: Issues and Indicators*, Expert Group on Development Issues. Available at: http://www.bistandsdebatten.se/wp-content/uploads/2012/10/1999_2-Aid-Dependence.-Issues-and-Indicators.pdf (accessed 22 March 2013).

Lizarralde, G. (2002) 'Multiplicity of choice and users' participation in post-disaster reconstruction: the case of the 1999 Colombian earthquake', in Conference Proceedings, Tiems 2002: Facing the Realities of the New Millennium, Tiems, Waterloo.

Lloyd-Jones, T. (2006) *Mind the Gap! Post-Disaster Reconstruction and the Transition from Humanitarian Relief*, report produced for the Royal Institution of Chartered Surveyors (RICS) by the Max Lock Centre at the University of Westminster.

Lyon, M. and Schinderman, T. with Boano, C. (eds) (2010) *After Disaster: Can Housing Reconstruction Bring Development?*, Rugby: Practical Action Publishing.

McBride, L. and D'Onofrio, A. (2008) 'Community-driven reconstruction: a new strategy for recovery', *Humanitarian Exchange Magazine*, 39. Available at: http://www.odihpn.org/report.asp?id=2909 (accessed 22 March 2013).

Menoni, S. and Pesaro, G. (2008) 'Is relocation a good answer to prevent risk? Criteria to help decision makers choose candidates for relocation in areas exposed to high hydrogeological hazards', *Disaster Prevention and Management*, 17(1): 33–53.

Moe, T.L., Gehbauer, F., Senitz, S. and Mueller, M. (2007) 'Balanced scorecard for natural disaster management projects', *Disaster Prevention and Management*, 16(5): 785–806.

Moe, T.L. and Pathranarakul, P. (2006) 'An integrated approach to natural disaster management: public project management and its critical success factors', *Disaster Prevention and Management*, 15(3): 396–413.

OED (2005) *Lessons from Natural Disasters and Emergency Reconstruction*, Washington, DC: World Bank.

ODI (2005) *The Currency of Humanitarian Reform. HPG Briefing Note, November 2005*. London: Overseas Development Institute. Available at: http://www.odi.org.uk/hpg/papers/Humanitarian_reform.pdf (accessed 22 March 2013).

Roy, A. (2006) 'Praxis in the time of empire', *Planning Theory*, 5(1): 7–29.

Sanderson, D. and Sharma, A. (2008) 'Winners and losers from the 2001 Gujarat earthquake', *Environment and Urbanization*, 20 (1): 177–86.

ShelterCentre/UNOCHA (2008) *Transitional Settlement and Reconstruction after Natural Disasters*, UNOCHA. Available at: http://www.sheltercentre.org/Transitional+Settlement+and+Reconstruction+after+Natural+Disasters (accessed 22 March 2013).

Skotte, H. (2004) 'Tents in concrete: what internationally funded housing does to support recovery in areas affected by war: the case of Bosnia-Herzegovina', PhD thesis, NTNU, Trondheim.

Slim, H. (2000) 'Dissolving the difference between humanitarianism and development: the mixing of a rights-based solution', *Development in Practice*, 10(3–4): 491–4.

Sphere Project (2011) *Sphere Handbook, Humanitarian Charter and Minimum Standards in Humanitarian Response*, Rugby: Practical Action. Available at: http://www.sphere project.org/handbook/ (accessed 22 March 2013).

Steinberg, F. (2007) 'Housing reconstruction and rehabilitation in Aceh and Nias, Indonesia: rebuilding lives', *Habitat International*, 31(1): 150–66.

Telford, J. and Cosgrave, J. (2007) 'The International Humanitarian System and the 2004 Indian Ocean earthquake and tsunami', *Disasters*, 31(1): 1–28.

Terry, F. (2002) *Condemned to Repeat? The Paradox of Humanitarian Action*, Ithaca, NY: Cornell University Press.

Turner, J.F.C. (1972) *Housing as a Verb: Freedom to Build*, New York: Macmillan.

Twigg, J. (2006) 'Technology, post-disaster housing reconstruction and livelihood security', Working Paper No. 15, Benfield Hazard Research Centre Disaster Studies.

UNEP (2008) *After the Tsunami: Sustainable Building Guidelines for South-East Asia*, United Nations Environment Programme and SKAT. Available at: http://www.relief web.int/rw/lib.nsf/db900sid/OCHA-7GZJW9/$file/Sustainable%20Building%20 Guidelines.pdf?openelement (accessed 22 March 2013).

UN-HABITAT (2007) *Anchoring Homes: UN-HABITAT's People's Process in Aceh and Nias after the Tsunami*, Nairobi: UN-Habitat.

UNHCR (1999) *Handbook for Emergencies*, Geneva: UNHCR. Available at: http://www. unhcr.org/cgi-bin/texis/vtx/publ/opendoc.pdf?tbl=PUBL&id=3bb2fa26b (accessed 22 March 2013).

—— (2005a) *Housing and Property Restitution for Refugees and Displaced Persons*, Sub-Commission on the Promotion and Protection of Human Rights Fifty-seventh session. Available at: http://daccess-ods.un.org/access.nsf/Get?Open&DS=E/CN.4/Sub.2/2005/L.4&Lang=E (accessed 22 March 2013).

—— (2005b) *Practical Guide for the Systematic Use of Standards and Indicators in UNHCR Operations*, Geneva: UNHCR.

UN/OCHA (2005) *Humanitarian Response Review: An Independent Report Commissioned by the United Nations Emergency Relief Coordinator & Under-Secretary-General for Humanitarian Affairs*, Geneva: OCHA.

Van Dyke, M. and Waldman, R. (2004) *The Sphere Project: Evaluation Report*, Washington, DC: Center for Global Health and Economic Development, Program on Forced Migration and Health.

Wamsler, C. (2006a) 'Mainstreaming risk reduction in urban planning and housing: a challenge for international aid organisations', *Disasters*, 30(2): 151–77.

—— (2006b) 'Integrating risk reduction, urban planning and housing: lessons from El Salvador', *Open House International* (OHI) (special issue on 'Managing Urban Disasters'), 31(1): 71–83.

Wilford, J. (2008) 'Out of rubble: natural disaster and the materiality of the house', *Environment and Planning D: Society and Space*, 26(4): 647–62.

World Bank (2001) *Complete Preliminary Gujarat Earthquake Damage Assessment and Recovery Plan, Joint Report*, Washington, DC: WB and ADB.

—— (2004) *Natural Disasters: Lessons from the Brink Countries and Donors Urged to Study Past Disaster Recovery Efforts to Avoid Repeating Mistakes*, Washington DC: World Bank.

—— (2009) *Community Drive Development*, Washington, DC: World Bank. Available at: http://go.worldbank.org/24K8IHVVS0 (accessed 3 August 2009).

World Habitat Awards (2007) *Integrated People Driven Reconstruction*. Available at: http://www.worldhabitatawards.org/winners-and-finalists/projectdetails.cfm?lang=00&theProjectID=742064F6-15C5-F4C0-9966E4B4F5449223 (accessed 22 March 2013).

Zetter, R.W. (1995) *Shelter Provision and Settlement Policies for Refugees: A State of the Art Review*, Studies on Emergencies and Disaster Relief, No. 2, Uppsala: Nordiska Afrikainstitute.

Zetter, R.W. and Boano, C. (2007) 'Gendering space for forcibly displaced women and children: concepts, policies and guidelines', Working Paper commissioned by Inter-University Committee on International Migration for UNFPA Women and Conflict Review, MIT.

Part III

Regional perspectives

14 Experiences from Sub-Saharan Africa

Dewald van Niekerk and Ben Wisner

Lessons for practitioners

- Most African governments still focus on preparedness and contingency measures and not on removing the **root causes** of **vulnerability** to **hazards**.
- These governments need to reconsider rhetorical and centralised, top-down instructions in favour of decentralisation and respect for local **knowledge** and initiative.
- Much successful integration of DRR and development is facilitated by civil society in partnership with communities.
- Without proof of tangible development outcomes, communities will not adopt a disaster risk reduction project.
- More effective DRR projects are linked with existing community-based services.

Introduction: Africa's hazard and vulnerability profile

Africa[1] takes up about a fifth of the Earth's total land mass and has a varied hazard profile which affects diverse habitats (Figure 14.1). The population is largely concentrated on the coasts, around large lakes such as those in the Great Rift Valley, along rivers and interior highlands. Africa is rapidly urbanising in a largely unplanned and uncontrolled manner, something that adds urban–industrial hazards to the threats many 'squatter citizens' already face (Hardoy and Sattertwaite 1989; Pelling and Wisner 2009).

The most prominent natural hazards are droughts, floods, epidemics and wild fires. Geological hazards such as earthquakes, landslides and surface collapse (e.g. sinkholes) are also present. Coping with both hazards and **poverty** is a population of 875 million in 2011 (World Bank 2012); 40 per cent of these are youth and children aged below 15 years of age. The main driver behind disaster risk remains the vulnerability of the population. Vulnerabilities on the continent are grounded in the legacy of colonialism, followed by years of authoritarian rule by African elites, a situation that has preserved and even widened class, regional and ethnic disparities and locked many people into a vicious cycle of poverty (ten of the poorest countries in the world are African), powerlessness and marginality (Chambers 1983; IMF 2012; Mascarenhas and Wisner 2012; Wisner 1988; Wisner *et al.* 2006).

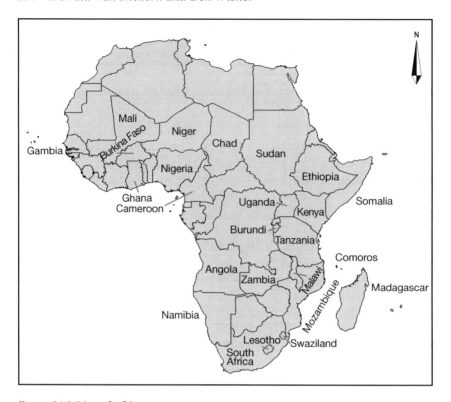

Figure 14.1 Map of Africa

History of planning in Africa

Africa has a legacy of colonial rule, followed by years of weak and even failed governance in many countries. The end of colonialism in the period from the 1960s through the 1980s brought many foreign experts who were housed in different government ministries. The planning priorities these expatriates brought concerned infrastructure development ('spatial modernisation' in the 1960s), extending market relations into the countryside ('economic modernisation' in the 1970s) and finally in the 1980s the implementation of 'structural adjustment' and the safety nets that were supposed to come along with it. In the midst of this busy, externally driven planning activity, there was little space for national capabilities to emerge, let alone innovations in the area of disaster risk reduction. Added to the colonial heritage of top-down planning and crisis intervention, Cold War 'aid' increased the prominence of Africa's militaries and fuelled ideologically driven conflicts. Food emergencies and floods were dealt with during this period as anomalies unrelated to 'development'. The notion that disasters might be the outcome of mal-development was rare (Meillassoux 1973; Wisner and Mbithi 1974).

Beginning with the 1984 famine in Sudan, some African leaders and intellectuals began to question the consequences of an export-driven growth model of development. Was something not systemically wrong if so many rural and urban poor were chronically at risk? The West African Great Sahel famine (1969–72) had caused questioning of this kind (Franke and Chasin 1980; Meillassoux 1973), but these questions had not entered the mainstream. Asking such questions in the late 1980s, a cohort of African planners was ready to respond to the opportunities provided by the International Decade for Natural Disaster Reduction (IDNDR), 1990–1999. Later, they responded to UN calls for creation of 'national platforms',[2] dedicated disaster prevention departments and new legislation.

Disaster and development planning

The idea of integrating disaster prevention and **mitigation** into development planning is not new (Blaikie *et al.* 1994; Cuny 1983; Lavell 1999; Van Niekerk 2006; Wisner *et al.* 2012). The idea became part of mainstream discourse from the 1990s onward (UNDP 2004; UNISDR 2004). The linkage of development and disaster seems inevitable when one considers the high costs that low-income countries pay for disasters relative to their gross domestic products (GDPs) (GFDRR 2011).

At the beginning of the 1990s, social scientists argued it was mistaken to view solutions to disaster as only the business of engineering and physical science (Bates *et al.* 1991: 288). The human dimension was also important. Lavell (1999) maintained that '**risk** and disasters are complex social problems'. Comfort *et al.* (1999) noted widespread failure to recognise changes in land use, settlement policies, population distribution and degradation of habitats as processes that increase hazard exposure and vulnerability. A consensus was emerging that disaster reduction required investments in environmental management and sustainable **livelihoods** that reduce vulnerability and exposure to hazards (Comfort *et al.* 1999; De Satge 2002; UNISDR 2004). This comprehensive approach to development and DRR would also include elements that address climate change (Cameron *et al.* 2012; Toulmin 2009).

However, even if there is verbal agreement by African leaders, one must ask how implementation of such a comprehensive approach to disaster reduction is likely to play out in a continent where human development (measured by movement towards the Millennium Development Goals) is seriously in question (AUC *et al.* 2012).

Disaster relief without development

In the 1970s and early 1980s, African countries were considered by former colonial powers and donor institutions to be largely defenceless in the face of natural hazards and in need of economic development as defined by external experts. Local communities were perceived to be helpless and requiring international intervention and assistance when affected by a hazard (Comfort *et al.* 1999). This led to a focus on provision of relief after a disaster has occurred (Lechat 1990) rather than investments to reduce potential loss and build capacity to cope and recover at the local level. This bias sparked a round of contingency planning, often involving national military authorities. However, the focus was response, not prevention. In this early period, governments and aid organisations did not consider linking disasters management and development.

Today, many Africa governments find themselves in the midst of a paradigm shift from traditional disaster management and preparedness towards disaster risk reduction as part of development planning (Table 14.1). But implementation must follow. Sustained political will is one of the conditions required for effective risk reduction (UNISDR 2004; Wisner *et al.* 2004). One has to ask whether these new African government laws, policies and plans created after 2005 are actually delivering a safer environment for the most vulnerable. Also, alas, some of the countries most at risk of disaster such as Sudan, Somalia, Chad and Malawi do not yet even have binding legal instruments or well-defined, developed and functioning institutional structures for disaster risk reduction.

National legislation and beyond

National legislation is a necessary but not sufficient condition for integrating disaster reduction and development planning. In the 1990s and 2000s, much new disaster management legislation passed through the parliaments of African countries. However, much of this legislation still fails to address disaster in the context of development. For example, Lesotho's Disaster Management Act of 1996 (Lesotho, Government of 1996) focuses on disaster response and provision of relief. Lesotho's government itself admits that the 'main challenge is that of mainstreaming of disaster risk reduction in development plans' (Phooko 2009). To this end, Lesotho has established a Disaster Management Authority, and developed a National Disaster Management Plan, which is operationalised through a Disaster Management Manual (Phooko 2007).

Disaster management in Malawi is governed by the Disaster Preparedness and Relief Act of 1991 (Malawi, Government of 1991) although a new disaster risk reduction **policy** was being created at the time of writing (end of 2012). Malawi does not have the UN-recommended national platform for disaster risk reduction (Malawi, Government of 2009). Malawi is one of the nine focal countries for the World Bank's Global Fund for Disaster Risk and Reduction (GFDRR). GFDRR provides support for institutional **capacity** development. Non-governmental organisations (NGOs) and community-based organisations (CBOs) in Malawi are active in DRR activities and aim to work within the disaster management framework created by government. For example, Action Aid International is working to build resilience in schools and implement flood mitigation projects (Action Aid Malawi 2012). The Sustainable Rural Growth and Development Initiative (SRGDI) has been active in the implementation of safe water and

Table 14.1 Examples of institutional DRR development in Africa

Country	Date of legislation	Institution	Observations
Burkina Faso	1973	Ministry of Social Action & National Solidarity	Began as unit to coordinate food aid in drought emergency & evolved
Ethiopia	1973	National Disaster Preparedness & Prevention Committee	Ditto
Niger	1974	Prime Ministers Office	Ditto
Nigeria	1976	National Emergency Management Agency	Ditto
Sudan	1985	Humanitarian Aid Commission	Ditto
Cameroon	1986	Ministry of Territorial Administration & Decentralization	
Malawi	1991	(a) National Disaster Preparedness & Relief Committee; (b) Joint Food Crisis Task Force (2002)	Response to recurring food emergencies
Ghana	1996	National Disaster Management Organization	
Burundi	1998	Ministry of Public Security	Response to IDPs due to civil conflict
Mozambique	1999	Ministry of International Economic Cooperation	Expanded and revised national system after 2000 floods
Uganda	1999	Prime Minister's Office	Response to displaced population due to conflict
South Africa	2002	Department of Provincial & Local Government	Immediate priority after 1994 elections ending apartheid & following Cape Flats floods
Angola	2003	Ministry of Interior	
Swaziland	2004	Deputy Prime Minister's Office	
Tanzania	2004	Prime Minister's Office	

Source: Ben Wisner from national reports to the World Conference on Disaster Prevention (UNISDR 2005).

sanitation programmes, landslide and flash flood prevention and advocating disaster risk reduction messages via the mass media and in schools. SRGDI has also been instrumental in partnering with the private sector and local communities to understand disaster risk and its impact on communities most at risk (SRGDI 2012).

The Swaziland government has made great strides in mainstreaming disaster risk reduction into its national poverty reduction strategy and national development strategy (Swaziland, Government of 2005). However, Ojo (2011) believes that most of the funding for disaster risk reduction and climate change adaptation projects is dependent on the NGO sector. Zambia has developed a National Disaster Management Policy which underscores the importance of disaster risk reduction and development integration (Zambia, Government of 2005). Following on the national policy, a national contingency plan for flood was developed (Zambia, Government of 2008) and is revised annually (Zambia, Government of 2009).

Tanzania has incorporated DRR into its development planning for local municipalities, and disaster risk reduction also forms part of its national strategy for growth and reduction of poverty (Tanzania, Government of 2009). Similarly in South Africa, the integration of DRR into development planning at local municipal level is a legislated requirement (South Africa, Government of 2000; 2002; 2005).

No specific national legislation or policies focused on DRR existed at the time of writing in Angola (Angola, Government of 2009), Burkina Faso (Burkina Faso, Government of 2009), Comoros (Bhavnani *et al.* 2008) and Burundi (Bhavnani *et al.* 2008; Burundi Government of 2009). Nevertheless, some progress has been made addressing disaster risk issues through a national coordinating mechanism in these countries. Legislation and policies are the first step in addressing disaster risk issues.

Box 14.1 Disaster risk management in Namibia

The Government of Namibia developed a National Action Plan for Capacity Development in Disaster Risk Reduction for the period 2006–2015. This plan was the first step by the national government to institutionalise disaster risk reduction. The Office of the Prime Minister developed a National Disaster Risk Management Policy (Namibia, Government of 2009), which was approved by cabinet and endorsed by the National Assembly in 2009. To ensure compliance and its enforcement, the Office of the Prime Minister also drafted a Disaster Risk Management Bill with support from the United Nations Development Programme. Namibia places an emphasis on the decentralisation of disaster risk management activities through its policies and legislation.

Integrating disaster risk reduction and development

Two benefits of an integrated approach

The inclusion of disaster in development planning opens up two opportunities. The first is provision of interventions that increase the capacity of communities to cope with and recover from hazard events. For example, a new housing project aimed at providing squatters with permanent dwellings can also address a number of socio-economic and physical vulnerability issues (World Bank 2001). Housing which is built according to accepted building standards not only protects against natural hazards, but it also creates 'homes' which may, in turn, strengthen the social cohesion within society. This may create an environment in which economic activities can thrive. Such small changes with long-term benefits are well documented by Hamdi (2004).

South Africa's Alexandra Township to the north of central Johannesburg is also a good example, where limited land and access to water resources forced communities for decades to settle in unsafe floodplains (Wisner 1995a, 1995b; World Bank 2001). A continuing development intervention (Alexandra Renewal Project) by the provincial and **local government** aims at creating permanent dwellings with the necessary basic infrastructure, thus gradually removing communities from the floodplain of the Jukskei River (Dlamini 2009).

The second opportunity created by integrating development and DRR is to reveal weaknesses and unintended consequences of development proposals that actually increase vulnerability to disaster. Viewing all development plans and schemes through the lens of disaster reduction provides an opportunity to take remedial action. In such a manner, high-risk developments can easily be identified and scrutinised using disaster risk reduction principles.

The West African nation of Mali presents a case where colonial development planning of a megaproject that ignored DRR has been transformed into a rice farming scheme that now takes risk to the small farmer-tenants into account. The French colonial authorities created an ambitious development in the 1930s to irrigate approximately one million hectares of land to grow cotton and rice and to develop hydropower over a 50-year period. More than 30,000 people were forced through an involuntary resettlement policy to move to this arid zone to work on the megaproject. However, tenants on the irrigation scheme largely ignored French attempts to change traditional agricultural practices. By 1982, only 6 per cent of the planned area had been developed, and the infrastructure was falling apart. The World Bank attempted to rehabilitate the project in 1985 and had improved success with rice farming, in part because of management reforms undertaken by a new government that came to power in Mali in 1991 (Aw and Diemer 2005). Geographical displacement of thousands of small farmers to the original scheme was bound to disrupt livelihood and dietary patterns. Resistance to the discipline of the scheme added to disruption, placing early tenants in a precarious situation – unable to practise their earlier farming methods but rejecting the agronomy required by the irrigation scheme.

Another example of a megaproject that did not take disaster risk into account is the Lesotho Highlands Water Project. The project aimed to divert fresh water for use in South Africa as well as to generate electricity. The lives of thousands of Lesotho citizens were affected, whose communal grazing land was appropriated without proper compensation (Thabane 2000). This led to livestock death (Pottinger and Horta 1999), and the diversion of water caused environmental and economic havoc downstream (Thabane 2000). If this scheme had been conceived with both disaster risk and development in view, such deficiencies would have been identified at the planning stage.

The challenge of implementation

Implementation remains a weak point in Africa. Malawi's implementation of its Poverty Reduction Strategy Paper (PRSP) – an exemplary case of a plan that integrates disaster reduction and development – provides an example of some very practical challenges to implementation. The Third Annual Report on the Malawi's PRSP by the International Monetary Fund (IMF) reports some macroeconomic gains due to the PRSP, but it also highlights setbacks: '[F]ood security crisis was deeper than anticipated, leading to higher expenditures' which in turn had an impact on poverty reduction at local level (IMF 2006: 3). The IMF review of Gambia's PRSP (IMF 2009: 7) indicated that 'progress has been relatively slow with regards to agricultural reforms and decentralisation' (ibid.). Although the Gambia PRSP already places significant emphasis on agriculture, the IMF's 2009 review recommends: 'developing a comprehensive agricultural sector strategy' (ibid.: 7).

How far, one must ask, has rhetoric by African governments resulted in concrete action? One might take the recommendations of the Millennium Report (UN 2000) as a case in point. It recommends a five-fold strategy for reducing losses from disasters which includes:

- strategies to reduce disaster losses to be mainstreamed in Poverty Reduction Strategy Plans;
- infrastructure investment to incorporate disaster risk reduction;
- social safety nets for the vulnerable, particularly through government provisions;
- early warning capacities and information campaigns supported by governments;
- pre-crisis emergency and contingency planning.

There is at least a verbal acceptance of these recommendations in most African government circles today, and, in fact, a study of a number of African national PRSPs shows that most suggest disaster reduction is an important focus within development. For example, the Madagascar Action Plan devotes a number of priority projects and activities to disaster risk reduction (Madagascar, Government of 2007). Similarly, the PRSP of Tanzania (Tanzania, Government of 2005) dedicates one of its operational targets to 'Vulnerability and Environmental

Conservation and Disaster Management', and the Malawian PRSP (Malawi Government of 2006) has 'Social Protection and Disaster Risk Management' as a poverty reduction theme. The Ethiopian PRSP (Ethiopia, Government of 2002) also emphasises the disaster profile of the country and links key sector development policies and strategies to disaster reduction actions (see Box 14.2).

In South Africa, the Disaster Management Act 57 of 2002 and the Municipal Systems Act 32 of 2000 require a disaster risk management plan as part of the integrated development planning process (NDMC 2007). The problem is that integration in itself is not a natural outflow of any planning process. Integration in planning can only occur if all the relevant role-players and stakeholders understand and are committed to such action (Knipe *et al.* 2002). The first step in achieving integration is to establish institutional capacity within the local government sphere. The aim of such institutional arrangements is to foster a common understanding of the key elements which constitute disaster risk and development (South Africa, Government of 2000). This is the great challenge facing Africa. In much of South Africa and a great deal of the rest of Africa, local government still lacks capacity, knowledge and skills for integrative activity.

Box 14.2 Relief to Development (R2D) in Ethiopia

The Government of Ethiopia has made some progress in the provision of relief as a development intervention. In partnership with USAID, Ethiopia implemented a series of projects aptly named Relief to Development, or R2D, in the mid-1990s. The aim of the R2D projects was to strengthen the Ethiopian food security early warning system through training of agricultural extension workers at the *woreda* (district/municipal) level. Measures were undertaken to increase the capacity of the Food Security Reserve Administration, including the construction of a large number of warehouses for reserve food stockpiles. In this period the government also established the National Disaster Prevention and Preparedness Fund. Employment Generation Schemes (EGS) were also implemented by government partners, mostly NGOs (Middlebrook 2005). Linked to the government's Productive Safety Net Programme, R2D further aimed to improve food security by providing animals to the poorest Ethiopians, along with help setting up financial savings, proper harvest storage and income-producing activities (USAID 2005). Although the initial assessment of the R2D scheme was not excessively positive, most of its tangible benefits could only be seen almost a decade after its implementation (ibid.). The Ethiopian experience shows the need for strong political will and proper institutional structures to use measures such as relief, emergency preparedness and development as disaster reduction initiatives.

Nevertheless, integration is now seen as central to successful implementation of DRR (AU 2004; South Africa, Government of 2005; UNISDR 2005). But what does 'integration' actually mean? Integration should mean that all development planning must consider disaster risk reduction issues and all disaster risk reduction planning must consider development outcomes, especially livelihoods (Bacon 2012; Wisner *et al.* 2012). In many African countries, progress towards thorough integration has been slow. In practice, one finds a DRR plan which forms a separate entity or annex to development plans.

Community-based disaster risk reduction

Another aspect of 'integration' involves the relationship between government's 'top-down' initiatives and spontaneous activity in communities from 'the bottom up' (Wangui *et al.* 2012). There is as yet untapped potential in **community-based disaster risk reduction (CBDRR)** (see Chapter 4) because top-down and bottom-up often inhabit parallel universes (see Chapter 6), or worse, government action contradicts or blocks what communities are trying to do (Delica-Willison and Gaillard 2012; Thompson 2012). CBDRR relies on the capacity of the community to remedy their disaster risk situation themselves and to help each other by creating a common understanding of their vulnerability linked to under-development (Shaw 2012).

NGOs and local government are in a good position to create the conditions that enable people to share knowledge and acquire expertise or generate new knowledge. In turn, these experts can learn from the locals by sharing experiences and exchanging knowledge (Wisner 1995b). With the exchange of information, local people acquire the capacity to experiment within the context of their own **cultures** and physical environments.

However, this process of sharing and co-learning is often threatened by biases. Biases may take many forms such as organisational preferences given to urban–industrialised regions or the neglect of rural areas for the benefit of urban development. In addition, there may be biases due to religion, ethnicity or language. There may also be a bias in favour of formally educated opinion as opposed to indigenous, folk, or experiential knowledge (Freire 1970; Wisner 2010). Such biases are important to consider because field workers, researchers and funders are not at all immune from them (Chambers 1983; 1997).

Political, economic, social, cultural and technological conditions change from one **community** to another, as do the natural and built environment. Thus there can be no 'one-size-fits-all' way to address disaster risk. Change and diversity will always influence disaster risk management, so the approach will need to be flexible enough to adapt to differences between and within communities.

While national-scale integration of development and disaster risk reduction is moving unevenly and slowly, locally based integration of disaster risk reduction and development takes place on a regular basis. For instance, in Kenya, projects in community-based water harvesting and storage were implemented in poor communities in Kitui district with the assistance of the German Welthungerhilfe. The main aim of the project was to address water shortage as a driving force of poverty (UNISDR 2008: 33). The project improved the availability of drinking water in dry periods, thus leading to better public health and strengthened livelihoods.

In Malawi, the UNISDR reported (2008: 45) that Tearfund (in partnership with River of Life Relief and Development):

> initiated a livelihood diversification project through micro and medium-scale enterprise development for poor women in the village. The initiative was taken following a risk assessment that identified low agricultural productivity and lack of alternative livelihoods as the sources of growing poverty and vulnerability. The project has enabled some women to build . . . houses with iron roofing from the proceeds of businesses. Others have invested in agriculture and reported bumper harvests that have made them food secure, selling excess crops to aid household asset recovery and buy items like soap and clothes. Girls are kept in school longer, thanks to the money earned from the businesses. The community members are confident that they can now deal with shocks, as they now have a coping mechanism.

From these examples we can draw two lessons. First, practice and local problems dictate the extent to which disaster risk reduction in development is being taken seriously, especially at the grassroots level. Without proof of tangible development outcomes, communities will not adopt a disaster risk reduction project. DRR efforts are also more effective and sustainable if they are linked with or integrated into existing community-based services (Von Kotze and Holloway 1996) and, above all, to improvements in livelihoods (Bacon 2012; Carney *et al.* 1999). Second, most successes recorded so far in the integration of development and disaster risk reduction are by non-governmental actors working in conjunction with local communities. This is a long-term, time-consuming process.

Conclusion

Reducing disaster risks across Africa requires a radical shift in the current thinking of governments and an even more radical shift from rhetoric and centralised, top-down instructions to decentralisation and respect for local knowledge and initiatives. Currently, disaster and risk management in a number of African countries still revolves around planning for disasters and reactive measures to disasters which might occur. Much attention is given to preparedness planning and contingency measures but not to removing the root causes of **vulnerability** to hazards. Some progress in integrating disaster risk reduction and development has been made. However, little has 'trickled down' from the national level, where much new legislation and many new institutions have been created (GNDR 2009). Critical and open evaluation of existing plans, policies and legislation is lacking.

Notes

1 Henceforth we will call this region 'Africa' for short.
2 National platforms for disaster risk reduction are multidisciplinary and multi-sectoral coordinating mechanisms at the national government level. These national platforms are responsible for the implementation of the principles of disaster risk reduction within all government sectors and all levels of government (Arnold 2012; Lavell *et al.* 2012).

References

Action Aid Malawi (2012) *We Survived the Worst: From Vulnerability to Resilience.* Available at: http://www.actionaid.org/malawi/we-survived-worst-vulnerability-resilience-0. (accessed 14 August 2012).

Angola, Government of (2009) *Angola: National Progress Report on the Implementation of the Hyogo Framework for Action*, National Commission for Civil Protection. Available at: http://www.preventionweb.net/files/7434_finalangola.pdf (accessed 28 October 2009).

Arnold, M. (2012) 'International planning systems for disaster', in B. Wisner, JC Gaillard and I. Kelman (eds) *The Routledge Handbook of Hazard and Disaster Risk Reduction*, London: Routledge, pp. 603–16.

AU (African Union) (2004) *Africa Regional Strategy for Disaster Risk Reduction*, Addis Ababa: African Union.

AUC, UNECA, AfDB, and UNDP–RBA (2012) *Assessing Progress in Africa towards the Millennium Development Goals*, Addis Ababa: African Union Commission.

Aw, D. and Diemer, G. (2005) 'Making a large irrigation scheme work: a case study from Mali', *Directions in Development. No. 31672*, Washington, DC: The World Bank.

Bacon, C. (2012) 'Disaster risk and sustainable development', in B. Wisner, JC Gaillard and I. Kelman (eds) *The Routledge Handbook of Hazards and Disaster Risk Reduction*, London: Routledge, pp. 156–68.

Bates, F., Dynes, R. and Quarantelli, E. (1991) 'The importance of the social sciences to the International Decade of Natural Disaster Reduction', *Disasters*, 15(3): 288–9.

Bhavnani, R., Owor, M., Vordzorgbe, S. and Bousquet, F. (2008) *Report on the Status of Disaster Risk Reduction in the Sub-Saharan Africa Region*, Washington, DC: Commission of the African Union, United Nations International Strategy for Disaster Reduction and the World Bank. Available at: http://www.unisdr.org/preventionweb/files/2229_DRRinSubSaharanAfricaRegion.pdf (accessed 28 October 2009).

Blaikie, P., Cannon, T., Davis, I. and Wisner, B. (1994) *At Risk: Natural Hazards, People's Vulnerability and Disasters*, New York: Routledge.

Burkina Faso, Government of, Conseil National de Secours d'Urgence et de Réhabilitation (2009) *Burkina Fasso: Rapport National de Suivi sur la Mise en Œuvre du Cadre d'Action de Hyogo.* Available at: http://www.preventionweb.net/files/7426_finalburkinafaso.pdf (accessed 28 October 2009).

Burundi, Government of, Ministère de l'Intérieur et de la Sécurite Publique (2009) *Burundi: Rapport National de Suivi sur la Mise en Œuvre du Cadre d'Action de Hyogo.* Available at: http://www.preventionweb.net/files/7427_finalburundi.pdf (accessed 28 October 2009).

Cameron, C., Norrington-Davies, G., te Velde, V. and Mitchell, T. (2012) *Managing Climate Extremes and Disasters in Africa: Lessons from the IPCC SREX Report*, London: Climate & Development Knowledge Network.

Carney, D., Drinkwater, M., Rusinow, T., Neefjes, K., Wanmali, S. and Singh, N. (1999) *Livelihoods Approaches Compared: A Brief Comparison of the Livelihoods Approaches of the UK Department for International Development (DFID), CARE, Oxfam and the*

United Nations Development Programme (UNDP), London: Department for International Development. Available at: http://www.start.org/Program/advanced_institute3_web/p3_documents_folder/Carney_etal.pdf (accessed 14 August 2012).

Chambers, R. (1983) *Rural Development: Putting the Last First*, London: Longman.

Chambers, R. (1997) *Whose Reality Counts? Putting the First Last*, London: Intermediate Technology Publications.

Comfort, L., Wisner, B., Cuter, S., Pulwarty, R., Hewitt, K., Oliver-Smith, A., Wiener, J., Fordham, M., Peacock, W. and Krimgold, F. (1999) 'Reframing disaster policy: the global evolution of vulnerable communities, *Global Environmental Change Part B*', *Environmental Hazards*, 1(1): 39–44.

Cuny, F. (1983) *Disaster and Development*, Oxford: Oxford University Press.

Delica-Willison, Z. and Gaillard, JC (2012) 'Community action and disaster', in B. Wisner, JC Gaillard and I. Kelman (eds) *The Routledge Handbook of Hazards and Disaster Risk Reduction*, London: Routledge, pp. 711–22.

De Satge, R. (2002) *Learning about Livelihoods: Insights from Southern Africa*, Cape Town: Periperi Publications.

Dlamini, N. (2009) 'ARP lands top UN-Habitat award'. Available at: http://www.joburg.org.za/content/view/4392/192/ (accessed 1 November 2009).

Ethiopia, Government of (2002) *Sustainable Development and Poverty Reduction Program*, Addis Ababa, Ethiopia: Ministry of Finance and Economic Development.

Franke, R. and Chasin, B. (1980) *Seeds of Famine*, Montclair, NJ: Allanheld Osmun.

Freire, P. (1970) *Pedagogy of the Oppressed*, New York: Continuum.

GFDRR (2011) *Natural Hazards, Unnatural Disasters: The Economics of Effective Prevention*, Washington, DC: GFDRR. Available at: https://www.gfdrr.org/gfdrr/NHUD-online (accessed 16 October 2009).

GNDR (2009) *'Clouds but Little Rain. . .'. Views from the Frontline: A Local Perspective of Progress Towards the Implementation of the Hyogo Framework for Action*, London: GNDR. Available at: http://www.globalnetwork-dr.org/images/documents/VFL%20archive/reports09/vflfullreport0609.pdf (accessed 29 July 2012).

Hamdi, N. (2004) *Small Change: About the Art of Practice and the Limits of Planning in Cities*, London: Earthscan.

Hardoy, J. and Sattertwaite, D. (1989) *Squatter Citizen*, London: Earthscan.

IMF (2006) *Malawi: Poverty Reduction Strategy Paper: Third Annual Progress Report*, Joint Staff Advisory Note, IMF Country Report No. 06/339, October. Available at: http://siteresources.worldbank.org/INTPRS1/Resources/383606-1165869436599/c0r6339_Malawi_PENDING.pdf (accessed 1 November 2009).

—— (2009) *The Gambia: Poverty Reduction Strategy Paper – Annual Progress Report*, Joint Staff Advisory Note, IMF Country Report No. 09/76, February. Available at: http://siteresources.worldbank.org/INTPRS1/Resources/Gambia_APR2_JSAN(Feb3_2009).pdf (accessed 1 November 2009).

—— (2012) *World Economic and Financial Surveys: World Economic Outlook Database*. Available at: http://www.imf.org/external/pubs/ft/weo/2012/01/weodata/index.aspx (accessed 13 August 2012).

Knipe, A., van der Waldt, G., van Niekerk, D., Burger, D. and Nel, K. (2002) *Project Management for Success*, Cape Town: Heinemann.

Lavell, A. (1999) 'The impact of disasters on development gains: clarity or controversy', IDNDR Programme Forum, 5–9 July. Geneva, Switzerland.

Lavell, A., Gaillard, JC, Wisner, B., Saunders, W. and van Niekerk, D. (2012) 'National planning and disaster', in B. Wisner, JC Gaillard and I. Kelman (eds) *The Routledge Handbook of Hazards and Disaster Risk Reduction*, London: Routledge, pp. 617–28.

Lechat, M.F. (1990) 'The international decade for natural disaster reduction: background and objectives', *Disasters*, 14(1): 1–6.

Lesotho, Government of (1996) *Disaster Management Act of 1996*, Maseru: Government Printer.

Madagascar, Government of (2007) *MAP: Madagascar Action Plan 2007–2012: A Bold and Exciting Plan for Rapid Development*. Available at: http://www.madagascar.gov. mg/MAP (accessed 1 November 2009).

Malawi, Government of (1991) *Disaster Preparedness and Relief Act of 1991*, Lilongwe: Government Printer.

—— (2006) *Malawi Growth and Development Strategy: From Poverty to Prosperity 2006–2011*, Lilongwe: Government Printer.

—— (2009) *Commission for Poverty and Disaster Management Affairs. Malawi: National Progress Report on the Implementation of the Hyogo Framework for Action*. Available at: http://www.preventionweb.net/files/8473_finalmalawi.pdf (accessed 29 October 2009).

Mascarenhas, A. and Wisner, B. (2012) 'Politics: power and disasters', in B. Wisner, JC Gaillard and I. Kelman (eds) *The Routledge Handbook of Hazard and Disaster Risk Reduction*, London: Routledge, pp. 48–60.

Meillassoux, C. (1973) *Qui se Nourrit de la Famine en Afrique?*, Paris: Gaillamard.

Middlebrook, P. (2005) 'Fighting hunger and poverty in Ethiopia: Ethiopia's experience in implementing employment generation schemes as part of the national policy for disaster prevention and management', PhD thesis, University of Durham.

Namibia, Republic of (2009) *National Disaster Risk Management Policy*. Available at: http://209.88.21.36/opencms/export/sites/default/grnnet/DDRM/Archive/national/DRM_Policy_Aug_09.pdf (accessed 14 August 2012).

NDMC (National Disaster Management Centre) (2007) *Inaugural Annual Report 2006/2007*, Pretoria, South Africa: NDMC. Available at: http://www.info.gov.za/view/DownloadFileAction?id=85468 (accessed 14 August 2012).

Ojo, J. (2011) *Swaziland Country Report: HFA Progress at Local Government and Community Perspectives. Views from the Frontline 2011*, Potchefstroom: African Centre for Disaster Studies.

Pelling, M. and Wisner, B. (eds) (2009) *Disaster Risk Reduction: Examples from Urban Africa*, London: Earthscan.

Phooko, M. (2007) 'Statement by honourable Dr Motloheloa Phooko, Minister in the office of the Prime Minister at the Global Platform for Disaster Reduction' presented in Geneva, Switzerland, on June 5, 2007. Available at: http://www.preventionweb.net/files/2250_LesothoStatementGP07.pdf (accessed 17 May 2011).

—— (2009) 'Statement by the honourable Dr. Motloheloa Phooko, Minister in the Prime Minister's Office', United Nations International Strategy for Disaster Reduction (ISDR) second session of the Global Platform for disaster Risk Reduction (DRR), 16 to 19 June, 2009, Geneva, Switzerland. Available at: http://www.preventionweb.net/files/globalplatform/Lesotho.pdf (accessed 29 October 2009).

Pottinger, L. and Horta, K. (1999) *Letter to the World Bank, Re: Lesotho Highlands Water Project*, International Rivers. Available at: http://www.internationalrivers.org/en/africa/letter-world-bank-re-lesotho-highlands-water-project (accessed 1 November 2009).

Shaw, R. (ed.) (2012) *Community-based Disaster Risk Reduction*, London: Emerald.

South Africa, Government of (2000) *Municipal Systems Act 32 of 2000*, Pretoria: Government Printer.

—— (2002) *Disaster Management Act No 57 of 2002*, Pretoria: Government Printer.

—— (2005) *National Disaster Management Policy Framework*, Pretoria: Government Printer.

SRGDI (Sustainable Rural Growth and Development Initiative) (2012) 'SRGDI DRR Activities', personal communication by authors with Mr. Maynard Nyirenda (Executive Director). Notes and documentation in possession of authors. 16 August.

Swaziland, Government of (2005) *Poverty Reduction Strategy and Action Plan. Vol. 1*, Mbabane, Swaziland: Ministry of Economic Planning and Development.

Tanzania, Government of (2005) *National Strategy for Growth and Reduction of Poverty*, Dodoma, Tanzania: Vice President's Office.

—— (2009) *Interim National Progress Report on the Implementation of the Hyogo Framework for Action*, Available at: http://www.preventionweb.net/files/8475_tanzania. pdf (accessed 14 August 2012).

Thabane, M. (2000) 'Shifts from old to new social and ecological environments in the Lesotho Highlands water scheme: relocating residents of the Mohale Dam area', *Journal of Southern African Studies*, 26(4): 633–54.

Thompson, M. (2012) 'Civil society and disaster', in B. Wisner, JC Gaillard and I. Kelman (eds) *The Routledge Handbook of Hazards and Disaster Risk Reduction*, London: Routledge, pp. 723–36.

Toulmin, C. (2009) *Climate Change in Africa*, London: Zed.

UN (2000) *We the People: The Role of the United Nations in the 21st Century*, Geneva: UN. Available at: http://www.un.org/millennium/sg/report/ (accessed 14 August 2012).

UNDP (2004) *Reducing Disaster Risk: A Challenge for Development,* Bureau for Crisis Prevention and Recovery, Geneva: UNDP. Available at: http://www.undp.org/content/ undp/en/home/librarypage/crisis-prevention-and-recovery/reducing-disaster-risk—a- challenge-for-development/ (accessed 14 August 2012)

UNISDR (2004) *Living with Risk: Turning the Tide on Disasters towards Sustainable Development*, Geneva: ISDR.

—— (2005) *Hyogo Framework for Action 2005-2015: Building the Resilience of Nations and Communities to Disasters*, Geneva: ISDR. Available at: http://www.unisdr.org/eng/ hfa/hfa.htm (accessed 18 April 2008).

—— (2008) *Linking Disaster Risk Reduction and Poverty Reduction: Good Practices and Lessons Learned*. A Publication of the Global Network of NGOs for Disaster Risk Reduction, Geneva: ISDR.

USAID (2005) 'Country spotlight: Ethiopia. Aid helps farmers with goats, grain banks, roads'. Available at: http://www.usaid.gov/press/frontlines/fl_jun05/spotlight.htm (accessed 25 October 2009).

van Niekerk, D. (2006) 'Disaster risk management in South Africa: the function and the activity – towards an integrated approach', *Politeia*, 25(2): 95–115.

von Kotze, A. and Holloway, A. (1996) *Reducing Risk: Participatory Learning Activities for Disaster Mitigation in Southern Africa*, Department of Adult and Community Education, University of Natal, Oxford: Oxfam Publishing.

Wangui, E., Smucker, T., Wisner, B., Lovell, E., Mascarenhas, A., Solomon, M., Weiner, D., Munna, A., Sinha, G., Bwenge, C., Meena, H. and Munishi, P. (2012) 'Integrated development, risk management and community-based climate change adaptation in a mountain-plains system in Northern Tanzania', *Revue de Géographie Alpine*, 100 (1). Available at: http://rga.revues.org/1701 (accessed 16 March 2013).

Wisner, B. (1988) *Power and Need in Africa*, London: Earthscan.

—— (1995a) 'The reconstruction of environmental rights in urban South Africa', *Human Ecology*, 23(2): 259–84.

—— (1995b) 'Bridging "expert" and "local" knowledge for counter-disaster planning in urban South Africa', *GeoJournal*, 37(3): 335–48.

—— (2010) 'Climate change and cultural diversity', *International Social Science Journal*, 61: 131–40.

Wisner, B., Blaikie, P., Cannon, T. and Davis, I. (2004) *At Risk: Natural Hazards, People's Vulnerability and Disasters*, 2nd edn, London: Routledge.

Wisner, B., Gaillard, JC and Kelman, I. (eds) (2012) *The Routledge Handbook of Hazards and Disaster Risk Reduction*, London: Routledge.

Wisner, B. and Mbithi, P. (1974) 'Drought in eastern Kenya: nutritional status and farmer activity', in G. White (ed.) *Natural Hazards: Global, National, Local*, New York: Oxford University Press, pp. 87–97.

Wisner, B., Toulmin, C. and Chitiga, R. (2006) 'Introduction', in B. Wisner, C. Toulmin and R. Chitiga (eds) *Towards a New Map of Africa*, London: Earthscan, pp. 1–50.

World Bank (2001) *Upgrading Urban Communities: A Resource for Practitioners.* Available at: http://web.mit.edu/urbanupgrading/upgrading/case-examples/overview-africa/alexandra-township.html (accessed 1 November 2009).

—— (2012) *Data.* Available at: http://data.worldbank.org/region/sub-saharan-africa (accessed 16 March 2013).

Zambia, Government of (2005) *National Disaster Management Policy*, Lusaka, Zambia: Government Printer.

—— (2008) *Zambia National Contingency Plan for Floods 2008/2009*, Lusaka: Disaster Management and Mitigation Unit of the Office of the Vice President.

—— (2009) *Zambia National Contingency Plan for Floods 2009/2010*, Lusaka: Disaster Management and Mitigation Unit of the Office of the Vice President.

15 Disaster risk management in Latin America and the Caribbean

Four decades of evolution and change, 1970–2010

Allan Lavell and Tania López-Marrero

Lessons for practitioners

- **Policy** and practice have shifted from a focus on disaster response to an emphasis on risk reduction in advance of a major **hazard**, but needs to continue to shift,
- To fully implement risk reduction, connections need to be made with wider topics, particularly land-use planning, environmental policy and livelihoods while focusing on community-based activities.
- To continue with these approaches in the face of climate change, disaster risk management should not be reduced to an adjunct of climate change adaptation. Instead, integration of programming and funding of climate change, disaster risk reduction and human development is required.

Introduction

Latin America and the Caribbean (LAC) (Figure 15.1) are exposed to the disastrous effects of different types of natural, socio-natural and technological phenomena – earthquakes, hurricanes, floods, landslides, tsunami, drought, extreme cold, fires and technological accidents, amongst the more prevalent. The region is periodically influenced by El Niño and La Niña ocean currents, annually subject to the Atlantic and Pacific hurricane season, affected by tectonic activity including the Pacific Ring of Fire and the Puerto Rico trench, and is projected to suffer from many effects of climate change. It is due to these characteristics, combined with high and increasing social **vulnerability** in many areas, that Mexico, Central America, the Andean and Caribbean countries figure prominently in disaster incidence and impact statistics (DESINVENTAR data base, 1997–2010 (www.desenredando.org); Lavell 1994; PREDECAN 2009; UNISDR 2009).

Between the 1950s and 1970s, most countries within the region established civil defense-type structures to deal with the threat of internal conflict and also with

Figure 15.1 Map of Latin America

emergencies and disasters. From the 1980s onwards, both in Latin America and the Caribbean countries (Figure 15.2) these traditional structures were modified as the field of disaster management widened to include a mandate beyond mere disaster response, with more emphasis on prevention and **mitigation**, rehabilitation and reconstruction. Also, in this period, tools for implementing this wider mandate became available.

Beginnings: disaster response and the role of civil defense from the 1940s

Most national civil defense organizations were created in the region because of the need for social control in situations of "internal war" against guerrilla

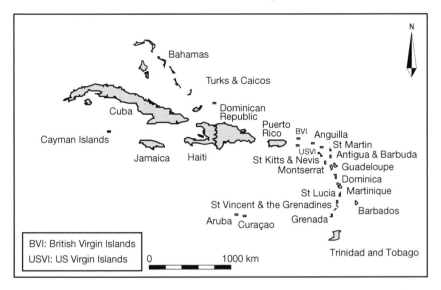

Figure 15.2 Map of the Caribbean region

movements (mostly in Latin America) pursued by national authorities under the influence of the USA during the early days of the Cold War. Set up to deal with internal security problems, these organizations quickly became the structural basis for institutional response to disasters triggered by natural hazards. The analogies between bombing and disaster could not be resisted and would lead to the dominance of military command and control mechanisms within disaster response for years to come. The exception was Costa Rica which disbanded its armed forces in 1949.

Up until the early 1970s, civil defense organizations limited themselves to response activities supported by the military armed forces, the Red Cross, fire, and medical services. Little concern for reconstruction and even less for prevention and mitigation could be seen in the region beyond traditional structural engineering work with buildings, dikes and dams. Scientific and technical support during this early period came predominantly from the engineering, medical and physical sciences. Disasters were considered either natural or acts of God (Wijkman and Timberlake 1984).

The case of the Costa Rican civil defense in 1963 is an interesting prelude to the advent of more widespread prevention notions. After massive flooding and landslides on the slopes of the Irazu volcano which had erupted intermittently for two years between 1961 and 1962, civil defense promoted tree reforestation as a means of ensuring the stability of slopes. This was a unique example of more advanced thinking on the topic of prevention. Such thinking is partly explained by the fact that the civil defense in Costa Rica was made up primarily of agricultural engineers and not career soldiers as in other countries (Lavell and Franco 1996).

The earthquakes in Peru, Nicaragua and Guatemala: preparedness and early warning, 1976 to mid-1990s

In 1970, a large earthquake off the coast of Peru led to one of the largest single disasters to affect Latin America during the last century (Oliver-Smith 1986, 1994). With 70,000 estimated deaths, many injuries, loss of housing, **livelihoods** and infrastructure, this event led to a large international response. Thousands of fatalities were concentrated in the small town of Yungay, situated below the White Cordillera mountain range of central Peru. The town was devastated by a massive landslide generated by the breaking off of the northern tip of the Huascaran Mountain as a consequence of the earthquake (Oliver-Smith 1986). Shortly thereafter, in 1972, the capital city of Nicaragua, Managua, was severely damaged by an earthquake with an estimated 8,000 deaths, a disaster whose aftermath would contribute to the downfall of the Somoza regime in 1979 with the Sandinista Revolution due to the **corruption** of the government in the reconstruction process. Then, in 1976, Guatemala was affected by a large earthquake that led to the death of approximately 20,000 persons and which was, due to the concentration of loss among poorer social groups, referred to by Alan Riding as a 'class-quake' (O'Keefe *et al.* 1976).

These events revealed the inadequacy of existing response mechanisms and procedures. Shortcomings were evident in early response, search and rescue, food and water supply, emergency housing, hospital and health services, appropriateness of foreign aid and its reception, not to mention the failings in rehabilitation and reconstruction that were subsequently documented (Abril-Ojeda 1982; Alexander 1993; Anderson and Woodrow 1989; Bates 1982; Bolin and Bolton 1982; Cuny 1983; Haas *et al.* 1977).

In response to these events, the Pan American Health Organization (PAHO) and later the USAID Office of Foreign Disaster Assistance (OFDA) put together their first disaster preparedness training schemes. PAHO focused on hospital emergency plans and response, while OFDA dealt with disaster response plans in general, including later efforts in the setting-up of emergency response centres in civil defense organizations. Between the end of the 1970s and the beginning of the 1980s these training programmes were fully established and over the next 30 years would train thousands of professionals and technicians in disaster response aspects. Both PAHO and OFDA have thus helped to create and implement a new school of thought and action in the region. Amplification of their approaches and schemes over the years would include PAHO's supplies and materials system for managing health-related aid donations (called SUMA http://www.paho.org/english/dd/ped/suma.htm), a hospital retrofitting programme, and early needs assessment methodology.

The developmental approach: Hurricane Mitch, Vargas and El Niño, 1997 to 1999

Hurricane Mitch in Honduras and Nicaragua (1998) and the deadly flooding and landslides in the Vargas region of Venezuela (1999), as well as El Niño-related floods, landslides and disease outbreaks (1997–98) may be considered collectively as 'windows of opportunity' that allowed concepts focused on relations between development (and maldevelopment) and disaster risk to take hold. Over the next ten years a focus on development and disaster began to influence the way **risk** was understood in the Andean and Central American countries. This new way of thinking was not yet dominant when it came to resources invested, actions taken, and how government institutions were structured. Nevertheless new concepts had been added to the policy debates, and the possibilities for change had gone beyond the inspiration offered by isolated examples of good practice at the local level by Maskrey (1987) and systematized in relationship to vulnerability by Wilches-Chaux (1989).

A period of increased innovation and overall acceptance of what were previously considered alternative models had begun. This transition was reflected in the relatively rapid disappearance over a ten-year period of the term 'disaster/emergency management' in national disaster organizations in favour of the now more widely accepted term 'disaster risk management'. The insights gleaned from the early research (Anderson and Woodrow 1989; Cuny 1983; Davis 1978; Hewitt 1983; Maskrey 1987; Wilches-Chaux 1988; Wisner *et al.* 1976; Wisner *et al.* 1977) were complemented by the work of an expanding network of academics and practitioners in the LAC region known as LA RED, from 1992 onwards.[1] This intellectual and practical work provided the underpinning for the transition towards a development-based approach to risk reduction in an increasing number of countries. By 1998 and the occurrence of Hurricane Mitch in Central America, most of the region had shifted their attention to such development-based approaches. Central to this transition were notions relating to the social construction of risk and the roles of environmental degradation, absence of land-use planning, the existing levels of social vulnerability, and lack of governance in the generation of **risk** (Blaikie *et al.* 1996; UNISDR 2009).

Hurricane Mitch in particular revealed land accumulation by the elite which meant that poor farmers lived in marginal, hazardous areas prone to landslides and flooding to be **underlying risk factors** or **root causes** of social vulnerability to the impact of hurricane Mitch (Wisner *et al.* 2004). A development pattern that favoured a narrow elite and external investors was thus clearly linked to the social construction of risk. Such disasters were now seen as 'unresolved development problems' in the phrase of Hagman (1984), and they came to be more widely accepted as such following Mitch because international agencies and civil society demanded processes of reconstruction with [socio-economic and political] transformation.

Damage and loss associated with climate-related disasters in the 1990s, especially damage associated with Hurricane Mitch, were widely and rapidly perceived to be associated with **poverty** and vulnerability created by marginality and subordinate social position, and lack of **access** to political power. Other factors discussed at the time included poorly located housing; lack of land-use control; environmental degradation, and the destabilizing of slopes by deforestation and road building. Such analysis was not just academic; there was widespread comment

---

Box 15.1 Disaster recovery as transformation: post-Mitch consensus

In mid-December 1998, following Hurricane Mitch, the Inter-American Development Bank hosted a Washington, DC meeting of the Central American governments, international agencies and civil society representatives who were part of the newly created 'Consultative Group for the Reconstruction and Transformation of Central America'. Diverse ideas were presented on reconstruction needs and the notions of social and ecological vulnerability reduction. The concept 'Reconstruction with Transformation' was commonly endorsed by all sectors present, establishing the guiding principle that reconstruction must be linked to development and poverty reduction. The resulting 'Stockholm Declaration' established general parameters for reconstruction finance. These included: the reduction of ecological and social vulnerability; transformation in social, economic and political structures; transparency and good governance; gender, race, ethnic and social equality; social participation; efforts to reduce external debt obligations; coordination of international assistance; and permanent monitoring of the reconstruction process.

---

on these issues in newspapers, by private sector and grass-roots organizations, even by some government and international agencies (see Girot 1999, 2002a, 2002b; Lavell 2000, for details of such discussion in the case of Mitch).

Despite failures in national implementation of the post-Mitch agenda (Wisner 2001), important institutions were created, including the Central American Coordination Centre for the Prevention of Natural Disasters (CEPREDENAC). Moreover, the impacts of Hurricane Mitch led to such agencies as the Central American Commission for Environment and Development (CCAD) and the Central American Commission for Hydraulic Resources (CRRH) accepting a risk reduction framework focused on development of **community-based disaster risk reduction (CBDRR)** (see Chapter 4) to an extent they had never done before.[2]

The transition to a more development-based view of risk and risk management was reinforced by priorities set by international development agencies such as German GTZ, The Swiss Development Agency (SDC), the European Union-financed Disaster Prevention Project for the Andean Countries (PREDECAN), and the Central American Environmental Vulnerability Reduction Project (PREVDA), and by regional, official, intergovernmental organizations such as the CEPREDENAC and the Andean Committee for Disaster Prevention (CAPRADE).

These changes were more prevalent in the Andean and Central American countries than in Southern Cone countries such as Argentina or Brazil, or Mexico. More impervious, nationalist ideologies and isolation from outside influences were major reasons for this. Mexico, in the case of the 2007 Tabasco and Chiapas floods, requested external support for only the second time in its history (the other instance being the 1985 earthquake) demonstrating the independence it shows in regard to disaster and risk management.

Fruits of a developmental approach to disaster risk reduction

The disaster prevention and response system concept

In a 1989 transformation, Colombia changed its institutional set-up for disaster management and created an inter-institutional, interdisciplinary, decentralized, development-based prevention and mitigation, preparedness and response system (Ramírez and Cardona 1996). Since then, other countries have followed the same road with varying levels of success and failure. During the early 2000s Nicaragua and Bolivia had progressed a fair way in terms of conceptualizing such a system, but ironically these two countries remain the most deficient in operation and implementation. Following a 2001 earthquake, El Salvador created the National Service for Territorial Studies (SNET) in 2003 that helped establish risk reduction and risk studies as something separate from disaster response. The most recent and radical change has been seen in Ecuador, where the government has created a Risk Management Secretariat, substantially reducing the military's role and incorporating civil defense into this new civilian-run organization. This was supported by the country's new Constitution that included language dedicated to the population's right to security and risk management. Finally, a new 2011 Peruvian risk management law and 2012 Colombian law have significantly advanced development-based interpretations of risk and risk management, and have increased control over risk management processes by development and finance agencies, as opposed to civil defense organizations.

Public investment and local level land-use plans

Peru has pioneered the use of public sector financing decisions for reducing risk. The Ministry of Finance and Economy with German GTZ (now GIZ) support has instigated regulations and produced a manual for operations in this area, elements of which have been gradually diffused into other Central American and Andean countries. The Costa Rican Planning Ministry is currently pushing this line of action as well.

Colombia has been the regional pioneer in promoting land-use planning, regional planning and environmental plans as vehicles for the introduction of risk management at the local level in its more than one thousand municipalities (the primary jurisdictions in the country). The use of such mechanisms in Bogota, Manizales, Medellin and other Colombian cities is now well developed. COSUDE in Nicaragua and the World Bank in Honduras and Nicaragua have promoted similar processes at the municipal level. The PREDECAN project in the Andean countries promoted the development of methods for land-use planning at the

---

Box 15.2 More effective early warning systems
(see Chapter 5)

Attempts to embed hazard early warning systems in local development plans and risk reduction schemes bode well for the future. Examples include the La Masica municipality project in Honduras. Here resident-based upstream observation of river heights and radio communication to the town centre provide flash flood early warning. The success of this scheme was fully noted during Hurricane Mitch when no deaths were reported in the municipality, this contrasting with the numbers of deaths occurring in surrounding jurisdictions under similar conditions of stress. IADB is now supporting early warning systems for volcanoes in Ecuador which provide for such systems to be embedded in local risk management structures as opposed to being a stand-alone scheme.

---

municipal level based on pilot projects in municipalities in all participating countries (Colombia, Ecuador, Peru and Bolivia). The Central American Federation of Municipalities (FEMICA) is following this line of action with its members, and the Spanish Agency for Development Cooperation (AECID) has also promoted studies that led to urban planning approaches that include risk reduction factors in Central American cities.

Risk management units in sectoral agencies

In some countries risk management units or secretariats have been inserted into existing ministries and departments such as agriculture, public works, planning and finance, education and health (Costa Rica, Peru, Colombia, Ecuador, for example). This is a positive sign of progress in focusing attention on risk in public sector activity and action throughout the region. Seen as a means for bringing greater attention to risk-related aspects, such an 'office approach' was instigated by PAHO support in health ministries in the 1980s and 1990s. However, with the growth of the number of sectoral disaster units in different ministries and municipalities throughout the region, a danger that could outweigh the advantage has arisen. This danger is that the issue of risk might become 'ghettoized' in small, marginal units where there is little political power (see Chapter 14).

The Caribbean: disaster risk management over three decades

As in Latin America, disaster outcomes in the Caribbean demonstrate the relationship between physical–environmental aspects associated with hazard exposure and the complex social and human settings in which hazards develop into disasters (see, for example, López-Marrero and Wisner 2012). We can argue, however, that the Caribbean shares many characteristics that are distinct from those of continental Latin American countries – characteristics that can influence differential vulnerabilities and disaster outcomes. The region is composed of small islands with great variety in terms of the countries' political ideologies and systems, economic situation and linkages, cultural background, and linguistic differences. The elements can influence disaster risk management and regional collaborations. For instance, the English-speaking countries of the Caribbean share a relatively high degree of connections; in terms of disaster risk management this is illustrated by their membership in the main regional disaster management body – the Caribbean Disaster Emergency Management Agency (CDEMA).

Because of their conditions as islands with limited land space, population densities are relatively higher compared to those of continental countries in Latin America. In the Caribbean, the majority of the population, particularly those on the smaller islands, are concentrated in coastal areas; the same goes for its major economic activities and infrastructure. Geographic isolation, limited natural resources, large exposed coastal zones also make Caribbean islands particularly prone to current hazards and to the potential effects of climate change and associated sea-level rise (Méheux *et al.* 2007; Mimura *et al.* 2007; Pelling and Uitto 2001).

Moreover, many islands, particularly the small islands developing states (SIDS), possess economies with little diversification. Tourism, for example, is a major economic sector in the region; and for some islands like Aruba, Turks and Caicos, the Cayman Islands, Saint Lucia, Antigua and Barbuda, Martinique, Guadeloupe, Saint Martin, Anguilla, and the US Virgin Islands, visitors' expenditures constitute more than 50 per cent of their gross domestic product (GDP) (Potter *et al.* 2004). This makes Caribbean islands highly susceptible to the impacts of natural hazards, as one single event can disrupt an island's economic base and can have great impact on their GDP. This was illustrated in the 2004 hurricane season when the passage of Hurricane Ivan over Grenada, for example, destroyed a large part of the country's infrastructure, including tourism-related facilities. In just a few hours, more that 90 per cent of hotel guest rooms were either completely destroyed or damaged (Nurse and Moore 2005; OECS 2004).

Natural hazards in the Caribbean are recurrent phenomena. Historically, different disasters have caused great damage and death within the region (see, for example, Tomblin 1981). Recent events like the 2010 Haitian earthquake (at least 217,300 fatalities), the passage of Tropical Storm Jeanne over Hispaniola on 2004 (at least 2,800 fatalities), and the 2004 floods on the Haiti–Dominican Republic border with at least 1,500 fatalities are just a few examples of events that remind us of the constant need to build on good practices and identify ways of reducing risks and disaster losses within the region (López-Marrero and Wisner 2012).

Beginnings of disaster risk management in the Caribbean

Comprehensive and explicit risk and disaster management initiatives in the Caribbean are mostly a post-1970s phenomenon. Prior to this time, national governments responded to disaster events independently, as disasters occurred, and with no concrete national organization or coordinated efforts to deal directly with such events; instead, decisions were handed over to the heads of state and entities like the police and the defense forces (Poncelet 1997). The late 1970s and early 1980s were particularly devastating years for the region in terms of disaster occurrences. Hurricane David and Frederick, and the eruption of Soufrière volcano in Saint Vincent (all in 1979) caused a great amount of damage. Hurricane David, for example, considered one of the most powerful hurricanes to have impacted the Caribbean during the second half of the twentieth century, resulted in at least 2,000 deaths and caused destruction to several islands of the Lesser Antilles, Hispaniola and Bahamas (Longshore 2008).

Such events prompted regional and country-level discussions in terms of the development of programmes, initiatives and institutional arrangements for disaster risk management, initially focusing on disaster response, but subsequently on preparedness as well (Collymore 2011; Poncelet 1997). Countries like Cuba, Puerto Rico, Barbados and Jamaica were among the first to create national organizations for disaster management; with the prime responsibilities lying on national-level ministries and governmental offices, the civil defense, and, in some instances, national disaster offices and committees (Jones 2011; Poncelet 1997). Over time, and just by looking at the changing names and objectives of different initiatives, one may see how the main focus of disaster management has changed. The original focus on *post-disaster management* – mostly relief – with state agencies in charge of disaster management and coordination, moved towards a focus on *pre-disaster management*, including prevention, preparedness, and mitigation, and with the participation of different government sectors, non-governmental organizations, the private sector, and the civil society more generally.

Evolution of regional disaster management in the Caribbean

As stated above, a series of disaster events in the late 1970s and early 1980s incited regional consultation and the development of regional initiatives for disaster management (Collymore 2011; Poncelet 1997). Different meetings, starting in 1981 in Dominican Republic, and subsequent ones, were the basis for today's initiatives, including the Caribbean Disaster Emergency Management Agency (CDEMA; http://www.cdema.org) and the development of the Comprehensive Disaster Management framework.

Regional initiatives have focused mostly on the English-speaking states that today constitute CDEMA, the leading body of disaster management on the region. At the 1981 meeting, the Pan Caribbean Disaster Preparedness Project (PCDPP), a multi-donor supported project[3] was created to improve regional disaster response (Poncelet 1997). A few years later, in 1984, the program developed into the Pan Caribbean Disaster Preparedness and Prevention Program (PCDPPP).

PCDPPP initiated disaster management and loss reduction with an emphasis on human capital – development education and awareness, training and workshops with representatives of member states – as well as the establishment of technical resources including warning systems and regional emergency telecommunications (Collymore 2011; Toulmin 1987). These resources were primarily associated with hurricane hazards. Activities under the PCDPPP certainly showed a shift from disaster relief and response to also include preparedness. This resulted in significant reduction of loss of lives and injuries, yet losses to property and infrastructure was high and continued to increase (Collymore 2011). Consequently the addition of prevention and mitigation activities became part of PCDPPP regional disaster management. Here, new activities were promoted, including vulnerability assessments of critical infrastructure and evacuation plans.

The development of building codes (i.e., the Caribbean Uniform Building Code), and land-use policies also started to inform strategies for disaster management (Chin 1997; Krimgold 2011). Activities under PCDPPP fomented the incorporation of a wider group of stakeholders, beyond government agencies, to include non-governmental organisations (NGOs) and professional groups like engineers, architects, and planners. Additionally, technical assistance was provided for the establishment of emergency offices and the development of national disaster plans. This was the case for countries like Antigua and Barbuda and Trinidad and Tobago (Collymore 2011).

The late 1980s was again a devastating period for the region in terms of disaster occurrence, particularly with the passage of Hurricane Gilbert in 1988 and Hugo in 1989. Hurricane Gilbert, for instance, has been regarded as the most destructive hurricane to strike Jamaica, resulting in about 500,000 people homeless, US$1 billion in property damage, and 45 people killed (Longshore 2008). Hurricane Hugo was one of the 20 most severe hurricanes to have affected the Caribbean region during the second half of the twentieth century, impacting particularly the Lesser Antilles and Puerto Rico. These events, along with the beginning of the International Decade for Disaster Risk Reduction in 1990, stimulated rethinking of regional disaster management and resulted in the establishment in 1991 of the PCDPPP successor – the Caribbean Disaster Emergency Response Agency (CDERA)[4] (Collymore 2011; Poncelet 1997). Moreover, events in the mid- and late 1990s such as Hurricanes Georges, Floyd, and Lenny, along with the 1997 Montserrat volcanic eruption also influenced in the development of CDERA objectives.

CDERA promoted inter-regional and intergovernmental partnership and cooperation, and included a wider range of activities, such as better structuring, organizing and channeling information to governmental agencies and regional NGOs in support of disaster preparedness and response, mobilizing and coordinating disaster relief (including neighboring countries' defense and police forces), disaster mitigation efforts and education, and institutional training among its participating states (Bisek *et al*. 2001; Poncelet 1997). While PCDPPP promoted activities beyond preparedness, the limited country capacities and resources to support prevention and mitigation restricted what they could do related to these phases of disaster management; it is under CDERA that these activities prospered and gained more precedence (Collymore 2011).

Under CDERA, an increased range of stakeholder engagement started to emerge; elements that later became part of the Comprehensive Disaster Management (CDM) framework. This is because CDERA embraced notions like the relationships between disaster and development along with the need to include disaster management in the wider context of government decision-making and its incorporation into national economic planning (Bisek *et al.* 2001; Collymore 2011).

In 2009, CDERA changed its name to CDEMA – the Caribbean Disaster Emergency Management Agency. New emphasis was placed on multiple hazards (including technological ones), and CDEMA embraces not only the management of current hazards and disasters but also those than can be intensified by

---

Box 15.3 Cuba: The Caribbean exception

Cuba provides a useful case of disaster reduction through the combination of personal and social protection. An examination of the number of people killed over the past three decades reveals that Cuba has had relatively few deaths from disasters, in spite of being the second country (after Haiti) reporting most hazard events (López-Marrero and Wisner 2012). This achievement of protecting lives has been registered in a country with the region's largest population and with one of the lowest GDP per capita. Cuba has also had to cope with an economic blockade imposed by the USA for over 50 years and the disappearance of subsidies and assistance from the former Soviet Union and its satellites.

Cuba's success in saving lives has been achieved through a variety of factors such as a well-organized and trained civil defense system, a country-wide early warning system, a high level of educational attainment and literacy among its population which permits a better understanding of warning systems, timely evacuations, community-based training programmes (including training and simulation exercises in schools), and **community** mobilization during the different phases of disaster (Llanes-Guerra and Montes de Oca Días 2002; Sims and Volgemann 2002; Thompson and Gaviria 2004; Wisner *et al.* 2005). Here, the impacts of policy and practice at various scales have proved to be effective in reducing disaster impacts. Cuba's achievements have been attained because disaster and risk management are not seen as different entities; but as an integral part of the country's and its people's development. Universal access to services such as health and education (in both urban and rural areas), policies to reduce social and economic disparities, investment in the country's infrastructure (including rural areas), and social organization have been among the priorities in Cuba's overall development over the years (Skelton 2004); **resources** that are put in place in the face of disaster occurrence.

climate change. CDEMA is meant to advance the work of CDERA, and will 'fully embrace the principles and practices of Comprehensive Disaster Management (CDM)' which 'seeks to reduce the risk and loss associated with natural and technological hazards and the effects of climate change to enhance regional sustainable development' (http://www.cdema.org/).

Collymore (2011) describes how disaster management in the region has developed over 25 years from primarily event-driven and relief activities to a broader approach including elements of preparedness, prevention, and mitigation, and more recently relating to topics of sustainability, development, and climate change. All these elements have advanced regional disaster management and have helped decrease the number of deaths and losses. Exceptions always occur, however, as this was the case of the extraordinary 2010 Haitian earthquake.

As with any initiative, it is easier to put strategies in words than to move forward and implement them in practice. In his reflection, Collymore raise some questions that need further thinking and discussion to advance regional Caribbean disaster management:

- How to tackle the dependency on external aid and interventions?
- How to balance disaster management with other development goals?
- What focus should **vulnerability assessment** have?
- How to develop possible solutions – should these be technologically or socially driven?
- Who should be the actors and stakeholders involved?
- On what level should we focus for capacity building – should it be a centralized, top-down mechanism, a decentralized one with focus on community-based capacity development, or a combination of both?

Community-based disaster risk reduction in LAC

Community-based disaster risk reduction (CBDRR) initiatives (see Chapter 4) provide a complementary approach to broader disaster risk management; emphasizing community and local action, while at the same time promoting community partnership with governmental, non-governmental, and other sectors of the society (Maskrey 2011). CBDRR is increasing in Latin American and Caribbean countries, albeit slowly.

In the Dominican Republic, for example, the governmental agency Asociación Dominicana de Mitigación de Desastres, in collaboration with NGOs, has been conducting workshops with vulnerable communities. Communities have developed plans and actions to address natural hazard vulnerability and reduce disaster impacts. They have constructed small-scale projects (e.g., drainage ditch embankments and containment walls), established emergency committees, evacuation plans, and organized clean-up brigades to put into place when a disaster is imminent (CGCED 2002). Participating communities had reduced impacts during the passage of Hurricane Georges in 1998.

CBDRR projects have also been undertaken elsewhere in Dominican Republic, in urban neighborhoods and rural communities (Bastidas *et al.* 2009). In this case, projects were undertaken in collaboration with the Dominican government and various NGOs, and emphasize early warning systems, community **vulnerability mapping**, local **capacity** building and training, public awareness and education, and small infrastructure projects. There is an emphasis on community organization and leadership, particularly among participating women and the youth. These initiatives, thus, have the dual functionality of preparing for disaster management but also to increase the well-being of participants.

Supporting CBDRR requires identifying elements that are important to community members in their everyday lives and identifying ways to mainstream those elements into disaster management (Delica-Willison and Gaillard 2012). Developing interventions that suit multiple purposes have a greater chance of acceptance by stakeholders. In Santo Domingo, in the Dominican Republic, for example, the construction of stairways and bridges in urban low-income sectors were valued and supported actions because they enabled market access that stimulated local businesses and social interaction between neighborhoods. In addition, they provide emergency access in the case of disaster occurrence (Pelling 2011). López-Marrero and Yarnal (2010) also advocate the identification of everyday concerns and **unsafe conditions** among residents of hazard-exposed communities as a starting point for CBDRR. In low-income communities in Puerto Rico, these authors found that health conditions, family well-being, economic factors, and land tenure were more immediate and worrying problems than floods.

Box 15.4 Microcredit and micro-insurance: mechanisms for risk reduction at the community level
(see Chapter 12)

In Colombia, the city of Manizales recently began an insurance scheme for the poor subsidized by the local population on a voluntary basis. Residents may voluntarily pay for insurance for disadvantaged groups when they pay their regular municipal taxes. Indigenous groups of highland Bolivia have a microcredit and insurance scheme in place that promotes risk reduction and provides financial security. The schemes do not just provide financial relief in times of loss, but also promote risk reduction by making compensation subject to the history of losses claimed by individuals – similar to the way National Flood Insurance is administered in the USA. If farmers have not protected themselves to a given standard established by local experts, then they receive no compensation for losses above that level. Both Colombia and Bolivia examples demonstrate efforts to get insurance off the ground as tools for risk reduction and not just risk transfer (Lavell and Lavell 2009).

All these problems are related to the creation of unsafe conditions that exacerbate disaster impacts; hence tackling these everyday life factors will both treat pressing daily concerns and strengthen capacity to cope with disasters.

Enhancing community capacity for disaster management also calls for the integration of diverse **knowledge** types (including local knowledge and experiences and external specialist knowledge), promoting effective links and collaborations between community members and other groups such and governmental emergency managers and NGOs, and cultivating new partners (see Chapters 5 and 6). All these elements are compatible with the objectives of the prevailing regional approach – the Comprehensive Disaster Management framework.

Climate change adaptation and disaster risk management: a new challenge

Latin America and the Caribbean suffer from a series of climate change-related conditions and greater impacts are projected for the future (Briones 2012; Mimura *et al.* 2007). An overall increase in average temperature of 1°C over the last century and 2–3 mm rise in sea levels are expected to bring severe consequences to the region's population, including, for example, coastal communities, urban populations and agricultural communities. El Niño is the name of the cyclical warming of water in the Pacific that affects the climate of the LAC region and elsewhere in the world. El Niño has increased in strength and intensity over the past 30 years, and there has also been an increase in intense hurricanes affecting the Caribbean islands and the Caribbean and Pacific coasts of Mexico and Central America (IPCC 2012). Increases in the number of forest fires and loss of forest may signal the process of conversion of Amazon regions from forest to savannah landscapes, accompanied with great loss of biodiversity (WWF 2012). Other warming impacts include loss of wetland in the southern Mexican Gulf coast zone, coral bleaching in the Caribbean and harm to delicate Andean high mountain ecosystems. The impact of increases in average temperatures on agricultural productivity of maize and other grains illustrates the sort of 'creeping' problem that places insecure weather-dependent livelihoods at risk (UNISDR 2009).

The conceptual separation of disaster risk reduction and climate change adaptation is disappearing (IFRC 2012), but funding and programming lag behind. It is the current position of most disaster risk specialists in the region that climate change adaptation can gain much from accumulated experience with disaster risk management already in place (O'Brien *et al.* 2006).

Conclusion

In both Latin America and the Caribbean a series of disasters in the period 1970–2000 coincided with changes in how experts framed and conceptualized the natural and human aspects of disaster risk and management. Punctuated by specific high profile, deadly and costly events, politicians in the region responded to demands of civil society and encouragement from international organizations and donors. Thus there has been an uneven but definite shift in policy and practice from mainly response to an emphasis on risk reduction. Links have been made with land-use planning, environmental policy, and livelihoods. Community-based activities have expanded. However, these positive changes have yet to be fully tested within the context of climate change. To meet these challenges, disaster risk management should not be reduced to an adjunct of climate change adaptation; rather an integrated approach to climate change, disaster risk and human development is required.

Notes

1   LA RED, the Network for the Social Study of Disaster Prevention was established in Limon, Costa Rica, in a meeting of 14 persons in August 1992 in order to stimulate the production of social-science-based thought and practice on risk and disaster (www.desenredando.org/).
2   In the Caribbean, another series of disasters led to the creation of the Caribbean Disaster Emergency Response Agency (CDERA) in 1991, renamed and strengthened under a name that substituted 'response' for 'management' (CDEMA) in 1999.
3   The project was supported by the Pan American Health Organization (PAHO), the United Nations Relief Organization, the Caribbean Community (CARICOM), the Canadian International Development Agency, the United States Agency for International Development (USAID), among others.
4   Supported by PAHO, the International Federation of Red Cross and Red Crescent Societies, USAID, among others.

References

Abril-Ojeda, G. (1982) *The Role of Disaster Relief for Long Term Development in LDC's with Special Reference to Guatemala after the 1976 Earthquake*, Monograph no. 6, Stockholm: Institute of Latin American Studies.

Alexander, D. (1993) *Natural Disasters*, New York: Chapman and Hall.

Anderson, M. and Woodrow, P. (1989) *Rising from the Ashes: Development Strategies at Times of Disasters*, Boulder, CO: Westview Press.

Bastidas, Pedro, María M. Santamaría, and Sussana Urbano. 2009. Community disaster preparedness in Dominican Republic: projects history by component. Santo Domingo, Dominican Republic: European Commission – Humanitarian Aid Office for the Caribbean.

Bates, F. (ed.) (1982) *Recovery, Change and Development: A Longitudinal Study of the 1976 Guatemalan Earthquake*, Athens, GA: University of Georgia Press.

Bisek, P., Jones, E. and Ornstein, C. (2001) *A Strategy and Results Framework for Comprehensive Disaster Management in the Caribbean*, CDERA, USAID UNDP. Available at: http://www.preventionweb.net/english/professional/publications/v.php?id=2518 (accessed 4 October 2012).

Blaikie, P., Cannon, T., Davis, I. and Wisner, B. (1996) *Vulnerabilidad: El Entorno social, economico y politico de los desastres*, trans. La Red/ ECCO, Peru: La Red. Available at: http://www.desenredando.org/public/libros/1996/vesped/ (accessed 23 March 2013).

Bolin, R. and Bolton, P. (1982) 'Recovery in Nicaragua and the USA', *International Journal of Mass Emergencies and Disasters*, 1(55): 125–44.

Briones, F. (ed.) (2012) *Perspectivas de Investigación y Acción Frente al Cambio Climático en Latinoamérica*, Special Issue of *Desastres y Sociedad* en el marco del XX aniversario de LA RED. Available at: http://www.desenredando.org/public/2012/LaRed_Desastres_y_Sociedad_2012-07_web.pdf (accessed 23 March 2013).

CGCED (Caribbean Group for Cooperation in Economic Development) (2002) *Natural Hazard Risk Management in the Caribbean: Revisiting the Challenge*, World Bank. Available at: http://siteresources.worldbank.org/INTDISMGMT/Resources/cgced_final.pdf (accessed 14 July 2012).

Chin, M. (1997) 'Possible mitigation strategies for hurricanes and earthquakes in the Caribbean', *Disaster Studies* 3: 88–95. Unit for Disaster Studies, University of West Indies, Mona, Jamaica.

Collymore, J. (2011) 'Disaster Management in the Caribbean: perspectives on institutional capacity reform and development', *Environmental Hazards*, 10(1): 6–22.

Cuny, F. (1983) *Disasters and Development*, Oxford: Oxford University Press.

Davis, I. (1978) *Shelter after Disaster*, Oxford: Oxford Polytechnic Press.

Delica-Willison, Z. and Gaillard, JC (2012) 'Community action and disaster', in B. Wisner, JC Gaillard and I. Kelman (eds) *The Routledge Handbook of Hazards and Disaster Risk Reduction*, London: Routledge, pp. 711–22.

Girot, P. (1999) *Reducción de la Vulnerabilidad ante Amenazas Naturales: Lecciones aprendidas del Huracán Match, Documento estratégico sobre gestión ambiental*, IADB, Washington, DC: Inter-American Development Bank.

—— (2002a) 'Scaling-up: resilience to hazards and the importance of cross-scale linkages', paper presented at UNDP Expert Group Meeting on Risk Management and Adaptation,' How to integrate disaster reduction and adaptation to climate change?' 17–19 June, Havana, Cuba.

—— (2002b) *Vulnerability, Risk and Environmental Security in Central America: Lessons from Hurricane Mitch*, Geneva: IISD/IUCN.

Haas, J., Kates, R. and Bowden, M. (1977) *Reconstruction Following Disaster*, Cambridge, MA: MIT Press.

Hagman, G. (1984) *Prevention Better than Cure: A Swedish Red Cross Report on Human and Environmental Disasters in the Third World*, Stockholm: Swedish Red Cross.

Hewitt, K. (ed.) (1983) *Interpretations of Calamity*, London: Allen and Unwin.

IFRC Climate Centre (2012) *Minimum Standards for Local Climate Smart Risk Reduction*, The Hague: IFRC Climate Centre. Available at: http://www.climatecentre.org/site/minimumstandards (accessed 23 March 2013).

IPCC (2012) *Managing the Risks of Extreme Events and Disasters to Advance Climate Change Adaptation*, Geneva: IPCC. Available at: http://www.ipcc-wg2.gov/SREX/ [overview] & http://ipcc-wg2.gov/SREX/images/uploads/SREX-All_FINAL.pdf (accessed 23 March 2013).

Jones, E. (2011) 'Then and now: a 30-year journey from the leading edge', *Environmental Hazards*, 10(1): 30–41.

Krimgold, F. (2011) 'Disaster risk reduction and the evolution of physical development regulation', *Environmental Hazards*, 10(1): 53–8.

Lavell, A. (1994) 'Prevention and mitigation of disasters in Central America: social and political vulnerability to disasters at the local level', in A. Varley (ed.) *Disasters, Development and Environment*, London: Belhaven Press, pp. 49–63.

—— (2000) 'Desastres y Desarrollo: Hacia un entendimiento de las formas de construcción social de un desastre: El caso del huracán Mitch en Centroamérica', in N. Garita and

J. Nowalski (eds) *Del Desastre al Desarrollo Sostenible: Huracán Mitch en Centro-américa*, Washington, DC: World Bank/CIDHCS.

Lavell, A. and Franco, E. (1996) *Estado, Sociedad y la Gestión de Desastres en América Latina: En Busca del Paradigma Perdido*, Peru: La Red, ITDG.

Lavell, A and Lavell, C. (2009) *Local Risk Management in the Andes*, Lima, Peru: CAPRADE-PREDECAN.

Llanes-Guerra, J. and Montes de Oca Días, M. (2002) 'Cuba: beyond a simple response to hurricanes', *Latin America and the Caribbean*, 6: 8–11.

Longshore, D. (2008) *Encyclopedia of Hurricanes, Typhoons, and Cyclones*, New York: Checkmark Books.

López-Marrero, T. and Wisner, B. (2012) 'Not in the same boat: disasters and differential vulnerability in the Insular Caribbean', *Caribbean Studies*, 40(2): 129–67.

López-Marrero, T. and Yarnal, B. (2010) 'Putting adaptive capacity into the context of people's lives: a case study of two flood-prone communities in Puerto Rico', *Natural Hazards*, 52 (2): 277–97.

Maskrey, A. (1987) *Community Based Disaster Risk Management*, Oxford: Oxfam and Oxford University Press.

—— (2011) 'Revisiting community-based disaster risk management', *Environmental Hazards*, 10(1): 42–52.

Méheux, K., Dominey-Howes, D. and Lloyd, K. (2007) 'Natural hazard impacts in small islands developing states: a review of current knowledge and future research needs', *Natural Hazards*, 40 (2): 429–46.

Mimura, N., Nurse, L., McLean, R.F., Agard, J., Briguglio, L., Lefale, P., Payet, R. and Sem, G. (2007) 'Small islands. Climate change 2007: Impacts, adaptation and vulnerability', in M. Parry, O. Canziani, J. Palutikof, P. van der Linden and C. Hanson (eds) *Contribution of Working Group II to the Fourth Assessment Report of the Inter-governmental Panel on Climate Change*, Cambridge: Cambridge University Press, pp. 687–716.

Nurse, L. and Moore, R. (2005) 'Adaptation to global climate change: an urgent requirement for Small Island Developing States', *Review of European Community and International Environmental Law*, 14(2): 100–7.

O'Brien, G., O'Keefe, P., Rose, J. and Wisner, B. (2006) 'Climate change and disaster management', *Disasters*, 30(1): 64–80.

OECS (Organization of Eastern Caribbean States) (2004) *Grenada: Macro Socio-economic Assessment of the Damages Caused by Hurricane Ivan*, OECS. Available at: http://www. gov.gd/egov/docs/reports/Ivan-Report-07-09-04.pdf (accessed 14 July 2012).

O'Keefe, P., Westgate, K. and Wisner, B. (1976) 'Taking the naturalness out of natural disasters', *Nature*, 260 (5552): 566–7.

Oliver-Smith, A. (1986) *The Martyred City: Death and Rebirth in the Andes*, Albuquerque, NM: University of New Mexico Press.

—— (1994) 'Perú: 31 de Mayo de 1970: Quinientos años de desastre', *Desastres y Sociedad*, 2(2): 2–15.

Pelling, M. (2011) 'Urban governance and disaster risk reduction in the Caribbean: the experiences of Oxfam', *Environment and Urbanization*, 23 (2): 383–400.

Pelling, M. and Uitto, J. (2001) 'Small island developing states: natural disaster vulnerability and global change', *Environmental Hazards*, 3 (2): 49–62.

Poncelet, J. (1997) 'Disaster management in the Caribbean', *Disasters*, 21(3): 267–79.

Potter, R., Barker, D., Conway, D. and Klak, T. (2004) *The Contemporary Caribbean*, Harlow: Pearson/Prentice Hall.

PREDECAN (Prevención de Desastres de la Comunidad Andina) (2009) *Atlas de las dinámicas del territorio Andino*. Lima, Peru: Secretaría General Comunidad Andina.

Ramírez, F. and Cardona, O. (1996) 'Sistema nacional para la prevención y atención de desastres de Colombia', in A. Lavell and E. Franco (eds) *Estado, Sociedad y Gestión de los Desastres en América Latina*, Bogotá: Red de Estudios Sociales en Prevención de Desastres en América Latina, Tercer Mundo Editores, pp. 214–55.

Sims, H. and Volgelmann, K. (2002) 'Popular mobilization and disaster management in Cuba', *Public Administration Development*, 22 (5): 389–400.

Skelton, T. (2004) 'Issues of development on the Pan-Caribbean: overcoming crises and rising challenges?' in T. Skelton (ed.) *Introduction to the Pan-Caribbean*, London: Arnold, pp. 42–71.

Thompson, M. and Gaviria, I. (2004) *Weathering the Storm: Lessons in Risk Reduction from Cuba*. Oxfam American Report. Available at: http://www.walterlippmann.com/oxfam-america-cuba-weathering-the-storm.pdf (accessed 14 July 2012).

Tomblin, J. (1981) 'Earthquakes, volcanoes and hurricanes: a review of natural hazards and vulnerability in the West Indies', *Ambio*, 10(6): 340–5.

Toulmin, L. (1987) 'Disaster preparedness and regional training on nine Caribbean islands: a long-term evaluation', *Disasters*, 11(3): 221–34.

UNISDR (United Nations International Strategy for the Reduction of Disasters) (2009) *Global Assessment Report on Disaster Risk Reduction*, Geneva: UNISDR.

Wijkman, A. and Timberlake, L. (1984) *Natural Disasters: Acts of God or Acts of Man?*, London: Earthscan.

Wilches-Chaux, G. (1989) *Desastres, Ecologismo y Formación Profesional*, Popayán, Colombia: SENA.

Wisner, B. (2001) 'Risk and the neoliberal state: why post-Mitch lessons didn't reduce El Salvador's earthquake losses', *Disasters,* 25(3): 251–68.

Wisner, B., Blaikie, P., Cannon, T. and Davis, I. (2004) *At Risk: Natural Hazards, People's Vulnerability and Disasters*, 2nd edn, London: Routledge.

Wisner, B., O'Keefe, P. and Westgate, K. (1977) 'Global system and local disasters: the untapped power of people's science', *Disasters*, 1(1): 47–57.

Wisner, B., Ruiz, V., Lavell, A., and Meyerles, L. (2005) 'Run tell your neighbor! Early warning during the 2004 hurricane season in the Caribbean', in *World Disaster Report 2005*, Geneva: IFRC, pp. 38–59.

Wisner, B., Westgate, K. and O'Keefe, P. (1976) 'Poverty and disaster', *New Society*, 9, pp. 546–8.

WWF (2012) *Climate Change in the Amazon*. Available at: http://wwf.panda.org/what_we_do/where_we_work/amazon/problems/climate_change_amazon/ (accessed 23 March 2013).

16 Disaster risk management in the Asia-Pacific

Emerging trends and directions

Krishna S. Vatsa

Lessons for practitioners

- Governments, NGOs, and international agencies need to work together to develop shared strategies and programmes for disaster risk management, especially focusing on community-based work to show the development risk reduction links.
- Urban development needs to be guided by planning, regulation and incentives towards increased disaster risk reduction.
- Disaster risk reduction can be successful only if the poor have greater **access** to improved shelter, diversified livelihoods, and more dependable social services, meaning that disaster risk management interventions need to link with these basic priorities.
- Disaster risk reduction programmes need to include livelihoods as a key component, and promote that through skill training, small enterprise development, and small grants.
- The urgency of dealing with climate change and variability means that an increased commitment of resources and expertise to disaster risk reduction, with an emphasis on **mitigation** as much as emergency preparedness and response, is needed.

Introduction

The Asia-Pacific region (Figures 16.1 and 16.2) is an extremely disaster-prone region because of the overlap between multiple hazards, population concentration and high levels of **poverty**. This chapter underscores the emerging trends and progress being made in the Asia-Pacific region (AP) for disaster risk reduction, and it underlines several issues that need prompt and well-coordinated action from governments, NGOs, international organizations, the private sector and academia.

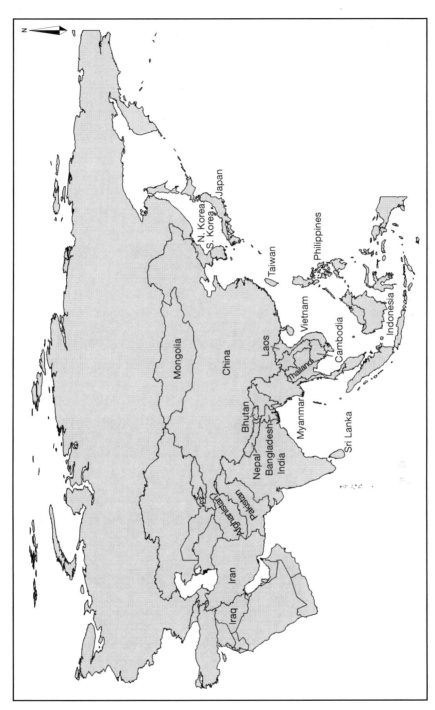

Figure 16.1 Map of Asia

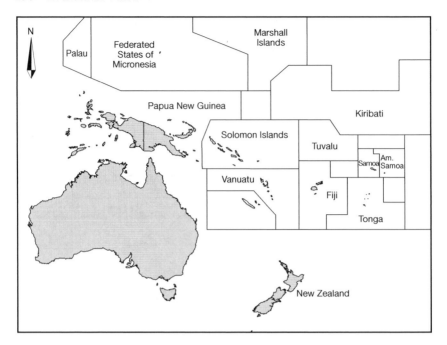

Figure 16.2 Map of the Pacific region

Disaster mortality and morbidity

Of the 21 largest disasters which have struck the world between 1975 and 2005, classified on the basis of more than 10,000 deaths, at least 12 disasters have occurred in Asia (UN 2007). The 1970 Bhola cyclone that struck East Pakistan (now Bangladesh) was the deadliest tropical cyclone recorded in modern times, with up to 500,000 people perishing in the disaster. A comparable number of people died as a result of the 1976 Tangshan earthquake in China, and the 2004 Indian Ocean tsunami, but because of uncertainty in the number of deaths in all three disasters, it may never be known which one was the deadliest (Wisner *et al.* 2004).

In 2008, two 'mega-disasters' occurred: Cyclone Nargis in Myanmar and the Sichuan earthquake in China. Cyclone Nargis killed over 138,000 people, while the Sichuan earthquake caused 87,000 deaths, significantly affecting the statistics on reported mortality, affected people, and economic damage costs of disasters worldwide during that year. These numbers intensified the trend of a small number of events responsible for the majority of the total losses during one year (CRED 2008).

Along with deaths and injuries, disasters can have other health impacts, such as waterborne diseases. A recent study using hospital visit data in Dhaka found that rates of disease increased during both high and low rainfall extremes.

The number of non-cholera diarrhoeal cases increased by approximately 4 per cent for every 10 millimetres increase in rainfall below a threshold of 52 millimetres and by 5 per cent for every 10 millimetres increase above this threshold (averaged over eight weeks). Diarrhoeal disease morbidity was also shown to increase at higher temperatures, particularly in populations with lower socio-economic status. After the floods of 2000 and 2001 in Mumbai, outbreaks of leptospirosis were reported in children living in informal settlements. The prevalence of leptospirosis increased eight-fold following the major flood event in July 2005 (Kovats and Rais 2008) (see Chapter 11).

These tragically high mortality and morbidity figures and other human impacts in AP are explained by looking at the interaction of two things: the **hazard** profile of the region and the **vulnerability** of the people who live there.

Hazard profile of the Asia-Pacific region[1]

The countries of the region which are badly affected by earthquakes include Japan, China, the Philippines, Indonesia, India, Nepal, Afghanistan, the Islamic Republic of Iran and the Pacific Islands. The earthquakes in Pakistan (October 2005) and China (May 2008) were the most severe among the recent earthquakes, while Indonesia has had major earthquakes on a regular basis in the recent past (May 2006 in Java; September 2009 in Sumatra). In the region, more than 50 cities with a population greater than one million are at significant risk from an earthquake.

Tsunamis may affect many of the coastal areas of the region. Important areas of tsunami generation in the Asia Pacific include the following major subduction zones, where plates composing the crust of the Earth override each other: the Sundra Arc, ranging from western Indonesia to the Philippines; the Philippine trench; the Manila trench; Makran, south of Pakistan; and the New Guinea trench. Moreover, the coastlines facing the Pacific are all exposed to the tsunamis generated along the so-called 'Ring of Fire' located along the perimeter of the Pacific Ocean. The December 2004 tsunami which had its epicentre off the west coast of Sumatra affected 14 countries bordering the Indian Ocean, though the hardest hit were Indonesia, Sri Lanka, India, and Thailand. Japan suffered a triple disaster in 2011, when it experienced a large earthquake and a very large tsunami hit the north-eastern coast of Honshu, the main island, destroying towns and villages and triggering the nuclear disaster at Fukushima Dai Ichi (Walenberger and Eilker 2013).

Volcanoes are also located mainly along the Pacific Rim. The countries in the region which are at risk from volcanic eruptions include the Philippines, Indonesia, Japan, North Korea, South Korea, Papua New Guinea, New Zealand, the Solomon Islands, Tonga, Samoa and Vanuatu. Those most frequently affected are Indonesia (129 active volcanoes), Japan (77 active volcanoes) and the Philippines (21 active volcanoes) (UNEP n.d.).

Floods include seasonal floods, flash floods, and urban floods due to inadequate drainage facilities, and floods associated with tidal events induced by typhoons in coastal areas. Every year, over 48 million people are affected by floods in rural areas in the Asia-Pacific countries, 40 per cent of whom are in Bangladesh and 32 per cent in India. Large areas of China, such as the Yangtze River basin, are subject to significant flood risk affecting large areas and large populations. Urban flooding, which is caused by inappropriate drainage and impervious surfaces, is also a serious hazard, particularly in large cities (Varley 2005).

Tropical cyclones, or typhoons,[2] affect large swathes of the Asia-Pacific region. A large number of depressions form over the northwest Pacific, just east of the Philippines, during June and November. On an average, about 30 typhoons a year strike the countries in the region (38 per cent of the world total), out of which around five to six inflict large-scale damage (UNEP n.d.). Tropical cyclones usually form over the southern end of the Bay of Bengal during April–December and then move to the eastern coast of India and Bangladesh often causing severe flooding and devastating tidal surges. The cyclones generated in the South Pacific ocean frequently cause damage in small island countries such as Fiji, Tonga, Vanuatu, the Solomon Islands, the Republic of the Marshall Islands, the Federated States of Micronesia and Samoa. Overall, the Philippines, Bangladesh and Vietnam suffer most frequently from these cyclonic activities.

Landslides are very common in the hilly and mountainous parts of the Asia-Pacific region. They occur frequently in mountainous parts of India, China, Nepal, Thailand and the Philippines. Though landslides are often triggered by storms and floods, human activities such as deforestation, cultivation and construction can also set them off or increase the likelihood that storms or floods will do so. Mountainous countries such as Nepal and Bhutan experience landslides on a large scale almost every year.

In most of the countries in the region, a large number of small and marginal farmers are dependent upon rain-fed farming. These farmers are most affected when the rains are deficient. A drought does not just reduce agricultural production; it also impacts drinking water, the livestock population and a large number of agriculture-based activities. Most countries in this region are drought-prone with examples including Kiribati, Tuvalu, the Republic of the Marshall Islands, Afghanistan, Iran, Iraq, the Philippines, Indonesia, China, Myanmar, Pakistan, Nepal, India, Sri Lanka and parts of Bangladesh.

Poverty, vulnerability and coping mechanisms

Poverty and vulnerability[3]

There are several features of poverty in Asia which are important to understand in the context of disaster risks. First, the incidence of poverty in rural areas is almost everywhere higher than that in urban areas. With rural populations accounting for a large proportion of Asian countries, rural poverty often accounts for two-thirds or more of total poverty. Second, a high incidence of one-US- dollar-a-day poverty and a large population mean that South Asia was home to almost two-thirds of Asia's extremely poor in 2002. Several countries in Southeast and East Asia – Cambodia, Laos, Mongolia and in some of the Pacific countries – have extreme poverty afflicting a fifth or more of these countries' populations. Third, poverty remains a problem even where the incidence of extreme poverty is low. In Indonesia, for example, only 7.5 per cent of the population lives below the one-US-dollar-a-day poverty line, but 52 per cent survive with less than US$2 a day (Balisacan *et al.* 2002).

A large-scale incidence of disasters has an immediate impact on poverty levels and indicators of well-being. In a single day the 2004 Indian Ocean tsunami killed over a quarter of a million people and disrupted the lives of millions more. In the Indonesian province of Aceh, poverty rates suddenly rose from 30 to 50 per cent (ReliefWeb 2008). Powerful earthquakes such as the ones in Gujarat, India, in 2001, or in Sichuan, China, in 2008, devastated basic social infrastructure, effectively locking thousands of children out of school. Likewise, cyclones such as Sidr in Bangladesh or Nargis in Myanmar have had disastrous human consequences, often hitting hardest at infants and their mothers (see Chapter 3). Disasters also compromise access to basic sanitation and safe water sources, impairing advances in maternal health and often allowing communicable diseases to proliferate (see Chapter 11).

A number of studies have found a significant correlation between poverty and disaster impact (Wisner *et al.* 2004) (see Chapter 2). It has worked both ways. Disasters have brought a decline in income and consumption levels, and increased poverty levels. At the same time, the poor suffer the disproportionate impact of disasters largely due to their lack of assets and coping mechanisms. In Orissa, India, part of the increasing levels of and deepening of poverty can be traced to recurrent shocks and the declining **capacity** of poor **households** to cope with both asset and income shocks: Mortality is concentrated in those districts of southern Orissa which are characterized by repeated droughts, floods, food insecurity, chronic income poverty and localized near-famine conditions (Shaw 2009).

Lal *et al.* (2009) conducted a study for Fiji which brings out a significant correlation between disasters and other indicators of well-being, suggesting that regular disasters have negative impacts on economic development, just as do external shocks in the form of political coups; plus the number of people affected by a disaster increased as unemployment increases. Another study comparing the impact of financial crisis and El Niño shock in the Philippines suggested through a regression analysis that the largest share of the overall impact on poverty was attributable to the El Niño shock, its share ranging between 47 per cent and 60 per cent of the total impact on measures of incidence, depth and severity of poverty (Datt and Hoogeveen 2003).

Disasters have also collided with conflicts (Wisner 2012). In the Asia-Pacific region too, disasters have interacted with conflicts: civil wars in Indonesia and Sri Lanka coincided with the 2004 Indian Ocean tsunami; the 2005 Kashmir earthquake occurred in a zone disputed by Pakistan and India; and the 2008 tropical cyclone *Nargis* (Myanmar) took place during a time when the military government was fighting separatist movements. While conflict indirectly may have contributed to the high death tolls in all these cases, the impact of the disasters on the conflicts differed considerably across the countries. While the peace process in Aceh was underway prior to the tsunami, there is little doubt that the disaster boosted the prospects for a lasting peace (Kelman 2011). Conversely, massive human and material destruction on Sri Lanka did little to halt the fighting and the violence escalated immediately after the tsunami.

Local coping mechanisms

A number of studies have shown that the cumulative impact of smaller, but frequent 'disasters' may be much greater than large disaster events (UNISDR 2009). Recurrent disasters have deeper impact on poverty and well-being of the people because these disasters deplete their **resources**, wear down their resilience, weaken their resistance to disease and undermine their ability to withstand future hazards (Brahmi and Poumphone 2002).

People have a highly varying perception of risks, and these are influenced by social structure and livelihood systems. In most of the floodplains in Asia, people seek to 'live with' with floods, rather than relocating. The flooding of land in deltas of the Ganges, Irrawaddy and Mekong Rivers brings benefits of enriched soil and leads to enhanced crop yields. The proximity of rivers is a major asset which provides a source of food as well as income, transportation and water for consumption and irrigation.

The trade-off between **risk** and **livelihoods** is also true of coastal and mountain communities, as evidenced during the 2004 tsunami and the 2005 Kashmir earthquake. Though the coastal communities are vulnerable to cyclones, they would not like to leave these coastal areas since they depend upon fishing for their livelihood. Similarly, despite the massive devastation caused by the earthquake in Kashmir, people continued to live in difficult situations because of the fear of livelihood insecurity if they left their traditional assets behind (Bhatti *et al.* 2006). Following the 1998 tsunami in Sissano, Papua New Guinea, survivors were told that tsunamis were likely to occur once every generation. Many people chose, nevertheless, to return to the original area because moving inland would have meant greater exposure to malaria and increased difficulties in accessing fisheries (World Bank 2006).

Thus people cope with disasters in multiple ways, depending upon their socio-economic status and geographical locations. The main challenge is that the poor end up being less able to cope with disasters, because of various internal and external factors imposed upon them (Roy *et al.* 2002). Whereas people with higher incomes tend to be in a position to undertake physical and economic measures to cope with disasters, the lower-income households tend to rely more on social networks and assistance from the government. They borrow largely from their friends and relatives, which make social networks extremely important for their survival. However, equally important is their access to the government relief assistance. For example, in the 2008 Kosi floods in Bihar, India, most households across all social groups expressed the need for government assistance to enable them to cope with the floods and their after-effects. Though dipping into previous savings and borrowings were important coping mechanisms, they did not have enough cash savings nor could they borrow from the moneylenders. Affected groups of men and women expected assistance from the government with respect to shelter, food, water and sanitation, and health and education for their survival and recovery (UNDP 2009).

Urbanization, climate change and increasing hazards

In 2005, the urban population in the Asia-Pacific region was 1,562 million or 40 per cent of the region's total. By 2030, it is estimated that 2,664 million people or almost 55 per cent of the total population in the region will be urban. This will involve an increase of 1.1 billion living in cities (Roberts and Fisher 2006). The majority of Asia's urban growth will be in six countries in terms of absolute numbers: Bangladesh, China, India, Indonesia, Pakistan, the Philippines and Vietnam (Shaw 2009), but proportionally many of the Pacific island states are experiencing substantial urban population increases.

The cities in Asia are prime drivers of economic growth. Per capita GDP of Ho Chi Minh City is more than three times Vietnam's national average; the per capita GDP of Shanghai is five times China's national average; incomes in Greater Jakarta, Seoul and Bangkok are at least 80 per cent higher than that in the surrounding areas (World Bank *et al.* 2008). However, the rapid urbanization and concentration of economic activities in the cities have serious consequences: unplanned informal settlements, water shortages, exposure to hazards and exposure to the impacts of climate change. Most Asian cities have very large populations living in informal settlements. These face shortages of all the essential urban services including water supply and sanitation. This is not just true of larger cities but also in smaller urban centres in small island countries such as Fiji. Almost 10 per cent of Fiji's national population of 850,000 residents now live in squatter settlements – a proportion that is rapidly increasing (Lal *et al.* 2009). These marginal populations are also seriously exposed to earthquake, floods, and cyclone hazards.

Urbanization and climate change

Many of the largest cities in Asia are located on the coast and within major river deltas, so they are highly susceptible to the impacts of climate change. WWF (2009) ranked the vulnerability of 11 cities in Asia due to the impact of climate change. Of these cities, Dhaka in Bangladesh is most highly exposed to climate change impacts since the city sits just metres above current sea levels, and it is regularly impacted by tropical cyclones and flooding. Its large population of relatively poor residents has limited adaptive capacity. Dhaka is followed by Jakarta in Indonesia and Manila in the Philippines, which also have large degrees of exposure (both experience frequent flooding), and relatively low adaptive capacity. Kolkata in India and Phnom Penh in Cambodia are tied for third most vulnerable city, largely because Kolkata is prone to saltwater intrusion and sea-level rise effects, while Phnom Penh has very low adaptive capacity (WWF 2009).

Table 16.1 Observed changes in extreme events and severe climate anomalies in Southeast Asia

Extreme events	Key trends
Heat waves	Increase in hot days and warm nights and decrease in cold days and nights between 1961 and 1998
Intense rains and floods	Increased occurrence of extreme rains causing flash floods in Vietnam; landslides and floods in 1990 and 2004 in the Philippines and floods in Cambodia
Droughts	Droughts normally associated with El Niño years in Indonesia, Laos, Myanmar, Philippines, and Vietnam; droughts in 1997 and 1998 causing massive crop failures and water shortages as well as forest fires in various parts of Indonesia, Laos, and Philippines
Typhoons	On average, 20 cyclones cross the Philippine area of responsibility with about eight or nine making landfall each year; an average increase of 4.2 in the frequency of cyclones entering the Philippine area of responsibility during the period 1990–2003

Source: IPCC (2007), cited in ADB (2009).

The evidence of changing hazard patterns is visible everywhere at the national as well as **community** levels, and needs systematic study and documentation (Table 16.1). In Vietnam, over the past 50 years, the peak month for typhoon landfalls has shifted from August to November, and most of the storms now occur later in the year. Typhoons have also tended to move to lower latitudes. In the Thùa Thiên Huê region, from 1952 to 2005, the area was hit directly by 34 typhoons (about seven per decade). Droughts and floods now occur with greater frequency than before and affect mostly the central coastal provinces. In the northern lowland part of the country, heat waves occur mainly in the summer, while in the south they occur in the spring-summer period (Cuong 2008, cited in ADB 2009).

As climate variability increases, it will have a far-reaching impact on different sectors such as agriculture and food, health, water availability and ecosystems. A World Bank study situated in Andhra Pradesh, India, suggests that with a modest-to-harsh climate change scenario, which could mean warming between 2.3°C to 3.4°C and a modest but erratic increase in rainfall (4–8 per cent), small farmer incomes could decline by as much as 20 per cent. In the arid regions, yields of all the major crops – rice, groundnut and sorghum – are expected to decline. Agriculture as it is practiced today will no longer be able to sustain large populations on small rain-fed farms.

Fragile housing

About 2.2 billion people live in Asia's rural areas, however, as noted, the region is urbanizing rapidly. In the urban centers, the housing stock is woefully short of the continually increasing demand created by the influx of migrants. As a result, some 554 million people in the Asia-Pacific region currently live in informal housing communities in urban areas. A large number of these houses have been poorly built, so they are most likely to be severely damaged in events such as high winds, flood, earthquake and urban fire.

In Kathmandu, Nepal, more than 90 per cent of the existing building stock is non-engineered (ADPC 2013). Every year about 5,000 more such non-engineered buildings are added. These houses have not incorporated earthquake-resistant designs, and are likely to be severely damaged in a large earthquake. Most of the developing countries face similar issues.

The non-engineered houses would perform better if constructed in accordance with traditional building technology and practices. However, over a period of time, people have lost the traditional building skills while they cannot afford modern professional design and construction. The 2009 earthquake in Bhutan clearly showed that stone masonry construction in the country suffered severe damages due to inappropriate design and building practices. Not just the houses, but the rich heritage of religious and cultural monuments too suffered serious damages due to discontinuity in building technologies (Bhutan, Royal Government of *et al*. 2009).

As people move from traditional building materials and methods to masonry construction, they may not be aware of or be willing or able to comply with the requirements of safe masonry construction. Limitation of resources (finance, **knowledge**, skills, building materials, etc.) has resulted in poor workmanship, and the situation tends to be deteriorating from year to year. In all the recent earthquakes in Maharashtra and Gujarat (India), Kashmir (Pakistan), and Yogyakarta (Indonesia), large-scale collapse of buildings could be attributed to the inadequate building skills and poor masonry construction standards. In China, in 2008, lack of attention to building codes along with poor construction standards resulted in large-scale collapse of schools in which 17,000 children perished (Wong 2009).

Institutional aspects of disaster risk reduction

Cross-boundary impact of disasters and the need for regional cooperation

As mentioned above, the 2004 Indian Ocean tsunami affected numerous countries. The 2005 Kashmir earthquake affected both Pakistan-administered and India-administered Kashmir. Cyclone Aila, which developed in the Indian Ocean in May 2009, affected India, Bangladesh, as well as landlocked Bhutan. Typhoon Ketsana which made its first landfall in the Philippines as a tropical storm on 26 September 2009 intensified and traveled further to cause serious loss of human life and property in Vietnam, Cambodia, Laos, and finally Thailand. Almost all the floods and inundation that affect Nepal have an impact on India as well as Bangladesh. The annual floods in the Mekong river basin, which yield a number of benefits as well, affect Vietnam, Cambodia, and Laos.

These have led to calls for greater regional cooperation in providing relief to the people and reducing disaster risks. Several efforts have been supported by regional institutions such as the Asian Disaster Preparedness Center (ADPC), headquartered in Bangkok and the Asian Disaster Reduction Center (ADRC), based in Kobe, Japan.

The Mekong River Commission began a flood management and mitigation programme in 2005. The programme is implemented through the Regional Flood Management and Mitigation Centre, which provides technical and coordination services to the four countries in the Lower Mekong Basin: Laos, Thailand, Cambodia, and Vietnam. Flood forecasts, flood data, technical standards, and training packages are key outputs of the programme. As part of this programme, the Mekong River Commission also plans to establish a Mediation and Coordination Section to facilitate dialogue and resolution of issues on land management and land-use planning, infrastructure development and cross-border emergency management of floods (Mekong River Commission 2013).

The South Asian Association for Regional Cooperation (SAARC) countries have came together to set up the SAARC Disaster Management Centre (SDMC) in October 2006. The Centre, which has been set up in New Delhi, has the mandate of providing capacity-building support and policy advice to the eight member-countries through training, system development, and exchange of information for effective disaster risk reduction.

The Association of Southeast Asian Nations (ASEAN) countries too established a Committee on Disaster Management (ACDM) in early 2003. The ACDM consists of heads of national agencies responsible for disaster management of ASEAN Member Countries. It assumes overall responsibility for coordinating and implementing the regional activities. As part of its objective of promoting disaster resilience in the region, the ACDM has developed an ASEAN Regional Programme on Disaster Management (ARPDM) to provide a framework for cooperation for the period of 2004–2010. The ARPDM outlines ASEAN's regional strategy on disaster management, as well as priority areas and activities for disaster reduction.

One of the most relevant examples of regional cooperation in the recent past has been the joint needs assessment in the wake of Cyclone Nargis in Myanmar in 2008. As the government was reluctant to accept international assistance in Myanmar, the Association of Southeast Asian Nations (ASEAN) assumed a leadership role, both in convincing the Myanmar government to cooperate with the international community and in managing the response itself. It constituted a two-tiered structure, consisting of a diplomatic body, the ASEAN Humanitarian Task Force (AHTF), and a Yangon-based Tripartite Core Group (TCG), consisting of ASEAN, the Myanmar government and the United Nations, to facilitate day-to-day operations. In so doing, it has helped to open up an unprecedented level of humanitarian space. ASEAN also took the lead in organizing the Post-Nargis Joint Assessment (PONJA), which was joined by the Myanmar government, ASEAN, the UN, international financial institutions and INGOs. Following the PONJA, ASEAN created a monitoring unit to measure the progress of the humanitarian response, dispatched ASEAN personnel to pre-established UN hubs in the field and commenced joint planning for the early recovery period (Creac'h and Fan 2008).

Regional centres like ADPC and ADRC have also worked closely with the governments of the countries in the Asia-Pacific region to improve their capacities for disaster risk reduction and to act as regional focal points for knowledge management and information sharing. These organizations have organized a large number of training programmes, meetings and conferences to discuss the status of disaster reduction activities.

Institutional and legislative system development

Since the 1990s, several countries in the Asia-Pacific region have taken steps to strengthen their institutional and legal systems for disaster management. This led to setting up of several national-level institutions and legislating national acts, which brought a renewed focus on disaster management in the country. Large-scale disasters in several countries presented the context for introducing such changes, though the declaration of International Decade for Natural Disaster Reduction (1990–2000) and the Yokohama Conference (1994) also spurred the process. However, many of these institutions became top-heavy and did not necessarily strengthen disaster management at the grass-roots level.

Consolidation of the National Disaster Coordination Council in the Philippines took place in 1990–1991 in the wake of the Baguio earthquake and the eruption of Mt. Pinatubo. The 1991 cyclone in Bangladesh led to the setting up of a separate Disaster Management Bureau in 1993. The Kobe earthquake in Japan (1995) led to a fundamental review of Japanese building regulations as well as national and regional disaster management institutions, and a similar process of extracting lessons and reforms is likely to follow Japan's triple Tohoku disaster (2011). After the 1996 and 1998 Anhui and Yangtze floods, China adopted a Natural Disaster Reduction Plan (1998–2010), which led the way for integration of risk reduction into development planning (Wisner *et al.* 2004: 362–3).

In Sri Lanka, the 2004 tsunami reaffirmed the urgent need for disaster risk management legislation. The Sri Lankan Parliament passed the Sri Lanka Disaster Management Act No 13 of 2005. The Act provided for the establishment of the National Council for Disaster Management (NCDM) and the Disaster Management Centre (DMC).

Yet these national disaster management authorities are mostly quite recent, and they are yet to attain maturity in terms of policies and strategies. Many apex institutions are top-heavy, and have not provided vision and leadership in the area of disaster risk reduction. These institutions need to develop strong linkages with local administration and community-based organizations in order to make their presence felt at the grass-roots level. They also need to work with academic and scientific institutions to improve early warning, mitigation and adaptation. It is important that an evaluation of the institutional and legal systems across AP countries be carried out to assess their contributions and to improve their partnerships with local governments and other national institutions.

Participation of NGOs

The role of NGOs

NGOs active in AP have had a role in disaster risk reduction that has evolved from relief and emergency response to disaster mitigation and preparedness, and recovery and reconstruction. A large number of NGOs working in the area of environment, poverty alleviation and livelihoods have started working in the area of disaster risk management as well. They have developed networks, worked with the governments and international agencies, and successfully influenced policies in many countries. However, the NGOs' influence as reflective of the political freedom and civil society has varied across the countries.

In South Asia, the NGOs have been a vibrant community, working in close cooperation with the governments, whereas in countries such as Myanmar, NGOs play a limited role. In East Asia, Japan has been a leading country in the promotion of NGO activities with special focus on disaster reduction (Shaw 2003). In Southeast Asia, the Philippines has been the leader with a well-established institutional and legal framework for disaster management and NGO involvement (ibid.). China too has started encouraging NGOs to participate in disaster relief. According to a study reported in *Asia Times*, a part of public donations to help disaster relief in the aftermath of the 2008 Sichuan earthquake was channeled through NGOs (Wang 2009). Though it is a small flow compared to the donations made by various government agencies, and government-designated Red Cross organizations, charities and foundations, it still is an important acknowledgement of the NGOs' role in disasters.

In successive disasters, NGOs have started playing an important role in recovery and reconstruction. In India, they participated in the reconstruction programme following the Latur earthquake (1993) and the Kutch earthquake (2001). However, the Indian Ocean tsunami in 2004 brought in the largest participation of local and international NGOs. The sheer number of NGOs participating in relief and recovery made coordination more difficult and more expensive. Many agencies had little or no experience or competence either in relief or recovery. A private company with no medical experience became responsible for building health centres and coordinating health assistance in one part of Aceh. Agencies provided more fishing boats than had been lost, even where overfishing had previously been a concern. It also raised the issue of professionalism of NGOs in handling relief and recovery issues, and ensuring accountability and transparency in the functioning of NGOs (TEC 2007).

Support for community-based disaster risk reduction programmes

An alternative perspective emerged in the practice of disaster risk management in the 1990s, which promoted **community-based disaster risk reduction (CBDRR)** (see Chapter 4). The CBDRR covers a broad range of local interventions to reduce disaster risks. These interventions are based on the recognition and study by communities of their own vulnerabilities and capacities. The most common elements of this approach are partnership, **participation**, empowerment, and ownership by the local people (Pandey and Okazaki n.d.). A large amount of literature has developed around the methodology and practices of CBDRR (Delica-Willison 2006).

The Cyclone Preparedness Programme (CPP), implemented by the Bangladesh Red Crescent Society, has been one of the most notable examples of CBDRR. Planned after the 1970 cyclone in Bangladesh, it is a volunteer-based early warning system with a large communication network of about 143 wireless stations. This communication network is used by its 33,000 volunteers in local villages, who transmit warnings to the local villagers through megaphones and hand-cranked sirens (ADRC 2005).

The Asian Urban Disaster Mitigation Program (AUDMP), started in 1995, was another important example of the CBDRR in the region. The ADPC started four community-based programmes in Bangladesh, Cambodia, Nepal and Sri Lanka, focusing on different hazards. It has been followed by several disaster risk management programmes in which community-based approaches have been actively promoted. Some of the most important programmes which have been supported by UNDP and other external donors are the Comprehensive Disaster Management Programme (CDMP) in Bangladesh and the Disaster Risk Management (DRM) programme in India. A number of NGOs too started community-based programmes in different countries, which, along with disaster risk management, focused on **livelihoods**, watershed management and shelter.

Though many of these community-based programmes have been individually evaluated, the collective outcome of these efforts is not sufficiently delineated. While these programmes have helped raise awareness and the profile of disaster risk management in these countries, they are largely donor-driven interventions and usually not sustainable. These interventions have not yet been integrated into national and local programmes, which reduces their long-term impact. Also, these programmes have largely pursued community-level preparedness, and not adequately stressed their linkages with development and natural resource management. The CBDRR is an area where the practitioners have accumulated a great deal of experience in Asia, but it needs to mature in terms of wide-ranging interventions and integration into government programmes.

The experience of recovery and reconstruction programmes

A large number of recovery and reconstruction projects (see Chapter 13) have been implemented in the Asia-Pacific region in the past two decades. These projects have generated a huge amount of learning which could be used to develop a more systematic approach to recovery. These lessons have spanned a large number of issues which emerge in the context of recovery, from needs assessment to temporary and permanent housing and livelihoods recovery. A large number of stakeholders – governments, NGOs, international agencies and community-based organizations – have participated in these recovery programmes and have developed a rich base of expertise in this area.

Recovery and reconstruction strategies have varied from one country to another, with the national context and the availability of resources playing an important part in developing the strategy. So in Japan, the resources for reconstruction following the 1995 Great Hanshin (Kobe) earthquake were mobilized through floating the government bonds in the market, and Hyogo Prefecture, the subnational/regional government, took the responsibility for leading reconstruction. However, in many low- and middle-income countries, such as India (Latur and Kutch earthquakes) and Pakistan (Kashmir earthquake), governments borrowed from the international financial institutions and set up specialized agencies for implementing reconstruction programmes. A large number of approaches to shelter have been promoted through these reconstruction programmes. There is an emerging consensus that a range of shelter options should be provided where possible and homeowners should be provided more choice and control over house design, technology, and implementation.

Conclusion

In view of the pervasive poverty in the Asia-Pacific region, a disaster risk reduction strategy can be successful only if the poor have greater access to improved shelter, diversified livelihoods, and more dependable social services. Governments, NGOs and other agencies need to link their interventions in this area with these basic priorities. People need to use the development resources to address their risks and uncertainties.

It takes some innovation and ingenuity to use development resources for disaster risk reduction. It also requires technical capacity and social facilitation to identify appropriate interventions and implement them at the household and community levels. If we take the example of the housing sector, there is a need to advocate safe building practices in the course of building both engineered and non-engineered houses. As most of the engineered houses are supported through housing finance and mortgage companies, building codes and by-laws should be made mandatory for all the projects supported by them. However, in case of non-engineered houses, which constitute the bulk of housing stock in the region, it is the revival of traditional building skills and practices that holds the key to safe housing. It needs to be promoted through a strong linkage with the social housing programmes, which can allocate resources for training and education of masons, carpenters, and other artisans, and create a mass awareness of safe building practices. It takes advocacy, policy support, and technical expertise to include disaster risk reduction in social housing programmes.

Similarly, livelihoods in the Asia-Pacific region have become increasingly fragile. Those who are dependent upon agriculture, fisheries and livestock for their livelihoods, are exposed to myriad risks, which arise from the depletion of natural resources, climate variability and other market-related uncertainties. A disaster risk reduction programme, therefore, needs to include livelihoods as a key component, and promote it through skill training, small enterprise development, and small grants.

A large number of small interventions have been attempted in the areas of shelter, natural resources, and livelihoods in several countries in the region (UNISDR 2008). Lessons emerging from these case studies demonstrate a close interaction of disaster risk reduction with other development programmes. There are larger programmes such as the Vulnerable Group Feeding (VGF) Programme in Bangladesh and National Rural Employment Guarantee Scheme (NREGS) in India, which can be utilized very effectively in disaster risk reduction.

Risk reduction interventions have acquired a greater urgency, as climate change and variability manifest. That requires an increased commitment of resources and expertise to disaster risk reduction, and an emphasis on mitigation as much as emergency preparedness and response. The development-risk reduction linkages need to be clearly demonstrated in community-based disaster risk reduction programmes, which are largely implemented as preparedness programmes.

Governments in the Asia-Pacific region have invested considerably in setting up national disaster management offices and authorities. Their impact in terms of technical and financial resources available for disaster risk reduction at the operational levels has not been impressive. The direction of institutional and legal development needs a change. There is a need to strengthen local governments and civil society organizations to support the disaster-affected people. It would mean setting up disaster management facilities in local governments, training people, and implementing local-level mitigation programmes, which reduce the impact of disasters. These are the areas where governments, NGOs, and civil society need to develop partnerships. Disaster risk reduction requires collaboration among agencies for a broad spectrum of programmes and services.

It is equally important that the governments identify the budget lines through which they can invest in preparedness and disaster risk reduction. At present, a large number of disaster management programmes in the region are externally funded and supported. While these programmes have provided the initial impetus, the momentum cannot be sustained without a steady commitment of national resources. Financial mechanisms such as an emergency reserve fund, a recovery facility, etc. need to be developed to support wide-ranging disaster management interventions.

Note

1 This section is based on UNEP (n.d.).
2 These storms are the same from a meteorological point of view whether they are called 'typhoons' or 'cyclones' in different parts of the Asia-Pacific region or, indeed, 'hurricanes' in other regions of the world.
3 This section is based on Wan and Sebastian (2011).

264   *Krishna S. Vatsa*

References

ADB (2009) *The Economics of Climate Change in Southeast Asia: A Regional Review*, Manila: Asian Development Bank.

ADPC (2013) Earthquake Vulnerability Reduction in Cities, Module 3, Session 1A, Bangkok: ADPC. Available at: http://www.adpc.net/casita/Course%20Modules/Earthquake%20 vulnerability%20reduction%20for%20cities/EVRC0301A_Earthquake_Vulnerability.pdf (accessed 24 March 2013).

ADRC (2005) *Cyclone Preparedness Programme in Bangladesh. Total Disaster Risk Management – Good Practices*, Kobe, Japan: ADRC, Chapter 3. Available at: http:// www.adrc.asia/publications/TDRM2005/TDRM_Good_Practices/PDF/PDF-2005e/ Chapter3_3.1.2-1.pdf (accessed 24 March 2013).

Asian Development Bank (2009) *The Economics of Climate Change in Southeast Asia: A Regional Review*. Manila.

Balisacan, A., Pernia, E. and Asra, A. (2002) 'Revisiting growth and poverty reduction in Indonesia: What do subnational data show?', ERD Working Paper No. 25, Manila: Asian Development Bank. Available at: http://www.adb.org/sites/default/files/pub/2002/wp025. pdf (accessed 24 March 2013).

Bhatti, A., Wisner, B. and Platt, L. (2006) *Tackling the Tides and Tremors: South Asia Disaster Report 2005*, Rwalpindi: Duryog Nivaran Secretariat and Practical Action.

Bhutan, Royal Government of, World Bank and United Nations (2009) *Bhutan Earthquake September 21, 2009: Joint Rapid Assessment for Recovery, Reconstruction and Risk Reduction*, Thimphu, Bhutan: Royal Government of Bhutan, World Bank and United Nations. Available at: http://gfdrr.org/docs/Bhutan_Rapid_Needs_Assessment_Report_ Oct_09.pdf (accessed 24 March 2013).

Brahmi, A. and Poumphone, K. (2002) *Study on Local Coping Mechanisms in Disaster Management: Case Studies from the Lao PDR*, Vientiane: Concern.

Cosgrave, J. (2007) *Synthesis Report: Expanded Summary. Joint Evaluation of the International Response to the Indian Ocean Tsunami*, London: Tsunami Evaluation Coalition. Available at: http://www.alnap.org/pool/files/Syn_Report_Sum.pdf (accessed 24 March 2013).

Creac'h, Y.K. and Fan, L. (2008) 'ASEAN's role in the Cyclone Nargis response: implications, lessons and opportunities', *Humanitarian Exchange Magazine*, 41. Available at: http://www.odihpn.org/report.asp?id=2965 (accessed 24 March 2013).

CRED (2008) *Annual Disaster Statistical Report*, Louvin, Belgium: CRED. Available at: http://www.cred.be/sites/default/files/ADSR_2008.pdf (accessed 24 March 2013).

Cuong, N. (2008) *Viet Nam Country Report: A Regional Review on the Economics of Climate Change in Southeast Asia. Report Submitted for RETA 6427: A Regional Review of the Economics of Climate Change in Southeast Asia*, Manila: Asian Development Bank.

Datt, G. and Hoogeveen, H. (2003) *El Niño or El Peso? Crisis, Poverty, and Income Distribution in the Philippines*, World Development 31(7): 1103–1124.

Delica-Willison, Z. (2006) *Community-based Disaster Risk Management: Gaining Ground in Hazard-Prone Communities in Asia*. Available at: http://www.snap-undp.org/elibrary (accessed 24 March 2013).

ESCAP (1995) *The State of the Environment in Asia and the Pacific 1995*. UNESCAP. Bangkok.

Government of Japan (1987) *Earthquake Disaster Countermeasures in Japan*. Tokyo.

Kelman, I. (2011) *Disaster Diplomacy: How Disasters Affect Peace and Conflict*, London: Routledge.

Kovats, S. and Rais, A. (2008) 'Climate, climate change and human health in Asian cities', *Environment and Urbanization*, 20 (1): 165.

Lal, P.N., Singh, R. and Holland, P. (2009) *Relationship Between Natural Disasters and Poverty: A Fiji Case Study*, SOPAC Miscellaneous Report 678, ISDR.

Mekong River Commission (2013) *Flood Management and Mitigation Programme*, Phnom Penh, Cambodia: MRC. Available at: http://www.mrcmekong.org/about-the-mrc/programmes/flood-management-and-mitigation-programme/ (accessed 24 March 2013).

Pandey, B. and Okazaki, K. (n.d.) *Community Based Disaster Management: Empowering Communities to Cope with Disaster Risks*, Japan: United Nations Centre for Regional Development. Available at: http://unpan1.un.org/intradoc/groups/public/documents/un/unpan020698.pdf (accessed 24 March 2013).

Roberts, B.H. and Fisher, K. (2006) 'Urban regional economic development in Asia: trends, issues and future challenges', *The Australasian Journal of Regional Studies*, 12(3): 359–82. Available at: http://search.informit.com.au/documentSummary;dn=020968760469630;res=IELHSS (accessed 24 March 2013).

Roy, B., Mruthyunjaya and Selvarajan, S. (2002) 'Vulnerability to climate induced natural disasters with special emphasis on coping strategies of the rural poor in coastal Orissa, India (Draft)', paper prepared for the UNFCCC COP8 Conference organized by the Government of India, United Nations Environment Programmes, and FICCI, October 23–November 1, 2002, New Delhi, India. Available at: http://unfccc.int/cop8/se/se_pres/isdr_pap_cop8.pdf (accessed 24 March 2013).

Shaw, R. (2003) 'Role of non-government organizations in earthquake disaster management: an Asian perspective', *Regional Disaster Dialogue*, 24(1): 117–29.

—— (2009) 'Thematic overview of urban risk reduction in Asia', submitted from the Asia Regional Task Force on Urban Risk Reduction as input to the Global Assessment Report on DRR. Available at: http://www.adrc.asia/events/RTFmeeting20080130/PDF_Presentations/2-Thematic_overview_URR_Asia.pdf (accessed 24 March 2013).

UN (2007) *Disaster Risk Reduction, Global Review 2007*. Geneva.

UNDP (2009) *Kosi Floods 2008. How We Coped! What We Need? Perception Survey on Impact and Recovery Strategies*, New Delhi: UNDP.

UNEP (n.d.) *Asia Pacific Environment Outlook*, Bangkok: UNEP. Available at: http://www.rrcap.unep.org/apeo/Chp1h-nathazards.html (accessed 24 March 2013).

UNISDR (2008) *Linking Disaster Risk Reduction and Poverty Reduction: Good Practices and Lessons Learned*, Geneva: UNISDR and GNDR. Available at: http://www.preventionweb.net/english/professional/publications/v.php?id=3293 (accessed 24 March 2013).

—— (2009) *Global Assessment Report on Disaster Reduction 2009*, Geneva: UNISDR. Available at: http://www.preventionweb.net/english/hyogo/gar/report/index.php?id=1130 (accessed 24 March 2013).

Varley, R.C.G. (2005) *The World Bank's assistance for water resources management in China*. Washington D.C. The World Bank. http://documents.worldbank.org/curated/en/2005/01/6049664/world-banks-assistance-water-resources-management-china.

Waldenberger, F. and Eilker, J. (2013) 'The economic impact of the Tohoku earthquake', Ecole des Haute Etudes en Sciences Sociales (EHESS)/Fondation France-Japon de l'EHESS, Paris. Available at: http://ffj.ehess.fr/index/article/283/the-economic-impact-of-the-tohoku-earthquake.html (accessed 24 March 2013).

Wan, G. and Sebastian, I. (2011) *Poverty in Asia and the Pacific: an update*, ADB Economics Working Paper Series No. 267, Manila: Asian Development Bank. Available at: http://www.adb.org/sites/default/files/pub/2011/Economics-WP267.pdf (accessed 24 March 2013).

Wang, S. (2009) 'NGOs tread lightly on China's turf', *Asia Times*, 12 September. Available at: http://www.atimes.com/atimes/China/KI12Ad02.html (accessed 24 March 2013).

Wisner, B. (2012) 'Violent conflict, natural hazards and disasters', in B. Wisner, JC Gaillard and I. Kelman (eds) *The Routledge Handbook of Hazards and Disaster Risk Reduction*, London: Routledge, pp. 71–82.

Wisner, B., Blaikie, P., Cannon, T. and Davis, I. (2004) *At Risk: Natural Hazards, People's Vulnerability and Disasters*, 2nd edn, London: Routledge.

Wong, E. (2009) 'Year after China quake, new births, old wounds', *New York Times*, 5 May. Available at: http://www.nytimes.com/2009/05/06/world/asia/06quake.html?page wanted=all&_r=0 (accessed 24 March 2013).

World Bank (2006) *Not If But When, Adapting to Natural Hazards in the Pacific Islands Region: A Policy Note*, Washington, DC: World Bank.

—— (2008) 'Indonesia: Aceh Poverty Assessment', Washington, DC: World Bank. Available at: http://reliefweb.int/report/indonesia/indonesia-aceh-poverty-assessment-2008 (accessed 24 March 2013).

World Bank, GFDRR and UNISDR (2008) *Climate Resilient Cities. 2008 Primer: Reducing Vulnerabilities to Climate Change Impacts and Strengthening Disaster Risk Management in East Asian Cities*, Washington, DC: World Bank.

WWF (2009) *Mega-Stress for Mega-Cities: A Climate Vulnerability Ranking of Major Coastal Cities in Asia*, Gland, Switzerland: WWF. Available at: http://www.prevention web.net/english/professional/publications/v.php?id=11822 (accessed 24 March 2013).

Part IV

Tools

17 Integrating people's capacities in disaster risk reduction through participatory mapping

Jake Rom D. Cadag and JC Gaillard

Lessons for practitioners

- Capacities refer to the set of **knowledge**, skills and **resources** people resort to in dealing with natural hazards and disasters.
- Many forms of participatory **mapping** enable people to identify and integrate capacities in community-based disaster risk reduction. Each of them has strengths and disadvantages.
- Participatory 3-Dimensional Mapping (P3DM) is a form of participatory mapping which is cheap, flexible, scaled, permanent and tangible for a large array of stakeholders.
- P3DM facilitates the integration of capacities in DRR by making people's knowledge, skills and resources tangible to outside stakeholders such as scientists and government officials.
- P3DM should be used in combination with other participatory tools for assessing all dimensions of people's capacities.

Introduction

Community-based Disaster Risk Reduction (CBDRR) relies upon the intrinsic ability of local communities to face disasters (Delica-Willison and Gaillard 2012) (see Chapters 4 and 5). Those who are vulnerable to natural and other **hazards** indeed display significant **capacities** to face such threats and are neither victims nor helpless people in time of hardship.

Capacities refer to the set of knowledge, skills and resources people resort to in dealing with natural hazards and disasters. The concept of capacity also encompasses the ability to claim, **access** and use this knowledge, skills and resources. Capacities are not the opposite end of **vulnerability** on a single spectrum, because highly vulnerable communities may display a large array of capacities (Davis *et al.* 2004). In fact, capacities are most often rooted in knowledge, skills and resources which are endogenous to the **community** and which rely on local knowledge, indigenous skills and technologies, traditional medicine and solidarity networks. In contrast, vulnerabilities often depend on structural constraints which are exogenous to the community, such as unequal distribution of wealth and resources within the society, market forces, political systems and governance (Wisner *et al.* 2012). It is thus essential that DRR considers both people's vulnerabilities and capacities in facing hazards.

Integrating capacities in DRR requires that the knowledge, skills and resources of people and communities are recognized by stakeholders outside of these communities. This often proves difficult as capacities partially rely upon intangible forms of knowledge, skills and resources (e.g. social network, folklore, memory of past events). One of the main issues therefore consists of making local capacities tangible in order to foster dialogue among actors in DRR. Such a dialogue is essential for integrating both bottom-up and top-down actions into DRR (Gaillard and Mercer 2013).

This chapter suggests a particular form of participatory mapping, i.e., Participatory 3-Dimensional Mapping (P3DM), as a tool for making people's capacities, as well as vulnerabilities, tangible so that these can be considered in DRR. It draws upon a project led by coastal communities of the municipality of Masantol on the island of Luzon, the Philippines, conducted between 2008 and 2009.

Maps, participatory maps and DRR

Maps constitute a powerful tool which gives visual expression to realities which are perceived, desired, or considered useful, thus often providing means for conveying ideas beyond the realms of those who produce maps (Chambers 2008). However, to communicate with outsiders, and make people's capacities tangible, maps need to be intelligible to all stakeholders, which is seldom the case for most of the maps used for DRR. Indeed, scientists supported by governments and sometimes international organizations usually provide very useful, highly detailed and scientifically accurate hazard maps and in rarer occasions vulnerability maps. Unfortunately, these maps often require particular skill to decipher. They are crafted after Western guidelines and semiologies, e.g., language, technical jargon, colour coding of the legend, orientation towards the North, which frequently make little sense to people threatened by the same hazards. They are therefore of limited use when fostering community-based DRR.

Participatory mapping has emerged as an alternative to better encompass the diversity of local communities' views on natural hazards and disasters (Chambers 2008; IFAD 2009). Participatory maps enable local communities, assisted by non-governmental organizations (NGOs), to draw a very insightful picture of their territory which features people's perception of natural hazards as well as their vulnerability and capacities (Twigg 2004; Benson *et al.* 2007). These maps are usually culturally embedded and thus reflect local needs and resources.

Different forms of participatory mapping are being used for DRR (Table 17.1). These include ground mapping, 'stone mapping', sketch mapping, GPS (Global Positioning System) mapping, and web-based and interoperable mapping – from the least to the most demanding in terms of resources.

Table 17.1 Main characteristics of the different forms of participatory mapping used for DRR

Type of participatory mapping	Principles	Advantages	Disadvantages	References
Ground mapping	People draw the map in the sand/ground with a stick or their fingers	– Very easy to set up and cheap – Familiar to most people – Less eye contact – Flexible (easy correction and adjustment)	– Temporary – Limited semiology – Neither scaled, nor georeferenced – Value often dismissed by government officials and scientists	– International Federation of Red Cross and Red Crescent Societies (2007)
Stone mapping	People draw the map using stones, branches, paper and other locally available materials	– Easy to set up and cheap – Familiar to most people – Less eye contact – Flexible (easy correction and adjustment)	– Temporary – Neither scaled, nor georeferenced – Value often dismissed by government officials and scientists	– International Fund for Agricultural Development (2009)
Sketch mapping	People draw the map on a sheet of paper with coloured marker pens	– Relatively easy to set up and cheap – Permanent – Large semiology – Most often stored locally	– Unfamiliar to many people – Rigid (difficult to correct and adjust) – Neither scaled, nor georeferenced – Value often dismissed by government officials and scientists	– von Kotze and Holloway (1996) – Oxfam (2002) – Abarquez and Murshed (2004) – International Institute of Rural Reconstruction and Cordaid (2007) – International Federation of Red Cross & Red Crescent Societies (2007)
Balloon and kite mapping	People use a camera attached to a balloon or kite to capture	– Accuracy – Permanent	– Unfamiliar to most people – Requires an external facilitator to	– Warren (2006) – Dosemagen et al. (2011)

continued

Table 17.1 continued

Type of participatory mapping	Principles	Advantages	Disadvantages	References
	aerial photographs. Data may eventually be included into a GIS or overlaid on existing maps	– Large semiology (if using GIS) – Scaled and georeferenced – Reliable to government officials and scientists	train participants – The balloon/kite component is relatively easy to set up and fairly cheap – The GIS component is costly and difficult to set up	
GPS Mapping	People walk around the area to be mapped and plot features with GPS. Data are eventually included into a GIS	– Permanent – Large semiology – Scaled and georeferenced – Reliable to government officials and scientists	– Unfamiliar to most people – Costly and difficult to set up – Requires an external facilitator to train participants – People seldom include the data themselves into the GIS – Flexible only to those who master the technology – May be manipulated by facilitators – Most often stored externally	– Kienberger and Steinbruch (2005) – Tran et al. (2008) – Peters et al. (2009)
Web-based and interoperable GIS mapping	People contribute to a web-based GIS database from their own computer	– Permanent – Scaled and georeferenced – Flexible for correction and adjustment – Credible to government officials and scientists	– Unfamiliar to most people – Costly and difficult to set up – Semiology controlled by facilitators – May be manipulated by facilitators – Stored externally	– White et al. (2010)

Ground and stone mapping are very flexible, easy to facilitate and do not require any resources. Participants resort to whatever materials are available in the environment (e.g. sand, stones, leaves, branches) to draw features on the ground, especially hazard-prone areas and the most important assets in the community (Figure 17.1). These forms of mapping are usually not permanent and dependent on climate conditions. Drawing sketch maps is the form of participatory mapping that is most frequently used for DRR because it is easy to set up and permanent (Figure 17.1). People use marker pens to draw spatial features associated with their community on a large piece of paper. Although some attempts have been made (Cronin *et al.* 2004), sketch maps remain poor for integrating people's knowledge, skills and resources into DRR initiatives driven by stakeholders outside of the community which drew the map. Since sketch maps, as well as ground and stone maps, are not scaled or georeferenced (i.e., associated with specific locations on the Earth's surface through longitude and latitude coordinates), they are often dismissed by government institutions and scientists which challenge the veracity of the data and thus fail to acknowledge people's capacities.

Figure 17.1 Top left: Participatory mapping activity conducted by school pupils using sand, stones, leaves, flowers and branches in Savo, Solomon Islands, in March 2011 (photograph by JC Gaillard). *Top right*: Sketch participatory map drawn by a local community on the slopes of Mt Merapi in 2009 (photograph by JC Gaillard). *Bottom left*: Scaled 2D mapping activity with college students in San Fernando, Philippines, in August 2009 (photograph by JC Gaillard). *Bottom right*: Participatory mapping activity conducted over an aerial photograph of Hastings, New Zealand, in November 2011. This picture shows the local civil defense officer and a district councillor collaborating with members of the local community (photograph by JC Gaillard)

On the other hand, GPS and web-based forms of participatory mapping are much more complicated to set up and most often require external assistance through costly technological resources. People plot the location of hazard-prone areas and vulnerable assets and resources either using a GPS device or directly onto an editable map available on a Web platform. Both rely upon the use of Geographic Information Systems (GIS) which refer to the combination of hardware, software and practices designed to capture, store, display, communicate, transform, analyze, and archive georeferenced information (Gregory *et al*. 2009; Goodchild 2005). Those GIS make people's capacities tangible to scientists and government institutions. However, people who are not acquainted with the technology associated with the tool often lose control over their own knowledge which is stored and used (if not manipulated) by outsiders.

In the wider field of natural resource management, attempts to overcome the limitations of the foregoing forms of participatory mapping have been made through Participatory 3-Dimensional Mapping (P3DM) (see http://www.iapad. org/). P3DM basically comprises the building of stand-alone scaled relief maps made of locally available materials (e.g. carton, paper, polystyrene) which are overlapped with thematic layers of geographical information (Rambaldi and Callosa-Tarr 2002). It enables the plotting of landforms and topographic landmarks, land cover and usage, and anthropogenic features, which are depicted using push-pins, yarn, and paint.

P3DM thus facilitates the interpretation, assimilation, and understanding of geo-referenced information by making it visible and tangible to everyone. P3DM raises local awareness of territories, provides stakeholders with powerful mediums for land-use management, and serves as an effective community-organizing tool (ibid.). Noteworthy is that most of the P3DM initiatives for natural resource management and land conflict resolution use a relatively small scale – often 1:10,000 – and, as such, rarely include details at the **household** level, including people's knowledge, skills and resources. Some initiatives have applied similarly small-scale P3DM to DRR but with an applicability limited to land-use and hazard mapping (Capelao 2007).

The subsequent sections provide insights into the way in which large-scale P3DM offers new opportunities for integrating people's capacities as well as their vulnerabilities in DRR.

The coastal communities of Masantol, the Philippines

This study focuses on six coastal communities of the municipality of Masantol in the Philippines. Masantol is located in the delta of the Pampanga River which drains a large part of Northern Luzon (Figure 17.2). The study area comprises six small and remote villages: Sagrada; Sapang Kawayan; Nigui; Balibago; Alauli; and Bagang. As of August 2007, 9,132 people inhabited these villages and made a living chiefly from aquaculture and fishing (National Statistics Office 2010).

Masantol suffers from frequent flooding and other natural hazards such as tropical cyclones, storm surges, earthquakes, and tsunamis. Over the past three

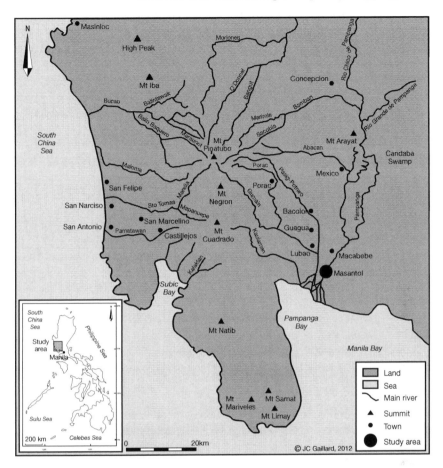

Figure 17.2 Location of Masantol in the Philippines

decades flooding has been worsening due to rapid land subsidence (Rodolfo and Siringan 2006). Land subsidence is aggravated by the extraction of groundwater for the maintenance of fishponds, agricultural lands, and domestic needs.

Negative impacts include direct damage to fishponds, houses, and property, disruption of electricity supply and transportation, delay of regular school activities, and an increase in the prices of commodities. Moreover, tropical cyclones and heavy rainfall often prohibit fishermen from engaging in their daily activities.

In response to increasing flooding, the Philippine government has focused on dredging activities and protective structures, such as dikes and river walls, whose efficiency has been challenged by Rodolfo and Siringan (2006). In fact, local people complain that flooding is worsening in Masantol despite the construction of huge dikes and sluice gates to control and channel floodwaters towards the sea from the late 1990s.

This background information on the study area has been collected during a long phase of relationship-building which spanned five years between 2002 and 2007. A consensus emerged on the importance of strengthening the ability of local communities to cope with natural hazards, particularly flooding. It is in this context that the decision was taken to conduct a P3DM for a DRR project.

Conducting P3DM in Masantol

The initial rapport-building stage enabled the constitution of a strong consortium of local stakeholders which shared the same objective of fostering DRR. These stakeholders included a local community-based organization, school communities, **local governments** at the municipal and village levels, a regional NGO and a pool of geographers and anthropologists from the University of the Philippines (UP) Diliman.

P3DM activities were conducted between August 2008 and August 2009. In participatory mapping, as for any CBDRR project, the schedule of activities should ideally be defined by the participants according to their own needs and availability and not according to outsiders' interests. Participants were selected by the local high school partner and the municipal government represented by its vice-mayor. Both were consensual enough in the project area to ensure a fair balance of representation. Participants included municipal and local officials, health workers, teachers, students, women, children, people with disabilities, fishermen, and owners and tenants of fishponds. P3DM is a tool and method which facilitates people's **participation** in consensual decision-making with a large array of stakeholders. Ensuring a large, representative and fair participation of the local community is therefore essential. Where it is not possible, then a series of sessions on the same map or different mapping exercises may be attempted with different social groups or stakeholders of DRR.

The facilitators initially prepared a scaled and georeferenced base map using a GIS and the latest available topographic map from the government. The scale was large (1:2,700) to facilitate mapping at the household level. The base map is a scaled map of the project area containing information that can be used as a basis for the construction of the 3D map. The preparation of the base map is usually a task for the local government (or the concerned partner government agency) or local NGO so that replication of the activity can be done without outside expertise. In Masantol, the base map included the river system to provide the participants with some landmarks. The local topography being flat, there was indeed no contour line to indicate major landforms as in usual P3DM. Despite the lack of verticality, the methodology used was identical to that of P3DM. For this reason the mapping activity depicted in this chapter is still called P3DM.

At the start of the mapping activities, participants were oriented and grouped to perform specific tasks. Men volunteered to prepare the wooden table which served as support for the P3DM. It is essential to rely upon such knowledge, skills and resources at all stages of any participatory mapping activities. The base map was eventually stretched over the table. Participants used pieces of paperboards

Figure 17.3 School pupils collaborating with adults, elders and women in plotting
 landmarks on the P3DM built in Masantol in August 2008

Source: Photograph by JC Gaillard.

and crepe paper to delineate and emphasize the dike separating and protecting the
villages from the Pampanga River.

Simultaneously, a group of students and local teachers prepared a legend which
was eventually agreed upon by the entire set of participants. The legend consisted
of a series of symbols represented by lines (yarn), points (push-pins of different
shapes and colours) and polygons (paint). The points symbolized individual
features such as houses, health centres, schools, public buildings, and other
important landmarks. The lines represented linear features such as rivers, roads,
trails and borders. Finally, polygons were used to depict land use. It is important
to anchor such data in people's life and experiences so that the information to be
plotted on the 3D map is tangible. It is therefore very useful to conduct a detailed
timeline of past disasters in the community in preamble of any participatory
mapping activities.

Participants eventually plotted major non-natural landmarks, such as schools,
churches, stores, village meeting centres, health centres and flood-control facilities, based on their own knowledge of the place (Figure 17.3). Different colours
of round push-pins were used to identify different types of houses based on building materials and the number of floors. Marker pens were used to indicate on the
top of the push-pins how many people live in each house. Participants eventually
proceeded with the plotting of natural landmarks such as mangrove areas,
fishponds, fishing grounds, roads and trail networks.

People also mapped the place of residence of the most vulnerable individuals as well as those with particular knowledge and skills within the different communities using flag-like push-pins. These include people with disabilities and permanent illness, elderly, children below five years old and pregnant women as well as midwives, local officials, schoolteachers and engineers. Participants finally plotted other local resources which might enhance communities' capacities to face natural hazards, i.e. boats, vehicles and fire hydrants. All this information proved to be crucial for assessing the **risk** of disaster.

Plotting data on a map needs to be a collective activity which involves everyone in the community. All people should collaborate and contribute their own knowledge to the map. This is an activity which is usually very lively and enjoyed by the participants whose knowledge is emphasized. It may, however, trigger intense discussions which sometimes may lead to potential conflicts. The facilitator must therefore be very careful in respecting momemtums and participants' initiatives as to how to sequence and organize the plotting of the different data. To level down power relationships between outsiders and members of the community and to avoid disempowering participants, the facilitator must never teach nor correct participants. Instead, he/she should foster discussion and spur reflection among them.

Assessing people's capacities and the risk of disaster

To make people's vulnerability and capacities tangible, it is essential to confront them with the potential threat of natural hazards. In Masantol, hazard mapping considered both local and scientific knowledge. This was done by overlaying people's knowledge of hazard-prone areas over the 3D map while taking into account the existing scientific hazard maps and consultations with the local officials. The participants first identified three types of floods, i.e., river floods, rain-fed floods and tidal floods. They also identified the degree and severity of the hazard, i.e., areas that were: (1) highly prone; (2) moderately prone; and (3) lowly prone to floods. In Sapang Kawayan, layers of black yarn were used to represent the depth of flood water. Further, participants identified weak points along fishpond dikes which often collapse under the pressure of tidal waters or heavy rains.

Plotting hazard-prone areas over vulnerable people and assets as well as skills and resources which constitute people's capacities allows participants to concretely appraise disaster risk in the immediate environment. Dangerous areas with a large number of houses made of wood and palm and with many children, pregnant women, elderly and people with disability or permanent illness were considered at high risk (Figure 17.4). Participants particularly realized that in Sapang Kawayan, there were many vulnerable people within an area they considered highly prone to flooding. This prompted them to consider this sector as a priority area for disaster risk reduction.

Similarly, people's capacities are more evident if people with particular skills and knowledge such as midwives and engineers as well as local resources such as vehicles and evacuation centres that are essential in the event of a disaster are depicted on the P3DM. In Sapang Kawayan, this was of particular concern because

Figure 17.4 Local elder plotting flood-prone areas on the P3DM built in Masantol. The map shows houses and housing materials (small cylinder push-pins), public buildings (big cylinder push-pins) and other facilities (ball-like push-pins) and vulnerable people as well as persons with particular knowledge and skills (flags), in August 2008

Source: Photograph by JC Gaillard.

the village is only accessible by boats which are available in limited number. P3DM made disaster risk assessment faster and more efficient.

Noteworthy is that disaster risk assessment also included other Participatory Learning and Action (PLA) tools such as disaster histories, hazard and resource calendars, capacity and vulnerability matrixes, all conducted as part of group discussions in parallel with P3DM (Wisner 2006). A larger array of tools enabled the appraisal of some dimensions of vulnerability and capacities which are difficult to plot on a map, e.g., interpersonal relationships and time-related issues.

Integrating people's capacities in DRR

A clear picture of whom and what is at risk, and of which capacities to face the natural hazards are available locally provides a solid basis for planning DRR. Action planning in Masantol was conducted as a priority in the village of Sapang Kawayan, which was considered by the participants as the community which most needed DRR activities. It consisted of framing a CBDDR plan in close collaboration with the government officials and scientists from UP. Such collaboration enabled the recognition of people's capacities by outside stakeholders. This plan particularly focused on disaster preparedness and required the preparation of a second large-scale (1:500) map specific for Sapang Kawayan.

People first discussed hazard monitoring to anticipate the occurrence of floods and other harmful phenomena. Rulers were set up near water pumps and strategic buildings to monitor the rate of land subsidence and anticipate which areas might be most exposed to floods in the future. Such data may eventually be added onto the P3DM. In parallel, people decided to use tricoloured bamboo posts to monitor the water level and serve as early warning devices for flooding. People differentiated between low water level (green), threatening water level (orange) and flood water level (red). Posts were located in strategic locations around the village identified on the P3DM.

The three-level colour-coded early warning system served as the basis for drawing the village emergency plan. People designed a set of specific activities to be conducted for each level of flood water. These activities included preparedness, warning and evacuation.

Evacuation schemes were defined on the P3DM based on the location of vulnerable people, persons with particular skills and knowledge, available vehicles, safe buildings and places, and potential routes. Evacuation zones for each tall building were defined on the P3DM. Such planning was rendered easy by the bird's eye view of the territory provided by the map.

A simpler warning and evacuation plan was defined in preparation for fire which often swept through the village. Another plan was designed for tsunami hazard which people were aware of, without prior experience. Posters and brochures made by government scientists were provided by the facilitators upon request from the participants. Participants carefully differentiated warning devices for fire (the church bell) and tsunami (clinking metallic cans) from that used for flooding (bamboo sound device).

Implementation of the emergency plan required a revival of the village disaster coordinating council. This includes different committees. One committee is tasked with checking the water level at the bamboo posts installed in the river. Another committee is responsible for conducting evacuation drills and to check regularly the readiness of the necessary warning devices. One committee should also ensure that the information depicted on the P3DM is regularly updated to keep disaster risk assessment up to date.

The emergency plan was eventually printed on a large tarpaulin and posted in front of the village hall so that everyone in the community could see it. Small laminated copies of the same plan were distributed to members of the disaster coordinating council and simple scientific brochures on tsunami in the local language were made available to the larger community.

Putting DRR to the test of disasters

The effectiveness and sustainability of P3DM for the DRR project conducted in Masantol were shortly put to a strong test in late September 2009 when back-to-back cyclones Ondoy and Pepeng brought severe flooding in the area. Fortunately, no one was killed although most people had to evacuate. The municipal vice-mayor eventually reflected,

> The project has helped me as a leader because during the time of calamity, I was able to apply what I have learned in ensuring the safety of the people such as identifying possible evacuation centres and finding solutions to the problems and needs of the people.

The P3DM was not the single factor in this success but it obviously contributed its share to enhancing people's capacities to face natural hazards. A fourth-year high school pupil summarized, 'It helped because people learned the meaning of being united.'

Eventually, another cyclone, Pedring, struck Masantol in late September 2011 and partially damaged one of the 3D maps which was stored in the local high school. This prompted the high school community to initiate a new series of mapping activities to rebuild the map. For such activities, the school pupils have been tasked to collect data in the surrounding villages to facilitate the identification of vulnerable assets and people as well as their capacities. In addition, the school principal has initiated a series of discussions on how to adopt DRR into the school curriculum. Some of gay and *bakla* (effeminate biologically male) young-sters have also been involved in preparing a participatory video featuring their own capacities in facing disasters. Such activity draws upon existing evidences that that particular social group display a large array of specific knowledge, skills and resources (Gaillard 2011).

In the aftermath of Cyclone Pedring, local community leaders who were involved in the P3DM activities in 2008 and 2009 gathered and reflected upon their own experience. They eventually decided to come up with a project intended to generate financial resources to strengthen the local community's preparedness in facing natural hazards. This consists in trading and distributing soft drinks in the neighbouring villages. Incomes generated through this activity are fully reinvested in buying relief goods to be distributed to those affected in the event of future cyclones and in funding further DRR activities, including the revival of the 3D map damaged during Cyclone Pedring initiated by the school and strengthening their action plan in facing natural hazards.

P3DM as an integrative tool for DRR

The project conducted in Masantol proved that P3DM can serve as a tool which facilitates the integration of people's capacities, along with their vulnerabilities, in DRR.

P3DM is a powerful tool for local communities to fully appraise disaster risk in their local environment as it provides a tangible view of vulnerabilities and capacities in facing natural hazards. P3DM further makes local knowledge, skills and resources credible to scientists and government officials. In contrast to most other forms of participatory mapping, the exact scale of P3DM allows scientists to delineate threatened sectors in their expected extent as they usually do on topographic maps or computer-based tools. Because the map is scaled and geo-referenced, scientists are further able to rigorously integrate people's data with their own knowledge. The possibility of integrating those data into a GIS (Gaillard and Maceda 2009) also enhances the tangibility and credibility of people's capacities for both scientists and government officials.

In that context, marginalized people, including the illiterate who may have limited grasp of scientific concepts, can discuss DRR with scientists, who, on the other hand, may have a poor understanding of the local context. In this study, P3DM was found to be credible to both the locals (including school pupils) who built the map and plotted most of the information, and the scientists and local government representatives who easily overlapped their own data. P3DM thus contributes to empowering the most marginalized by granting them access to scientific knowledge and by rendering credible their own knowledge and larger capacities to the eyes of local officials and scientists. It henceforth balances power relationships between locals and scientists and therefore unlocks one of the crucial problems identified in the literature for integrating bottom-up and top-down actions in DRR (Dekens 2007; Gaillard and Mercer 2012; Mercer *et al.* 2009, 2010).

Making people's capacities tangible opens grounds for discussion within the local community and between the community and outside stakeholders involved in DRR. Building a P3DM is a collective learning experience which stimulates the exchange of information through the search for consensus around the type and the location of information to be plotted on the map. P3DM thus facilitates the exchange of information and dialogue within and among members of local communities, especially those who are usually excluded from **policy** planning because they are marginalized, e.g., children, the elderly, women, people with disabilities. All have roles in the construction of a concrete, easy-to-access and long-lasting tool.

P3DM also facilitates the dialogue between members of the local communities and scientists, local government officials and NGOs. It provides the common, trusted ground which enables all stakeholders to collaborate on DRR. P3DM enables all stakeholders to assess the needs and capacities of local communities and to plan from the inside what could and should be done at the community level. The same tool enables NGOs and local government officials to plan and plot, in collaboration with the locals, top-down actions intended to sustain local needs. Such a common tool for collaboration is essential to integrate bottom-up and top-down DRR measures (Gaillard and Mercer 2013). Those measures and actions are obviously more credible and more easily endorsed by all stakeholders because all collaborate in the same activity.

P3DM further enables the integration of DRR into larger development planning. In Masantol, participants plan to use the map to find the best location for the construction of a bridge linking the six isolated villages to the rest of the municipality, according to not only disaster risk-related needs (evacuation, access for rescue teams) but also the need to access public services and commercial places on a daily basis. Plans for such a bridge have eventually been designed and a budget prepared so that the local community support by its partner NGO is now lobbying different government agencies and donors to provide enough financial assistance. People also consider the P3DM in settling conflicts around fishing grounds between fishermen of different communities. Finally, because it is cheap and easy to reproduce, P3DM helps in making DRR much easier to integrate and to prioritize within the larger framework of development for local authorities who often struggle with limited resources.

Conclusion

P3DM contributes to making local knowledge, skills and other resources tangible to outside stakeholders (Table 17.2). Conducting P3DM to facilitate the integration of people's capacities in DRR, however, requires careful groundwork. Consultation with potential stakeholders is crucial to ensure the participation of a representative group of people, including the usually marginalized. The most marginalized are, however, often invisible within the community. Therefore, a good initial knowledge of the local community and a cautious assessment of the needs and expectations of all potential stakeholders are crucial. Such groundwork also helps in anticipating issues such as the lack of anonymity of data plotted on the map and potential misuse of P3DM by the most powerful stakeholders to the detriment of the larger community.

Other different forms of participatory mapping have been derived from early experiences in using P3DM to facilitate the integration of people's capacities in DRR (Table 17.2). Those include two-dimensional scaled mapping which is a quick and lighter version of P3DM. People here plot and delineate spatial information, especially hazard-prone areas, vulnerable resources and people as well as their capacities on a base map sketched to scale by the facilitators beforehand (Gaillard and Pangilinan 2010). As in P3DM those information are depicted using push-pins and yarns (but no paint to shorten the activity) (Figure 17.1). In contexts where people are acquainted with aerial photographs and satellite images (through open access mapping applications available from the Internet), similar mapping activities may be conducted. People use push-pins and yarn to locate on an aerial photograph or a satellite image of their place hazard-prone areas, vulnerable resources and people as well as their capacities. Such tools have been recently used in New Zealand (Figure 17.1).

Like the other forms of participatory mapping, P3DM cannot stand alone in integrating people's capacities, along with their vulnerability, in DRR. It should be combined with calendars, ranking and scoring, and other tools common to vulnerability and capacity analysis (VCA) and PLA (Wisner 2006). A combination of tools is particularly important in assessing those dimensions of disaster risk which are poorly addressed by P3DM such as client–patron relationships, gender-related inequalities, social networks and the variation of vulnerabilities and capacities with time (especially in the short run) according to people's mobility.

For all these activities as for the core participatory mapping activities both the process and the outcomes should be considered. The objective of a P3DM activity is not to come up with a stunning and perfectly accurate map if this is through disempowering the participants. Tangible outcomes should not overcome the process through which these outcomes are achieved. Therefore, it is sometimes better to end up with a poorly finished map because, for example, the participants discovered painting for the time in their life. If the use of the 3D map is for the

Table 17.2 Principles, advantages and disadvantages of P3DM and derived forms of participatory mapping for facilitating the integration of people's capacities in DRR

Type of participatory mapping	Principles	Advantages	Disadvantages	References
P3DM	People built a 3-dimensional model of their place with locally available materials. They then overlap thematic layers of geographic information	– Relatively easy to set up and cheap – Permanent – Flexible (easy correction and adjustment) – Large semiology – Scaled and georeferenced – Reliable to government officials and scientists – Enable dialogue with government officials and scientists – Most often stored locally	– Unfamiliar to many people – Often require an external facilitator to provide the base map	– Maceda et al. (2009) – Gaillard and Maceda (2009)
Scaled 2D mapping	People draw a scaled map of their place then plot spatial data with push-pins and yarns	– Relatively easy to set up and cheap – Permanent – Large semiology – Flexible (easy correction and adjustment) – Scaled – Enable dialogue with government officials and scientists – Most often stored locally	– Unfamiliar to many people – Often require an external facilitator to provide the base map	– International Federation of Red Cross and Red Crescent Societies (2008) – Gaillard and Pangilinan (2010)
Aerial photograph or satellite image mapping	People plot spatial data with push-pins and yarns on top of an aerial photograph or a satellite image of their place	– Relatively easy to set up – Permanent – Large semiology – Flexible (easy correction and adjustment) – Scaled – Enable dialogue with government officials and scientists – Most often stored locally	– Unfamiliar to many people when access to the Internet is limited – Aerial photographs and satellite images may be outdated – Often require an external facilitator to provide the base map	n/a

sole use of the community and depending upon the context, minor inaccuracies in the plotting of data may be acceptable. It may cause more harm if the facilitator tries to correct such errors, thus leading participants to feel disempowered. Accountability downward in the direction of the community must always take precedence over upward accountability in the direction of outsider stakeholders or donor agencies. In that sense, the practice of participatory mapping to facilitate the integration of people's capacities in DRR should therefore always respect the key principles of CBDRR as outlined in Chapter 4 in this volume.

Acknowledgement

This chapter is modified from an article published in *Area*, (2012) 44(1): 100–9.

References

Abarquez, I. and Murshed, Z. (2004) *Community-Based Disaster Risk Management: Field Practitioners' Handbook*, Pathumthani: Asian Disaster Preparedness Center.

Benson, C., Twigg, J. and Rossetto, T. (2007) *Tools for Mainstreaming Disaster Risk Reduction: Guidance Notes for Development organisations*, Geneva: ProVention Consortium.

Capelao, P. (2007) *Raumoco Watershed Vulnerability Mapping East Timor*, Lospalos: Concern Timor Leste.

Chambers, R. (2008) *Revolutions in Development Inquiry*, London: Earthscan.

Cronin, S.J., Petterson, M.J., Taylor, M.W. and Biliki, R. (2004) 'Maximising multi-stakeholder participation in government and community volcanic hazard management programs; a case study from Savo, Solomon Islands', *Natural Hazards*, 33 (1): 105–36.

Davis, I., Haghebeart, B. and Peppiatt, D. (2004) *Social Vulnerability and Capacity Analysis*, Discussion paper and workshop report, Geneva: ProVention Consortium.

Dekens, J. (2007) *Local Knowledge for Disaster Preparedness: A Literature Review*, Kathmandu: International Centre for Integrated Mountain Development.

Delica-Willison, Z. and Gaillard, JC (2012) 'Community action and disaster', in B. Wisner, JC Gaillard and I. Kelman (eds) *Handbook of Hazards and Disaster Risk Reduction*, London: Routledge, pp. 711–22.

Dosemagen, S., Warren, J. and Wylie, S. (2011) 'Grassroot mapping: creating a participatory map-making process centered on discourse', *The Journal of Aesthetics and Protest*, 8. Available at: http://joaap.org/issue8/GrassrootsMapping.htm (accessed 16 March 2013).

Gaillard, JC (2011) *People's Response to Disasters: Vulnerability, Capacities and Resilience in Philippine Context*, Angeles City: Center for Kapampangan Studies.

Gaillard, JC and Maceda, E.A. (2009) 'Participatory 3-dimensional mapping for disaster risk reduction', *Participatory Learning and Action*, 60: 109–18.

Gaillard, JC and Mercer, J. (2013) 'From knowledge to action: bridging gaps in disaster risk reduction', *Progress in Human Geography*, 37 (1): 93–114.

Gaillard, JC and Pangilinan, M.L. (2010) 'Participatory mapping for raising disaster risk awareness among the youth', *Journal of Contingencies and Crisis Management*, 18 (3): 175–9.

Goodchild, M.F. (2005) 'Geographic information systems', in K. Kempf-Leonard (ed.) *Encyclopedia of Social Measurement*, Amsterdam: Elsevier, pp. 107–13.

Gregory, D., Johnston, R., Pratt, G., Watts, M.J. and Whatmore, S. (2009) *The Dictionary of Human Geography*, 5th edn, Chichester: Wiley-Blackwell.

IFAD (2009) *The IFAD Adaptive Approach to Participatory Mapping*, Rome: International Fund for Agricultural Development.

IFRC (2007) *VCA Toolbox with Reference Sheets*, Geneva: International Federation of Red Cross and Red Crescent Societies.

—— (2008) *Bridging the Gap: Integrating Climate Change and Disaster Risk Reduction*, Geneva: International Federation of Red Cross and Red Crescent Societies.

International Institute of Rural Reconstruction and CordAid (2007) *Building Resilient Communities: A Training Manual on Community-Managed Disaster Risk Reduction*, Silang/The Hague: International Institute of Rural Reconstruction/CordAid.

Kienberger, S. and Steinbruch, F. (2005) *P-GIS and Disaster Risk Management: Assessing Vulnerability with P-GIS Methods – Experiences from Búzi, Mozambique*, International Conference on Participatory Spatial Information Management and Communication – PGIS'05, Nairobi, 7–10 September.

Maceda, E.A., Gaillard, JC, Stasiak, E., Le Masson, V. and Le Berre, I. (2009) 'Experimental use of participatory 3-dimensional models in island community-based disaster risk management', *Shima: The International Journal of Research into Island Culture,* 3 (1): 46–58.

Mercer, J., Kelman, I., Suchet-Pearson, S. and Lloyd, K. (2009) 'Integrating indigenous and scientific knowledge bases for disaster risk reduction in Papua New Guinea', *Geografiska Annaler B*, 91 (2): 157–83.

Mercer, J., Kelman, I., Taranis, L., and Suchet-Pearson, S. (2010) 'Framework for integrating indigenous and scientific knowledge for disaster risk reduction', *Disasters*, 34: 214–39.

National Statistics Office (2010) *2007 Census of Population*, Manila: National Statistics Office. Available at: http://www.census.gov.ph/data/census2007/index.html (accessed 29 October 2012).

Oxfam (2002) *Participatory Capacities and Vulnerabilities Assessment: Finding the Link between Disasters and Development*, Quezon City: Oxfam Great Britain – Philippine Programme.

Peters, G., McCall, M.K. and van Westen, C. (2009) *Coping Strategies and Manageability: How Participatory Geographical Systems can Transform Local Knowledge into Better Policies for Disaster Risk Management*, Disaster Studies Working Paper 22, London: Aon Benfield UCL Hazard Research Centre.

Rambaldi, G. and Callosa-Tarr, J. (2002) *Participatory 3-Dimensional Modelling: Guiding Principles and Applications*, Los Baños: ASEAN Regional Centre for Biodiversity Conservation.

Rodolfo, K.S. and Siringan, F.P. (2006) 'Global sea-level rise is recognised, but flooding from anthropogenic land subsidence is ignored around Northern Manila Bay, Philippines', *Disasters*, 30 (1): 118–39.

Tran, P., Shaw, R., Chantry, G. and Norton, J. (2009) 'GIS and local knowledge in disaster management: a case study of flood risk mapping in Vietnam', *Disasters*, 33: 152–169

Twigg, J. (2004) *Disaster Risk Reduction: Mitigation and Preparedness in Development and Emergency Programming*, Good Practice Review No. 9, London: Humanitarian Practice Network.

von Kotze, A and Holloway, A (1996) *Reducing Risk: Participatory Learning Activities for Disaster Mitigation in Southern Africa*, Geneva/Durban: International Federation of Red Cross and Red Crescent Societies/University of Natal.

Warren, J.Y. (2006) *Grassroot Mapping: Tools for Participatory and Activist Cartography*, MSc Thesis, Massachusetts Institute of Technology, Cambridge, MA.

White, I., Kingston, R. and Barker, A. (2010) 'Participatory geographic information systems and public engagement within flood risk management', *Journal of Flood Risk Management*, 3 (4): 337–46.

Wisner, B. (2006) 'Self-assessment of coping capacity: participatory, proactive and qualitative engagement of communities in their own risk management' in J. Birkmann (ed.) *Measuring Vulnerability to Natural Hazard: Towards Disaster-Resilient Societies*, Tokyo: United Nations University Press, pp. 328–40.

Wisner, B., Gaillard, JC and Kelman, I. (eds) (2012) *The Routledge Handbook of Handbook of Hazards and Disaster Risk Reduction*, London: Routledge.

18 A knowledge integration tool for disaster risk reduction including climate change

Ilan Kelman and Jessica Mercer

Lessons for practitioners

- No single form of **knowledge**, such as science or traditional knowledge, should be relied on for disaster risk reduction, including dealing with climate change.
- Climate change should not be isolated, but should be placed within other disaster, development, and livelihoods challenges.
- Climate change concerns should be addressed without causing or exacerbating other problems, since climate change is only one of many major **hazards** facing communities.
- A useful starting point for local disaster risk reduction is to identify community goals, needs, and priorities, followed by linking those local concerns to the global situation.

Introduction

Communities around the world have long experienced the challenges and opportunities of dealing with **vulnerabilities** that lead to disasters (Dearing *et al.* 2006; Hewitt 1983; Lewis 1999; Wisner *et al.* 2004, 2012). The importance of applying different knowledge forms for community-based activities to address such vulnerabilities is increasingly receiving deserved recognition, especially in light of the hazard of climate change (Brokensha *et al.* 1980; Fernando 2003; Mercer 2012; Sillitoe 1998).

Nevertheless, no single form of knowledge and no single approach can be a panacea for dealing with multiple hazards (Kelman *et al.* 2012). For example, land-use changes and the changing climate, among other factors, are causing such rapid environmental changes that in some cases, the relevance of local knowledge about the **community**'s environments is reduced (Shaw *et al.* 2009). Similarly, climate projections produced by external scientists are frequently too coarse to support decision-making in small communities. Community-based approaches, local knowledge, and external knowledge should therefore be combined to overcome the limitations and to build on the respective strengths of each (e.g., Glantz 1997; Mercer *et al.* 2009, 2010; Wisner 1995; Wisner *et al.* 1977).

This chapter outlines a tool for integrating community-based approaches (see also Chapter 4) and local knowledge with external knowledge for disaster risk reduction, which explicitly includes climate change adaptation. Mercer *et al.* (2009; 2010) developed and piloted the original tool (Process Framework) to address disaster risk reduction in small island developing states (SIDS; http://www. sidsnet.org) and this chapter draws extensively on that work. This tool was then subsequently revised to focus on and incorporate the specific hazard of climate change (Kelman *et al.* 2009), another source on which this chapter relies.

SIDS are 52 island states and territories facing similar sustainability challenges, including displaying exceptional **vulnerability** to environmental hazards including climate change (Pelling and Uitto 2001). Many SIDS communities have extensive local knowledge and traditional approaches that have helped their people deal with these challenges for centuries (e.g., Campbell 2009; Nunn *et al.* 2007). Based on such literature, this chapter draws extensively from Kelman *et al.* (2009) and Mercer *et al.* (2009, 2010) to further apply an assessment of work covering climate change impacts, vulnerability, and adaptation across SIDS (CICERO and UNEP/GRID-Arendal 2008). This assessment was prepared under the Many Strong Voices (MSV) programme (http://www.manystrongvoices.org) which brings together the peoples of the Arctic and SIDS to meet the challenges of climate change within wider development and sustainability contexts. The programme seeks to catalyse local initiative and action through **capacity** building, research, education, and outreach. The MSV assessment work indicates that valuable SIDS community knowledge and community-based approaches are available for disaster risk reduction including climate change adaptation, even though external methods and data are needed and assist.

A community-based knowledge integration tool for disaster risk reduction

The Knowledge Integration Tool described here was originally developed for isolated communities in the SIDS of Papua New Guinea (PNG; Figure 18.1). PNG achieved independence from Australia in 1975, prior to which, its economy was largely based on agriculture. Post-independence, PNG has increasingly exploited its natural resources for export, especially mining (Connell 1997) and more recently timber (Shearman and Bryan 2011; Shearman *et al.* 2009). PNG, however, has remarkable social and environmental diversity and independence failed to generate a spirit of national development. Additionally, natural resource exploitation has been hindered by poor governance and **corruption** along with a rugged terrain requiring expensive infrastructure (Connell 1997; Transparency International 2008). Consequently, subsistence agriculture remains the main livelihood for the majority of PNG's population.

Most of PNG's population is indigenous, with over 800 tribal languages spoken and 87 percent of the residents living in rural areas (PNG National Statistical Office 2003). Over 400 food crop species are grown across the country – mainly on land passed down through families for generations – reflecting the country's enormous

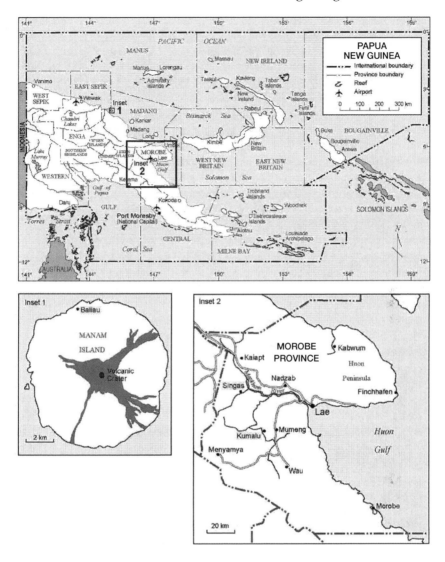

Figure 18.1 Map of PNG illustrating the village locations

Note: Based on http://un.org/Depts/Cartographic/map/profile/papua.pdf.

environmental variations (Department of Lands and Physical Planning 2005; Connell 1997). Many communities have developed coping mechanisms to deal with environmental changes and extremes that lead to food scarcity (e.g., Waddell 1983). Yet much community knowledge and its practices are being undermined by a combination of local values such as 'modernisation' and views of what 'modern' means, national pressures including urbanisation, and global changes, including climate change (Mercer *et al.* 2009, 2010).

To develop and test a tool to apply to dealing with those changes, pilot studies were undertaken in Singas, Kumalu and Baliau villages covering all of disaster risk reduction. Respectively, these communities are affected by mainly floods, floods and landslides, and an erupting volcano (see also Mercer and Kelman 2008, 2010). These villages were selected based principally on their previously expressed interest in participating in disaster risk reduction activities after community members had approached the PNG authorities for assistance. These original contacts became the entry point into each village. Afterwards and throughout the consultations, rapport and trust were built by this chapter's second author who participated in community tasks, including playing with children, cooking, gardening, and going to market to buy and sell goods.

Singas, Kumalu and Baliau community members rely on subsistence agriculture **livelihoods**. The main food staples in Singas and Baliau are plantains and fish, while in Kumalu it is sweet potato due to the village's higher altitude. All three villages further benefit from some form of cash input. Kumalu community members have close ties with community members in Bulolo, the district centre and a gold-mining area, and earn cash to send home through panning for gold and working in the mine. Baliau village's main cash crop is copra. Singas community members earn cash incomes mainly from selling surplus agricultural produce at a nearby market.

In each village, with the community members' agreement, the fieldwork method used was 'guided discovery' (Bruner 1961). Community members use past experiences and existing knowledge to discover new knowledge and relationships that assist them on their own terms. The guided discovery process is affected through participatory techniques such as **mapping** exercises, timelines, and matrix ranking (see Mercer *et al.* 2008, 2009, 2010). The specific tasks in each specific context were decided with local partners in each location (e.g. Chambers 2002; Wilcox 1994), factoring in the need to be able to draw generalisations and to aggregate lessons (Mercer *et al.* 2009).

Part of 'guided discovery' involves developing a Process Framework (Figure 18.2) with community members. This framework is a Knowledge Integration Tool, enabling structured and straightforward learning leading to action while being flexible enough to adapt to different contexts and community interests. It guided community members through an in-depth exploration of factors contributing to their community's vulnerabilities to hazards, while identifying and integrating different knowledge forms that could be used to address those vulnerabilities. To enable knowledge integration, four steps were used (Mercer *et al.* 2009, 2010).

Step one collected background information for the community through participatory group work identifying general community information, interests, and goals. Examples of the information gleaned are village history, maps, hazard and disaster timelines, and social and environmental trends.

With this baseline, communities completed step two identifying underlying vulnerability factors, both external and internal (Lewis 2009; Wisner 1993). External factors are effectively beyond a community's control, such as storms and volcanic eruptions. Internal factors can be controlled by the community to a large

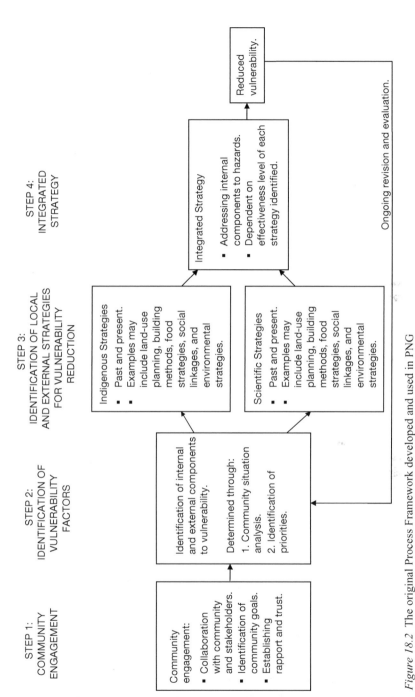

Figure 18.2 The original Process Framework developed and used in PNG

Source: Mercer *et al.* (2009), with some text adjusted.

extent, such as changing crops or cropping patterns along with structures in flood plains or landslide run-out zones.

Climate change was mentioned as an external factor in all three villages. That is, through guided discovery, the villagers – not outsiders introducing the concept – determined that climate change for them was a hazard that should be addressed. Villagers in the three settlements discussed weather patterns, raised concerns about recently changing weather patterns, and connected those experiences to climate change.

Concentrating on the internal vulnerability factors, community members covered step three by separating into groups to identify past and present local and external strategies used to cope with these internal factors for vulnerability reduction. This group work assisted in ensuring that voices were heard from both genders (see also Chapter 3) and most ages within the ethnically homogeneous villages. Once these strategies for vulnerability reduction were identified, community members scored the effectiveness of each strategy in reducing vulnerability.

For step four, the scores enabled community members to establish their views of the most effective strategies to address their vulnerability and to prioritise possible vulnerability reduction strategies which integrated various knowledge sources. The scoring system was viewed as a guide rather than accepted as being absolute. Occasionally, the results from the scoring sparked qualitative discussion that led to further revisions of the scoring in order to better reflect community members' views. As such, the process was iterative, factoring in intangible, qualitative views rather than rigidly adhering to numbers. That is an important principle within the Knowledge Integration Tool and for any tool aiming to apply community views and knowledge. Identifying and prioritising the most effective strategies represented the integrated approach for reducing vulnerability, combining local and external knowledge forms.

Feedback from community members indicated that this approach enabled them to identify strategies that they felt were achievable with existing **resources** and knowledge. The tool also supported them in identifying stages and forms of vulnerability through time, including pinpointing how their own decisions – for instance, changing building materials and land-use practices – could have contributed. Guided discovery through the Knowledge Integration Tool therefore encourages awareness and responsibility within the communities to contribute to addressing their own vulnerabilities on their own terms, especially the internal factors, but within the context of external factors.

Highlighting climate change

The original Process Framework or Knowledge Integration Tool targeted mainly event-specific environmental hazards that the communities had previously experienced. Climate change as a long-term trend is likely to alter the timing, severity, and frequency of many of these environmental hazards along with affecting weather seasonality. Consequently, the Knowledge Integration Tool provides a useful entry point for discussing how and why communities could be vulnerable to, and could deal with, longer-term climate change within disaster risk reduction.

The appropriateness of revising the Knowledge Integration Tool to directly address climate change hinges to a certain extent on leaving step one unchanged. A danger could exist if forcing climate change onto the agenda of community goals and concerns. The experience in PNG and through MSV suggests that this danger is minimal. Aside from the three communities in PNG identifying climate change as an external concern, SIDS communities frequently report climate change challenges (e.g., http://www.climatefrontlines.org) and are actively seeking and supporting endeavours to address climate change (e.g. CICERO and UNEP/GRID-Arendal 2008).

The following revisions to the Knowledge Integration Tool are suggested to fully account for climate change within wider disaster risk reduction contexts (from Kelman *et al.* 2009; see Figure 18.3) and thereby are also applicable to other creeping (long-term, slowly evolving) environmental problems (Glantz 1994):

Revision to Step 2

(a) Rather than focusing on internal and local factors, the engagement created through this knowledge integration process should also be used to highlight a global situation analysis, with global climate change causes and trends linked to local impacts and vulnerabilities. External knowledge indicating historical and potential future consequences of climate variability and change – for instance, satellite observations along with climate modelling and projections over different time scales – could be presented and discussed to connect with internal vulnerability factors identified by local and external participants. Convergence areas could then be identified for a complete situation analysis, setting the stage for strategies to deal with climate change and other creeping environmental problems suggested in step three and integrated in step four.

(b) Rather than separating internal and external factors as mutually exclusive categories, climate change links them. For example, land-use changes have increased flood damage in Kumalu as an internal factor that can be partly redressed locally. That must be done in the context of uncertainty in how flood characteristics will change due to climate change. Including climate change suggests that contingency and flexibility, rather than fixed strategies or rigid goals, should be considered for flood risk reduction.

Revision to Step 3

(a) One part of identifying local strategies for reducing vulnerability to both environmental hazards and climate change should focus explicitly on determining how people have responded to longer-term changes in the past. Community members in collaboration with partners outside the community – regionally, nationally, and globally – could then determine the extent to which past responses and knowledge might be applicable under current local

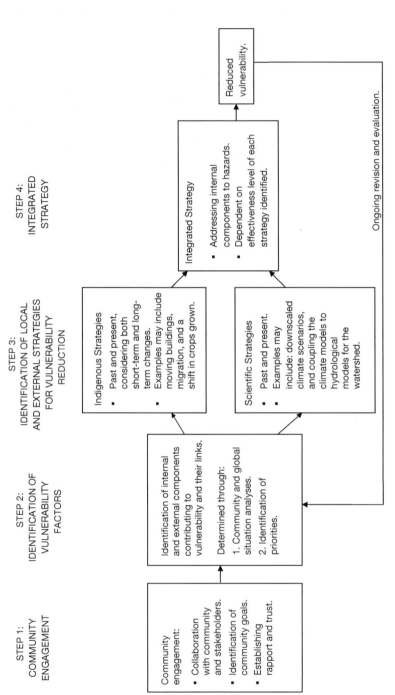

Figure 18.3 The revised Process Framework: A Knowledge Integration Tool which highlights climate change

Source: Kelman *et al.* (2009).

realities, as well as under projected future changes. An example is construction methods for buildings. For instance, constructing homes on stilts avoids flooding in Singas (Mercer and Kelman 2008) while in Baliau, steeply sloped roofs avoid fire and collapse risk from volcanic ash and ensure run-off during heavy rainfall (Mercer and Kelman 2010).

(b) One part of identifying external strategies should be requesting data that the community decides would be useful for long-term planning. Examples are downscaled climate scenarios or regularly updated remotely sensed observations. This information could enable communities to prepare for expected hazards over different time scales.

Revision to Step 4

(a) Strategies should include measures for addressing climate change, specifically paying attention to how community vulnerability is affected by climatic variability and change beyond already experienced environmental hazards. One example is the potential for invasive species (e.g., Wilkie 2002) that could change the pests or diseases affecting established crops.

Lessons and recommendations

The advantages from this work, and the lessons to highlight and to apply elsewhere, are the Knowledge Integration Tool's ability to relate local and global topics, especially by combining community knowledge and experiences with external information and approaches. Two main points are detailed here.

First, by identifying community goals and priorities, and by connecting these to local and global situation analyses, all hazards within disaster risk reduction are supported simultaneously. The starting point is the community's needs, not the specific hazards such as landslides, climate change, or volcanic eruptions.

For example, all three villages in PNG identified increased vegetation burning as potentially exacerbating floods and erosion. The Knowledge Integration Tool helps to consider how land use has changed over past decades, affecting community vulnerability. By considering local and external strategies that improve land-use practices and reduce burning, flood and erosion vulnerability is reduced, irrespective of climate change affecting those hazards.

The second point, also emphasised in MSV, is that disaster risk reduction, including climate change adaptation, should be integrated into wider development and sustainability contexts in which it is frequently embedded already (Lewis 1999; Wisner *et al.* 2004, 2012). The three PNG villages exemplify the development challenges faced by many SIDS communities, irrespective of climate change. The Knowledge Integration Tool enables solutions to be identified to adjust livelihoods to tackle many challenges simultaneously using all available and applicable knowledge.

One possible option to explore for the PNG villages could be reversing land-use changes to reduce flood and erosion risk by expanding the crop profile grown.

Crops could include local species with multiple uses, covering combinations of erosion prevention, building materials, nutrition, and livestock fodder. The potential could be explored for growing small amounts of cash crops alongside food crops. That could supplement income while maintaining sufficient diversity in case of shifts in external markets and/or environmental conditions. If such livelihood adjustments were deemed to be appropriate, implementing and monitoring them would require local and external knowledge. Local knowledge would be needed regarding appropriate cropping patterns and land use. External knowledge could assist in identifying suitable crops that might not have been grown before in the community along with identifying potential long-term environmental trends.

Caution is essential before implementation in order to fully analyse the potential positive and negative consequences. The uncertainties in future environmental and market analyses must be weighed carefully against analysis of who may win and lose, in the short term and long term, when livelihood and land-use systems are adjusted. For instance, the introduction of cash cropping for coffee in Kumalu in 1954 was identified by the community as leading to later vulnerability (Mercer *et al.* 2009). Power relations must be carefully managed in all such decisions.

This discussion highlights the challenges of ensuring that climate change concerns are addressed without causing or exacerbating other problems. Climate change is only one of many major hazards facing these communities; it should neither dominate nor be neglected. The Knowledge Integration Tool enables communities to find solutions to adjust and expand livelihoods to tackle many hazard challenges simultaneously – exactly the ethos underlying disaster risk reduction.

Conclusion

The revised Process Framework or Knowledge Integration Tool has the potential to demonstrate the usefulness of placing climate change adaptation directly within disaster risk reduction processes (Kelman and Gaillard 2008). Key commonalities between the original tool and the tool highlighting climate change are the four-step structure; community members identifying the factors that should be addressed to reduce vulnerability; and the strategies combining different knowledge forms. Key differences are highlighted by Figures 18.2 and 18.3.

A key strength of the Knowledge Integration Tool is recognising different knowledge forms as resources upon which to build successful local strategies for vulnerability reduction. The 'guided discovery' method adheres to principles within disaster risk reduction and wider development processes, providing step-by-step guidelines for applying a community-based tool that moves away from solely top-down approaches.

Instead, top-down approaches are combined with bottom-up participatory processes 'guided' by the people involved (Gaillard and Mercer 2013). In this way, the tool represents guidelines to assist communities in identifying problems and in combining different knowledge bases to seek potential solutions for themselves on their own terms, without neglecting outside support. These key principles of the Knowledge Integration Tool ensure its appropriateness for wider application in SIDS as well as in non-SIDS regions with similarities, notably isolated mountain communities and Arctic communities.

In describing the tool and suggesting its application, this chapter does not analyse the tool's implementation or evaluation. Mercer *et al.* (2009) discuss some advantages and challenges of implementing and evaluating the first Process Framework (Figure 18.2). The lessons are poignant for the revised tool focusing on knowledge integration for multiple hazards including climate change (Figure 18.3).

The main expected outcome of implementing the Knowledge Integration Tool presented here is reduced community vulnerability through considering climate change as one hazard among many within disaster risk reduction. That explicitly recognises and acts on both immediate and long-term challenges (i.e. the creeping environmental changes from Glantz 1994). A second outcome is establishing long-term cooperative partnerships between communities and collaborators outside the community at regional, national, and international levels. These partnerships would provide a platform for exchanging and applying local and external knowledge and expertise to design vulnerability reduction strategies that are locally contextual, without neglecting wider contexts.

References

Brokensha, D., Warren, D.M. and Werner, O. (1980) *Indigenous Knowledge Systems and Development*, Lanham, MD: University Press of America.

Bruner, J. (1961) 'The act of discovery', *Harvard Educational Review*, 31(1): 21–32.

Campbell, J. (2009) 'Islandness: vulnerability and resilience in Oceania', *Shima: The International Journal of Research into Island Cultures*, 3(1): 85–97.

Chambers, R. (2002) *Participatory Workshops: A Sourcebook of 21 Sets of Ideas and Activities*, Brighton: Institute of Development Studies, University of Sussex.

CICERO and UNEP/GRID-Arendal (2008) *Many Strong Voices: Outline for an Assessment Project Design*, CICERO Report 2008:05, Oslo and Arendal Norway: CICERO (Center for International Climate and Environmental Research – Oslo) and UNEP/GRID.

Connell, J. (1997) *Papua New Guinea: The Struggle for Development*, London: Routledge.

Dearing, J.A., Battarbee, E.R.W., Dikau, I. and Oldfield, E.F. (2006) 'Human–environment interactions: learning from the past', *Regional Environmental Change*, 6 (1–2): 1–16.

Department of Lands and Physical Planning (2005) *Land Tenure System in Papua New Guinea*, Port Moresby, Papua New Guinea: Department of Lands and Physical Planning.

Fernando, J.L. (2003) 'NGOs and production of indigenous knowledge under the condition of postmodernity', *The Annals of the American Academy*, 590: 54–72.

Gaillard, JC and Mercer, J. (2013) 'From knowledge to action: bridging gaps in disaster risk reduction', *Progress in Human Geography*, 37(1): 93–114.

Glantz, M.H. (1994) 'Creeping environmental problems', *The World & I*, June: 218–225.

—— (ed.) (1997) 'Using science against famine: food security, famine early warning, and El Niño', Special issue, *Internet Journal of African Studies*, 2. Available at: http://ccb.colorado.edu/ijas/ijasno2/ijasno2.html (accessed 13 June 2011).

Hewitt, K. (ed.) (1983) *Interpretations of Calamity from the Viewpoint of Human Ecology*, London: Allen and Unwin.

Kelman, I. and Gaillard, JC (2008) 'Placing climate change within disaster risk reduction', *Disaster Advances*, 1(3): 3–5.

Kelman, I., Mercer, J. and Gaillard, JC (2012) 'Indigenous knowledge and disaster risk reduction', *Geography*, 97(1): 12–21.

Kelman, I., Mercer, J. and West, J. (2009) 'Combining different knowledges: community-based climate change adaptation in small island developing states', *Participatory Learning and Action Notes*, 60: 41–53.

Lewis, J. (1999) *Development in Disaster-prone Places: Studies of Vulnerability*, London: Intermediate Technology Publications.

—— (2009) 'An island characteristic: derivative vulnerabilities to indigenous and exogenous hazards', *Shima: The International Journal of Research into Island Cultures*, 3(1): 3–15.

Mercer, J. (2012) 'Knowledge and disaster risk reduction', in B. Wisner, JC Gaillard, and I. Kelman (eds) *The Routledge Handbook of Hazards and Disaster Risk Reduction*, London: Routledge, pp. 89–100.

Mercer, J. and Kelman, I. (2008) 'Living with floods in Singas, Papua New Guinea', in R. Shaw, N. Uy and J. Baumwoll (eds) *Indigenous Knowledge for Disaster Risk Reduction: Good Practices and Lessons Learned from Experiences in the Asia-Pacific Region*, Bangkok: UNISDR, pp. 46–51.

—— (2010) 'Living alongside a volcano in Baliau, Papua New Guinea', *Disaster Prevention and Management*, 19(4): 412–22.

Mercer, J., Kelman, I., Lloyd, K. and Suchet-Pearson, S. (2008) 'Reflections on use of participatory research for disaster risk reduction', *Area*, 40(2): 172–83.

—— (2009) 'Integrating indigenous and scientific knowledge bases for disaster risk reduction in Papua New Guinea', *Geografiska Annaler: Series B, Human Geography*, 91(2): 157–83.

Mercer, J., Kelman, I., Taranis, L. and Suchet, S. (2010) 'Framework for integrating indigenous and scientific knowledge for disaster risk reduction', *Disasters*, 34(1): 214–39.

Nunn, P.D., Hunter-Anderson, R., Carson, M.T., Thomas, F., Ulm, S. and Rowland, M.J. (2007) 'Times of plenty, times of less: last-millennium societal disruption in the Pacific Basin', *Human Ecology*, 35 (4): 385–401.

Pelling, M. and Uitto, J.I. (2001) 'Small island developing states: natural disaster vulnerability and global change', *Environmental Hazards*, 3 (2): 49–62.

PNG National Statistical Office (2003) *Census 2000: Population and Social Statistics*. Available at: http://www.spc.int/prism/country/pg/stats/Pop_Soc_%20Stats/popsoc.htm (accessed 20 February 2009).

Shaw, R., Sharma, A. and Takeuchi, Y. (eds) (2009) *Indigenous Knowledge and Disaster Risk Reduction: From Practice to Policy*, Hauppauge: Nova Publishers.

Shearman, P.L., Ash, J., Mackey, B., Bryan, J.E. and Lokes, B. (2009) 'Forest conversion and degradation in Papua New Guinea, 1972–2002', *Biotropica*, 41 (3): 379–90.

Shearman, P.L. and Bryan, J. (2011) 'A bioregional analysis of the distribution of rainforest cover, deforestation and degradation in Papua New Guinea', *Australian Ecology*, 36(1): 9–24.

Sillitoe, P. (1998) 'The development of indigenous knowledge', *Current Anthropology*, 39(2): 223–52.

Transparency International (2008) *Global Corruption Report 2008*, Cambridge: Cambridge University Press.

Waddell, E. (1983) 'Coping with frosts, governments and disaster experts: some reflections based on a New Guinea experience and a perusal of the relevant literature' in K. Hewitt (ed.) *Interpretations of Calamity: From the Viewpoint of Human Ecology*, London: Allen & Unwin, pp. 33–43.

Wilcox, D. (1994) *The Guide to Effective Participation*, Brighton: Delta Press.

Wilkie, M.L. (2002) 'Climate change, forests and SIDS', *International Forestry Review*, 4(4): 313–16.

Wisner, B. (1993) 'Disaster vulnerability: scale, power, and daily life', *GeoJournal*, 30(2): 127–40.

—— (1995) 'Bridging "expert" and "local" knowledge for counter-disaster planning in urban South Africa', *GeoJournal*, 37(3): 335–48.

Wisner, B., Blaikie, P., Cannon, T. and Davis, I. (2004) *At Risk: Natural Hazards, People's Vulnerability and Disasters*, 2nd edn, London: Routledge.

Wisner, B., Gaillard, JC and Kelman, I. (eds) (2012) *Handbook of Hazards and Disaster Risk Reduction*, London: Routledge.

Wisner, B., O'Keefe, P. and Westgate, K. (1977) 'Global systems and local disasters: the untapped power of people's science', *Disasters*, 1(1): 47–57.

19 Conclusion

Addressing all vulnerabilities

Alejandro López-Carresi, Maureen Fordham, Ben Wisner, Ilan Kelman and JC Gaillard and Members of the Practitioner Advisory Panel

Learning across sectors

At the beginning of this book we defined 'practitioner' broadly. If we have been successful, the person holding this book might work in a government ministry or department, as a field coordinator for a humanitarian organisation, or in a role such as a volunteer, a campaigner or lobbyist. It is also likely that you do not have 'disaster risk reduction' or 'disaster management' specifically spelled out in your job description. So we have tried to digest lessons and insights from the world of disaster management and disaster risk reduction research and practice in ways that are helpful for people working in other areas – education, health, economic policy, insurance and financial services, human rights, engineering, food security and agriculture – just to mention a few.

Have we succeeded?

The litmus test is whether or not the lessons make sense across many contexts from many perspectives. For this book, that means ensuring that the lessons and insights apply to whichever **hazards** a practitioner deals with from whichever perspective they are dealing with those hazards.

The Emergency Capacity Building consortium (ECB; http://www.ecbproject. org) focuses on seven sectors in its attempts at building learning bridges. Those learning bridges aim to enable win–win practice by those who do not specialise in disasters and hazards (including climate change) yet who nevertheless contribute to disaster risk reduction and the ability of people to live well despite hazards including climate change (Turnbull *et al.* 2013: 47–91). Box 19.1 explores the case for taking all hazards seriously within each of these sectors – the all-hazards approach championed by many practitioners. The sector names have been updated and modified in places, plus we must keep in mind that all sectors link to, and are encompassed by, people's day-to-day and decade-to-decade struggle to create and maintain productive **livelihoods**.

Do all these sectors and the discussion make sense within the context of all hazards, from long-term global hazards such as climate change to rapid onset, to local hazards such as earthquakes and landslides? One of the ways of answering this question is to consider a usual pair of specific hazards in a specific location. Russia has been severely affected by both meteorites and diphtheria, providing an unusual yet intriguing matching pair to test the relevance of an all-hazards approach.

In the 1990s, a resurgence of the deadly childhood disease, diphtheria, killed 5,000 in Russia, the CIS and the Baltic States (Lo 2012). This was accompanied by an epidemic of alcoholism, HIV-AIDS and tuberculosis that still challenges economic and social development in the region. These threats are pervasive and highly erosive to the wide definition of health, including social relations and well-being. They belong in the group of hazards leading to disasters that are sometimes called 'neglected', 'silent' and 'extensive' (Rowling 2013; UNISDR 2009: 59–85; Wisner and Gaillard 2009). It seems reasonable to assume that no matter what 'practice' the reader is pursuing, wherever in the world, the way that Russians and their partners are and are not grappling with these problems may have valuable lessons to teach.

Then, in February 2013, a meteorite entered the Earth's atmosphere and disintegrated over a medium-sized town in Russia. More than a thousand people were injured, mainly by glass from windows shattering from the shock wave, with more than a hundred requiring hospitalisation. Are threats from so-called 'near-Earth objects' (NEO), such as asteroids and comets which might enter the Earth's atmosphere, simply too rare to care about? In the wake of the meteorite strike in Russia, a lively discussion took place, and it seems that more public and private funding will go to **mapping** and monitoring possible extraterrestrial hazards, as was suggested even before this event (McGuire 2012).

But what of dealing with the vulnerabilities discussed in the sectors in Box 19.1? The question still remains: should the reader who grasps this book stop right now and think about how unusual hazards might impact the work they normally do?

Does focusing on the sectors, especially highlighting vulnerabilities and capacities as evidenced throughout this entire book, present a convincing case that sectoral practitioners should, and can easily, integrate NEO and disease hazards into their work? If so, since NEO impacts are rare, while diseases are prevalent but not always prominent in disaster-related work, then the case for considering sectors, vulnerabilities and capacities for all hazards seems to have been made.

But we, as editors, must leave that question up to you – for feedback to us. Have we addressed your needs as a practitioner? What challenges do you face in your institution or work place when you try to break down the walls of silos named 'project', 'department', 'sector' or 'discipline' in order to take a more wide-ranging approach to development and disaster risk reduction, encompassing climate change adaptation, as advocated in our book? Please send comments, criticism and suggestions to bwisner@igc.org if you want to discuss with the editors privately or see https://www.jiscmail.ac.uk/cgi-bin/webadmin?A0=RADIX for a public email list.

Because, ultimately, while we as editors are labelled as 'experts', everyone has their own expertise from which we can learn. We need to take our own advice regarding the next section 'Listening to People' – by listening to you.

Box 19.1 Sectoral implications of hazards

- *Food security.* Consideration should be given to regional stockpiles and alternative logistical arrangements for getting food to disaster survivors as well as, for smaller hazards, decentralised municipal stockpiles at different locations. Examples include **community** stockpiles, supplemental home gardens, alternate sources of nutrition, nutritional programs and local sourcing, drought-resistant varieties, additional crops in higher rainfall, and foods tailored to locally specific climate forecasts. Good health and nutrition status, along with solid primary health care, reduce the **vulnerability** of a population to the stress and impacts of various hazards.

- *Remittances.* In 2012, over US$400 billion was estimated to have been remitted in an officially recorded manner to families by people working as migrants – approximately four times the official development aid for that year (World Bank 2012). This is expected to grow more than 8 per cent a year, plus many remittances in goods, services, and cash are sent outside of official channels. For disaster recovery, remittances can be an important lifeline and means of support. People sending remittances use many forms for the transfer, suggesting that efforts should be made to support people with alternatives to large companies and banks that take large commissions. That should involve a mix of remittance-related and non-remittance-related livelihood support, often focused on vulnerability reduction. Examples are setting up non-farm and off-farm livelihoods during times of drought, cash-for-work programmes for local level disaster-related and vulnerability reduction tasks, building up local water and food sources, and sourcing local suppliers for emergency relief supplies. That will contribute to protection of livelihoods and livelihood assets against routine hazards, while reducing vulnerability to non-routine hazards. Disaster risk reduction and disaster management as an additional skill or full-time or supplemental occupation can also be supported. For instance, masons and construction workers need to be trained in safe design and construction at the building and community levels.

- *Natural resource management.* The protective function of ecosystems is often overlooked when natural resources are viewed as only an income source. Forests, wetlands and river bank vegetation are often protective against hazards. So alongside livelihood considerations, natural resource management needs to be seen as a basis for ecosystem protection as part of disaster risk reduction. Also, after disasters, relocation and resettlement of survivors need to be planned carefully. Lessons from decades of post-disaster relocation (and from forced relocation for 'development' projects such as large dams) teach that people need support for applying and supplementing their own **knowledge** of natural resource management, because the new location often has different natural resource characteristics.

- *Water, sanitation and hygiene (WASH)*. Infrastructure damage from hazards can lead to fires, chemical spills, and other forms of pollution contaminating water sources over a large area. Post-disaster plans need to provide for rapid delivery of water from regional sources, rapid decontamination of local water supplies and public education about home or local small-scale decontamination of water.

- *Education*. Schools are key buildings in a community and should be built to the highest standards. This means safe school construction for all new schools, **vulnerability assessment** and retrofitting/relocation for existing schools and school preparedness plans and disaster exercises. Care must also be taken in the siting of schools. Safe transport needs to be available for children's access to schools in times of long-duration hazards, such as floods with standing water. Teachers and parent-teacher associations should be involved in preparedness planning, as well as in disaster management and disaster risk reduction activities. That will further assist them in understanding and providing community support when schools are requisitioned for evacuation. Fire safety and awareness of emergency exits are part of this process, but students should be drilled in sheltering in place for a variety of hazards, alongside evacuation drills for hazards such as earthquakes and fires. Those drills should also be used as opportunities for highlighting disaster management and disaster risk reduction skills.

- *Health*. The definition of 'health' includes physical, psychological and social well-being. For short-term disaster management, actions include pre-positioning first aid materials and ensuring that people are trained in using them, plus anticipating and addressing public health concerns which arise in post-disaster shelter. That covers, for instance, WASH (see above), gender and maternal health needs, and grief counselling. For disaster risk reduction over the longer term, a strong primary health care and referral system with buildings and functions that are constructed to withstand hazards is needed for health resilience and wider vulnerability reduction.

- *Capacities of the groups labelled as being most vulnerable*. Development specialists have gradually realised that farmers, fishers, herders, small manufacturers and business owners, and traders have a great deal of knowledge, wisdom and skills. Other groups, often considered primarily to be 'vulnerable' also have knowledge, wisdom and skills. These include people living with disabilities, youth, women, sexual and gender minorities and elderly people.

Listening to people

A common feature of this book's chapters is awareness and engagement with ordinary people's capacities including their perceptions, knowledge, **wisdom**, skills and ideas. Despite the best of intentions, women, sexual and gender minorities, youth, elderly and people with disabilities are often left out. They are still considered to be only 'vulnerable groups' who receive assistance but who do not give it – not as groups who could even contribute to designing appropriate development to render assistance unnecessary. Here, even the chapters that, conventionally, might be expected to be 'technical' and exclusively 'top-down' in approach – such as those on early warning, emergency management, infrastructure and health – argue in favour of engagement with communities.

As an example, people-centred early warning has at its heart an interaction between external knowledge and local knowledge. If getting to people where they live and work in a timely way with information that is actionable and practical is, indeed, the 'last mile' problem, then prior and thorough organisation of, and especially by, local people, along with trust and dialogue with outside 'experts' are essential. That turns the 'last mile' around and instead advocates for the 'first mile'. That is, the people themselves should be first, not last, for early warning design and implementation.

Emergency management likewise is shown to involve timely organisation at the community scale including local identification and mapping of hazards and, in the event of a disaster, response by trained volunteers in coordination with professionals. The chapter on disaster myths emphasises that trust has to be two-way. Just as ordinary people should trust planners and uniformed professionals (such as fire, ambulance, police and the military) – even though reality can preclude that – the false stereotypes of the 'rioting' and 'looting' rabble who panic should be set aside. Where there has been a history of allegations of abuse by authorities, trust is particularly difficult to establish.

Community activists and other ordinary people need to be aware of the kinds of physical damage to buildings and infrastructure that can occur, as discussed in that chapter. We do not need to be trained engineers to ask key questions of project managers, contractors and policymakers. Awareness of related effects of many disasters including factory fires, toxic emissions and environmental contamination adds urgency to demands by many ordinary people for greater and accountable oversight and regulation by governments and authorities.

In the health chapter, we find numerous good examples of the ways in which local level, normal activities can help with disaster management and disaster risk reduction. This includes primary health care workers, midwives and psychological counsellors. Also, assessment of health impacts and epidemiological surveillance involves trust and good relations with communities. Yet that can be increasingly difficult given incidents such as the murder of polio vaccination workers in Pakistan and Nigeria in 2013.

The chapters devoted to regional perspectives demonstrate positive movement towards meaningful participation by and engagement with ordinary people through partnerships with local professionals and administrators. The connection among national, subnational and local programmes needs to be elaborated. Understanding government programmes and schemes enables local community organisations to become part of these schemes. That also assists in engaging with multi-jurisdictional approaches, such as management of watersheds, coastal areas, mountains and forests.

Finally, the 'tools' chapters deal with the implementation and difficulties of inviting local voices and contributions to disaster management and disaster risk reduction. Participatory tools should be designed to allow for integrating people's capacities – including their knowledge, skills and **resources** – with supportive actions initiated by outside stakeholders, such as government officials and scientists. This warrants that people's capacities are made tangible to outside stakeholders, so that everyone is engaged in a balanced dialogue which builds up trust.

Principles and practicalities

The approach advocated by the chapter authors, editors and practitioner advisers is based on some fundamental principles summarised in numerous projects and publications, respected by academics and practitioners, examples of which are:

- The ECB Project (http://www.ecbproject.org) especially through *Toward Resilience* (Turnbull *et al.* 2013: 12–13).
- The Humanitarian Charter that begins the Sphere Project handbook produced by a broad consensus among NGOs and the IFRC over several years (http://www.sphereproject.org/; Sphere 2011).
- The recommendations of the Global Network of Civil Society Organisations for Disaster Reduction (http://www.globalnetwork-dr.org/; GNDR 2009, 2011).
- *The Routledge Handbook of Hazards and Disaster Risk Reduction* (Wisner *et al.* 2012).

These principles are:

- Increase understanding of hazards. An example is incorporating the climate change context, mainly climate change as an influencer of hazards, in hazard analysis.
- Increase understanding of vulnerabilities and capacities – and their interaction. An example is recognising that everyone, even the most vulnerable groups, have capacities which a community needs.
- Recognise rights, responsibilities and duties.
- Strengthen participation of, and action by, ordinary people. An example is designing, testing, implementing and evaluating low-cost slower-paced actions, consistent with levels of capacities which are enhanced slowly, so as to achieve true ownership and sustained action.

- Foster interactions among multiple governance levels. An example is linking community organisations with **local government** people responsible for disaster management and disaster risk reduction.
- Draw on and build diverse sources of knowledge and wisdom. An example is using a community's self-reliant action to deliver demonstrable results while serving as an inspiration to surrounding communities.
- Instil flexibility and responsiveness.
- Address and connect different time and space scales. An example is reducing vulnerability to rare hazards by improving day-to-day health.

The chapters that deal with prevention and risk reduction, which start the book, all advocate or assume a framework of such principles. The same is true of the subsequent chapters which address response and recovery. Turning to the three regional perspectives, challenges emerge in the details of implementation. Principles can have a wide gap from the reality of action on the ground. Some progress has been made, and is documented, in the regional chapters. Where most progress has been made, all of the above principles have been applied. The final chapters on tools are more operational, indicating how the principles can be applied in practice.

Challenges and difficulties which emerge in using the principles are suggested in Box 19.2. These challenges and difficulties should not be viewed as 'problems' and should not be discouraging, because they can all be overcome. Box 19.2 provides some hints how but the key is in the chapters throughout this book. We hope that no issue becomes insurmountable, but instead that the pages in this volume provide the support and guidance necessary for each reader to contextualise their situation – and to overcome any challenges or difficulties.

The future

At the beginning of each chapter, we have listed bullet points particularly relevant to practitioners. These lists aim to provide guidance for each reader to know the on-the-ground relevance of each chapter. In particular, those bullet points try to move away from the hazard-orientated approach which so many of us are used to, theoretically and operationally. Instead, they highlight what the authors universally note is the challenge of disasters and disaster risk: vulnerabilities.

That is not to say that hazards can or should be ignored. On the contrary, we fully accept the need to understand, monitor, and analyse a wide range of hazards. In fact, the all-hazards approach which is often taken in disaster risk reduction – to cover all forms of hazards simultaneously, rather than just focusing on one threat – is needed. If implemented properly, it will contribute towards ensuring that we do not get blindsided by an unusual or forgotten hazard. Examples, as discussed earlier in this chapter, are meteorites and diphtheria.

But more than an all-hazards approach is needed. We must never forget the people, communities, and societies who are being affected by the hazards. Without them, there is no disaster.

Box 19.2 Challenges to implementing the principles

- *Increased understanding.* Despite rhetorical commitment to 'participa-tion', many agencies still privilege Western-based professional science and technology. Increased understanding requires taking local knowledge seriously and facilitating a dialogue between outside specialist knowledge and local knowledge. In the routine operation of sectors such as food security, natural resource management and health, a minority (although increasing) number of programmes respect local practices, perceptions, knowledge, wisdom and skills.

- *Rights, responsibilities and duties.* Across all sectors and in many countries, the issue of rights, responsibilities and duties is difficult in practice because it is highly political and can begin from different bases of ethics. A **culture** of accountability needs to be fostered within development and humanitarian organisations and pushed by lobbying and campaigning at national and international levels. Indications of how vexed these issues can be are the attempts by the United Nations to deny compensation to Haitians affected by cholera from 2010, despite the fact that all evidence points at the cholera coming from the United Nations troops stationed in Haiti following the January 2010 earthquake (Lall and Pilkington 2013).

- *Strengthen **participation**.* Few projects, programmes and **policy** state-ments neglect to mention 'community participation' or the involvement of 'stakeholders'. Yet several elements work against seeing vigorous engagement by ordinary people. The first is that 'participation' takes many forms, from one-off consultations to community control. The latter is politically challenging in many countries. Second, sustained community participation takes time and resources, often unavailable in typical short-term project cycles and project budgets. Third, community norms might dictate that only a certain sector of the community can and should speak for everyone, despite the principle of inclusiveness. Finally, ordinary people often have scarce time to 'participate' and need to be highly motivated to do so – perhaps by seeing tangible and immediate benefits resulting from the time that they invest. The challenges can be overcome by seeing participation, not as an outcome, but as a process. It is pointless and misleading to have nice pictures of many participants in a report if the people only attended because they were paid to attend but did not have much real control over the activities or results. In particular, accountability should be downward to the community as well as upward from the community to the funding agency.

- *Multiple level and diverse knowledge.* Administrative barriers and poor internal communication are spoilers when aiming to put these principles into practice. Behind the scenes, it is often real or imagined competition for budget resources that is the culprit. Structural changes in governments, institutions and agencies – such as creating commissions and sponsoring reports – do not help if the commissions have little power and if the reports' recommendations are not adhered to. Decentralisation can assist if the lower levels have sufficient capacities and resources, including but not limited to financing, for fulfilling the promise of partnerships with communities.

- *Flexibility, timescales and responsiveness.* Flexibility is hard unless budget managers allow it. If one is committed to 'strong' participation by ordinary people (Wisner 1988), then there must be flexibility in programming and project implementation in order to accommodate people's input and feedback throughout the continual process. Slow-onset hazards and pervasive environmental change are also difficult because political administrations come and go with elections or non-democratic changes, the cyclicity of which is usually much shorter than the time scale of these hazards. Vulnerabilities, naturally, are long term.

They have vulnerabilities. They also have capacities. If vulnerabilities are reduced and if capacities are enhanced, then by definition (see, for example, Chapter 2), all hazards are embraced. That is, an all-vulnerabilities approach takes on all hazards – reducing vulnerability and improving **capacity** for all the hazards – so that people, communities, and societies are ready to deal with whatever hazard they experience.

Again, that is not saying that specific hazards or characteristics of hazards can or should be ignored. If people are living in a floodplain, then potential flood heights, velocities, and contaminants among other factors are useful to project and analyse. If seismologists are certain regarding the potential seismicity of a location, then earthquake-related building codes can be tailored to that seismicity.

The key message is that an all-vulnerabilities approach by definition includes – not supersedes and not overrides – an all-hazards approach. Meteorites and diphtheria are important, as are floods and earthquakes. Continually reducing all vulnerabilities and building all capacities is disaster risk reduction. That will make your life easier, as a practitioner for disaster management and disaster risk reduction, no matter what hazards or combination of hazards is experienced.

References

GNDR (2009) *Clouds but Little Rain: Views from the Frontline: A Local Perspective of Progress Towards Implementation of the Hyogo Framework for Action*, Teddington: Global Network of Civil Society Organisations for Disaster Reduction. Available at:

http://www.preventionweb.net/english/professional/publications/v.php?id=9822 (accessed 17 November 2012).

—— (2011) *If We Do Not Join Hands: Views from the Frontline 2011,* Teddington: Global Network of Civil Society Organisations for Disaster Reduction. Available at: http://www. globalnetwork-dr.org/views-from-the-frontline/voices-from-the-frontline-2011/ (accessed 17 November 2012).

Lall, R. and Pilkington, E. (2013) 'UN will not compensate Haiti cholera victims, Ban Ki-moon tells president', *The Guardian*, 21 February. Available at: http://www.guardian. co.uk/world/2013/feb/21/un-haiti-cholera-victims-rejects-compensation (accessed 22 February 2013).

Lo, B.M. (ed.) (2012) *Diphtheria in Emergency Medicine*. Available at: http:// emedicine.medscape.com/article/782051-overview (accessed 20 February 2013).

McGuire, B. (2012) 'Hazards from space', in B. Wisner, JC Gaillard and I. Kelman (eds) *The Routledge Handbook of Hazards and Disaster Risk Reduction*, London: Routledge, pp. 399–410.

Rowling, M. (2013) 'European media campaign shines spotlight on "silent" disasters' *Thompson Reuters Foundation*, 18 February. Available at: http://www.trust.org/ alertnet/news/european-media-campaign-shines-spotlight-on-silent-disasters/#. UST_TxSCzqk.twitter (accessed 20 February 2013).

Sphere (2011) *Humanitarian Charter and Minimum Standards in Humanitarian Response*, Geneva: The Sphere Project. Available at: http://www.sphereproject.org/handbook/ (accessed 20 February 2013).

Turnbull, M., Sterrett, C. and Hilleboe, A. (2013) *Toward Resilience: A Guide to Disaster Risk Reduction and Climate Change Adaptation*, Rugby: Practical Action and Catholic Relief Services. Available at: http://www.ecbproject.org/new-practitioners-guide-to-disaster-risk-reduction-drr/practitioners-guide-to-drr—cca (accessed 19 February 2013).

UNISDR (2009) *Global Assessment Report on Disaster Reduction 2009*, Geneva: UNISDR. Available at: http://www.unisdr.org/we/inform/publications/9413 (accessed 20 February 2013).

Wisner, B. (1988) *Power and Need in Africa*, London: Earthscan.

Wisner, B. and Gaillard, JC (2009) 'An introduction to neglected disasters', *Jàmbá*, 2(3): 151–9. Available at: http://acds.co.za/uploads/jamba/vol2no3/wisner_gaillard.pdf (accessed 20 February 2013).

Wisner, B., Gaillard, JC and Kelman, I. (eds) (2012) *Routledge Handbook of Hazards and Disaster Risk Reduction*, London: Routledge.

World Bank (2012) *Migration and Development Brief 19*, Washington, DC: Migration and Remittances Unit, Development Prospects Group, the World Bank. Available at: http://siteresources.worldbank.org/INTPROSPECTS/Resources/334934-1288990 760745/MigrationDevelopmentBrief19.pdf (accessed 22 February 2013).

Glossary

Most of the specialised terms used in this book are defined by the chapter authors. Other terms that are commonly used by people studying and dealing with hazards and disasters (including climate change) follow the consensus usage that can be found in two lists of terminology, one by the UNISDR (2009) (http://www.unisdr.org/we/inform/terminology) and one by the IPCC (2012) (http://www.ipcc.ch/pdf/special-reports/srex/SREX-Annex_Glossary.pdf). We recognise that there are sometimes differences between these glossaries, and even between (and within) the IPCC and the UN agency dealing with climate change (the UNFCCC), so where there are discrepancies, we suggest selecting the definition according to the audience's main background.

The words below, by contrast, belong to the overlapping languages of development studies and disaster risk reduction (Wisner *et al.* 2012a; Wisner *et al.* 2004) and are commonly used throughout this book. Chapters 1 and 2 in this volume also provide some advice regarding specific terms.

Access – Ability to meet the financial, economic, political and/or sociocultural requirements that formally or informally govern control and use of resources (Wisner *et al.* 2004).

Capacity – Individual, household or community abilities, strengths and resources to take action to achieve a goal on the basis of locally available knowledge, skill, resources and assets. Sometimes capacity is supplemented by infusions of knowledge or other resources from outside the community, usually on the basis of social entitlements (e.g., remittance of wages, goods, services or tuition fees from a family member) or political entitlements (e.g., demands on government for public goods) (Wisner *et al.* 2012a). Other similar words are 'capability' and 'ability'.

Community – A group of people with a range of demographic, economic and even cultural characteristics who nevertheless live their daily lives interacting and, to one degree or another are mutually dependent (Delica-Willison and Gaillard 2012) or supportive. No implication is made that communities are homogeneous or speak with a single voice. Indeed, within a single geographic community there may be a variety of, sometimes competing, communities of interest, circumstance or identity. There may also be geographical communities, communities of interest, communities of circumstance, communities of supporters and communities of identity (Deeming and Fordham 2012: 35–38).

Community-based disaster management (CBDM) – Planning and prior arrangements, often in collaboration with local government, NGOs, scientists, faith groups, school communities, grassroots groups, etc., for community involvement in all aspects of disaster management – risk reduction, warning, response, relief and recovery (Wisner 2006).

Community-based disaster risk reduction (CBDRR) – Planning and continuous activity by a community in monitoring the hazards it faces, the vulnerability of various groups of people in the community, their capacities and community attempts to reduce risk by affecting hazards, reducing vulnerability and/or increasing capacities (Delica-Willison and Gaillard 2012). There are family resemblances with an array of methods including 'rapid rural appraisal', 'participatory rural appraisal' and 'participatory action learning'. A common feature of all is 'organised common sense' (Thompson and Guijt 2011: 174).

Corruption – Abuse of power or authority for gain. This broad definition would cover misuse of political power by government officials and staff at all levels, abuse of physical power by police and the military, abuse of economic power by more affluent people and abuse of authority by traditional and religious leaders (Transparency International 2013), (I)NGOs and other organised groups.

Culture – Behavioural norms, beliefs, rituals, social organisation, language, artefacts and forms of land use, resource management and spatial settlement which form the characteristics of a group of people who self-identify as a distinct group within a larger society. In the domain of disaster management, climate change and human development, culture plays an important role in local/inside emic understandings of natural hazards versus non-local/outside/etic understandings and the practical consequences of these differences in, for example, warning systems. (Gaillard 2012).

Hazard – A process whose normal function or extreme manifestation potentially threatens people's lives, health, livelihoods and assets. Usually in this book the authors mean 'natural hazard' by hazard; however, a number of technological hazards may also manifest as secondary to a natural hazard event or process (see Chapter 8). In the words of the UNISDR (2005: 17), 'A dangerous phenomenon, substance, human activity or condition that may cause loss of life, injury or other health impacts, property damage, loss of livelihoods and services, social and economic disruption or environmental damage.'

Hazard assessment – A wide range of methods used to measure, map or describe the hazards potentially affecting a given locality/community (Wisner *et al.* 2004: 333–42; Serje 2012).

Household – A group of people who live in the same house or home compound and usually eat together. These people may or may not be related by blood, and members who are not present for periods of time may be considered *de jure* members of the household.

Hyogo Framework for Action – The so-called 'HFA' is a set of non-binding guidelines accepted by 168 countries in 2005, the implementation of which was supposed to lead to a 'substantial decrease of losses from natural hazards' by 2015 (UNISDR 2005; see http://www.unisdr.org/we/coordinate/hfa).

Knowledge – Non-material capacities stored in individual brains, muscles, family, community narratives, practices and more formal storage media such as books, works of art and information and communication technology. People may be conscious or unconscious of the knowledge they possess or to which they have access. Knowledge may be gendered, linked to occupations, age-graded, public, private and secret (Mercer 2012).

Livelihood – Activities of individuals and households that use a variety of resources to produce their well-being (Wisner *et al.* 2004).

Local government – The primary government unit at the local end of a hierarchy that descends from central government thorough various subnational administrative units.

Locality – A primary formal or informal geographical settlement unit.

Mapping – The representation in reduced scale (usually but not always in two or three dimensions) of landscape, the built environment and spatial relations. A wide variety of media may be used including the ground itself with stones and sticks, paper, cardboard or even clay models and computers.

Mitigation – In the work of disaster risk reduction this term is used to refer to a variety of actions taken to reduce risks by affecting the hazards themselves, reducing exposure and vulnerability and/or increasing the capacity of the potentially affected population. In the work of climate change, the term refers to steps taken to reduce emissions that contribute to climate change or to increase the sinks for emissions. The brief definition given by UNISDR (2005: 19) is '[t]he lessening or limitation of the adverse impacts of hazards and related disasters'.

Participation – A continuum of processes used to engage local people in discussions of their own situation, for example, of their strengths and weaknesses as well as the opportunities they have and threats they face (SWOT), and in actions towards reducing the risk of disaster. The continuum of processes or 'ladder' of participation includes very weak and superficial forms of 'consultation' through to fully community-controlled learning and action (Chambers 2013).

Policy – Formal or informal agreements or courses of action at various governance levels on goals and the means for their attainment.

Poverty – Both the state of relative or absolute deprivation of the means of well-being at any point in time and the process by which this deprivation is produced and reproduced or 'locked in'. Absolute poverty refers to the inability to provide for basic human needs for food, safe water, sanitation, health care and housing (see Wisner 1988).

Resource – Material and immaterial means through which someone or groups of people are able to achieve their ends. Most commonly one thinks of 'natural' resources (land, water, natural vegetation, etc.); however, topographic characteristics such as slope and aspect may also be resources as well as spatial and temporal relations such as proximity. Knowledge and information as well as public infrastructure may also be considered resources in the broad sense, as well as social networks and cultural values (Wisner *et al.* 2012b).

Risk – The combination of hazard and vulnerability yielding the potential for negative consequences, in this case as might be expected in the form of a disaster. This coincidence of hazard and vulnerability seldom occurs in a pure form unmediated by efforts to self-protect and efforts (or their absence) by government or other external body to provide social protection. The term is also used commonly in the phrase 'disaster risk' (Wisner *et al.* 2012b).

Root cause – Underlying factors or drivers that lie in social, cultural, economic, political and institutional arrangements in society that are basic to its structure and function. These are often unrecognised or 'taken for granted' and are often generations old. Examples include racial and other forms of discrimination, class and caste systems, militarism, corruption, etc. (Wisner *et al.* 2004).

Underlying risk factors – Term used by the UNISDR for the socio-economic and environmental conditions that the UNISDR considers to be fundamental in creating risk. Such factors include 'changing social, economic, environmental conditions and land use' (UNISDR 2005: 10–12). Underlying risk factors in this sense should not be confused with 'root causes', which the editors consider to lie at a deeper level (and often remotely in historical time and geographical space) and are needed to explain why the underlying risk factors arise.

Unsafe conditions – Physical and/or biological conditions at the micro-scale at the moment just before damage or harm by exposure to a natural hazard. Examples include poor house construction (just before impact of an earthquake), clogged drainage canals next to a home (just before heavy rainfall and flooding) and lack of vaccinations by children (just before relocation of the family to a shelter following destruction of their home) (Wisner *et al.* 2004).

Vulnerability – '[T]he characteristics of a person or group and their situation that influence their capacity to anticipate, cope with, resist and recover from the impact of a natural hazard' (Wisner *et al.* 2004: 11).

Vulnerability assessment – Process of quantitative and qualitative description and analysis of vulnerability (methods that complement each other). On the quantitative side there may be use of indicators such as health status or income, while qualitative assessment usually depends on bringing to light the relative susceptibility to harm of various sub-groups through community-based, participatory discussion (Birkmann 2006).

Wisdom – 'The soundness of an action or decision with regard to the application of experience, knowledge and good judgment' (Oxford English Dictionary 2013). Some conceive a hierarchy of socially situated mental abilities beginning with capture of primary data, the collation of data into information, manipulation of information in order to create knowledge and, finally, the exercise of good judgment in the use of knowledge (hence 'wisdom') (Ackoff 1989).

References

Ackoff, R. (1989) 'From data to wisdom', *Journal of Applied Systems Analysis*, 16: 3–9.

Birkmann, J. (ed.) (2006) *Measuring Vulnerability to Natural Hazards*, Tokyo: United Nations University Press.

Chambers, R. (2013) 'Participation or development: Why is this a good time to be alive?', *Participation, Power and Social Change*, Brighton: IDS. Available at: http://participation power.wordpress.com/tag/robert-chambers/ (accessed 4 April 2013).

Deeming, H. and Fordham, M. (2012) 'Problematising the concept of "community"', in *Early Discussion and Gap Analysis on Resilience*, Work Package 1, emBRACE: Building Resilience Amongst Communities in Europe, Available at: http://www.embrace-eu.org/documents/emBRACE-D1-1_LitReview_040412_Final.pdf (accessed 10 April 2013).

Delica-Willison, Z. and Gaillard, JC (2012) 'Community action and disaster', in B. Wisner, JC Gaillard and I. Kelman (eds), *The Routledge Handbook of Hazards and Disaster Risk Reduction*, London: Routledge, pp. 711–22.

Gaillard, JC (2012) 'Caste, ethnicity, religious affiliation and disaster', in B. Wisner, JC Gaillard and I. Kelman (eds), *The Routledge Handbook of Hazards and Disaster Risk Reduction*, London: Routledge, pp. 459–69.

IPCC (2012) 'Glossary of terms', in C. Field, V. Barros, T. Stocker, D. Qin, D. Dokken, K. Ebi, M. Mastrandrea, K. Mach, G.-K. Plattner, S. Allen, M. Tignor and P. Midgley (eds), *Managing the Risks of Extreme Events and Disasters to Advance Climate Change Adaptation*, A Special Report of Working Groups I and II of the Intergovernmental Panel on Climate Change (IPCC), Cambridge: Cambridge University Press, pp. 555–64. Available at: http://www.ipcc.ch/pdf/special-reports/srex/SREX-Annex_Glossary.pdf (accessed 4 April 2013).

Mercer, J. (2012) 'Knowledge and disaster risk reduction', in B. Wisner, JC Gaillard and I. Kelman (eds), *The Routledge Handbook of Hazards and Disaster Risk Reduction*, London: Routledge, pp. 97–108.

Oxford English Dictionary (2013) *Oxford Dictionaries On Line*, Available at: http://oxforddictionaries.com/us/definition/american_english/wisdom (accessed 4 April 2013).

Serje, J. (2012) 'Data sources on hazards', in B. Wisner, JC Gaillard and I. Kelman (eds), *The Routledge Handbook of Hazards and Disaster Risk Reduction*, London: Routledge, pp. 179–90.

Thompson, J. and Guijt, I. (2011) 'Whose knowledge counts? Tales of an elective participatory pluralist', in A. Cornwall and I. Scoones (eds) *Revolutionizing Development: Reflections on the Works of Robert Chambers*, London: Earthscan, pp. 173–80.

Transparency International (2013) 'How do you define corruption?' Berlin: Transparency International. Available at: http://www.transparency.org/whoweare/organisation/faqs_on_corruption#defineCorruption (accessed 4 April 2013).

UNISDR (2005) *The Hyogo Framework for Action*, Geneva: UNISDR. Available at: http://www.unisdr.org/we/coordinate/hfa (accessed 4 April 2013).

—— (2009) *Terminology*, Geneva: UNISDR. Available at: http://www.unisdr.org/files/7817_UNISDRTerminologyEnglish.pdf (accessed 4 April 2013).

Wisner, B. (1988) *Power and Need in Africa*, London: Earthscan.

—— (2004) 'Assessment of capability and vulnerability', in G. Bankoff, G. Frerks and D. Hilhorst (eds), *Mapping Vulnerability*, London: Earthscan, pp. 183–93.

—— (2006) 'Self-assessment of coping capacity', in J. Birkmann (ed.), *Measuring Vulnerability to Natural Hazards*, Tokyo: United Nations University Press, pp. 316–28.

Wisner, B., Blaikie, P., Cannon, T. and Davis, I. (2004) *At Risk: Natural Hazards, People's Vulnerability and Disasters*, 2nd edn, London: Routledge.

Wisner, B., Gaillard, JC and Kelman, I. (eds) (2012a) *The Routledge Handbook of Hazards and Disaster Risk Reduction*, London: Routledge.

—— (2012b) 'Framing disaster: theories and stories seeking to understand hazards', in B. Wisner, JC Gaillard and I. Kelman (eds), *The Routledge Handbook of Hazards and Disaster Risk Reduction*, London: Routledge, pp. 18–34.

Index

Note: page numbers in *italic* type refer to Figures; those in **bold** refer to Tables.

Made in the USA
San Bernardino, CA
20 June 2020